COUNCIL UNBOUND

COUNCIL UNBOUND:

THE GROWTH OF UN DECISION MAKING ON CONFLICT

AND POSTCONFLICT ISSUES AFTER THE COLD WAR

MICHAEL J. MATHESON

UNITED STATES INSTITUTE OF PEACE PRESS
Washington, D.C.

UNITED STATES INSTITUTE OF PEACE
1200 17th Street NW
Washington, DC 20036

First published 2006

Printed in the United States of America

The paper used in this publication meets the minimum requirements of American National Standard for Information Sciences—Permanence of Paper for Printed Library Materials, ANSI Z39.48-1984.

Library of Congress Cataloging-in-Publication Data
Matheson, Michael J.
    Council unbound : the growth of UN decision making on conflict and postconflict issues after the Cold War / Michael J. Matheson
    p. cm.
    Includes bibliographical references and index.
    ISBN-13: 978-1-929223-78-7 (softcover : alk. paper)
    ISBN-10: 1-929223-78-1 (softcover : alk. paper)
    ISBN-13: 978-1-929223-79-4 (hardcover : alk. paper)
    ISBN-10: 1-929223-79-X (hardcover : alk. paper)
    1. United Nations. Security Council--Decision making. 2. United Nations--Peacekeeping forces. 3. Sanctions (International law) 4. Intervention (International law) 5. Aggression (International law) I. Title.
    KZ5036.M38 2006
    341.5'8--dc22
                                          2005035179

To my wife Patricia,
who has sustained and supported me
in every way

Contents

FOREWORD

Although scholars, students, and policymakers will find Michael Matheson's *Council Unbound* a masterful survey of the newly renascent powers of the United Nations Security Council, two distinct readerships will significantly benefit from this book: those who believe that the United Nations is an ineffective entity, and those who believe it is becoming a global government. *Council Unbound* will dispel many cherished (if not well-informed) beliefs among both of these readerships.

Regarding the former, Matheson lays out the myriad tasks of the world organization in halting incipient conflagrations between or within states the world over, and in managing the Herculean job of guiding the reconstruction of states and societies recovering from the human and physical destruction of mass violence.

For the latter readership, the title of this work does not imply a world body run amok. In fact, as the author explains in detail, the United Nations Security Council has its own limits within the UN Charter, and it must find concurrence among nine of its fifteen members (including the veto-wielding "Permanent Five") before deciding to act on a "threat to the peace"—including international terrorism—or to undertake complex peacekeeping operations. Although the UN

Security Council is now *unbound* from the Cold War constraints of superpower competition that prevented full implementation of the UN Charter's provisions for stemming aggression, it is not free from the strictures of that same charter, which stands as the basic legal authority for the Council's actions in summoning either sanctions against a miscreant member or assistance for a collapsing one.

Nor is the Council immune to the effects of disputes that arise over conflicting national interests. The organization continues to be plagued by disagreements among its permanent members—witness the objections of China and Russia regarding various UN-mandated peacekeeping missions and, more recently, the decision of the Bush administration to forgo a specific UN mandate for intervention in Iraq, relying on previous UN Security Council resolutions.

Regardless of these limitations on the Security Council's operations, any reader of this book cannot fail to acknowledge that the Council has surely expanded its roles in the maintenance of peace over the past decade and a half, extending its purview into not only "third-generation" peacekeeping tasks—entailing the establishment of representative political institutions in "failed" states that have collapsed under the weight of their profound social divisions, and the restoration of effective public security architectures—but also the criminal prosecution of political and military leaders, including even heads of state. Indeed, Matheson expertly documents the Security Council's assumption of an enormous conflict management agenda and the challenges of constructing responsive political institutions worldwide.

Mike Matheson is highly qualified to write about the U.S. response to the Council's expanded functions. He came to the Institute as a senior fellow after serving as deputy legal adviser and acting legal adviser at the U.S. State Department during the beginning of the Security Council's assumption of new tasks in the post–Cold War period, starting with the first Gulf War. He also serves on the executive council of the American Society of International Law, as well as being a member of the UN International Law Commission. Currently he is a member of the international law faculty at George Washington University's School of Law.

As with any large institution that has expanded its functions, there are bound to be problems with management, and *Council Unbound* comes at a time when the United Nations faces the weighty task of assessing proposals for the world organization's reform. Practically every program and project of the United States Institute of Peace involves the United Nations or its specialized agencies, and we are now in the process of following up on the work of the Institute-supported bipartisan Task Force on the United Nations. The task force's report, *American Interests and UN Reform,* called for myriad changes in the way the organization is managed and run, many of them paralleling Secretary-General Kofi Annan's own agenda for organizational reform of the world body. The Institute's UN-related programmatic work also reflects many of the in-depth studies of how international organizations manage conflict and postconflict peacebuilding that have been published by the U.S. Institute of Peace Press, starting with Mihaly Simai's *The Future of Global Governance* (1994). We now proudly offer Mike Matheson's excellent survey of the UN's expanded global repertoire as the latest addition to this important body of policy-relevant scholarship.

Richard H. Solomon
President
United States Institute of Peace

PREFACE

THIS BOOK IS AN ATTEMPT TO DESCRIBE the development and expanded use by the United Nations Security Council during the post–Cold War period of its legal authority to deal with threats to the peace. It is not a broad treatise on the political role of the Council, its effect on the events of the period, or its place in the foreign policy of the United States. Rather, the book reflects my experience and perspective as an attorney in the U.S. State Department over a period of almost thirty years, and in particular my experience during the 1990s, when my colleagues and I in the Office of the Legal Adviser resorted again and again to the legal authority of the newly renascent Security Council to help policymakers deal with the crises of the post–Cold War period. In doing so, we often made use of that authority in ways that may have seemed ambitious at the time but have since been generally accepted as legally valid by the major actors of the UN system.

Although this book draws on my experience in the U.S. State Department, of course it does not purport to represent the views of the U.S. government. It was the product of a year's work as a senior fellow at the U.S. Institute of Peace, but, likewise, it does not necessarily represent the Institute's views. It is based entirely on the public record of this period, though it is wholly consistent with my own personal recollection of the events and issues described. Most of the major events in the development of the Council's authority occurred between 1990 and 2000 (when I left the State Department), but the book continues the story through 2005. The discussion herein is extensively annotated with references to the major UN decisions in each context, as reflected in the resolutions of the UN Security Council, and to the legal debates surrounding those decisions, as reflected in a variety of secondary sources, including leading law reviews (principally the *American Journal of International Law*). For readers interested in surveying more broadly the primary sources of U.S. and international law pertaining to the Council's expanded powers, as well as the legal commentary on these powers, I offer a selected bibliography at the end of this volume. Although I have made most citations to the scholarly and professional literature conform to the guidelines set forth in *The Chicago Manual of Style,* 15th ed., most of the references to public documents (treaties, international legal cases, etc.) follow a modified system of commonly accepted legal citation.

I want to thank Peter Pavilionis and Timothy Docking of the U.S. Institute of Peace for their inspiration, suggestions, and editing on this project, and Charles Henderson for his outstanding work as my research assistant at the Institute. I also want to acknowledge the many colleagues with whom I worked at various times in the State Department and elsewhere on the issues described in the book, particularly Edwin Williamson, Conrad Harper, David Andrews, the late Edward Cummings, Sean Murphy, Bruce Rashkow, Ronald Bettauer, John Crook, Theodor Meron, David Scheffer, James O'Brien, Crystal Nix, Alan Kreczko, James E. Baker, and Kathleen Suneja.

LIST OF ACRONYMS*

CSCE: Conference on Security and Cooperation in Europe
ECOMOG: ECOWAS Monitoring Group
ECOWAS: Economic Community of West African States
EU: European Union
FRY: Federal Republic of Yugoslavia
IAEA: International Atomic Energy Agency
ICC: International Criminal Court
ICJ: International Court of Justice
ICTY: International Criminal Tribunal for the Former
                    Yugoslavia
IFOR: Implementation Force (Bosnia)
ILC: International Law Commission
INTERFET: International Force for East Timor
ISAF: International Security Assistance Force (Afghanistan)

---

* A listing of acronyms for UN peacekeeping operations discussed in this work
can be found in Appendix 2.

KFOR:	Kosovo Force
NATO:	North Atlantic Treaty Organization
OAS:	Organization of American States
OSCE:	Organization for Security and Cooperation in Europe
SFOR:	Stabilization Force (Bosnia)
SRSG:	Special Representative of the (UN) Secretary-General
UN:	United Nations
UNCC:	UN Compensation Commission
UNITAF:	Unified Task Force (Haiti)
UNMOVIC:	UN Monitoring, Verification, and Inspection Commission (Iraq)
UNSCOM:	UN Special Commission (Iraq)
WMD:	weapons of mass destruction

Council Unbound

INTRODUCTION

THE FOUNDERS OF THE UNITED NATIONS made it clear that the overriding priority of the new international order created in 1945 would be to maintain international peace and security. As the opening words of the UN Charter proclaimed, the "peoples of the United Nations" were above all "determined to save succeeding generations from the scourge of war, which twice in our lifetime has brought untold sorrow to mankind . . . ."

If the prevention and resolution of armed conflict is the first essential function of the international system, then the creation of legal authority and mechanisms to assist in this task must be one of the essential functions of international law. The international legal system must provide effective legal tools to assist political leaders in preventing the outbreak of armed conflict and, if such conflict occurs, in ending it on acceptable terms and dealing with its consequences in a manner that will discourage future conflict. This is true whether armed conflict takes the form of hostilities between states, serious fighting between a state and armed insurgents, or large-scale attacks by terrorist groups against a government and the population it serves.

Although legal principles and mechanisms rarely will be the most important element in suppressing armed conflict and dealing with its consequences, experience shows that uncertainty about the international legal authority for a response to armed conflict can seriously impair that response's political viability, as well as create complications for its implementation by national authorities. Legal debates often come to embody underlying conflicts about power and policy, and an effective answer to legal objections will often help to deal with challenges that are fundamentally political in character. There are a number of specific areas in which the consequences of armed conflict cannot be addressed successfully unless effective legal mechanisms can be put in operation—some obvious examples being the prosecution of crimes, compensation of victims, and the governance of affected communities. Finally, when states or international organizations take actions that have no credible basis in international law, they tend to corrode the integrity and viability of the international order and move international relations away from predictability and rationality toward the arbitrary use of force and economic power.

Some national political leaders naturally prefer to address these issues on a unilateral basis, or at least on the basis of joint action by states having similar political and legal systems and priorities. This approach can be simpler and can produce more timely and direct results in some situations. However, in many circumstances, such an approach limits the degree of international support for the effort and may be ineffective if it does not secure the cooperation of other states or international bodies that could make an important contribution. For example, states may find it simplest to try war criminals entirely on the basis of national laws and resources, but in certain situations some form of international prosecution or involvement would be very useful in creating a fair and effective process, encouraging the surrender of accused persons, and building international support. Likewise, it may be easier to initiate and conduct military operations without the complication of seeking a legal mandate from an international or regional body, but doing so may result in the loss of important military and other assistance and may impair the political viability of the effort.

For most of the twentieth century, the international system was remarkably unsuccessful in providing effective legal tools to assist in suppressing armed conflict and dealing with its consequences. Extensive efforts were made at the beginning of the century to create international arbitration mechanisms that would prevent or terminate conflict, but these efforts collapsed with the outbreak of World War I. Between the world wars, the international community renounced war and attempted to create a new international security system through the League of Nations, but these efforts failed in the face of defiance by the Axis powers.

In 1945, the international community was determined to put in place an effective system for preventing and suppressing armed conflict that would rely on both legal principles and the power of the major Allied nations. To achieve this goal, the UN Charter included a new prohibition against the use of force among states (with certain exceptions) and created a Security Council with sweeping powers to address threats and breaches of international peace and security. In due course, these steps were strengthened by the adoption of a series of declarations and international agreements aimed at elaborating on the prohibition of the use of force and creating new norms for the control of armed conflict.

Nevertheless, this system largely failed during the Cold War because it depended on a community of interests among the major powers that did not then exist. The Security Council, although entrusted with unprecedented authority to control armed conflict, could not act in the face of a veto by any of the five permanent members. This fact essentially excluded it from any effective role in major international conflict situations where the interests of the great powers diverged. As a result, the enormous potential of the Council as a source of authority remained mostly dormant. The international community struggled from conflict to conflict with no other legal basis for action but the inadequate authority of other UN organs, the uncertain authority of regional organizations, occasional authority drawn from specific treaties, and the residual sovereign powers of states.

The fall of the Soviet Union made it possible for the Council to act without being immobilized by the fundamental conflicts of interests and attitudes among its permanent members that had been characteristic of the Cold War period. This circumstance enabled the

Council to begin to carry out the role envisioned for it under the UN Charter as the supreme arbiter of international peace and security. It had the effect of unleashing the dormant legal authority of the Council and turning it into a great engine for the creation of legal obligations and mechanisms for suppressing armed conflict and dealing with its results, many of which would have surprised even the founders of the United Nations. The Council was thus unbound from its Cold War political constraints but not from the legal constraints of the UN Charter.

This new period of UN authority first manifested itself with the Iraqi invasion of Kuwait, which led to important innovations in the application of economic sanctions and the authorization of military operations by the Security Council. It continued with the imposition by the Council of a comprehensive cease-fire regime to end the first Gulf War, including unprecedented provisions for the resolution of boundary disputes, the control of armaments, and the compensation of victims of the conflict. After a period of indecision, the Council finally began to apply some of the same tools to situations involving the dissolution of a state (Yugoslavia) and to conflicts that were essentially internal in character (for example, Somalia and Rwanda). These applications of authority led in turn to a series of actions to provide for international trial of crimes committed during armed conflict (Yugoslavia and Rwanda) or to provide international involvement in national or "hybrid" trials (for example, Sierra Leone). The Council even found it necessary to take over the governance of entire territories devastated by armed conflict (Kosovo and East Timor). Finally, the Council applied some of these tools to deal with serious terrorist actions that threatened the peace (such as the *Lockerbie* bombing, and the attacks in New York City and Washington, D.C., on September 11, 2001) and with the threat of the proliferation of weapons of mass destruction (WMD).

Moreover, the Council's robust exercise of its authority to address threats to the peace became a powerful engine for international action to serve important collateral objectives—particularly to deal with severe repression of human rights, the overthrow of democratic regimes, and humanitarian crises. The Council did so by substantially broadening the concept of "threats to the peace" to include such internal crises where there was a plausible concern that their continuation might lead to regional and international escalation.

This book reviews these developments, focusing on the Council's decision in each case to assert new authority and to create new legal mechanisms, as well as the manner in which they were used in practice. It assesses the objections that were made to the adequacy of the legal basis for the Council's actions. It asks whether those actions are likely to be a useful precedent in other situations, whether the Council could validly assert even greater authority under the Charter should it find it useful to do so, and what legal limits there may be on the Council's authority.

Of course, for political and practical reasons it has not been possible, even during the post–Cold War period, for the Council to act vigorously or to use its authority effectively in all situations. In some instances (such as Rwanda and Sudan), this failure to act had tragic consequences; in other instances (such as Kosovo), states acted, but without the secure legal basis that Council action would have provided. In the recent conflict in Iraq, the differences among the permanent members largely immobilized the Council at the critical point and made a difficult crisis worse. Further, the processes created by the Council have sometimes experienced serious problems, as the recent disclosures about the Iraq Oil-for-Food Program and the conduct of UN peacekeepers has shown. Nonetheless, the precedents established by the Council's action in the post–Cold War period have clearly shown the wide scope and importance of the Council's legal authority, and it is essential that neither the international community as a whole nor the major powers within it lose sight of this fact or underestimate the tremendous potential of the Council as a means for acting on conflict situations.

Because the expansion in the exercise of authority by the Council has essentially been a pragmatic response to a long series of crisis situations, it is best approached on a historical rather than a theoretical basis. For this reason, the account that follows tracks the historical development of each aspect of the Council's authority in relation to the specific sequence of crises and events that produced it. I have, however, attempted to relate this sequence of events to the main theoretical questions about the Council's legal authority that tend to engage legal scholars. The result is neither a history nor a legal treatise, but an analytical survey that hopefully will be of some interest to not only both policy and legal experts but also to others who have taken a recent interest in this seemingly ubiquitous player in the arena of international law and politics.

The book begins in chapter 1 with a brief description of the general framework for Council action contained in the UN Charter and the practice of the Council, including its relationship with other UN organs and the rules and practices that shape its decision making. Chapter 2 considers the jurisdiction and mandate of the Council and, in particular, the development of the Council's perception of its authority under Chapter VII of the UN Charter to deal with threats to the peace. Chapter 3 examines the Council's use of various types of sanctions, including the problems of enforcing sanctions and of collateral damage to persons and states that are not the object of sanctions. Chapter 4 addresses UN peace operations, from traditional, limited peacekeeping missions to the "second-generation" and "third-generation" operations that have extended to complete governance of territories. Chapter 5 examines the Council's authorization of the use of force by both UN operations and non-UN entities, including states, regional organizations, and coalitions. Chapter 6 describes the new technical commissions that the Council has created, including those dedicated to resolving boundary disputes, providing compensation for victims of armed conflict, and conducting inspections to verify compliance with arms limitations. Chapter 7 considers the ways in which the Council has facilitated the prosecution of criminal offenses, including the creation of ad hoc tribunals and assistance to domestic trials. The book concludes with some thoughts about the significance of the expansion of the Council's legal authority and its relationship to larger policy questions about the Council and the role of the United States in the United Nations.

In the end, legal norms and mechanisms can never be an adequate substitute for effective political decisions and (where necessary) the use of economic and military power in the right cause. Nonetheless, international legal norms and mechanisms can be important in authorizing, supporting, and constraining political, economic, and military action. It is therefore important for both policymakers and lawyers to understand the scope and the limits of international legal authority in this area, and this book aims to contribute to that process of understanding.

1   THE FRAMEWORK FOR COUNCIL ACTION

A S A GENERAL MATTER, AN EFFECTIVE SYSTEM for dealing with armed conflict would have several fundamental legal features. First, it would require that states resolve their disputes by peaceful means and prohibit nondefensive use of force without appropriate sanction by the international community. Second, it would authorize one or more international organs to take action to prevent and resolve armed conflict, including dispute-resolution measures, sanctions, and, if necessary, the use of force. Third, it would authorize international organs to address the consequences of armed conflict in a way that provides justice to the victims of the conflict and resolves issues that might cause a resumption of conflict. Fourth, it would confirm the right of states (either individually or collectively) to take action—including, where necessary, the use of force—to protect themselves from armed attack if the international community were unable or chose not to take action.

Although the need for these features may seem obvious, the fact is that international law prior to the twentieth century was almost entirely lacking in all but the last point, and the attempts of the international community to remedy this deficiency during the first forty-five years of the twentieth century were fundamentally unsuccessful.

Only with the adoption of the UN Charter was there a coherent scheme to address all of these points, and even that scheme was so constructed that it could not function as intended for another forty-five years.

This study begins by looking at the general framework for action by the Security Council that has been created by the UN Charter and the Council's own practice. This chapter starts with a review of the state of international law concerning the resolution of armed conflict that existed prior to the adoption of the Charter, and then of the system created by the Charter to remedy the shortcomings of pre-existing law. In doing so, the chapter highlights the essential changes made by the Charter regarding the legal authority of the international community to deal with armed conflict, most of which did not bear fruit during the Cold War because of the political divisions that made it impossible for the Security Council to act.[1] The chapter then addresses the decision-making process of the Council and some of the important innovations made in the post–Cold War period to enable the Council to cope with its expanded role. Of course, most of this information will be familiar to those who have studied the Charter and the Council's functions.

INTERNATIONAL LAW PRIOR TO THE UN CHARTER

The international system prior to the twentieth century was based on the sovereignty and autonomy of states, with relatively little constraint on their use of force to achieve political objectives. States were considered to have the right to wage war for political purposes, including the redress of wrongs of all kinds, the acquisition of territory, or the imposition of political terms and constraints on other states. The only recognized legal requirements were that war first be formally declared, that neutral states be given a certain degree of protection from the effects of the conflict, and that some basic rules on the conduct of hostilities be observed to limit the infliction of unnecessary harm during the course of the fighting. Doctrines were also developed to justify the use of force outside a formal state of war—for example, armed "reprisals" to secure the rights of states or their nationals, or "humanitarian interventions" to protect populations threatened with serious atrocities.[2]

At the same time, international procedures for the peaceful resolution of disputes were fairly rudimentary—consisting primarily of precedents for the ad hoc arbitration of disputes by third parties where the states in question agreed to do so. Likewise, there were no global institutions with general legal authority to intervene in disputes between states, to command states to refrain from the use of force, or to take coercive measures to prevent or terminate an armed conflict.

Several serious attempts were made at the end of the nineteenth century and the beginning of the twentieth century to establish a system to resolve disputes peacefully and to prevent or resolve armed conflicts. One was the series of Hague Peace Conferences held between 1899 and 1907, which attempted to bring together the entire community of states to adopt legal systems for the peaceful resolution of disputes and the development of more ambitious constraints on the means and methods of warfare. (A number of the Hague Conventions adopted during this process continue in force to this day, although many of the restrictions on armed conflict have largely been obviated by subsequent developments in military technology and doctrine.) This series of conferences (the next of which would have been held in 1915) was ended by the outbreak of World War I.[3]

A related effort was a series of international agreements concluded around the turn of the century (for which the United States was a particularly strong proponent) that attempted to substitute arbitration or other forms of peaceful dispute resolution for the use of force. Often these agreements provided for the creation of a bilateral commission to investigate disputes between the parties, and for a "cooling-off period" while the commission worked, during which time the parties would refrain from resorting to hostilities. Unfortunately, these agreements proved powerless to stop the general outbreak of war in 1914.[4]

Following the carnage of World War I, the international community made more comprehensive efforts to prevent or resolve armed conflict. The 1920 League of Nations Covenant attempted to create a general system for the peaceful resolution of disputes and for collective action against states that instead resorted to war. Article 12 of the Covenant required League members to submit any disputes between them to arbitration, judicial settlement, or inquiry by the League Council. It required the parties to the dispute to refrain from resorting to war until three months after the award by the arbitrators or the judicial decision or the report of the Council, as the case might be. Articles 13 and 15 required that League members carry out any arbitral award, judicial decision, or Council report that might be rendered, and not resort to war against any member that complied with it.[5]

Article 16 of the Covenant provided that if any League member resorted to war in violation of these requirements, it was then to be deemed to have committed an act of war against all League members. In that event, League members agreed to sever all trade and financial relations with the offending state and its nationals. The Council was then under a duty to "recommend to the several governments concerned what effective military, naval, or air force the members of the League shall severally contribute to the armed forces to be used to protect the covenants of the League." However, the Council could act only with the unanimous vote of its members, and its authority was rarely used in the face of widespread aggression during the 1930s. Obviously the effectiveness of the League was sharply limited by the fact that one major power (the United States) was never a member, and several others (Germany, Japan, Italy, and the Soviet Union) were members only during a part of the League's existence.[6]

A second major attempt to constrain the use of force in the interwar period was the 1928 Kellogg-Briand Pact.[7] Article I stated that the parties "solemnly declare in the names of their respective peoples that they condemn recourse to war for the solution of international controversies, and renounce it as an instrument of national policy in their relations with one another." This statement was a striking change from the nineteenth century tolerance of war as an instrument of national policy. In fact, the Kellogg-Briand Pact remains in force to this day and was a primary basis for the holding by the Nuremberg Tribunal that a war of aggression is an international crime for which there is personal criminal liability.[8]

Nonetheless, the articulation in the Pact of a prohibition against war, without effective international machinery and national political will to enforce it, proved impotent in the face of determined aggression. Further, there was ambiguity as to whether the Pact prohibited uses of force that fell outside the traditional concept of "war," such as armed reprisals and other forcible interventions.[9]

On the whole, the combination of the League of Nations and the Kellogg-Briand Pact represented a considerable change in international norms concerning the use of force. They were a serious attempt to provide two of the missing components of an effective international system for resolving armed conflict—namely, a requirement that states resolve their differences only by peaceful means and the creation of international machinery to prevent or terminate conflict. However, the system had serious shortcomings and ambiguities, did not have sufficient participation and support from the great powers, and did not have adequate means for resolving issues that might cause a resort to armed conflict. In the end, the system collapsed in the face of Axis aggression.

UN CHARTER PROVISIONS ON MAINTENANCE OF THE PEACE

The catastrophic events of World War II led directly to the creation of the UN system. The primary objective of the founders of the United Nations was to prevent and suppress any resumption of armed conflict, and this is clearly reflected in many provisions of the UN Charter. (The text of all relevant provisions is contained in Appendix 1 of this book.)

The List of Purposes of the United Nations in Article 1 starts with the following: "1. To maintain international peace and security, and to that end: to take effective collective measures for the prevention and removal of threats to the peace, and for the suppression of acts of aggression or other breaches of the peace, and to bring about by peaceful means, and in conformity with the principles of justice and international law, adjustment or settlement of international disputes or situations which might lead to a breach of the peace." To meet this objective, the Charter set forth a prohibition against the use of force by one state against another (subject to certain exceptions) and created a very ambitious institutional structure to suppress threats and breaches of the peace.

The prohibition on the use of force and the parallel duty to resolve disputes by peaceful means are stated in Article 2 as follows:

"3. All Members shall settle their international disputes by peaceful means in such a manner that international peace and security, and justice, are not endangered. 4. All Members shall refrain in their international relations from the threat or use of force against the territorial integrity or political independence of any state, or in any other manner inconsistent with the Purposes of the United Nations."

Unlike the Kellogg-Briand Pact, the formulation in Article 2(4) is not limited to "war," but embraces any "threat or use of force." On the other hand, there has been considerable debate over the years as to whether Article 2(4) constitutes a total prohibition on the threat or use of force (subject to the later exceptions in the Charter for the use of force in self-defense or with Council authorization) or, rather, is only a partial prohibition that permits forcible unilateral actions that are allegedly not directed at depriving another state of its territory or political independence (such as intervention to promote democracy or to deal with widespread atrocities).[10] This question will be explored in chapter 5.

In any event, to enforce this prohibition on the use of force, the Charter went on to create an institutional structure centered on the new Security Council, which was given sweeping and unprecedented authority. Article 24 states, "1. In order to ensure prompt and effective action by the United Nations, its Members confer on the Security Council primary responsibility for the maintenance of international peace and security, and agree that in carrying out its duties under this responsibility the Security Council acts on their behalf."

The authority of the Council for the maintenance of peace is contained in two chapters of the Charter: Chapter VI on "Pacific Settlement of Disputes," and Chapter VII on "Action with Respect to Threats to the Peace, Breaches of the Peace, and Acts of Aggression." Chapter VI details the authority of the Council to take nonmandatory actions to assist in the resolution of disputes before they endanger the peace. Chapter VII, on the other hand, deals with situations that have become a threat to or breach of the peace and gives the Council extensive mandatory powers.

Chapter VI begins in Article 33 by reaffirming that parties to a dispute, "the continuance of which is likely to endanger the maintenance of international peace and security," must attempt to resolve the dispute by any of a variety of peaceful dispute-resolution techniques, including negotiation, arbitration, judicial settlement, and resort to regional arrangements. It states that the Council shall, when it deems necessary, call on the parties to settle their dispute by such means. Article 34 authorizes the Council to "investigate any dispute, or any situation which might lead to international friction or give rise to a dispute, in order to determine whether the continuance of the dispute or situation is likely to endanger the maintenance of international peace and security." Article 35 authorizes any UN member to bring any such dispute or situation to the Council's attention. Together, these articles give very broad scope to the Council to involve itself at any time in any situation that might affect international peace or security, either on its own initiative or at the request of the states involved.

Article 36 authorizes the Council to recommend procedures for the settlement of such a dispute or situation at any stage, and Article 37 authorizes it to recommend specific terms of settlement if it determines that the continuance of the dispute is in fact likely to endanger international peace and security. Curiously, Chapter VI does not mention the possibility of the deployment of peacekeeping forces or similar missions that operate with the consent of the states involved; but, as detailed in chapter 4 of this book, this has become the most important of the Council's nonmandatory powers for the maintenance of the peace.

Chapter VII of the Charter begins in Article 39 with a definition of the threshold for the Council's more sweeping authority to deal with situations that have developed into actual threats or breaches of the peace: "The Security Council shall determine the existence of any threat to the peace, breach of the peace, or act of aggression and shall make recommendations, or decide what measures shall be taken in accordance with Articles 41 and 42, to maintain or restore international peace and security."

Over the years, there has been considerable debate as to what could properly be considered a "threat to the peace"—particularly with respect to conflicts arising within a single state. Chapter 2 of this book will deal at length with this question, and with the way in which the concept of a "threat to the peace" has been expanded considerably during the post–Cold War period.

The provisions that follow Article 39 spell out the types of measures the Council may take to deal with such a threat to the peace. Article 40 provides that the Council may, at the outset, call on the parties to comply with "provisional measures" to prevent any aggravation of the situation. Article 41 provides that the Council may decide on measures not involving the use of armed force and gives an illustrative list of some of these types of measures, including diplomatic and economic sanctions. Chapter 3 of this study will look at the very expansive use that the Council has made of this authority in the post–Cold War period.

Article 42 then provides that if the Council considers that measures under Article 41 have been or would be inadequate to resolve the situation, it may authorize armed action, including action by the armed forces of member states. This is, of course, the ultimate form of coercive action that could be taken by the international community and lies at the heart of the Charter system of collective security. Articles 43 through 47 provide for a system through which it was intended that the Council would carry out this authority, involving special agreements with member states to provide forces and facilities to the Council, and to operate under the strategic direction of a "Military Staff Committee" consisting of the chiefs of staff of the permanent members or their representatives. However, for political reasons these arrangements never materialized, and, as chapter 5 examines, the Council has turned to other means of authorizing and supervising the use of armed force under Article 42.

In addition to the basic core of responsibilities for international peace contained in Chapters VI and VII, the Charter gives the Security Council a number of secondary authorities that are relevant to the maintenance of international peace and security. Article 4 gives joint responsibility to the Council and the General Assembly for the admission of new UN members (which must be "peace-loving states"). Article 5 empowers the Assembly, upon recommendation by the Council, to suspend a UN member from the exercise of rights and privileges of membership if preventive or enforcement action has been taken against it by the Council. Article 6 provides in the same way for possible expulsion of any UN member "which has persistently violated" the principles of the Charter. Article 26 provides that the Council is responsible for formulating "plans to be submitted to the Members of the United Nations for the establishment of a system for the regulation of armaments." Article 29 says that the Council may establish "such subsidiary organs as it deems necessary for the performance of its functions." Article 83 gives the Council all the functions of the United Nations with respect to any areas under the UN Trusteeship system that are designated as "strategic areas." Finally, Article 94 authorizes the Council to "make recommendations or decide upon measures to be taken" to enforce decisions of the International Court of Justice.

Although the Security Council has "primary" responsibility for international peace and security, that responsibility is not exclusive under the Charter system. Under Article 11, the General Assembly may discuss and make recommendations concerning any questions relating to peace and security, and may call the attention of the Security Council to situations that are likely to endanger the peace. However, under Article 12, the General Assembly may not make any recommendations with respect to a situation in which the Council is exercising its functions. The Assembly has sometimes used this power to make "recommendations" as an asserted basis for involvement in conflict situations—a source of considerable controversy.

The Charter also gives the UN secretary-general certain responsibilities that have developed into a very significant role in the maintenance of peace and security. Specifically, Article 99 provides that the secretary-general may bring to the Council's attention any matter "which in his opinion may threaten the maintenance of international peace and security," and also empowers him to perform such other functions as may be entrusted to him by the Council or the Assembly. Over the years, these authorities have provided the basis for the secretary-general's efforts to provide political leadership in conflict resolution, to direct UN peacemaking efforts, and to provide a variety of services that have been essential to UN actions in this area.

Further, the Charter gives a potentially significant role in the maintenance of peace to regional agencies or arrangements. This role is provided for in Chapter VIII, which was added in light of the developing inter-American system for the maintenance of peace in the Western Hemisphere. Article 52 says that UN members "shall make every effort" to resolve disputes peacefully through regional arrangements before referring them to the Security Council. Article 53 says the Council "shall, where appropriate" use regional arrangements for enforcement action under its authority, but then adds that enforcement action may not be taken by regional arrangements without the Council's authorization.

Finally, in light of the possibility that effective action might not be taken promptly (or at all) by these international organs to deal with armed attack against a member state, Article 51 confirms that nothing in the Charter impairs the "inherent right of individual or collective self-defense . . . until the Security Council has taken measures necessary to maintain international peace and security." Chapter 5 of this study will consider some of the issues that have arisen with respect to this right, including the authority of the Council to take action that restricts the exercise of self-defense and the question of "anticipatory" or "pre-emptive" self-defense by states.[11]

This brief summary shows that the Charter system does include the fundamental legal features for the resolution of armed conflict listed above. The Charter does require that states resolve their disputes by peaceful means and does prohibit their use of force without appropriate sanction by the international community. The Charter does authorize the Security Council to take action to prevent and resolve armed conflict including, if necessary, the use of force. The Charter does give extensive powers to the Council that can be used to address the consequences of armed conflict, as considered in some detail in later chapters. And the Charter does confirm the right of states to take action to protect themselves from armed attack if the international community is unable to or chooses not to act effectively to deal with the threat.

However, it is also clear that the Security Council is the indispensable heart of this system, and that the Charter structure works only if the Council is able to act effectively. When the Council has been immobilized by political divisions, other actors—particularly states, regional organizations, and other UN organs—have attempted to fill the gap, but often with unsatisfactory results and a serious lack of international legitimacy. Accordingly, the end of the Cold War—

which made it possible for the Council to begin exercising its Charter authority—was an event of fundamental importance in bringing the Charter system for the resolution of conflict closer to fruition. But at the same time, the end of the Cold War has obviously not put an end to divisions among the permanent members, which have on a number of occasions inhibited or prevented the Council from taking effective action. Therefore, the manner in which the Council makes decisions continues to be of considerable importance.

SECURITY COUNCIL DECISION MAKING

In light of the very extensive power and responsibility that was to be given to the Security Council, the question of decision-making procedures for the Council was a central issue in the negotiation of the Charter, since it involved the degree to which decisions on collective security and mandatory measures would be taken by the victorious great powers or by the other member states of the United Nations. The answer to this question is contained in Article 27, which provides that decisions of the fifteen-member Council on "procedural" matters shall be made "by an affirmative vote of nine members," and decisions on all other matters shall be made "by an affirmative vote of nine members, including the concurring votes of the permanent members." Article 27 provides that any Council member that is a "party to a dispute" before the Council must abstain from voting on any Chapter VI decision relating to that dispute, but this requirement does not apply to decisions under Chapter VII.

The practice of the Council over its first few decades resolved some of the ambiguities inherent in Article 27. In particular, the language requiring the "concurring votes" of the permanent members for nonprocedural decisions was treated by the Council as permitting a decision even if one of the permanent members abstained, declined to vote, or was absent.[12] Although, in the abstract, this was an unusual interpretation of the phrase "concurring votes," it was nonetheless very useful, as a practical matter, since it permitted permanent members to register their objections clearly and conspicuously, but without having to assume the political onus of preventing a decision from being taken. Without this interpretation, for example, several important resolutions during the post–Cold War period might have been defeated by Chinese abstentions.[13]

Considerable attention was also paid during the early years of the United Nations to the question of what constituted a "procedural" decision that might be adopted without regard to the veto. Essentially, the negotiating record of the Charter and the practice of the Council after its adoption have led to the treatment of a number of categories of decisions as nonprocedural, including enforcement actions under Chapter VII, other measures that might lead to such enforcement (such as conducting an investigation or making recommendations for action to the parties), and the creation of subordinate bodies with a mandate to take such actions.[14] All of these matters are subject to the veto.

The result is that any of the five permanent members can prevent the adoption of any significant decisions under Chapter VII. But the permanent members cannot secure the adoption of such a decision without the concurrence of at least four of the other ten members. In practice, this has meant that such Council action requires substantial support across regional or political lines.

This will be all the more true if the Council's membership is expanded, as has been proposed for a number of years.[15] In particular, in December 2004, a high-level panel appointed by Secretary-General Kofi Annan proposed that nine additional members be added, to result in an allocation of six seats each to Africa, Asia, Europe, and the Americas. Under one proposed option, six of the new members would be permanent; under another proposed option, there would be no new permanent members, but eight of the new members would be "semi-permanent" with renewable four-year terms. Under either option, none of the new members would have the veto. Preference for election to the permanent or "semi-permanent" seats would be given to states in each region that are the top financial or troop contributors to the United Nations.[16]

In any event, with the end of the Cold War, the use of the veto has substantially declined.[17] Nonetheless, it is true that the use or threat of the veto has effectively prevented the Council from acting at certain critical points in the post–Cold War period. This has led to a renewal of proposals to eliminate or limit the exercise of the veto—

for example, to require that the veto not be effective unless at least two permanent members exercise it in any given case, or to permit the overruling of a veto of one permanent member by a majority of the Council or the General Assembly.[18] But such changes would require amendment of the Charter, which itself requires acceptance by all the permanent members,[19] and this seems to be out of the question.[20]

In the alternative, it is sometimes suggested that the permanent members might agree not to exercise the veto under certain circumstances. For example, the Canadian-sponsored International Commission on Intervention and State Sovereignty recommended in 2001 that the permanent members agree not to use the veto "in matters where their vital state interests are not involved, to obstruct the passage of resolutions authorizing military intervention for human protection purposes for which there is otherwise majority support."[21] Similarly, the 2004 UN high-level report asked the permanent members to limit use of the veto to "matters where vital interests are genuinely at stake" and to refrain from its use "in cases of genocide and large-scale human rights abuses."[22] The permanent members would do well to pay attention to these proposals, but they are unlikely to agree to limit their exercise of the veto, and in any event would surely retain the prerogative of judging for themselves whether their national interests would require its exercise.

There seems therefore to be little prospect of the elimination or restriction of the veto. But the formal voting procedures of Article 27 are not the only way in which decisions may be taken under the authority of the Council. Along with the great increase in the scope and variety of the Council's business in the post–Cold War period has come an increasing use by the Council of different means of taking action in ways that do not necessarily follow the pattern of Article 27.

Action by consensus

Frequently the Council acts without vote on the basis of consensus within the Council—that is, as a result of consultations in which none of the members of the Council objects to the action.[23] Such an action typically takes the form of a written announcement by the president of the Council reciting a "statement on behalf of the Council."

During the post–Cold War period, the number of these actions has been substantial and has sometimes exceeded the number of formal resolutions in a given year.[24] This procedure can be a means of achieving prompt action where the adoption of a formal resolution by vote may be politically awkward or time-consuming. As a legal matter, it can be reconciled with Article 27 in that the consensus obtained includes all the members whose votes would have been necessary for formal adoption under Article 27.[25]

Usually these statements are used for expressions of the Council's attitudes and recommendations with respect to immediate developments in a particular situation, and such expressions are not binding. However, these statements sometimes contain provisions having direct legal impact, such as determinations that a state or other entity had acted in violation of its obligations,[26] decisions about the continuation or modification of sanctions,[27] or decisions on the scope of the authority of a subordinate body.[28]

Implied action

From time to time it has been argued that the Council's authorization for a particular course of action should be implied, even though it has not given express authorization. For example, such arguments were made with respect to the following situations:

- ❖ The 1962 Cuban missile crisis, during which the Organization of American States recommended that its members use armed force to the extent necessary to prevent Soviet offensive missiles from reaching Cuba, but Security Council authorization (as contemplated by Article 53) was not available because of the Soviet veto. The United States argued (among other things) that the Council's failure to disapprove the quarantine was legally equivalent to authorizing it.[29]
- ❖ In the early 1990s, the armed intervention of the Economic Community of West African States (ECOWAS) in the Liberian internal conflict, where the Council never expressly authorized the intervention, but from time to time commended the actions

of ECOWAS and called on parties to the conflict to comply with its cease-fire.[30] Some commentators characterized this as implicit (though retroactive) authorization by the Council.[31]

❖ In 1991, the Western intervention in northern Iraq after the end of the Gulf War for the purpose of protecting and providing humanitarian relief to large numbers of Kurdish refugees, where the Council did not expressly authorize the intervention, but (with apparent knowledge that it was about to occur) condemned Iraqi repression, demanded that Iraq desist and allow access by international humanitarian organizations, and appealed to all states to contribute to international relief efforts.[32] Some commentators suggested that this amounted to implicit authorization.[33]

❖ The 1999 North Atlantic Treaty Organization (NATO) military campaign against the Federal Republic of Yugoslavia (FRY) to compel the withdrawal of Serb forces from Kosovo, in which the Council never expressly authorized the NATO campaign but condemned Serb repression and directed that it cease, imposed an arms embargo on the FRY under Chapter VII, defeated a Russian proposal condemning the NATO air campaign, and (after the conclusion of the NATO campaign) authorized an international security presence in Kosovo under NATO command to carry out the terms imposed by NATO through its use of force.[34] Some suggested that the Council's actions constituted a form of implicit approval of the NATO bombing campaign.[35] (In contrast, as explored in chapter 5, the United States and its supporters argued that their 2003 intervention in Iraq was based on *express* prior authorization by the Council for action to restore and maintain the peace in the region.)

Each of these military interventions was also justified by its proponents on other grounds. But, as for the claim of implicit authorization by the Council, much depends on the circumstances in each case. For example, in the case of Liberia, the Council's endorsement of the ECOWAS intervention came after the fact, but at least it seems to be the case that the ECOWAS actions were favored at the time by the members of the Council, whose acceptance would have been needed for an express decision to authorize the intervention. Express advance authorization is always preferable, but if the Council were to indicate clearly its acceptance of such a regional intervention without formally authorizing it, the failure to obtain prior formal authorization would not be a serious challenge to the Charter structure.

However, in other cases, the Council did not affirmatively authorize military action precisely because one or more permanent members were prepared to veto it. In such circumstances, to argue that the Council had acted by inaction would stand the basic decision-making structure of the Charter on its head, permitting the authorization of the use of force in the face of overt opposition by one or more of its permanent members. Such a result would hardly be in the long-term interests of the United States or any other permanent member. The acceptance of such a doctrine would, in any event, be self-defeating, since the permanent member or members opposing such a result would in the future simply prevent the Council from taking the actions that constituted "implicit authorization." This would be an unfortunate and counterproductive outcome, since it might, for example, cause a permanent member to veto a Council decision to find a threat to the peace, or to condemn repressive actions, or to require that those actions be terminated.

Delegation of decisions

Sometimes the Council may prefer to delegate a decision to another body or person rather than make the decision itself. This practice of delegation has increased substantially during the post–Cold War period and has taken new and more important forms. One important consequence is that such decisions may then be taken by persons or bodies that are much better suited to the character of the decision required. Another is that such decisions can be taken by the delegated actor without following the procedure for substantive decisions specified in Article 27.

This sort of delegation may take several forms. First, the Council may delegate authority to the UN secretary-general, who of course may draw upon the substantial resources of the Secretariat to exercise that authority. During the post–Cold War period, the Council assigned many important tasks to the secretary-general, including the conduct of peacekeeping operations and the administration of significant new programs. In the course of doing so, the Council has from time to time given to the secretary-general the authority to make decisions or has made Council decisions contingent on determinations by him.

Some of these delegations are relatively ministerial in character—for example, when the Council provides that its sanctions become effective or cease to be effective when the secretary-general reports that a specific notification has been received or a specific action taken.[36] In other cases, however, the determinations to be made by the secretary-general require considerable judgment and discretion. For example, in the case of Haiti, the Council provided that sanctions would come into force on a specific date unless the secretary-general reported that "the imposition of such measures is not warranted at that time."[37] In the case of the National Union for Total Independence of Angola (or UNITA, the Angolan insurgent movement of Jonas Savimbi), the Council provided that sanctions would come into force if the secretary-general reported that UNITA had broken the cease-fire or had "ceased to participate constructively" in the implementation of the relevant peace accords and Council resolutions.[38]

Acting under authority from the Council, the secretary-general may create bodies to make the decisions necessary to carry out the tasks assigned to him. One prominent example of this was the Iraq-Kuwait Boundary Demarcation Commission, created by the secretary-general pursuant to the Council's decision at the end of the Gulf War that it was necessary to have a definitive resolution of the dispute over the boundary, which had been one of the ostensible causes of the conflict.[39] (The commission was composed of one representative of Iraq and one of Kuwait, plus three independent experts appointed by the secretary-general.[40]) In due course, the commission completed the demarcation of the boundary, after which the Council declared that the demarcation was final and guaranteed the inviolability of the boundary as demarcated.[41] The work of the Boundary Commission will be examined in greater detail in chapter 6.

Even more extensive were the broad governance powers over Kosovo and East Timor that were given by the Security Council to the secretary-general and his "special representatives," including the authority to make all necessary laws, appoint all necessary executive and judicial officers, and take all appropriate administrative measures.[42] These special representatives in turn created a variety of local courts and councils to carry out these functions. The governance of territories under the authority of the Council will be discussed in greater length in chapter 4.

Second, the Council may delegate decisions to persons or bodies outside the UN structure. For example, the Council provided in September 1994 that various sanctions against Yugoslavia would be suspended if the co-chairmen of the Steering Committee of the International Conference on the Former Yugoslavia certified that the authorities of the Federal Republic had effectively closed their border with Bosnia.[43] The scheme for the governance of Kosovo involved significant delegations of responsibility to the Organization for Security and Cooperation in Europe (OSCE) and the European Union (see chapter 4).

Third, the Council is authorized by Article 29 of the Charter to "establish such subsidiary organs as it deems necessary for the performance of its functions," and it may delegate decision-making authority to subsidiary organs on such terms and conditions as it chooses.[44] Many subordinate organs have no formal decision-making authority, such as the committees and working groups created from time to time to study or recommend solutions to specific problems, or the many peacekeeping and other missions created by the Council to carry out specific tasks in the field.[45] However, during the post–Cold War period, the Council has also created a number of subsidiary organs to which it has delegated the authority to make significant substantive decisions.

One important example—which will be discussed at greater length in chapter 3—is the series of sanctions committees created to enforce the sanctions regimes imposed by the Council during the past fifteen years. Each of these committees is composed of representatives of all of the Council members. These committees typically have many important nondecision functions, such as monitoring and reporting on compliance with Council sanctions, providing information and assistance to states to assist in compliance, and providing expert advice to the Council on sanctions enforcement.[46] But in addition, these committees have been given important decision-making authority in many cases.

For example, sanctions committees have often been given the authority to grant exceptions from sanctions on a case-by-case basis for specific purposes—the most common being the approval of shipments of food, medicine, or other humanitarian items, or of travel for religious purposes.[47] Sometimes the committees have been given more general authority to grant exceptions in their discretion.[48] In several instances, these committees have been given the authority to promulgate binding rules for the implementation of sanctions (as well as recommendatory guidelines).[49]

In a number of cases, sanctions committees have been authorized to draw up lists of persons or organizations that are judged to fall within categories against whom sanctions will apply (such as the members of certain ruling circles that are thought to be responsible for offensive conduct), or lists of organizations to which sanctions will not apply.[50] For example, the Sanctions Committee for Iraq was given substantial authority to regulate imports for the maintenance and improvement of the Iraqi oil production and transportation networks;[51] it was also given the task of drawing up lists of items whose import would be permitted.[52]

Another subsidiary organ to which considerable decision-making authority was given by the Council is the UN Compensation Commission, which was created in 1991 to adjudicate and pay claims against Iraq arising out of its invasion and occupation of Kuwait. Among other things, the Governing Council of the commission—whose membership is identical to that of the Security Council itself—was given the authority to determine what categories of claims could be submitted for losses suffered by states, individuals, and business entities; to determine the procedures for adjudication of those claims and to approve the awards to be issued; to establish priorities for payment of the various categories of claims; and to govern the administration of the fund that would pay these claims, to be drawn from Iraqi oil export revenues.[53] This immense process—involving more than a hundred billion dollars of claims—is discussed in greater detail in chapter 6.

Yet another set of subordinate organs with considerable delegated authority are the two international criminal tribunals created by the Council for the prosecution of international crimes in Rwanda and the former Yugoslavia. These tribunals consist of independent judges elected by the General Assembly and Security Council who have been given the power to indict, convict, and punish offenders for crimes relating to specific conflict situations, as well as to require states to surrender such persons for trial.[54] The work of these tribunals will be considered in chapter 7.

These various delegations of authority were essential for several reasons: (1) to ensure that decisions requiring legal, financial, or other technical expertise would be made by persons with the necessary professional background; (2) to give assurance that certain kinds of decisions (such as the guilt or innocence of accused persons) would be made on a nonpolitical basis; (3) to relieve the Council of the burden of decisions that might be politically difficult if the Council were forced to make them; and (4) to enable the Council to focus on urgent policy and political issues and to avoid being swamped by a great volume of administrative questions better handled elsewhere.

One striking aspect of all these delegations of decision-making authority is that the process by which decisions are made by these bodies varies considerably and in no instance conforms to the voting rules of Article 27 of the Charter. The sanctions committees make decisions by consensus. The Governing Council of the Compensation Commission has, to date, made all its decisions by consensus, but its rules provide for the possibility of decisions on most issues by a vote of nine members, with no veto applying.[55] The Iraq-Kuwait Boundary Demarcation Commission made decisions by majority vote.[56] In the international criminal tribunals, indictments are confirmed and orders are issued for the arrest and surrender of accused persons by a single judge, while judgments by the trial and appellate chambers are decided by a simple majority of the members of the chamber.[57] The secretary-general and his special representatives of course make individual decisions, while the bodies created by the special representatives to govern Kosovo and East Timor have had a variety of different decision-making procedures.

Thus, while the permanent members are still very unlikely to give up their formal veto power under the Charter, the Council has not felt obligated to replicate the permanent-member veto and other aspects of its formal voting procedures in all situations, and it has instead been prepared to create flexible decision-making structures specifically designed for particular situations during the post–Cold War period. While the basic decision to exercise Chapter VII authority must still be made by the Council in accordance with Article 27, there now seems to be no reason why the Council cannot delegate and structure other decisions involving the application of Chapter VII powers in such manner as it finds appropriate.

Termination of decisions

Because of the great number and importance of Council actions in the post–Cold War period, the mechanism for termination of these measures has become a frequent and significant issue.

This question first arose in Council practice with respect to the sanctions against Southern Rhodesia, which had been imposed by the Council in 1966 without time limit or expiration mechanism.[58] When the white minority regime finally gave up its assertion of independence in 1979, the United Kingdom terminated its observance of sanctions, apparently on the view that the sanctions had expired automatically, while the Soviet Union and African states insisted that the sanctions had to be observed fully until the Council terminated them. The matter was obviated when the Council affirmatively decided to terminate the sanctions a short time later.[59]

On a number of occasions during the post–Cold War period, the Council again decided on measures without providing a fixed duration or a definite triggering event for termination.[60] Some of these decisions stated that sanctions would remain in effect until the Council decided otherwise, without prescribing the criterion for such a decision. For example, in 1991, the Council imposed an arms embargo on Yugoslavia, to be observed "until the Council decides otherwise following consultation between the Secretary-General and the Government of Yugoslavia."[61] At the end of the Gulf War, the Council decided that the arms embargo against Iraq would continue to apply "until it takes a further decision."[62] In November 1992, the Council imposed an arms embargo against Liberia, to be effective "until the Security Council decides otherwise."[63]

In some cases, the Council provided that the measures in question would terminate when it determined that a particular criterion or condition had been met. For example, in 1992, the Council imposed economic sanctions against the Federal Republic of Yugoslavia, which were to apply "until the Council decides" that the FRY had fulfilled the requirements of a previous Council resolution with respect to Bosnia (including the cessation of hostilities, withdrawal of military units, and disbanding of irregular forces).[64]

In other cases, the Council gave other individuals or bodies the role of determining or advising as to when such criteria or conditions had been met. For example, in June 1993, the Council imposed an arms and petroleum embargo on Haiti, while stating its readiness to review those measures with a view to lifting them if the secretary-general reported that the "de facto authorities" in Haiti had agreed to reinstate the Aristide government and had begun to implement that agreement in good faith.[65] In March 1998, the Council imposed an arms embargo on the Federal Republic of Yugoslavia for its conduct in Kosovo, to be reconsidered with a view to termination if the secretary-general reported that various steps had been taken, including the initiation of a "meaningful dialogue" with the Kosovar Albanian community on political status issues.[66] In October 1999, the Council imposed certain sanctions against the Taliban for its support of terrorist groups, which were to terminate once the secretary-general reported that the Taliban had turned Osama bin Laden over to "appropriate authorities in a country where he will be arrested and effectively brought to justice."[67]

On many other occasions, the Council's decisions carried a specific time limit, at which point a further affirmative decision to renew was required. This had already become common practice for the deployment of peacekeeping forces. The majority of resolutions authorizing states or regional organizations to use force have no fixed time limit, but time limits have been imposed in a few cases.[68] The imposition of several recent sanctions regimes was accompanied by a fixed time limit, but this was not the case for most sanctions regimes.[69] Certain other Council regimes (such as the use of Iraqi oil export revenues for humanitarian supplies) had fixed time limits, while others (such as the use of Iraqi oil export revenues for compensation for Gulf War damage) did not.[70]

Where a Council decision does not expire by its own terms after a fixed period of time (or on the occurrence of an objective event), any permanent member can use its veto to prevent the termination or modification of that decision. This has sometimes been referred to as a "reverse veto," and has been criticized for enabling any permanent member to perpetuate sanctions regimes or authorizations to use force indefinitely, even if they no longer serve their original purposes or have lost the support of the majority of the Council or the international community as a whole.[71] On the other hand, if a Council decision terminates automatically on the expiration of a fixed period, then the sanctions regime or peacekeeping authorization in question might end, contrary to the wishes of the majority of the Council, because of the opposition to renewal of one or two permanent members.

Therefore, when making its initial decision on a program, the Council needs to exercise judgment as to whether it is more important to avoid the risk of undue prolongation of the regime, in which case a fixed duration is called for, or to ensure the durability and credibility of the regime, in which case the regime should end only when the Council affirmatively decides it is time.[72] If a fixed duration is chosen, the Council must carefully choose a period of time that does not compromise the effectiveness of the program by inviting its premature demise. Or, as suggested by the previous discussion, the Council may choose to delegate the authority to terminate a program by a process that does not include the veto.

THE LEGAL CHARACTER OF COUNCIL DECISIONS

The Charter gives extraordinary power to the Council for the purpose of restoring and maintaining the peace, including the power to impose binding obligations on UN members. Specifically, Article 25 provides that UN members "agree to accept and carry out the decisions of the Security Council in accordance with the present Charter." Article 48 provides that action required to carry out the Council's decisions "shall be taken by all of the Members of the United Nations or by some of them, as the Security Council may determine." While there has been debate on the extent to which Council decisions outside of Chapter VII may have binding effect,[73] there is no doubt that the Council can take binding decisions within Chapter VII.

Furthermore, decisions under Chapter VII take precedence over other sources of international law. Article 103 of the Charter specifically provides that in the event of a conflict between the obligations of UN members under the Charter and their obligations under any other international agreement, "their obligations under the Charter shall prevail." The International Court of Justice (ICJ) has confirmed that this applies to obligations created by decisions of the Council under Chapter VII.[74] As will be examined in chapter 3, this is an essential feature of Chapter VII sanctions regimes, which would be ineffective if they did not override other international agreements (such as trade treaties and aviation agreements). While it has been argued in Council debates that the Council cannot or should not modify existing treaty regimes,[75] nonetheless the Council clearly has the authority to require states to take actions that would otherwise be prohibited by other treaties. (Of course, there are certain types of treaty obligations that the Council would rarely if ever find it appropriate to override, such as the basic protections for prisoners of war and detained civilians in the 1949 Geneva Conventions.[76])

Article 103 does not literally apply to the obligations of states under customary international law—that is, principles generally accepted in state practice as having international legal force.[77] However, it is generally accepted that the obligation of states under Articles 25 and 48 to carry out decisions of the Council lead to the same result,[78] and in fact it would be anomalous if the Council were able to override obligations under treaties but not under customary law.[79] (Once again, there are some customary norms that the Council would rarely if ever find it appropriate to override, such as fundamental human rights.)

However, the Council's authority under Chapter VII is not without limits, and there has been increased attention in recent years to the question of what these limits may be.[80] One limit has already been mentioned—namely, the requirement that the Council find the existence of a threat to the peace, breach of the peace, or act of aggression as a predicate to Chapter VII action. This important limit will be the subject of chapter 2 of this book. Further, the Council must of course comply with the procedural requirements of the Charter for Council decisions, as has been described earlier.

In addition, Article 24(2) of the Charter provides that the Council "shall act in accordance with the Purposes and Principles of the United Nations," which are spelled out in Articles 1 and 2. The purposes include the maintenance of international peace and security; the development of friendly relations on the basis of equal rights and self-determination of peoples; international cooperation in the economic, social, cultural, and humanitarian fields; and the promotion of human rights. The principles include the sovereign equality of UN members, the fulfillment of Charter obligations in good faith, the settlement of international disputes by peaceful means, abstention from the use of force, and nonintervention into internal affairs.

As Article 24(2) says, the Council is obligated to act in accordance with these purposes and principles, but it is not clear how much this obligation actually limits the Council in practice. The purposes and principles are very general statements that are not defined and are subject to a wide range of interpretation, and some by their nature do not seem to have specific legal content. Further, the application of some of these purposes and principles is limited by specific Charter provisions. For example, Article 2(7) specifically states that the principle of nonintervention does not prejudice the application of enforcement measures under Chapter VII; and, notwithstanding the principle of non-use of force in Article 2(4), Article 42 specifically authorizes the Council to take military action to maintain or restore international peace and security.

In addition, conflicts will often arise among the various purposes and principles in specific circumstances, requiring the Council to choose between them or make some compromise among them. For example, the Council may find it necessary, in order to maintain the peace or advance human rights in a particular situation, to take actions that will, at least to some degree, limit the exercise of self-determination or impair economic development. The list of purposes and principles does not establish a clear order of priority among them in the event of conflict, but the maintenance of peace and security is the first stated, and there is no reason to suppose that the others were meant to take automatic precedence. The logical conclusion is that the Council has the discretion and responsibility for deciding how to resolve such conflicts, though it is fair to assert that the Council should, to the extent possible, maintain the peace through methods that are also consistent with the other principles. In any event, these are important questions to which we will return at greater length in later chapters in the context of specific types of Council action, such as sanctions, governance of territories, the use of force, territorial disputes, and criminal prosecutions.

It is interesting to note that Articles 1 and 2 do not include a general requirement that the Council act in accordance with international law in carrying out its functions. Article 1(1) says that one of the purposes of the United Nations is "to bring about by peaceful means, and in conformity with the principles of justice and international law, adjustment or settlement of international disputes or situations which might lead to a breach of the peace." But the article does not apply the language about international law when it states that another of the purposes is "to take effective collective measures for the prevention and removal of threats to the peace, and for the suppression of acts of aggression or other breaches of the peace." Apparently this difference was quite deliberate, in that a proposal was made but rejected to apply the requirement of conformity with international law to the maintenance of international peace and security as well, evidently because such a requirement was thought to unduly inhibit the Council's flexibility in dealing with conflict situations.[81]

The question then arises as to whether Council decisions should be subject to review and possible nullification on legal grounds by some other body—the obvious candidate being the ICJ, which is the "principal judicial organ of the United Nations."[82] The Charter does provide one possible avenue for review by the court of the legality or legal effect of Council actions, in that either the Security Council or the General Assembly may ask the court for an advisory opinion on any legal question, which could include a request by either body for the court's advice on the legality or legal effect of actions taken or under consideration by that body.[83] This authority was used by the General Assembly to obtain an opinion on the legality of its authorization of expenditures for peacekeeping operations in the Congo in the early 1960s,[84] and by the Council on the legal effect of its actions concerning the termination of the mandate of South Africa over South-West Africa (Namibia).[85] Such opinions are "advisory" and not legally binding, but nonetheless the Council might be expected to pay attention to the court's views on the legality of its actions if it had requested them.[86]

Otherwise, neither the charter nor the statute of the court provides any right of appeal to the court (or any other body) to review or nullify a Council decision on the grounds that the Council may have acted illegally, and the court has never asserted that such a right exists.[87] However, one party to a case before the court may attempt to rely on a decision of the Council and the other party may challenge the legality of that decision; the question then arises as to whether the court may decline to apply the Council decision on the grounds that it was beyond the Council's authority.[88] This is precisely the question presented to the ICJ in the *Lockerbie* case (concerning the destruction of an American airliner over Scotland by Libyan agents), in which the United States and United Kingdom relied on Chapter VII decisions of the Council and Libya challenged the legality of those decisions.[89] The Council never decided whether it could or should review the legality of Council decisions in such a situation, because the *Lockerbie* case was resolved by agreement of the parties before a decision on the merits was handed down.

It has been argued that the exercise by the court of this form of judicial review is legitimate and appropriate, given the broad power of the Council and the asserted desirability of having some external check on unlawful action by the Council.[90] However, the *Lockerbie* case illustrates the possible pitfalls of such action by the court. Libya brought its case before the court just as the Council was considering the imposition of sanctions on Libya to compel it to cease support for terrorism and to surrender the accused Libyan agents for trial; the immediate Libyan objective was to persuade the ICJ to hand down an immediate order ("provisional measures") that would prevent the United States and the United Kingdom from pursuing such sanctions before the Council, or to persuade the Council to refrain from acting until the court had considered its case. Fortunately, neither the Council nor the court heeded Libya's demands: the Council imposed sanctions,[91] and the court denied Libya's request for provisional measures.[92]

But if the court were aggressively to assert a broad power to review the legality of Council decisions in such cases, then the Council might feel constrained to stay its hand until the court passed on the issue. Even if the Council acted, dissatisfied states might refrain from complying in the hopes that the court would later hold in their favor. Given the length of time that the court often takes to resolve cases before it, this could mean that Council decisions might effectively be in a state of suspended animation for extended periods.[93] This situation could result in serious damage to the credibility and effectiveness of the Council's action in crisis situations. It suggests that the court should be cautious about asserting a right to review Council decisions, particularly its exercise of Chapter VII powers.

But even if the court were to decide that it could and should review the legality of Council decisions, the question would remain as to which decisions under Chapter VII would be reviewable and what the standard of review would be. The Charter specifically gives the Council the responsibility for deciding whether there is a threat to the peace and what measures are to be taken in response.[94] Such a decision is typically a matter of political judgment and policy, which rests on an evaluation of complex circumstances at the time of the decision that would be difficult for a court to second-guess. These decisions are therefore not readily subject to judicial review, and it is difficult to see how the court could reasonably substitute its judgment for that of the Council in such a case.

At the very least, the ICJ would have to give very substantial deference to the Council's judgment on such matters. Even in advisory opinion cases, where matters have been expressly referred to the court by the Security Council or General Assembly, the court has made clear that "a resolution of a properly constituted organ of the United Nations which is passed in accordance with that organ's rules of procedure . . . must be presumed to have been validly adopted."[95] The Appeals Chamber of the International Criminal Tribunal for the Former Yugoslavia affirmed that the Council "exercises a very wide discretion" in finding the existence of threats to the peace[96] and, likewise, that it enjoys "a wide margin of discretion" in deciding what measures are to be taken as a result.[97]

For these and other reasons, it seems neither appropriate nor likely that the court will substantially constrain the ability of the Council to act under Chapter VII. This makes it all the more important for the Council itself to pay attention to legal constraints and considerations in making Chapter VII decisions and, in particular, to take seriously its duty to make reasonable judgments about threats to the peace and to act in a manner consistent with the requirements of the Charter.

ASSESSMENT

The UN Charter contains all the fundamental legal authority necessary for effective international action to deal with armed conflict, including the ability of the Council to take a very wide range of measures to restore and maintain the peace. Specifically, the Council's actions under Chapter VII are binding on states and override other obligations.

Nonetheless, the system depends in the end on the ability of the Council to act promptly and decisively. The basic prerequisite for this ability has been and will always be the development of political consensus, particularly among the permanent members, on the course to be taken, which in turn requires both leadership and compromise by the United States and other major players.

At the same time, the development of appropriate decision-making procedures can play an important role in this process, and considerable progress has been made in the post–Cold War period in developing such procedures. There is little prospect for significant restriction of the right of veto itself, but the Council has shown increasing willingness to delegate authority to a variety of actors—to the secretary-general, to subordinate bodies or officials created by the Council, or to outside entities—and to do so in a flexible manner that may not include the right of veto. This delegation will not lead to the end of the veto in basic decisions on the use of Chapter VII powers, but it does open up useful alternatives, particularly with respect to UN programs of governance, justice, and sanctions that may be necessary to handle conflict situations.

Finally, while the Council exercises very broad legal authority under the Charter, and its decisions under Chapter VII have very broad legal effect, there are still important legal principles to which the Council must give due attention in exercising this power. No judicial authority seems likely to act as a significant constraint on Council action in this regard, but the Council itself must take seriously its own responsibility to act in a manner consistent with the Charter.

2

JURISDICTION
AND MANDATE

D URING THE COLD WAR, the Security Council could rarely exercise the full scope of its powers because of conflict between the permanent members and a cautious attitude among states generally about the intrusion of international organs into what they regarded as their internal affairs. With the end of the Cold War, the conflict between the permanent members greatly eased, and states increasingly came to accept international involvement in resolving all forms of armed conflict. This shift resulted in not only the unleashing of the latent authority that the Council had always been recognized to have under the Charter, but also an interpretation and application of that authority more expansive than what the Charter's founders might have contemplated. In recent years, political conflicts among the permanent members have re-emerged, which has on some important occasions inhibited the Council from exercising the full scope of its authority. Nonetheless, an expansive view of the Council's jurisdiction and mandate is now well established and is available wherever its members are prepared to act.

A fundamental aspect of the legal authority of any international institution is the scope and character of its jurisdiction and mandate. This chapter considers the Security Council's jurisdiction, both in theory as spelled out in the Charter and in practice as it has developed in coping with actual conflict situations.

As emphasized in the preceding chapter, the primary authority of the Security Council is defined in terms of international peace and security. The Council's jurisdiction under Chapter VI—which gives it recommendatory but not binding authority—is stated in very broad terms. According to Articles 33–34, it includes "any dispute, the continuance of which is likely to endanger the maintenance of international peace and security" and "any situation which might lead to international friction or give rise to a dispute." It is hard to imagine any situation of actual or potential conflict that could not fit within this mandate.

The predicate for Council action under Chapter VII—which gives the Council extensive mandatory powers—was designed to be more demanding. According to Article 39, there must be a determination by the Council of "the existence of any threat to the peace, breach of the peace, or act of aggression." In fact, the great majority of Council actions have been based on a finding of a "threat to the peace," rather than on the "breach of the peace" or "aggression" criteria. This fact reflects in part a frequent desire to avoid a characterization of a situation that might be premature, counterproductive, or give the appearance of taking sides in the conflict. It also reflects the fact that the criterion of a "threat to the peace" is a more flexible and open-ended standard.

A determination that a situation constitutes a threat to the peace is obviously a matter of judgment, and the criterion necessarily gives great latitude and discretion to the Council in deciding whether it has jurisdiction in any particular case. The negotiating history of Article 39 indicates that the UN founders deliberately resisted more limiting formulations and intended to give broad discretion to the Council in deciding what might constitute such a threat.[1]

One curious aspect of the Charter language on this point is that Article 39 provides for a determination by the Council of the existence of a threat to or breach of "the peace," whereas the Charter refers elsewhere in Article 39 and other articles in Chapters VI and VII to the maintenance or restoration of "international peace and security." There is no indication that the omission of the word "international" in the beginning of Article 39 had some deliberate purpose. At one early point, the United States attempted to use this language difference to argue that internal disorders could fall within Article 39 without a showing of a threat to peace outside the country in question, but in general, states do not seem to have accepted this view.[2] In fact, the great majority of Chapter VII resolutions refer either to a threat to "international" peace and security, or to a threat to peace and security in the region, or both. In the relatively few cases in which the Council referred simply to a threat to or breach of "the peace," there does not seem to be any reason to think that the Council meant that the situation presented no threat to peace outside the country concerned.[3]

This question—of what constitutes a threat to or breach of the peace—is of fundamental importance, because it determines to a large extent the boundary between national sovereignty and international jurisdiction under the Charter system. Article 2(7), which provides that nothing in the Charter authorizes the UN to intervene "in matters which are essentially within the domestic jurisdiction of any state," then provides that "this principle shall not prejudice the application of enforcement measures under Chapter VII." In other words, if the Council determines that an internal situation (such as a conflict against domestic insurgents or internal ethnic violence) constitutes a threat to the peace, then the international community—through the Council—has the power to intervene dramatically and powerfully, if necessary, through sanctions or the use of force. In such a case, national sovereignty gives way to international authority in the most direct and forceful way.

It is therefore not surprising that this question of the legitimate scope of the Council's jurisdiction under Chapter VII, and in particular the extent of its right to treat an internal situation as a threat to the peace, has been an important element in defining the relationship between international and national authority in the post–Cold War period. This development has occurred at the same time that the international community has begun to take a much more restrictive view of the scope of matters that are reserved to the "domestic jurisdiction" of states, as is evidenced by the very considerable increase in

UN human rights activities aimed at scrutinizing and reforming the treatment by governments of their own nationals.[4]

THE COLD WAR PERIOD

Of course, any situation involving actual or imminent armed conflict between states would clearly fall within the Security Council's jurisdiction, and the Council never doubted its authority to find a threat to or breach of the peace in such circumstances—even during the Cold War, when political differences among the permanent members were largely paralyzing effective Council action. For example, the Council determined that there was a threat to the peace with respect to the Palestine conflict in 1948, and that there was a breach of the peace with respect to Korea in 1950, the Falkland Islands (Islas Malvinas) in 1982, and the Iran-Iraq conflict in 1987.[5]

The real questions about the Council's jurisdiction arise with respect to situations in which armed conflict between states is not in progress and does not appear to be imminent. In such cases, there was a considerable difference in the Council's practice during the Cold War, depending on whether it was considering action under Chapter VI or Chapter VII. From the beginning, the Council was ready to exercise freely its nonmandatory Chapter VI authority, even in internal situations that did not seem to present any immediate risk of hostilities between states. For example, it investigated complaints of internal oppression by the Franco regime in Spain and pronounced on the Israeli abduction and trial of Adolf Eichmann, even though the possibility of armed conflict among states was very remote.[6]

However, the Council proceeded more cautiously in using its mandatory Chapter VII authority. In the case of Southern Rhodesia, following a proclamation of independence by the white minority regime under Ian Smith in November 1965, the Council determined that the "continuance in time" of the situation would constitute a threat to international peace and security. As a result, the Council called upon the United Kingdom (the recognized "administering Power") to take all appropriate measures to bring that regime "to an immediate end."[7] This resolution drew on the language of Article 37 of Chapter VI and was only recommendatory in character. Almost five months later, the Council determined that the situation was now "a threat to the peace" and called on the United Kingdom "to prevent, by the use of force if necessary" the shipment of oil for Rhodesia to the port of Beira in Portuguese Mozambique.[8] Then in December 1966, the Council invoked Articles 39 and 41 under Chapter VII to impose a partial economic embargo on trade and other financial transactions with Southern Rhodesia.[9] Finally, in May 1968, the Council imposed a comprehensive embargo.[10]

The U.S. State Department defended the Council's determination of a threat to the peace on the grounds that "in the political context of the African Continent, such action could lead to civil strife that might involve other parties on one or both sides of the conflict."[11] However, others argued that the Council's action was invalid because the Rhodesian minority regime had merely declared its independence and presented no threat to any other state.[12]

In 1960, in the case of South Africa, the Council reacted to the repressive apartheid system by declaring that the situation "is one that has led to international friction and if continued might endanger international peace and security" and calling on the South African government to abandon its racist policies.[13] This, again, was a use of Chapter VI terminology to support Chapter VI recommendations. In 1963, the Council declared that "the situation in South Africa is seriously disturbing international peace and security," and called on all states to cease arms sales to South Africa, but did not invoke Chapter VII.[14] The United States explained that it had accepted this resolution because it did not use language that would have implied a Chapter VII situation. The U.S. delegate stated: "There are in this troubled world many disturbances of international peace and security, but even in those parts of the world where there is now sporadic fighting on international frontiers, this organization has been wisely cautious about invoking the powers of the Security Council under Chapter VII."[15]

It was not until 1977, in the wake of widespread violence, increased government repression, and the threat of the acquisition of nuclear weapons by South Africa, that the Council finally determined that "the acquisition by South Africa of arms and related materiel constitutes a threat to the maintenance of international peace and security," and invoked Chapter VII to impose a mandatory arms embargo.[16]

In fact, both the Rhodesian and South African situations did present clear threats to the peace in any objective sense of the phrase, even though they were primarily internal conflicts. In both cases, surrounding states became a base for insurgents fighting the white minority regimes, and those regimes in turn conducted a number of military operations against their neighbors, culminating in the occupation of a large part of Angola for an extended period. The acquisition of nuclear capabilities by the South African government—an event to which the Council called particular attention in its 1977 decision—made this threat even more clear and serious. Under these circumstances, the reluctance and delay of the Council in finding a threat to the peace and in applying Chapter VII demonstrated that the Council still had a relatively cautious view of the applicability or appropriateness of the use of this important authority in such situations.

Such caution is underlined by the Council's failure to invoke Chapter VII with respect to a number of other serious internal conflicts during the same period, including those in the Congo, Biafra, Cambodia, and various countries in Central America—each of which clearly had serious implications for the peace of its region. Indeed, it is fair to say that the Council's use of Chapter VII for Rhodesia and South Africa was less a reflection of a desire to deal aggressively with threats to the peace as such than a determination to eradicate odious racial discrimination and oppression. In that sense, the Council's actions on Rhodesia and South Africa can be seen as first steps toward the use of Chapter VII to achieve human rights objectives that became much more frequent after the end of the Cold War.

CONFLICTS IN THE POST–COLD WAR PERIOD

During the post–Cold War period, the basis for international intervention under Chapter VII was vastly expanded, not only to encompass all sorts of ongoing internal armed conflicts, but also to deal with internal problems that could lead to such conflicts in the future, such as humanitarian disasters, internal repression, and threats to democracy. The following is a discussion of some of the more important examples of this development.[17]

The Gulf War

The Iraqi invasion of Kuwait in August 1990 did not present any real difficulty about the jurisdiction of the Council to act, because it involved serious armed conflict between states from the very beginning. The invasion was a clear violation of Article 2(4), since it was not a response to Kuwaiti attack and was openly designed to extinguish the existence of Kuwait as a sovereign state and to incorporate it into Iraq. In the language of Article 2(4), it was a use of force against the "territorial integrity" and the "political independence" of Kuwait, as well as "inconsistent with the Purposes of the United Nations." It also posed a serious political and economic threat to both the Gulf Arab states and to the West in general. With the end of the Cold War, the Soviet Union (whose seat on the Council would soon be taken over by the Russian Federation) no longer had any inclination to use its veto in the Council to back client states like Iraq in aggressive military actions against states oriented toward the West.

Accordingly, on the very first day of the invasion, the Council determined that Iraqi actions constituted "a breach of international peace and security," invoked Articles 39 and 40 of Chapter VII, and demanded immediate Iraqi withdrawal.[18] Four days later, the Council invoked Chapter VII again to impose a comprehensive economic embargo,[19] beginning a series of increasingly vigorous Chapter VII measures that will be examined in detail in later chapters of this book. No member of the Council took issue with the right of the Council to exercise its Chapter VII authority under these circumstances. Nor, as will be examined in later chapters, did the Council hesitate after the war to find a continuing threat to the peace in Iraq's noncompliance with the Council's demands concerning the elimination of weapons of mass destruction, or to use its Chapter VII authority to deal with the consequences of the Gulf War (such as compensation of war victims) or to minimize Iraqi threats to its neighbors (including the maintenance of an arms embargo).

However, there was considerable disagreement when the war ended over the proper response to Iraqi repression of internal factions, particularly the Kurdish population of northern Iraq. During March 1991, after crushing Shiite dissidents in the south, Iraqi forces moved against Kurdish rebels in the north, causing hundreds of thousands of Kurdish refugees to escape into the mountainous areas bordering Turkey and Iran. The lack of food, shelter, sanitation, and medical attention threatened to cause a serious humanitarian catastrophe and to overwhelm the resources of neighboring states.[20]

On April 4, 1991, the Council adopted Resolution 688 by a vote of 10–3. (The negative votes were cast by Cuba, Yemen, and Zimbabwe; China and India abstained.) The resolution condemned Iraqi repression of its civilian population and stated that it was a threat to international peace and security in the region. The resolution went on to demand that Iraq, "as a contribution to removing the threat to international peace and security in the region," immediately end that repression and allow access by international humanitarian organizations to all in need of assistance. The resolution further appealed to all UN member states and humanitarian organizations to contribute to such humanitarian relief efforts. In the weeks that followed, the resolution formed the political and legal cornerstone for an extensive international intervention in northern Iraq that included the deployment of substantial numbers of U.S., British, and French troops to secure safe areas for the protection of Kurdish civilians and the provision of humanitarian relief.[21]

There was considerable controversy as to whether this resolution provided adequate legal authority for military intervention. The resolution itself did not expressly authorize the use of force, nor did it expressly invoke the Council's authority under Chapter VII. Nonetheless, the resolution did include the finding of a threat to peace and security that is the predicate for Chapter VII action, and this finding was a matter of considerable debate within the Council prior to its adoption.

Several Council members argued that such a finding was inappropriate because the situation in northern Iraq was a domestic situation that did not constitute a threat to international peace, and that accordingly the resolution was unlawful intervention into the internal affairs of a member state, contrary to Article 2(7) of the Charter. Yemen argued:

The draft resolution claims that there is a problem threatening international peace and security. We do not share that view. There is no conflict or war taking place across the borders of Iraq with its neighbors. The draft resolution also refers to political developments within Iraq, but according to Article 2 of the United Nations Charter it is not within the Council's purview to address internal issues in any country. Further, the draft resolution calls for internal dialogue, and that is obviously an attempt to intervene in the internal affairs of Iraq.

However, our position with regard to the draft resolution is based not only on certain provisions in its text but also on our objection to the fact that the whole issue is not within the competence of the Security Council. The Security Council is mandated only to safeguard international peace and security. . . . We wonder what State, big or small, has no internal problems; what State will not at some point in time encounter internal difficulties and experience transborder problems? In our opinion the text of the draft resolution is a first departure from the rule of maintaining a strict focus on the Council's responsibilities under the Charter. Over the past 40 years the Council has consistently refrained from intervention in the internal affairs of States.[22]

Similarly, Zimbabwe stated:

We recognize that a serious humanitarian situation has arisen as a result of these developments. However, this is in our view essentially an internal matter, as defined in paragraph 7 of Article 2 of the Charter. It is our view that addressing this situation in the manner suggested by the draft resolution would be inconsistent with the clear parameters of the Council's competence as provided for in the Charter.

The draft resolution refers directly to the confrontation between the Government of Iraq and its population. It prescribes specific measures which it expects the Government of Iraq to take in resolving what is a domestic conflict. In our view, this would be inconsistent with the Charter.[23]

Cuba added that the powers of the Council "do not include the questions of a humanitarian nature about which concern has been expressed in this Chamber" and that such questions should be addressed to the General Assembly.[24]

In fact, it is fairly clear that the situation did—in an objective sense—constitute a threat to regional peace and security, as the supporters of the resolution pointed out.[25] The crisis had arisen out of the conduct of a major armed conflict and there was a genuine possibility of a resumption of hostilities between Iraqi and coalition forces that were still present in the region in considerable numbers. Turkey, in particular, had made clear that it could not tolerate the entry of so many destitute Kurds into its territory, and there was a real risk of Turkish military intervention (as in fact occurred later in the decade). According to Turkey, Iraqi forces were conducting active military operations along its border and had already fired mortar rounds into Turkish territory.[26]

However, much of the argument by supporters of the resolution focused not on the immediate threat to regional peace, but on the repression conducted by the Iraqi government and the severe humanitarian catastrophe that threatened many hundreds of thousands of civilian refugees. France argued:

> The Security Council . . . would have been remiss in its task had it stood idly by, without reacting to the massacre of entire populations. . . . It is a matter of urgency that an end be put to the brutal repression of the Iraqi population . . . . Violations of human rights such as those now being observed become a matter of international interest when they take on such proportions that they assume the dimension of a crime against humanity.[27]

Britain rejected the argument that the resolution was an entirely internal matter that was outside the Council's mandate, asserting that:

> . . . Article 2, paragraph 7, an essential part of the Charter, does not apply to matters which, under the Charter, are not essentially domestic, and we have often seen that human rights—for example in South Africa—are defined in that category. . . . There are Iraq's international obligations, under Article 3 of the Geneva Conventions of 1949, to protect, in the case of internal armed conflicts, all innocent civilians from violence of all kinds to life and person.[28]

In its narrowest terms, Resolution 688 demonstrated that the prospect of moving large numbers of refugees across international borders could justify a Council determination of a threat to the peace (and consequently could form the basis for the exercise by the Council of its Chapter VII powers). This theme would be repeated on many occasions in the following decade.

In a deeper sense, however, the difference among Council members as to whether the Council had the authority to act in this situation was only partly a disagreement about whether there was a genuine threat to the peace. More fundamentally, it was a difference about whether the international community should intervene in a case where the actions of a state within its own territory had produced a severe humanitarian crisis and should in such a case take action directed at that state's internal policies. In effect, the Council's decision with respect to northern Iraq was a significant step in the development of the proposition that the Council could and should use its Chapter VII authority to deal with internal policies that threatened a humanitarian disaster where that disaster presented some plausible threat to the peace of the region.

Yugoslavia

The next development on this fundamental question came in September 1991, when the Council adopted Resolution 713, concerning the outbreak of fighting within Yugoslavia. That resolution stated that "the continuation of this situation constitutes a threat to international peace and security" and, acting under Chapter VII, imposed an embargo on arms shipments to Yugoslavia. The stated purpose of the embargo was "establishing peace and stability in Yugoslavia," and the resolution noted that the Council was "deeply concerned by the fighting in Yugoslavia, which is causing a heavy loss of human life and material damage, and by the consequences for the countries in the region, in particular in the border areas of neighboring countries."

The international community was clearly ambivalent at this point about the character of the conflict in Yugoslavia. Two of the Yugoslav republics had already declared independence, and many states were beginning to apply concepts that deal with relations between states—such as aggression, non-use of force, and the integrity of borders—to the conflict between the Yugoslav republics. Nonetheless, at the time of the adoption of this resolution, the international community still treated Yugoslavia as a single state and the regime in Belgrade as its government.[29]

Therefore, intervention by the Council into the internal affairs of Yugoslavia was a serious issue for some Council members, who went out of their way to point out various aspects of the situation that, in their view, justified the use of the Council's Chapter VII authority and distinguished it from intervention into internal affairs. Several Council members stressed that Yugoslavia itself had asked for the Council's action (presumably to inhibit arms shipments to seceding republics).[30] Some pointed to the numbers of refugees who were crossing Yugoslav borders and burdening neighboring countries.[31] Others argued that the conflict itself had begun to spill across these borders and threaten the stability of the entire region, where there were similar ethnic conflicts and separatist movements.[32]

Nonaligned Council members were particularly clear in insisting that the Council's action was not a precedent for open-ended intervention by the Council in internal situations. India stated:

> Let us therefore note here today in unmistakable terms that the Council's consideration of the matter relates not to Yugoslavia's internal situation as such, but specifically to its implication for peace and security in the region. Internal conflicts are for the State concerned to address, with assistance from its friends or well-wishers, if it so desires. The Council's intervention becomes legitimate and acceptable only when any conflict it faces has serious implications for international peace and security.[33]

China stressed that "a country's internal affairs should be handled by the people in that country themselves."[34]

Once again, there was ample objective basis for the Council to have judged that the Yugoslav situation constituted a threat to the peace and security of the region, as was abundantly demonstrated over the years that followed. The Council's action in adopting Resolution 713 reaffirmed the proposition that refugee flows could constitute a threat to the peace, and added the concept that political turmoil within a country could threaten the peace by stimulating similar conflicts among factions in other countries in the region. This concept would be used to justify Council action with respect to a number of other internal conflicts in the following decade.

Somalia

The invocation of Chapter VII authority to address humanitarian crises was pressed even further in the case of Somalia. After the overthrow of the government of Siad Barre in 1991, the country had descended into anarchy and civil conflict that, in combination with severe droughts, threatened the lives of millions of Somali civilians and caused many hundreds of thousands of Somali refugees to cross into neighboring countries.[35] On January 23, 1992, the Security Council invoked Chapter VII to impose an arms embargo for the purpose of encouraging a cessation of hostilities within the country and promoting a political settlement that would enable relief efforts to resume. The Council stated that it was "gravely alarmed" at the heavy loss of life resulting from the conflict in the country, was "aware of its consequences on stability and peace in the region," and was "concerned that the continuation of this situation constitutes . . . a threat to international peace and security."

After a series of Chapter VI resolutions that attempted unsuccessfully to handle the situation through the deployment of peace-keeping forces, the Council again returned to Chapter VII on December 3, 1992, this time to authorize the United States and others to deploy military forces to establish a secure environment for humanitarian relief operations. In doing so, the Council determined that "the magnitude of the human tragedy caused by the conflict in Somalia, further exacerbated by the obstacles being created to the distribution of humanitarian assistance, constitutes a threat to international peace and security." During the debate on this resolution, Council members asserted that the peace was threatened by the heavy refugee flows into adjacent countries and, more generally, by the fear that civil conflict and warlord violence—if unchecked—would spread throughout the Horn of Africa.[36] Yet it was obvious that the real motivation for invoking Chapter VII was the general feeling that the international community simply could not tolerate a humanitarian disaster of the scale that was looming. A number of members tried to limit the precedent-setting impact of the Council's action by asserting that the Somali situation was "unique," "unprecedented," "exceptional," and "sui generis," but, as Zimbabwe pointed out, "any unique situation and the unique solution adopted create of necessity a precedent" for future actions "under equally unique circumstances."[37]

Unlike the previous situation in northern Iraq, the Somali situation did not present any immediate credible threat of interstate armed conflict. The judgment that the situation was a threat to the peace was based, rather, on the feared destabilizing effect on internal peace and order in neighboring countries of massive refugee flows and uncontained civil conflict. But without doubt, the primary objective and motivating factor behind the use of Chapter VII was not the threat to peace as such, but the threatened loss of hundreds of thousands of Somali lives.

Haiti

In 1990, it appeared that decades of political instability and authoritarian rule in Haiti had come to an end with the country's first democratic election, in which Jean-Bertrand Aristide became president. However, within a year, Aristide was overthrown by a military coup that was followed by widespread human rights abuses and a renewal of refugee flows into neighboring countries. The international community—and particularly the inter-American community, which feared a reversal of the democratization process that had gained strength in Latin America during the preceding decade—strongly opposed the coup and continued to treat Aristide as representing the legitimate government of Haiti, even though he was in exile in Washington.[38]

After the failure of a voluntary economic embargo and other measures under the auspices of the Organization of American States (OAS), the Security Council decided to use its Chapter VII powers to assist in the effort to restore Aristide. On June 16, 1993, the Council adopted Resolution 841, imposing a mandatory embargo on shipments of arms and petroleum products that was to continue in force until the de facto regime in Haiti had agreed to the restoration of the Aristide government. The resolution stated the Council's concern that "the persistence of this situation contributes to a climate of fear of persecution and economic dislocation which could increase the number of Haitians seeking refuge in neighboring Member States," as a result of which the Council determined that, "in these unique and exceptional circumstances, the continuation of this situation threatens international peace and security in the region."

The Council debate suggested some residual concerns about the possible precedent-setting effect of the use of Chapter VII in such a situation. The Council president noted that "Members of the Council have asked me to say that the adoption of this resolution is warranted by the unique and exceptional situation in Haiti and should not be regarded as constituting a precedent."[39] A few members noted that the situation in Haiti was a threat to the peace of the region because of the prospect of increased refugee flows (though these were on a considerably smaller scale than in the Iraqi and Somali cases).[40] In fact, however, the dominant concern was that the coup, if not reversed, could have a ripple effect on other democratic governments in the region. In effect, a threat of adverse political and human rights consequences in other states was now accepted as a sufficient threat to the peace, even if there was no imminent prospect of armed conflict among states. As the decade progressed, this concept was applied frequently to the mounting conflicts in Africa.

Africa

During the 1990s, the Council found the existence of a threat to the peace in several internal conflicts in Africa that were thought to have the potential for destabilizing the region, including Liberia, Rwanda, Angola, and the Central African Republic.[41] In most of these conflicts, there was a substantial noninternal element in the form of cross-border insurgencies or direct outside intervention, but the Council was also concerned that disorder and the failure of democracy in one country would, by example, produce similar results in other states in the region.

The most striking example of this was the situation in Sierra Leone, which largely paralleled the case of Haiti. In May 1997, the democratically elected government of Tejan Kabbah was overthrown by a military coup, which was generally condemned by the international community and was the object of an economic embargo by the West African regional organization, ECOWAS. As in the case of Haiti, the Security Council then stepped in, adopting Resolution

1132 on October 8, 1997, which used the Council's Chapter VII authority to impose a mandatory arms and petroleum embargo. The resolution stated that the Council was "gravely concerned at the continued violence and loss of life in Sierra Leone following the military coup of 25 May 1997, the deteriorating humanitarian conditions in that country, and the consequences for neighboring countries," and consequently determined that the situation "constitutes a threat to international peace and security in the region." During the debate on the resolution, a few members noted the threat of refugee flows into neighboring countries.[42]

But the overwhelming thrust of the members' justification for the judgment that a threat to the peace existed was the fear that the military coup in Sierra Leone, if allowed to stand, might inspire by example a series of similar coups against other democratic governments in the region. For example, Sweden repeated the secretary-general's assertion that: "At stake is a great issue of principle, namely, that the efforts of the international community for democratic governance, grounded in the rule of law and respect for human rights, shall not be thwarted through illegal coups."[43] Korea argued: "This unacceptable coup has had a very serious destabilizing impact on the whole region by reversing the new wave of democracy that is spreading across the African continent."[44] Portugal observed that: "The crisis in Sierra Leone is, of course, worrying in itself on account of the usurpation of constitutional order. But it is also a destabilizing factor for the region, in particular for neighbouring countries, such as Liberia, where the still-fragile process of national reconciliation is trying to take hold."[45] The United States noted that the purpose of the resolution was the restoration of a democratically elected government and that, with this resolution, "the Security Council makes clear its willingness to exercise the enforcement powers of Chapter VII of the United Nations Charter in the service of this goal."[46]

By this point, Council members were no longer agonizing about the appropriateness of invoking Chapter VII to deal with an internal conflict that threatened the political stability of the region, or whether or not there was an immediate prospect of armed conflict among states. The harsh reality of the conflicts of the 1990s in Africa had demonstrated that serious chaos and instability in one country had a high risk of encouraging similar developments elsewhere in the region, and this was accepted as a form of threat to the peace of the region that was sufficient to justify the use of Chapter VII.

The Council has continued to act on this premise right up to the present. In April 2003, the Council determined that the persistent internal chaos in Somalia constituted a threat to international peace and security in the region, and on that basis acted under Chapter VII to enforce the long-standing arms embargo on Somalia.[47] In May 2003, the Council determined that the outbreak of internal conflict in Cote d'Ivoire also constituted such a threat, and on that basis introduced a UN mission to work jointly with French and ECOWAS forces in that country.[48] In the same month, the Council determined that renewed fighting among Congolese insurgent factions constituted "a threat to the peace process in the Democratic Republic of the Congo and to the peace and security of the Great Lakes region," and on that basis acted under Chapter VII to authorize the introduction of a multinational force to restore order.[49] In August, the Council determined that the deteriorating internal conflict in Liberia constituted "a threat to international peace and security, to stability in the West Africa subregion, and to the peace process for Liberia" and authorized the introduction of a multinational force to address the situation.[50]

In February 2004, the Council determined that the collapse of internal order in Haiti constituted a threat to international and regional peace, and authorized the deployment of a multilateral force to restore the situation.[51] In May, the Council determined that the ongoing internal conflict in Burundi was a threat to peace and security in the region sufficient to justify the deployment of a UN peacekeeping operation with authority to use force to enforce a cease-fire.[52] In July 2004, the Council determined that the humanitarian disaster in Sudan was a threat to "international peace and security and to stability in the region," justifying the imposition of sanctions and other measures under Chapter VII.[53]

This does not mean that the Council was always aggressive in using its Chapter VII authority in the African conflicts of the 1990s. The Council lost its impetus for vigorous Chapter VII action in Somalia after U.S. forces suffered significant casualties in Mogadishu.

It intervened too late in Rwanda, and was painfully slow in using its Chapter VII authority in Sierra Leone, Liberia, the Congo, Burundi, and Sudan. No source of legal authority is effective where there is no political will to use it, but the Council's actions in Africa during the past decade show the scope of jurisdiction that the Council has available to it when that political will exists.

International terrorist acts

The concept of a threat to or breach of the peace has recently been further expanded in the context of the Council's response to international terrorism.[54] There is, of course, no doubt that serious acts of international terrorism may constitute such a threat to or breach of the peace. The Council confirmed this on March 31, 1992, when it determined in Resolution 748 that there was a threat to international peace and security as a result of the destruction of two commercial airliners by Libyan agents and Libya's refusal to take a series of steps to redress these actions, including the renunciation of support for terrorism and the surrender of the accused Libyan agents for trial. As a result, the Council invoked Chapter VII and imposed a series of economic and diplomatic sanctions that were to remain in force until Libya met the Council's demands. During the debate on the resolution, there was no dispute that such acts of international terrorism were indeed a serious threat to international peace and security that could properly invoke the Council's jurisdiction under Chapter VII.[55] The five members that abstained did so on other grounds.[56]

Similarly, on April 26, 1996, the Council determined that a threat to international peace and security existed as a result of the failure of Sudan to take certain steps relating to the terrorist assassination attempt on the life of the president of Egypt, including the extradition of the suspected terrorists. As a result, the Council imposed a series of diplomatic and other sanctions against Sudan.[57]

The Council took this a step further in response to the activities of the al Qaeda terrorist network and the Taliban regime that gave them sanctuary and assistance. In August 1998, the Council condemned the attacks on the U.S. embassies in Kenya and Tanzania, called on states to take action against such terrorist operations, and expressed its concern over the presence of terrorists in Afghanistan, but it did not immediately invoke Chapter VII or take measures against al Qaeda or the Taliban.[58] It was more than a year later that the Council determined that al Qaeda activities in Afghanistan constituted a threat to international peace and security, and at that point the Council began to take concrete Chapter VII measures against the Taliban, demanding that it surrender Osama bin Laden for prosecution and imposing economic sanctions against the Taliban until it complied.[59] After the attacks of September 11, 2001 on the World Trade Center in New York and the Pentagon outside Washington, D.C., and the successful military response of U.S.-led forces in Afghanistan, the Council reaffirmed that the situation in Afghanistan constituted a threat to international peace and security, and invoked Chapter VII to authorize the deployment of an international security assistance force to assist the new Afghan government.[60]

GENERIC THREATS TO THE PEACE

Another important development in the past few years has been the willingness of the Council to address threats to the peace that are not restricted to any particular conflict or crisis, and to adopt generic measures designed to deal with them.[61] Over the years, the Council has increasingly addressed generic problems outside Chapter VII, including the impact of HIV/AIDS on peacekeeping,[62] and the impact of armed conflict on women and children.[63] More recently the Council has used Chapter VII as well for such purposes.

After the September 11, 2001 attacks, in addition to acting specifically with respect to the situation in Afghanistan, the Council decided in Resolution 1373 (2001) that all acts of international terrorism constituted a threat to international peace and security, and adopted a series of measures to address international terrorism generally. These measures included the freezing of terrorist assets, prohibition of activities in support of terrorist groups, prevention of the movement of terrorists, and assistance to other states in prosecuting terrorists. In Resolution 1377 (2003), the Council declared that "acts of international terrorism constitute one of the most serious threats to international peace and security in the twenty-first century," and in Resolution 1456 (2003) adopted a comprehensive declaration to meet this threat, calling on states to take a long list of actions to prevent and prosecute terrorist acts "wherever they occur."

Another significant step in this evolution was the Council's adoption in April 2004 of Resolution 1540, which determined that the generic problem of the proliferation of weapons of mass destruction constituted a threat to international peace and security. The Council imposed a series of measures under Chapter VII, including: (1) requiring all states to refrain from providing any support to non-state actors that attempt to acquire WMD; (2) requiring all states to take effective domestic measures to secure WMD-related materials and trafficking; and (3) establishing a committee to oversee implementation of the resolution.

This resolution was highly controversial within the Council and was the subject of intense debate during a series of open-ended sessions in which more than fifty UN members took part. Pakistan initially objected that "the threat of WMD proliferation by non-State actors may be real, but it is not imminent. It is not a threat to peace within the meaning of Article 39 of the United Nations Charter."[64] However, Pakistan later voted in favor of the resolution when certain other changes were made. A number of other members objected that the Council was assuming the role of a "global legislature" in requiring such a far-reaching menu of domestic measures, and some clearly feared that a Chapter VII resolution might be used to justify coercive unilateral actions against states that might be accused of violations. These questions will be explored in later chapters. Pakistan's delegation was alone in its initial assertion that the generic problem of WMD proliferation was not a threat to the peace; the others that addressed this question insisted that it could and did constitute such a threat for Chapter VII purposes. In the end, the resolution was adopted unanimously.

Setting aside for the moment the question of the appropriateness of the measures taken to deal with these generic threats, it is now apparent that the Council and the UN community generally have accepted that such generic threats can constitute a threat to the peace and therefore are an appropriate subject of action by the Council. This view is not inconsistent with the Charter. Although much of the language of Chapters VI and VII seems to contemplate action by the

Council in the context of a specific dispute or situation, the key provisions of Chapter VII—Articles 39, 41, and 42—are not so limited. The authorities contained in these articles apply whenever the Council determines the existence of any threat to or breach of the peace—whether specific or generic in character.

The Council's actions with respect to these problems are also significant because they confirm that the authority of Chapter VII is available to address threats to the peace from any source—whether from action by states, from action by nonstate actors, or from inaction of states in the face of dangerous activities in their territories. This confirmation was implicit in the Council's earlier use of Chapter VII to deal with the actions of nonstate actors in Somalia, Sierra Leone, and Yugoslavia. It was made even more clear by the Council's action against al Qaeda and the Taliban authorities that acquiesced in or assisted al Qaeda activities. Indeed, the Council's generic programs against international terrorism and WMD proliferation are essentially focused on nonstate terrorists (together with states that might tolerate their activities).

ASSESSMENT

The expansion of the Council's exercise of its jurisdiction and mandate during the post–Cold War period is clearly shown in the number of situations in which Chapter VII was invoked and the number of Chapter VII resolutions adopted. From the creation of the UN until the Iraqi invasion of Kuwait, fewer than ten Chapter VII resolutions were adopted with respect to only three countries. From the Iraqi invasion of Kuwait until the end of 2004, more than 250 Chapter VII resolutions were adopted with respect to more than twenty countries. To be sure, many of these Chapter VII resolutions were simply extensions, modifications, suspensions, or terminations of previous Chapter VII actions. Nonetheless, the frequency and importance of the Council's use of its Chapter VII authority during this period of less than fifteen years far exceeded that of the previous forty-five years of the Cold War.

At the beginning of the 1990s, various members of the Council—particularly the nonaligned members—were still uncertain about the legality or propriety of the use of Chapter VII with respect to con-flicts that were primarily internal in character, even where real threats to other states from the effects of those conflicts were apparent. In time, the Council came to accept that the effect on neighboring states of cross-border fighting, refugee flows, economic disruption, or the spread of political instability would suffice to qualify as a threat to the peace for the purpose of Chapter VII.

But the real debate in these cases was not so much about the technical question of whether the Article 39 threshold had been met, but whether it was appropriate for the international community to intervene with the coercive tools of Chapter VII in internal conflict situations. At first, many members of the Council were reluctant to accept such intervention where international action was directed against the policies and actions of a state concerning its own nation-als. However, over the course of the post–Cold War decade, the Council came more and more to accept that this could indeed be an appropriate way to deal with severe humanitarian crises (as in north-ern Iraq and Somalia), serious violations of fundamental human rights (as in Bosnia and Rwanda), significant threats to democracy (as in Haiti and Sierra Leone), or other serious threats to regional sta-bility (as in various crises in the Balkans and Africa).[65] By the end of the decade, the Council was often taking decisions to intervene in such cases with little or no debate about whether it had the authority to do so under the Charter.

This development is of fundamental significance for the inter-national order. There will be very few serious internal armed conflicts that would not present at least some credible threat of cross-border fighting, international terrorism, refugee flows, economic dislocation, or political instability to the affected state's neighbors. As will be explained in later chapters, this means that the full array of Chapter VII powers—including the application of force and other coercive measures—are now available with respect to such conflicts. Further, it seems that the Council now is willing to apply these powers to generic problems that threaten the peace, and to take steps that may not be limited to a particular dispute or situation. In effect, the Coun-cil has asserted a general power to impose obligations on states in response to general problems that threaten the peace.

Although these developments may not necessarily be what the negotiators of the UN Charter originally contemplated, they are not inconsistent with the Charter and are in fact a much-needed development of the Charter system to meet the urgent requirements of the post–Cold War international system. It is not unreasonable for the Council to judge that internal conflict involving severe humanitarian disasters, serious repression, ethnic conflict, or political instability constitute a threat to international peace and security. It is essential for the international community to have an effective source of legal authority to address such threats and, in doing so, to advance the fundamental values that are now widely accepted by states.

Nor is it unreasonable for the Council to deal with such problems on a general basis (in appropriate circumstances) instead of limiting itself to responding to specific situations. The Council has already decided that some generic threats to the peace—specifically, international terrorism and the proliferation of WMD—must be tackled by general measures going beyond particular conflicts or countries. In the future, other generic problems—such as the commission of war crimes or the control of inhumane or destabilizing weapons—may also require such generic treatment. There is no reason Chapter VII should not be seen as a source of authority to take such action.

This does not mean that the jurisdiction and mandate of the Council under Chapter VII is unlimited. Most economic, political, and social problems—however serious and urgent—do not present a threat to the peace in the sense contemplated in Chapter VII, nor would it be sensible to treat Chapter VII as a general authorization for mandatory Council action to handle such issues. It is obvious, however, that the line between problems that threaten the peace and those that do not is not self-evident. It will always be a matter of judgment that will be influenced by the degree to which the community of states is prepared to accept international intervention into what would otherwise be considered the internal affairs of states, and the degree to which that community is prepared to accept the Security Council as the proper vehicle for such intervention.

Chapter 1 of this book considered the possibility that the Council's actions under Chapter VII of the Charter might be significantly constrained by judicial decisions, particularly by those of the International Court of Justice, and suggested that this was unlikely. In particular, a decision that a situation does or does not constitute a threat to the peace seems to be a matter of policy and factual appreciation that must be judged by the Council and is not readily subject to judicial criteria or competence. The appeals chamber for the International Criminal Tribunal for the Former Yugoslavia has held that the Council "exercises a very wide discretion" in making such a decision, and specifically that the Council has the authority to decide if civil war or internal strife constitutes such a threat.[66] This makes it all the more important that the Council act responsibly in such matters.

The political differences that have emerged in recent years among the permanent members—particularly those that split the Council over Kosovo in 1999 and Iraq in 2002–03—do not signal a retreat in the Council's expansive reading of its authority. In fact, the year in which the greatest number of Chapter VII decisions was adopted was 2005, and in 2004 alone the Council invoked Chapter VII with respect to ten essentially internal conflict situations and two generic threats to the peace. Although the Council's ability to act—as always—will be dependent on the political will and substantial consensus of its members, the jurisdiction and mandate of the Council remains as broad and potent as ever.

3

SANCTIONS

THE INTERNATIONAL COMMUNITY has made extensive use of collective sanctions as a means of dealing with threats to the peace. Such sanctions have been seen as an intermediate step between diplomacy and the use of armed force, providing an emphatic statement of the position of the international community, denying access to vital resources by states that threaten the peace, and exerting pressure on such states to alter their behavior.[1] The Security Council imposed sanctions under Chapter VII on two occasions during the Cold War, but in each case with some hesitation and with uncertain results. However, since the end of the Cold War, the Council has dramatically expanded its use of sanctions. This expansion has resulted in a considerable body of precedent and practice that has given the international community a new range of tools to address threats to the peace, while at the same time presenting a number of problems that the Council has still not wholly resolved. This chapter examines these developments and considers the legal issues that have arisen in the process.

THE DEVELOPMENT OF COLLECTIVE SANCTIONS

The use of collective sanctions was not an invention of the UN Charter. Article 16 of the League of Nations Covenant provided,

> Should any Member of the League resort to war in disregard of its covenants under Articles 12, 13 or 15, it shall *ipso facto* be deemed to have committed an act of war against all other Members of the League, which hereby undertake immediately to subject it to the severance of all trade or financial relations, the prohibition of all intercourse between their nationals and the nationals of the covenant-breaking State, and the prevention of all financial, commercial, or personal intercourse between the nationals of the covenant-breaking State and the nations of any other State, whether a Member of the League or not.

Although Article 16 seemed on its face to contemplate an immediate, mandatory, and total severance of all commercial and personal connections with the sanctioned state, in fact the League did not operate in this way. Its major use of sanctions was against Italy, with the objective of compelling it to abandon its invasion of Ethiopia in 1935. The League assembly established a committee of experts that recommended a series of arms and financial embargoes and a partial trade embargo. These measures did result in a substantial reduction in Italy's international trade but, in the end, failed to end Italy's occupation of Ethiopia, partly because the critical element of an oil embargo was not imposed and because the League sanctions were not applied by all major trading states.[2]

The drafters of the UN Charter nonetheless recognized the importance of giving the Security Council the power to impose coercive measures short of armed force. Article 41 of the Charter provides, "The Security Council may decide what measures not involving the use of armed force are to be employed to give effect to its decisions, and it may call upon the Members of the United Nations to apply such measures. These may include complete or partial interruption of economic relations and of rail, sea, air, postal, telegraphic, radio, and other means of communication, and the severance of diplomatic relations."

This provision is a more flexible instrument than Article 16, and potentially more powerful. The imposition of sanctions under the Charter is not automatic but a matter for the decision and discretion of the Security Council. The Charter allows the Council to decide how rapidly and how comprehensively to apply sanctions. It might decide to impose an immediate and total interruption of commercial and diplomatic relations, to begin with limited sanctions and increase them over time, or to continue with limited sanctions throughout. The Council may impose sanctions whenever it determines that there is a threat to or breach of the peace, which (as we have seen) can include situations that are well short of actual war between states. Finally, the list of specific sanctions in Article 41 is nonexhaustive, and (as will be seen in later chapters) the Council has wide discretion to take other measures not involving the use of force under this article.

However, the Council was slow to use the full potential of Article 41 during the Cold War, partly because there were few occasions when the permanent members could agree on the desirability of imposing coercive sanctions against one side or the other in disputes among states, and partly because the Council was reluctant even in those cases to apply the full scope of possible sanctions. Sanctions were imposed in two situations that have already been referred to in chapter 2: Southern Rhodesia and South Africa.

In the case of Southern Rhodesia, the Council initially reacted to Ian Smith's unilateral declaration of independence in 1965 by calling on governments to withhold recognition and diplomatic relations, to observe an arms embargo, and "to do their utmost" to sever all economic relations, including observing an oil embargo.[3] When these voluntary measures did not succeed in breaking the white minority regime, the Council invoked Article 41 (more than a year later) to require UN members to prevent the following activities with respect to Southern Rhodesia: (1) the import of a list of specific Rhodesian commodities; (2) any activities by their nationals or in their territories promoting such trade; (3) shipment of such commodities in ships or aircraft of their registry; (4) any activities by their nationals or in their territories promoting the sale or manufacture of arms and related items; (5) any activities by their nationals or in their territories promoting the supply or manufacture of aircraft or motor vehicles; (6) any participation by their nationals or vessels, or in their territory, in the supply of oil; and (7) any financial or economic assistance to the minority regime.[4] Six months later, the Council, concerned that these measures were not being universally complied with, established a committee to seek information from states concerning their compliance and to report to the Council on violations.[5]

From time to time over the next eleven years, the Council reiterated and fine-tuned these sanctions but was unable to prevent serious violations that kept the minority regime alive, particularly through South Africa and the adjoining Portuguese colonies.[6] The white minority regime finally collapsed and sanctions were terminated at the end of 1979, but it is usually thought that the sanctions made only a partial contribution to this result.[7]

In the case of South Africa, the Council's actions were less comprehensive. In the early 1960s, the Council began to adopt Chapter VI resolutions calling on South Africa to refrain from oppressive enforcement of its apartheid laws, and calling on states to refrain from supplying arms and related items to South Africa.[8] But it was not until the end of 1977 that the Council made this arms embargo mandatory through the invocation of Chapter VII, and the embargo did not prevent the South African regime from acquiring or manufacturing the arms it needed.[9] Apart from the arms embargo, the Council limited itself to urging UN members to adopt additional measures against South Africa, such as the suspension of new investments.[10] The latter national sanctions, rather than those imposed by the United Nations itself, probably had the more significant effect on the end of the apartheid regime.

This relatively modest use of Article 41 sanctions changed dramatically with the end of the Cold War and the Iraqi invasion of Kuwait. During the single week following the Iraqi invasion, the Council enacted sanctions that were more stringent and comprehensive than any adopted before.[11] Over the years that followed, the Council adopted additional mandatory sanctions with respect to a number of countries: Iraq, Kuwait, Yugoslavia, Somalia, Libya, Liberia, Haiti, Rwanda, Bosnia, Sudan, Angola, Afghanistan, Ethiopia and Eritrea, Sierra Leone, and the Congo.[12] Some of these sanctions regimes were immediate and comprehensive (Iraq); some began as partial measures and later became comprehensive (Yugoslavia and Haiti); others remained partial. In adopting these sanctions, the Council has intro-duced significant innovations in the scope and application of sanc-tions, in enforcement techniques, and in measures for dealing with collateral damage to countries and persons that were not the object of sanctions.

Scope and Application

Arms sanctions

The most common type of sanction in the Council's practice is a pro-hibition on the supply of arms to the sanctioned country, either by itself or as part of a broader trade embargo. Specific arms embargoes were imposed on Southern Rhodesia, South Africa, Yugoslavia, Somalia, Libya, Liberia, Haiti, Rwanda, Ethiopia and Eritrea, and Afghanistan.[13] The supply of arms to Iraq was prohibited by the comprehensive sanctions imposed at the time of the invasion of Kuwait.[14]

An arms embargo may be stated in simple and generic terms: "a general and complete embargo on all deliveries of weapons and mili-tary equipment" to the sanctioned country.[15] Sometimes specific ref-erence is made to paramilitary or police equipment,[16] to the provision of weapons-related technical assistance or training,[17] to licenses, pat-ents or other arrangements for the manufacture or maintenance of arms in the sanctioned country,[18] or to investment in companies manufacturing arms in the sanctioned country.[19] Even without such specific references, the scope of a general arms embargo can be very broad. For example, the Council has recently confirmed that its long-standing general arms embargo against Somalia was to be interpreted as prohibiting any financing of arms purchases and any direct or indirect supply of technical advice, training, or other assistance related to military activities.[20]

Such embargos may serve one or more of a number of purposes: (1) to restrict the flow of arms to both sides of an ongoing armed conflict, so as to make more difficult its continuation or escalation (Yugoslavia or Eritrea-Ethiopia); (2) to degrade the military capabili-ties of a state or group that is or may become involved in fighting with UN-authorized forces or is perceived as a continuing threat to other states (Iraq); (3) to constrain the ability of a repressive regime to use military, paramilitary, or police forces to oppress its own population (Haiti and South Africa); (4) to decrease the power of warlords in internal conflict situations (Somalia); (5) to limit the supply of arms to terrorist groups that might be used to commit acts of terrorism abroad (Afghanistan); or (6) simply to send a conspicuous message that the Council is not pleased with the conduct of the sanctioned entity and might consider stronger measures if that conduct is not changed.

In their early form, these arms embargos did not impose obligations on the sanctioned state to refrain from acquiring or developing arms but only imposed obligations on other states not to supply them. In fact, some sanctioned states, such as South Africa, developed a substantial indigenous arms industry and used those arms in ways that were contrary to the purposes of the Council's sanctions.

However, at the end of the Gulf War, the Council went further with respect to Iraqi weapons of mass destruction and long-range ballistic missiles. As part of its omnibus cease-fire resolution, the Council required Iraq to refrain from acquiring and to accept the elimination of (1) all chemical and biological weapons and related systems and facilities; (2) all ballistic missiles with a range of 150 kilometers and related facilities; and (3) all nuclear weapons or related materials, components, or facilities. An elaborate system of declarations and UN inspections was imposed to monitor and enforce these prohibitions, which will be discussed in chapter 6. These obligations went well beyond those Iraq had already assumed under the major nonproliferation treaties.[21] Further, the resolution provided that the general sanctions imposed on trade and financial transactions would continue until the Council agreed that Iraq had complied with these requirements.[22] The United Nations encountered serious problems in enforcing those requirements, but it is now apparent that these sanctions (together with the UN inspection regimes) did in fact significantly degrade Iraq's ability to reconstitute its military forces and its WMD programs.[23] In any event, the Council's actions against Iraq were an important precedent that may be essential in dealing with future threats of proliferation.

Would the Council have the authority to impose such restrictions on a more generic basis, as opposed to imposing them in a specific situation on a specific country that is the object of sanctions? For example, would the Council have the authority to impose restrictions on transfer, acquisition, or use in a particular region of land mines, nuclear weapons, small arms, or other weapons thought to be having a destabilizing effect on the peace of that region and the safety of its civilian population? Would the Council have the authority to impose worldwide restrictions on acquisition or transfer of WMD, even with respect to countries that have not ratified the treaties that address these subjects?

In fact, the Council has already invoked Chapter VII of the Charter to impose mandatory measures on a generic basis to deal with general threats to the peace and, in particular, to prohibit the supply of WMD and related items to nonstate actors under Resolution 1540. During the consideration of that resolution, a number of states argued that obligations of this kind should be accepted by states on a voluntary basis pursuant to treaty, and that it was unlawful or inappropriate for the Council to impose such obligations under Chapter VII.[24] But in the end, the Council did so by unanimous vote, a result that some Council members accepted as an exceptional measure urgently required to fill a serious gap in current nonproliferation treaties.[25] It is undoubtedly preferable, as a general matter, for such obligations to be adopted through multilateral treaty negotiations, particularly where states will need to take extensive regulatory and enforcement actions in their territories to carry them out, and it is apparent that states will resist any attempt by the Council to become a "global legislature" with a general mandate to supersede the treaty process. Nonetheless, action by the Council may be called for when immediate steps are necessary that cannot wait for the lengthy process of treaty negotiation and ratification or when it is necessary to impose obligations on recalcitrant states, and it is now clear that the Council has the authority to take such action.[26]

Finally, one might suppose that restrictions on trade and acquisition of arms would not be vulnerable to legal challenge, given the long Council practice of imposing such restrictions and their obvious close connection to the Council's mandate under Chapter VII to restore and maintain the peace. Nonetheless, a challenge to the Council's arms embargo against Yugoslavia was brought in the International Court of Justice in the context of Bosnia's suit against the Federal Republic of Yugoslavia alleging the commission of genocide by the FRY and its Bosnian Serb surrogates. The embargo was imposed prior to the secession of Bosnia, but the Council made clear after the secession that it continued to apply to all parts of the territory of the former Yugoslavia. Bosnia then argued to the ICJ that the embargo could not validly be applied to Bosnia because it would abridge Bosnia's right of self-defense and render it helpless against FRY aggression and genocide.[27]

The court never decided on this argument because Bosnia withdrew it. But in any event, the argument is contrary to the Charter itself, in that Article 51 provides that "measures taken by Members in the exercise of this right of self-defense . . . shall not in any way affect the authority and responsibility of the Security Council under the present Charter to take at any time such action as it deems necessary in order to maintain or restore international peace and security." If the Bosnian argument were correct, the Council could not impose arms embargos, cease-fires, or other restrictions on both sides of an armed conflict, because in theory, one is the aggressor and the other the victim acting in self-defense. The consequence of the Bosnian argument would be that before acting, the Council would always have to determine which side was in the right and impose restrictions only on the other side. In some cases (such as the Iraqi invasion of Kuwait), this would be appropriate. But in many other cases, it would make the Council's task of restoring the peace difficult or impossible.[28] Yet the Bosnian situation does point out the need for the Council to assess the likely consequences of imposing such restrictions, as well as the possibility that it may be politically infeasible to repeal or modify them at a later time, even though they might bear more heavily on the victim of aggression. (Other aspects of the relationship between Article 51 and action by the Council are considered in chapter 5.)

Trade and financial transactions

As noted, the mandatory sanctions the Council imposed during the Cold War on trade and financial transactions were imposed incrementally and directed (at least initially) at specific types of commodities or services—such as the export of specific mineral and agricultural products, and the import of oil and aircraft. One frequent criticism of the Council's early practice in this regard was that imposing such partial sanctions piecemeal and over an extended period of time diluted their economic and political effect and gave the sanctioned entities the time and opportunity to adjust to and circumvent sanctions. In particular, it was argued that the piecemeal application of limited sanctions allowed the white minority regime in Southern Rhodesia to develop alternative export products and routes, and allowed the South African regime to develop a robust indigenous arms industry.[29]

When Iraq invaded Kuwait, the Council was determined to apply maximum economic and political pressure at once, and not to rely on a gradual escalation of partial measures. This determination was the product of a number of factors, including the clear and brazen character of the Iraqi aggression and the declared intent of Iraq to annex another UN member state; the brutal character of the Iraqi occupation from the start (including its violation of third-country diplomatic rights); the severe threat posed to other Gulf states, to the stability of oil markets, and to the entire balance of power in the region; the absence of any serious political opposition among the permanent members (given the impending collapse of the Soviet empire); and the need for immediate and comprehensive action to prevent Iraq from looting Kuwaiti assets around the world.

As a result, within days the Council imposed a comprehensive prohibition on all forms of trade and financial transactions with Iraq and Iraqi-occupied Kuwait. It included requirements that states prohibit (1) import of any commodities and products originating in Iraq and Kuwait; (2) any sale or supply by their nationals, from their territories, or by their flagships of commodities or products to any person or body in Iraq or Kuwait, except for medical supplies and, in humanitarian circumstances, foodstuffs; (3) any activities by their nationals, in their territories, or by their flagships promoting such prohibited trade; and (4) any supply of funds or economic resources to any entity in Iraq or Kuwait by themselves, their nationals, or persons within their territory, except for medical or humanitarian purposes or, in humanitarian circumstances, foodstuffs.[30]

Sanctions of this scope and rigor were new in the practice of the Security Council but were not unprecedented in national practice. In particular, the United States had adopted several comprehensive sanctions regimes against communist countries under the authority of U.S. sanctions legislation.[31] As a result, the United States was in a position to adopt comprehensive unilateral sanctions on the very day of the invasion, and four days before the Security Council adopted its own sanctions.[32] Given the U.S. leadership in organizing sanctions against Iraq, it is clear that the U.S. action and prior experience played an important part in shaping the scope of the Council's resolution.

At the end of the Gulf War, the sanctions against Iraq were kept in place, but with an important distinction. The prohibitions against the supply of arms, and particularly items related to weapons of mass destruction and long-range missiles, were to remain in force indefinitely. On the other hand, the prohibitions against exports to Iraq were to be reviewed every sixty days in light of Iraq's policies and practices, including its compliance with Council resolutions, for the purpose of determining whether to reduce or lift those prohibitions. Further, the prohibitions against the import of Iraqi products were to be lifted once the Council decided that Iraq had complied with its obligations concerning the elimination of WMD and long-range missiles.[33] However, in light of Iraq's continuing intransigence and its failure to comply with the Council's requirements, these provisions for lifting of sanctions were never implemented. In the end, sanctions were terminated only in May 2003 after the removal of Saddam Hussein's regime.[34]

Later in 1991, the Council began a long series of sanctions measures against the Federal Republic of Yugoslavia that in time became comprehensive in scope. But, unlike its sanctions against Iraq, the Council did not move directly to comprehensive sanctions and then maintain them at that level over time but, rather, tightened or relaxed sanctions against the FRY and its surrogates depending on the Serb response to the Council's requirements.

The Council started with the adoption of an arms embargo in September 1991 that, as we have seen, applied to all the contending parties in the territory of the former Yugoslavia.[35] In May 1992, the Council reacted to the FRY military intervention against other Yugoslav republics by adopting comprehensive economic sanctions against the FRY that closely paralleled the earlier sanctions against Iraq.[36] In April 1993, the Council took the further step of providing for the freezing of the funds of the FRY and Yugoslav enterprises.[37] In September 1994, as a means of pressuring the Bosnian Serbs to accept a territorial settlement that had been put to the parties to the conflict in Bosnia by various elements of the international community, the Council imposed comprehensive sanctions on persons and entities of the area controlled by the Bosnian Serbs.[38] At the same time, the Council provided for the suspension of certain sanctions against the FRY if it effectively closed its border with the Serb-controlled areas of Bosnia.[39] Following the conclusion of the Dayton Peace Agreement, the Council provided for the suspension and then the termination of sanctions.[40] An arms embargo was later reimposed on the FRY as a result of its repression in Kosovo,[41] and subsequently terminated when Serbia met the Council's demands.[42]

Similarly, in the case of Haiti, the Council did not impose comprehensive sanctions immediately but started with lesser sanctions and strengthened them as the Haitian military junta refused to respond to the Council's requirements. In June 1993, following the failure of Organization of American States sanctions to compel the Haitian military junta to restore power to the democratically elected Aristide government, the Security Council invoked Chapter VII to impose an oil embargo and to require the freezing of the funds of the Haitian junta and entities controlled by it.[43] Shortly thereafter, the junta agreed to negotiations in New York and signed the Governors Island Agreement providing for Aristide's return, and in response, the Council suspended the sanctions.[44] However, the junta did not carry through on its commitments, and in May 1994, the Council imposed comprehensive economic sanctions on Haiti until such time as the junta departed, the Aristide government was restored, and the terms of the Governors Island Agreement were carried out.[45] In the end, these comprehensive sanctions also failed to dislodge the junta, and it was not until the Council authorized the use of force to restore

Aristide that the junta relented and departed.[46] (This authorization for the use of force will be discussed in chapter 5.)

Apart from these three cases of comprehensive sanctions, however, the sanctions imposed by the Council have been partial in character and directed against specific actors or specific types of trade and financial transactions. In recent years, these partial sanctions have been referred to as "targeted sanctions" or "smart sanctions"—that is, they are designed to focus on the ruling elites that are the object of the Council's actions, rather than the economy or population of the sanctioned country as a whole.[47]

In several cases, partial or targeted sanctions were imposed against regimes that had given sanctuary or support to groups that had committed serious acts of international terrorism. In the case of Libya, the Council prohibited air traffic and the supply of aircraft and related components and services, and later required the freezing of Libyan funds, until Libya had surrendered for trial the persons accused of the destruction of Pan Am Flight 103.[48] These sanctions were suspended when the two accused were surrendered six years later,[49] and lifted permanently in 2003 when Libya finally accepted the rest of the Council's demands.[50]

In the case of Sudan, following an assassination attempt on Egyptian president Hosni Mubarak by persons who had been given sanctuary in Sudan, the Council acted in August 1996 to prohibit air traffic with Sudan until it had ceased giving sanctuary and support to terrorists.[51] Five years later, the Council declared itself satisfied with the steps taken by Sudan and terminated the sanctions.[52]

In the case of Afghanistan, in response to the granting of sanctuary and support by the Taliban regime to terrorist groups, the Council required states to freeze Taliban funds and to deny landing or takeoff rights to aircraft owned or operated by the Taliban, unless and until it surrendered Osama bin Laden and ceased its support for terrorists.[53] Sanctions against Afghanistan were terminated in January 2002 with respect to the Afghan national airlines following the demise of the Taliban regime,[54] but sanctions have continued against individuals associated with the Taliban and al Qaeda, including the freezing of their assets and denial of entry, economic transactions, and arms supplies.[55]

In other cases, the Council imposed partial or targeted economic sanctions against parties to civil conflicts that were thought to be primarily responsible for the continuation of violence and atrocities. For example, in the case of Angola, the Council imposed a package of sanctions in August 1997 against the insurgent group UNITA in an attempt to compel it to comply with the Lusaka Protocol, an agreement for the resolution of the conflict; the measures imposed included a prohibition on travel of senior UNITA officials and their families and on flights of UNITA aircraft.[56] These sanctions were suspended and eventually terminated after UNITA began to cooperate in the implementation of the Lusaka Protocol.[57]

In the case of Sierra Leone, the Council adopted a series of measures to control the illicit trade in diamonds that had financed the brutal insurgency in that country, including controls on the import of rough diamonds from Sierra Leone and the institution of a system of certificates of origin to enforce them.[58] These measures were later supplemented by sanctions directed at the Liberian government, which had supported the insurgents in Sierra Leone, including a prohibition on travel of senior members of the Liberian government and its armed forces.[59] When Liberian president Charles Taylor left Liberia, the Council terminated sanctions against Liberia but imposed sanctions against Taylor and his associates to degrade their ability to threaten the Liberian peace process from outside.[60]

The Council also used targeted sanctions as a supplementary measure with respect to particular individuals in the case of the comprehensive sanctions regimes imposed on Iraq, Yugoslavia, and Haiti. In the case of Iraq, the Council required states to deny entry to Iraqi officials who were involved in obstructing the operations of UN weapons inspectors.[61] In the case of Yugoslavia, states were required to prevent the entry of persons holding positions of authority in the areas of Bosnia controlled by the Serbs, or persons who had violated Council sanctions with respect to those areas.[62] In the case of Haiti, the Council required states to deny permission to enter to Haitian military and police officers, coup participants, and their families, and to freeze their funds and financial resources.[63]

Because targeted sanctions apply only selectively and not to all persons in a country, a variety of different factual and subjective judgments are needed in their enforcement: for example, which individuals are responsible for the policies the Council opposes, which entities and assets they control, which of their relatives or associates are also subject to sanctions. This situation suggests the need for some form of regular process and transparency in making such designations, and the sanctions committees have been criticized for failing to provide adequate procedures for this purpose. For example, the 2004 report of the secretary-general's high-level panel concluded that "the way entities or individuals are added to the terrorist list maintained by the Council and the absence of review or appeal for those listed raise serious accountability issues and possibly violate fundamental human rights norms and conventions."[64] No doubt, the committees and the Secretariat need to do more in this regard.

Often the application of economic sanctions requires other states to violate obligations they may have to the sanctioned country under bilateral or multilateral trade agreements, friendship and commerce treaties, agreements regulating the use of canals or rivers, and the like. This is not a legal barrier to the enforcement of sanctions imposed by the Council under Chapter VII. As noted previously, Article 103 of the Charter provides that, in the event of a conflict between obligations under the Charter and obligations under any other international agreement, the former prevails. Since member states are obligated under Articles 25 and 48 to carry out binding Council decisions, that obligation prevails over any inconsistent agreement—past, present, or future. The ICJ recognized this in denying Libya's request in the *Lockerbie* case for a preliminary order that would have effectively disregarded a Chapter VII decision in favor of Libya's asserted rights under a multilateral agreement (the Montreal Convention).[65]

Likewise, the Council typically provides in its sanctions decisions that states must comply, notwithstanding anything to the contrary in contracts or licenses in effect prior to the imposition of sanctions.[66] On occasion, the Council takes the extra step of providing that no claim can be brought by the sanctioned state (or any person or body in that state) in connection with any contract or other transaction because the performance of the contract was affected by the Council's sanctions.[67] In short, Council sanctions prevail over other obligations, whether public or private in character.

In the post–Cold War era, the Security Council has developed a wide spectrum of possible measures against trade and financial transactions—ranging from comprehensive to highly selective—that it may choose from to meet the needs of a particular situation. Where urgent, dramatic action is required to deal with an aggressive regime that is using force against its neighbors (as in the case of Iraq and Yugoslavia), and comprehensive measures may be necessary. On the other hand, where the objective is to inhibit or put pressure on specific actors in an internal conflict situation (as in the case of Liberia and Sierra Leone), targeted sanctions may be more appropriate, even though they will not usually have the coercive force of comprehensive sanctions and are more susceptible to evasion. Targeted sanctions may also be necessary when there is insufficient political support for the imposition of comprehensive sanctions or when it would not be feasible to maintain and enforce comprehensive sanctions over an extended period.

Diplomatic sanctions

Article 41 of the UN Charter lists "the severance of diplomatic relations" as one of the measures the Council may order as a means of giving effect to its decisions under Chapter VII. In fact, the Council has used a variety of measures relating to diplomatic relations and recognition that have required it to make fundamental decisions about the legal status of states, governments, and regimes.

In the case of Southern Rhodesia, the Council decided at the outset that the declaration of independence by the white minority regime was a "usurpation of power" that had "no legal validity," called on the United Kingdom to bring that regime to an end and called on all other states not to recognize it or entertain diplomatic relations with it.[68] Later, the Council required UN member states to sever "all diplomatic, consular, trade, military and other relations" with the regime, and to take action to suspend any form of membership of Southern Rhodesia in UN specialized agencies and regional organizations.[69] Although the Council's resolutions made repeated references to the fact that the United Kingdom was the lawful sovereign over Southern Rhodesia, the Council's rejection of the minority regime clearly was based on its denial of self-determination and civil rights to the majority of the population rather than a desire to confirm the rights of a colonial power over one of its colonies.

On the other hand, in the case of Namibia, the Council affirmed the right of the people of Namibia to freedom and independence, declared that the continued presence and acts of South African authorities in Namibia were illegal, called on South Africa to withdraw from the territory, and called on all states to refrain from any dealings with the South African government that would be inconsistent with these conclusions.[70] The ICJ then confirmed the Council's authority to take these actions and the obligation of all member states to comply.[71] In 1978, when South Africa had finally agreed to withdraw, the Council created a UN Transition Assistance Group to bring about Namibian independence through free elections under UN supervision.[72]

Similarly, in the case of East Timor, the Council condemned the Indonesian invasion in 1975, recognized the right of the people of East Timor to self-determination and independence, and called on all states to respect those rights.[73] The Council took the same position when it assumed interim governance over East Timor nearly thirty-five years later, pending a transition to independence.[74]

Immediately after the Iraqi invasion of Kuwait, the Council declared that Iraq's asserted annexation of Kuwait "has no legal validity, and is considered null and void," and it called on all states and international organizations not to recognize that annexation and to refrain from any action that might be interpreted as such.[75] It likewise declared null and void the Iraqi orders for the closure of Kuwaiti diplomatic missions and the withdrawal of the diplomatic immunity of their personnel.[76]

The Council likewise had to make decisions during the Yugoslav conflict—often in conjunction with the General Assembly—about the status and recognition of the former Yugoslav republics. When it imposed an arms embargo in 1991, the Council continued to treat Yugoslavia as a single state, while declaring unacceptable any "territorial gains or changes within Yugoslavia brought about by violence."[77] By May 1992, however, the Council began to treat Bosnia as an independent republic of the former Yugoslavia and to demand the withdrawal of Yugoslav army units from Bosnia.[78] Later in the same month, it formally recommended to the General Assembly that Bosnia, Croatia, and Slovenia be admitted as UN members.[79] From that time forward, sanctions were imposed by the Council on the "Federal Republic of Yugoslavia (Serbia and Montenegro)" as an independent entity.[80] However, the Council refused to recognize the new FRY as the successor to the former Yugoslavia, and pronounced that the FRY could not claim the Yugoslav membership in the United Nations but would have to apply separately for admission.[81] Only after the fall of the Milosevic regime did the FRY apply for separate admission, which the Council immediately approved.[82]

On the other hand, the Council rejected the desires of the majority of the inhabitants of Kosovo for independence from the FRY, even after the Council assumed interim governance over the territory following the NATO air campaign in 1999. Rather, the Council reaffirmed the territorial integrity of the FRY and decided that the interim administration of Kosovo would provide only "substantial autonomy within" the FRY.[83] As discussed further in chapter 4, the final status of Kosovo remains a potentially difficult issue for the Council and the other parties involved.

In the case of Afghanistan, the Council endorsed the agreement reached in December 2001 on provisional governing arrangements to replace the Taliban regime.[84] The following year, after the creation of a transitional administration in Kabul, the Council recognized that administration as "the sole legitimate Government of Afghanistan, pending democratic elections in 2004."[85]

Finally, after the coalition military intervention in Iraq in 2003 and the demise the Saddam Hussein regime, the Council made a series of decisions about the status and duties of coalition authorities and the emerging Iraqi political structures. Among other things, the Council (1) determined that the United States and the United Kingdom were occupying powers for the purposes of the Geneva and Hague Conventions;[86] (2) welcomed the establishment of the Iraqi Governing Council in July 2003 "as an important step towards the formation by the people of Iraq of an internationally recognized, representative government that will exercise the sovereignty of Iraq,"[87] and (3) determined that the Governing Council "embodies the sovereignty of the State of Iraq" during the transitional period.[88] In 2004, the Council endorsed the formation of the "sovereign Interim Government of Iraq, . . . which will assume full responsibility and authority by 30 June 2004 for governing Iraq while refraining from taking any actions affecting Iraq's destiny beyond the limited interim period until an elected Transitional Government of Iraq assumes office."[89]

In each of these instances, the Council exercised the authority to make definitive judgments on some of the most fundamental aspects of international relations—whether an entity was entitled to be treated as a sovereign state; whether its people had the right of self-determination, independence, or autonomy; and whether a particular regime or movement had the right to be treated as the government of such a state. In each case, the Council made its judgment based in part on its understanding of international law and its appreciation of political and moral factors, but also, most important, on its judgment of what would best serve the Council's fundamental mandate—the restoration and maintenance of peace. Such action is both an inevitable aspect of the discharge of the Council's responsibilities and, as asserted in chapter 5, an appropriate aspect of its Chapter VII authority.

Even in cases where a sanctioned entity is accepted as the government of a state, the Council has occasionally used diplomatic sanctions as a means of demonstrating its displeasure with the actions of the sanctioned state and of exerting political pressure by making it more difficult for the state to conduct effective diplomacy in support of its national political objectives. For example, as part of its response to the Libyan involvement in the destruction of Pan Am Flight 103 and other acts of international terrorism, the Council decided that all states must "significantly reduce the number and the level of the staff at Libyan diplomatic missions and consular posts and restrict or control the movement within their territory of all such staff who remain."[90] Similarly, as part of its reaction to Sudanese involvement with terrorist groups, the Council directed that states reduce Sudanese diplomatic personnel and restrict their travel, and called upon international and regional organizations not to convene any conferences in Sudan.[91]

Enforcement of Sanctions

One of the most serious problems faced by the Council over the years in the imposition of sanctions has been the perennial difficulty of enforcing them in the face of determined efforts by the sanctioned entities to evade them. This difficulty has typically been compounded by the relative inexperience of most countries in sanctions enforcement and the ambivalence of many governments and economic actors about the necessity or desirability of the sanctions. In the face of these problems, the Council has developed a variety of enforcement techniques.

The basic features of these techniques could be seen in the Council's imposition of comprehensive sanctions in the case of Iraq. The Council gave primary responsibility for enforcement to member states through the application of national laws and the actions of national enforcement authorities. The key provision of the Council's initial resolution imposing sanctions on Iraq required that "all States shall prevent" imports into their territory, sale or supply of goods and services from their territory, activities in support of such trade by their nationals or their flag vessels, and the provision of funds and other resources by their nationals and persons within their territory.[92] In effect, the Council required states to exercise the various elements of national jurisdiction permitted under international law to accomplish the Council's purposes. Unfortunately, while some states (like the United States and the United Kingdom) already had extensive experience with sanctions enforcement and an extensive structure of domestic laws and enforcement authorities for the purpose, most states were less prepared and required considerable time and effort to create the legal and practical basis for effective enforcement.[93]

The Council then adopted specific enforcement procedures to plug obvious avenues for Iraqi evasion of national controls. Within the first month after the Iraqi invasion, the Council called on member states that had maritime forces in the Gulf area to halt all maritime shipping bound to or from Iraq or Kuwait for the purpose of inspecting and verifying their cargos and destinations and ensuring strict compliance with Council sanctions.[94] The following month, the Council required every state to deny permission to any aircraft to take off from its territory if that aircraft was carrying any cargo to or from Iraq or Kuwait (subject to certain humanitarian and other exceptions), and to deny permission to any aircraft destined for Iraq or Kuwait to overfly its territory unless the aircraft landed for inspection to ensure that it contained no prohibited cargo.[95]

Further, the Council gave certain enforcement responsibilities to the sanctions committee created at the time sanctions were first imposed on Iraq. These responsibilities included receiving reports and seeking information from member states on their implementation of sanctions, and then reporting back to the Council with recommendations for further measures.[96]

These basic enforcement elements were repeated and developed in subsequent sanctions regimes. All of these later regimes depended first on enforcement through national laws and authorities. In the case of Sierra Leone, the Council required the establishment of a certificate of origin system to ensure that rough diamonds from Sierra Leone were imported into other countries only under the control of the government of Sierra Leone.[97] (Later, the Council concluded that Liberian government officials were complicit in the illicit shipment of diamonds through Liberia, and consequently required all states to prohibit import of all rough diamonds from Liberia, whatever their state of origin.[98])

Each of the Council's sanctions regimes has also involved the creation of a sanctions committee with the tasks of accumulating information from states, monitoring enforcement, making recommendations to the Council for improvement, and granting or denying exceptions. In some cases, the committees were given specific enforcement tasks, such as the authorization and monitoring of transshipments and the approval of border-crossing points for traffic into or out of the FRY,[99] the designation of members of the Sierra Leone junta who were to be denied entry into other states,[100] and the identification of specific parties that had violated Council sanctions with respect to transactions with UNITA and the illicit sale of Angolan diamonds.[101]

In the cases of Haiti and Yugoslavia, member states were called upon to halt maritime shipping, to inspect and verify cargos and destinations, and to prevent any prohibited trade.[102] States were required to deny takeoff, landing, and overflight to aircraft bound to or from the FRY, unless previously approved by the sanctions committee.[103] Special measures were required in the case of Yugoslavia because a considerable volume of goods are transshipped through the area by way of the Danube and other routes. As a result, the Council required that states take steps (including halting and inspecting cargoes) to prevent diversion to the FRY of goods supposedly destined for other countries, and permitted transshipments on the Danube only where specifically authorized by the sanctions committee and monitored to preclude diversions.[104] Freight vehicles and rolling stock were permitted to pass into or out of the FRY only at a limited number of border-crossing points, and any vessels or vehicles found to have violated sanctions were to be impounded.[105]

In short, the Council now has developed legal tools and precedents to deal with evasions—for example, by authorizing the use of force to constrain violations or by imposing secondary sanctions on states that abet or tolerate such violations—but, as with any other aspect of Chapter VII, enforcement will ultimately depend on the determination of Council members to use those tools and to provide the resources to use them effectively. For example, in the years following the Gulf War, a very substantial degree of evasion of the sanctions against Iraq developed, sometimes carried on in plain view with the tacit acquiescence of the Council (as will be described later in this chapter). Further, enforcing sanctions and granting and monitoring exceptions is a very complex task that requires substantial expertise and administrative resources, and one cogent criticism of the UN administration of sanctions during this period has been that the resources made available by the sanctions committees and the UN Secretariat have been inadequate.[106] This situation contrasts with the Council's creation of autonomous organizations with large, expert staffs to handle criminal prosecutions, compensation, and arms inspections, which is examined in chapters 6 and 7.

COLLATERAL DAMAGE

A frequent point of criticism of Council sanctions has been the damage that can be caused to parties that are not the object of the sanctions. This criticism usually focuses on the damage done to the population of the target state and to the economic interests of other states (particularly neighboring states that depend on transshipments through the target state, or states with significant trading relations with the target state). The sanctions against Iraq were often criticized as causing undue harm to neighboring states such as Jordan and to the civilian population of Iraq.[107] The sanctions against the FRY were sometimes criticized as strengthening the domestic political position of the Milosevic regime because of Serb resentment of the economic damage done to the Serb population.[108] The sanctions against Haiti were criticized for causing further deprivation to the already poor population of Haiti and for enriching the Haitian elites who profited from black-market operations.[109]

Obviously, the members of the Council who voted for these sanctions regimes were aware of the risks of such collateral damage but considered that the assumption of those risks was justified by the purposes to be served by the sanctions—the end of the Iraqi occupation of Kuwait and the elimination of Iraqi WMD, the termination of the Yugoslav conflict and the atrocities committed by the Belgrade regime and its surrogates, and the end of the repressive Haitian junta and the restoration of the democratically elected government. But it is obviously useful to develop means of minimizing collateral damage while preserving the effects of sanctions. During the past fifteen years, the Council has developed various techniques for doing so.

The civilian population of the target state

Every sanctions regime of the past decade has included exemptions for humanitarian and other purposes designed to minimize the effect of sanctions on the population of the target country. The first sanctions resolution against Iraq exempted the sale of "supplies intended strictly for medical purposes, and, in humanitarian circumstances, foodstuffs," as well as payments for the same purposes.[110] Similar exceptions were made with respect to the prohibition on aircraft flights to and from Iraq or Kuwait.[111] The Council's comprehensive cease-fire resolution at the end of the Gulf War exempted medicine, health supplies, and foodstuffs notified to the sanctions committee and, with the committee's approval under a "simplified and accelerated 'no-objection' procedure," materials and supplies for "essential civilian needs" as identified by the secretary-general or the committee.[112]

There was, however, continuing criticism over the years that the sanctions committee was not sufficiently forthcoming in giving timely approval for humanitarian requests and in permitting imports to restore Iraqi infrastructure needed to maintain the health and well-being of the civilian population.[113] Eventually this criticism led to steps by the Council to expedite the process and expand the scope of items permitted. For example, the sanctions committee was directed to approve lists of humanitarian items and lists of items for agriculture, education, electric power, housing, and other civilian requirements, with the proviso that items on the lists would not require specific submission and approval.[114]

The committee was also directed to review other applications more expeditiously and decrease the number of applications on "hold" by committee members.[115] The Council adopted a Goods Review List designed to simplify and expedite imports of items needed for civilian purposes, while excluding dual-use items that could be misused to support weapons programs.[116] The list and procedures to implement it were reviewed and revised right up to the point at which the U.S.-led coalition finally opted to abandon reliance on sanctions and to use force to end Saddam Hussein's regime.[117]

Recognizing that additional sources of funding had to be allowed for the purchase of such items, the Council decided in August 1991 that states would be permitted to import up to $1.6 billion worth of Iraqi petroleum products, the proceeds of which would be deposited in an escrow account administered by the United Nations, and used partly for humanitarian items and partly to fund the costs of UN operations in Iraq and compensation for war victims. This arrangement became commonly known as the Oil-for-Food Program. The purchase of humanitarian items was to be subject to UN monitoring and supervision for the purpose of "assuring their equitable distribution to meet humanitarian needs in all regions of Iraq and to all categories of the Iraqi civilian population."[118] If accepted, further purchases presumably would have been approved.

However, the Iraqi government refused these sales of oil and deliveries of humanitarian items, objecting that UN monitoring would violate its sovereignty.[119] As a substitute source of funding, the Council then decided that states would transfer to the UN escrow account proceeds from prior Iraqi oil sales that had been frozen around the world.[120] However, only the United States made substantial contributions of Iraqi funds, which kept UN programs concerning Iraq in operation but did not provide sufficient funds for humanitarian purposes.[121]

The Council tried again in April 1995, authorizing states to import Iraqi petroleum products in amounts that would produce $1 billion every ninety days. These sales were to be monitored by the sanctions committee, and the proceeds were to be paid into an escrow account established by the secretary-general. The funds in the account were to be used in part to pay the costs of oil export and maintenance of pipelines, in part to compensate war victims (as will be described in chapter 6), in part to meet the costs of UN programs in Iraq (including weapons inspections), and the rest for humanitarian relief for the Iraqi population (including food, health supplies, and other items for "essential civilian needs"). Between $130 and $150 million were to be used each ninety days for relief distributed directly by the United Nations in the three northern provinces under Kurdish control, and the rest was to be distributed by Iraq in the rest of the country under UN supervision to ensure equitable distribution to all parts of the population.[122]

Iraq did permit oil exports under this Oil-for-Food Program, though from time to time over the years it suspended, obstructed, or harassed UN operations to evade effective supervision of humanitarian distributions or to make other political points. Nonetheless, the Council continued to expand the size and scope of the program, eventually lifting altogether the limits on the amount of oil that could be imported for such purposes.[123] Over time, the amount of humanitarian relief financed through this mechanism was substantial: some $31 billion worth of humanitarian items were delivered between December 1996 and the coalition intervention in 2003, and a further $8 billion worth were in the pipeline.[124] After coalition forces occupied Iraq, the Council provided for the transfer of the surplus funds in the account to a development fund controlled by the occupying powers, to be used "to meet the humanitarian needs of the Iraqi people, for the economic reconstruction and repair of Iraq's infrastructure, for the continued disarmament of Iraq, and for the costs of Iraqi civilian administration, and for other purposes benefiting the people of Iraq."[125] In November 2003, the Oil-for-Food Program was terminated, and a total of more than $9 billion was eventually transferred to the development fund.[126]

The Council's other sanctions programs had similar exceptions for sales of food, medicine, and other humanitarian items, for flights serving humanitarian purposes, and the like.[127] In some cases, express prior approval by the relevant sanctions committee was required for each transaction; in other cases, expedited procedures were adopted, such as the "simplified and accelerated 'no objection' procedure" developed in connection with Iraq.[128]

However, in none of these cases did the Council have any source of funding from the resources of the sanctioned country that was comparable to Iraqi oil exports, which offered a very large margin of revenues over production costs and could be readily monitored and controlled by the international community. As a result, nothing comparable to the Iraqi Oil-for-Food Program was created with respect to these other sanctions programs to finance humanitarian imports. In theory, however, the Iraqi program might still be a precedent for future Council action if any comparable source of sanctioned-country resources (such as oil, diamonds, or other high-value raw materials) were available.

It is possible—in one degree or another—to mitigate the damage to the civilian population caused by sanctions, but it will never be possible to eliminate it altogether, and in some cases the damage will still be severe, as was evidently the case in Iraq. This creates a dilemma for the Council, in that sanctions are typically imposed for serious reasons, and their lifting is often conditioned on compliance with specific requirements that are thought to be essential to restoring and maintaining peace (such as the elimination of Iraqi WMD after the first Gulf War). Any lifting or serious weakening of sanctions before such conditions are met therefore carries with it the risk of degrading the effectiveness and credibility of the Council's actions and increasing the threat to the peace. Weighing these competing considerations is a difficult matter for the Council, requiring political judgment, strength, and common sense.

In addition, any program for humanitarian exceptions on the scale of the Iraqi program can present opportunities for sanctions evasion, diversion of funds to illicit purposes, and manipulation by the targeted regime. Serious allegations have been made that these things occurred on a significant scale in the Iraqi Oil-for-Food program, and in 2004, an independent high-level inquiry into these allegations (headed by former U.S. Federal Reserve System chairman Paul Volcker) was instituted by the UN secretary-general with the blessing of the Council.[129] An interim report of the committee charged with this inquiry suggested that the arrangements for the administration of the program that were negotiated by the UN secretariat with Iraq in 1996 gave Iraq considerable influence over the selection of the companies that would buy oil and sell humanitarian goods, and that Iraq used this influence to obtain substantial kickbacks and to reward countries, companies, and individuals that were thought to be favorably inclined toward Iraq.[130] The report also suggested that there were serious improprieties and violations of established financial and procurement rules in the selection of the major UN contractors that administered the program and in the allocation of oil contracts.[131]

A further report of the Volcker Committee in September 2005 confirmed these conclusions.[132] The committee found serious flaws in the way in which the program was structured and administered, including the following:

> 1. However well intentioned the program was in principle, the Security Council failed to define clearly the practical parameters, policies, and administrative responsibilities. Far too much initiative was left to the Iraqi regime in the program's design and subsequent implementation. . . . Neither the Security Council nor the Secretariat leadership was clearly in command. . . .
>
> 2. The administrative structure and personnel practices of the organization—certainly within the Secretariat—were simply not fit to meet the truly extraordinary challenges presented by the Oil-for-Food Program. . . .
>
> 3. Most notable among the United Nations' structural faults is a grievous absence of effective auditing and management controls. . . . The Oil-for-Food Program has exposed chronic weaknesses of plan-

ning, sorely inadequate funding, and the simple absence of enough professional personnel to implement controls and auditing. . . .

4. The isolated instances of corruption detailed in the earlier Committee Reports extend to the top of the program administration—one important reflection of the managerial weaknesses. . . .

5. Finally, the particular nature of the Oil-for-Food Program placed in stark relief the difficulties of effective cooperation among United Nations agencies. . . .[133]

But, on the other hand, these serious errors in the administration of the Oil-for-Food program should not obscure the fact that the program was an essential part of the overall UN program for Iraq, and that such humanitarian relief programs must remain part of the Security Council's toolbox to ameliorate the effects of necessary sanctions programs. The Volcker Committee itself found that:

> Conceived as a means for reconciling strong sanctions against a corrupt Iraqi regime with needed supplies of food and medicines to an innocent and vulnerable population, the program did achieve important successes. Its existence helped maintain the international effort to deprive Saddam Hussein of weapons of mass destruction. Furthermore, a new study commissioned by the committee confirms that minimal standards of nutrition and health were maintained in the face of a potential crisis.[134]

The committee also pointed out that such humanitarian requirements were bound to recur, and that in the absence of the United Nations, no other national or international entities would likely be able to accomplish such "complex missions cutting across national boundaries and diverse areas of competence."[135]

These findings underscore the importance of the recommendation of the 2004 UN high-level report that when the Council imposes any sanctions regime, "it should routinely establish monitoring mechanisms and provide them with the necessary authority and capacity to carry out high-quality, in-depth investigations."[136] Further, such programs can be effectively run only if sufficient autonomous expertise and resources are devoted to the task, as has been done, for example, in the program for compensation for damage resulting from the Gulf War, to be discussed in chapter 6. Finally, the Council must take responsibility for effective, continuing oversight of the entire process, and, in particular, for ensuring that decisions are made on the basis of valid technical and policy considerations, and not to accommodate political and economic interests of individual Council members.

Damage to other states

Because economic sanctions typically rely on the interruption of economic relations that were of benefit to both sides of the relationship, the imposition of such sanctions will inevitably cause damage to both sides. The UN Charter recognizes this problem, but the solution it offers is at best only a reminder to the Security Council that some action may be appropriate. Article 50 provides, "If preventive or enforcement measures against any state are taken by the Security Council, any other state, whether a Member of the United Nations or not, which finds itself confronted with special economic problems arising from the carrying out of those measures shall have the right to consult the Security Council with regard to a solution of those problems." During the negotiations on the Charter, a proposal was made to substitute a right to assistance for this right to consultation, but the proposal was rejected.[137] The result is that it is entirely up to the Council to take or refrain from action to prevent or relieve such damage.

The problem of damage to other states was a matter of serious concern with respect to the sanctions program against Southern Rhodesia, whose newly independent and economically weak neighbors had been heavily dependent on Rhodesian and South African trade, investment, and communications. The Council responded by sending special missions to assess the needs of neighboring states, and by requesting states and international organizations to give assistance to these neighbors as a matter of priority, but it made no exceptions to sanctions on their behalf.[138]

The Iraqi invasion of Kuwait and the imposition of UN sanctions had serious economic effects on many countries, as a result of the suspension of trade, financial, and contractual relationships, the expulsion of large numbers of foreign workers, and the severe reduction of tourism and other business activities in the region. Jordan and other heavily affected states invoked Article 50, and the Security Council responded by assigning to the sanctions committee the task of examining these requests and making recommendations for action.[139] The committee in turn created a working group that produced a series of reports asking states to grant assistance to the affected countries.[140] In fact, assistance was provided in a variety of forms, including increased oil production to replace lost Iraqi and Kuwaiti exports, bilateral economic assistance, and loans by international financial institutions.[141]

The committee did not recommend exemptions from the sanctions for states affected by them, nor did the Council grant any express exemptions. Yet it is apparent that the committee and the Council were aware that Jordan and other states in the region evaded sanctions from time to time (particularly by accepting Iraqi oil or allowing it to transit their territory), but chose not take action against these states.[142] The Oil-for-Food Program was in some sense also an exception to sanctions in that it allowed states to purchase large amounts of Iraqi oil and sell large quantities of items for the civilian population.

At the conclusion of the Gulf War, the Council created the UN Compensation Commission for the purpose of providing compensation (drawn from Iraqi oil export revenues) to states affected by the invasion and occupation of Kuwait (as described in chapter 6). However, the Governing Council of the commission decided that compensation would not be offered for losses caused by the embargo and the economic situation caused by it.[143] This decision took account of the fact that these losses were very large and ill-defined and would heavily deplete the resources of the commission, to the detriment of more urgent claims for damage that was more directly caused by the invasion and occupation.

In adopting sanctions against the FRY, the Council recognized that other states in the region could be economically affected, given their extensive commercial relations with the FRY and their dependence on transshipment of goods across FRY territory. The right of states to seek consultation under Article 50 was acknowledged in the Council's first resolution imposing comprehensive sanctions.[144]

At first, the Council provided that sanctions would not apply to the transshipment through the FRY of products originating elsewhere.[145] However, as noted previously, the Council subsequently found it necessary to restrict such transshipments, particularly with respect to traffic on the Danube. These restrictions created problems for neighboring states and caused them to seek relief or exceptions from the sanctions committee. For the most part, the committee insisted on strict enforcement of the sanctions, but on a few occasions it granted minor exceptions to deal with special circumstances: for example, allowing Romania to release FRY vessels suspected of sanctions violations from a Danube port where their presence was creating a safety hazard, and allowing the provision of fuel to operate FRY ice-breaking vessels.[146]

The possibility of serious economic damage to other states has been a significant factor in the Council's decisions about the scope of partial sanctions in other cases. In particular, the dependence of several European states on Libyan oil exports was clearly a significant element in the Council's decision not to include oil transactions in its initial sanctions against Libya,[147] and its later freeze on Libyan funds included an express exception for funds derived from the sale of petroleum products.[148]

Various efforts have been made in the UN community in recent years to consider additional means of avoiding or relieving sanctions' economic damage to other states, including resolutions of the General Assembly,[149] reports of the secretary-general,[150] and proposals by member states.[151] Among the steps proposed have been the development of methodologies for assessing such damage; the adoption of a standard process of assessments, on-site inspections, and consultations to bring these matters to the Council's attention at an early stage in the consideration of possible sanctions; and the sharing of the costs of sanctions by all UN members, either by action of the Council or of international financial institutions.[152] Nonetheless, any significant sanctions program will cause economic damage to other states, a fact that the Council must carefully weigh in imposing sanctions.

LEGAL CONSTRAINTS ON SANCTIONS

As noted at the beginning of this book, the UN Charter imposes certain legal constraints on the Security Council in exercising its Chapter VII authority. These of course apply to the imposition of sanctions, but their practical effect as legal constraints is limited by various factors. As a predicate for the imposition of sanctions, the Council must find the existence of a threat to or breach of the peace or act of aggression, but the Council has taken a very robust view in the post–Cold War period of what may constitute such a threat. Articles 41 and 48 give the Council discretion to determine what sanctions are to be applied, and by whom, as a result of such a finding.

It has also been acknowledged earlier that in accordance with Article 24(2), the Council must act in accordance with the "Purposes and Principles of the United Nations" contained in Articles 1 and 2. This includes principles that may be relevant to sanctions decisions, such as the protection of human rights (such as the "right to life") and the promotion of adequate standards of living, and it has been argued that these principles have been violated by sanctions against Iraq and Haiti because of the serious deprivations caused to their civilian population.[153]

Yet the "Purposes and Principles of the United Nations" contain a number of objectives, the first and foremost of which are the restoration and maintenance of the peace, and when these objectives conflict in a particular situation, it is the responsibility of the Council to decide how to reconcile them or to what degree to compromise some of them to accommodate others. As the secretary-general has said, "The international community should be under no illusion: these humanitarian and human rights policy goals cannot easily be reconciled with those of a sanctions regime. It cannot be too strongly emphasized that sanctions are a tool of enforcement, and, like other methods of enforcement, they will do harm."[154]

It is also the case that certain provisions of international humanitarian law may apply to sanctions imposed during armed conflict. For example, it is unlawful to intentionally use the starvation of civilians as a method of warfare by depriving them of items indispensable to their survival, including willfully impeding relief supplies as provided for under the 1949 Geneva Conventions.[155] But these provisions would not be violated by sanctions programs exempting shipments of food and medical supplies, allowing reasonable measures to pay for such shipments, and providing exceptions for relief operations.

It has also been suggested that the principle of proportionality—
the rule in the law of armed conflict that prohibits any attack likely
to cause loss or injury to the civilian population that is clearly disproportionate to the military advantage of the attack—should be applied
to the imposition of economic sanctions.[156] Although the principle of
proportionality in the law of armed conflict does not technically
apply to acts not involving the use of force, it would be reasonable for
the Council to apply such a principle in assessing the possible effects
of its sanctions on the civilian population. Certainly the Council
should consider the possible effects on civilians when adopting and
maintaining sanctions, and reasonable arguments can be made that
in certain cases the harm caused by the sanctions was excessive in
light of the limited effect of sanctions on the ruling elites that were
the object of those sanctions.

ASSESSMENT

The post–Cold War period has seen a very great expansion in the
scope, frequency, and importance of the use of sanctions by the Security Council. Sanctions have been used as an alternative to the use of
force, as a complement to the use of force, or in the aftermath of the
use of force. Different types of sanctions (partial and comprehensive)
have been used that have (1) increased or decreased in severity and
scope to reflect changing circumstances and policy requirements, or
(2) targeted particular sectors or particular persons and entities. Sanctions decisions have included within them determinations by the
Council on the legal status of states, governments, and territories.
    The Council has faced three recurring problems in its imposi-
tion of sanctions during this period: the difficulty of maintaining
and enforcing them—particularly in the long-term application of
comprehensive sanctions against determined regimes; the problem of
minimizing undesired collateral effects of sanctions on untargeted
states and civilian populations; and the problem of avoiding fraud
and manipulation by the sanctioned country. The Council has developed various techniques for dealing with these problems, although
they will never be wholly resolved.

The aspect that has attracted the most attention and criticism over the years has been the degree of injury and loss that sanctions have caused for vulnerable parts of the civilian population that have had little or no involvement in the conduct of their targeted governments. Such injury or loss may sometimes be the bitter but unavoidable cost of effective Council action, and no legal constraint or external review of Council decisions can preclude it. The Council can and should apply a principle of proportionality in such cases to weigh the likely damage to civilians against the likely utility of sanctions in fulfilling vital objectives. But the application of such a principle can be very difficult in practice. What level of suffering by the civilian population is justified as a means of defeating aggression and unlawful occupation of one state by another, or of preventing an aggressive regime from acquiring WMD, or of ending widespread atrocities against a particular ethnic group?

Such decisions must rest in the judgment and discretion of the Council, and general legal principles will rarely give clear answers. What is important is that the Council take this matter very seriously and give every consideration to the use of the techniques that have been developed during the past decade to minimize collateral damage, and to provide relief or compensation for damage that cannot be avoided.

4

UN PEACEKEEPING
AND GOVERNANCE

O
NE OF THE MORE PROMINENT forms of UN involvement in
the resolution of armed conflicts during the Cold War took
the form of the deployment of peacekeeping missions to
areas of actual or potential hostilities. After the end of the Cold War,
the number, size, and mandates of such missions greatly expanded,
including many forms of nonmilitary activity, and eventually some
UN missions assumed the function of governing particular territories
for transitional periods. Yet there is no express provision in the UN
Charter for such missions, and the legal and policy ground rules for
them had to be invented through trial and error under the stress of
urgent circumstances.

This chapter will consider the development of the legal framework for UN peacekeeping missions during the Cold War and the
considerable and important changes that have occurred in the past
fifteen years, including the new and expanded functions that such
missions have come to serve.[1] It will look in particular at the Security
Council's use of Chapter VII in authorizing peacekeeping missions,
which has significantly expanded the legal basis for their operations
and has largely resolved many of the issues about the lawful scope of
their actions. These developments have obviated, as a legal matter,

some of what were considered to be inherent limitations on peace-keeping missions. But other serious policy issues about UN peace-keeping in the more demanding missions of the post–Cold War era remain, including the need for clear mandates, adequate finances and personnel, strong command structures, and political resolve in the face of adversity. The chapter concludes with a look at the recent UN experience in governing territories affected by conflict, in particular Kosovo and East Timor.

First off, though, a brief note on terminology. A number of different terms have been used over the years to identify different aspects of UN efforts to prevent, constrain, and terminate conflicts. The secretary-general's 1992 *Agenda for Peace* defined "peacekeeping" as "the deployment of a United Nations presence in the field, hitherto with the consent of all the parties concerned, normally involving United Nations military and/or police personnel and frequently civilians as well." Peacekeeping was distinguished from "preventive diplomacy" (action to prevent disputes from arising), "peacemaking" (action to bring hostile parties to agreement, essentially through peaceful means), and "postconflict peacebuilding" (action to avoid a relapse into conflict).[2] The term "peace operations" has been used to include both consensual "peacekeeping" and nonconsensual "enforcement" operations.[3]

In fact, UN operations do not fall into well-defined, mutually exclusive categories, any more than do the conflicts they address, and many of the missions treated by the United Nations as peacekeeping operations have functions that fall within more than one of the above categories.[4] In particular, most of the post–Cold War missions on the official UN list of peacekeeping operations have had Chapter VII mandates, many have been authorized to use force other than in self-defense, and some have operated without the consent of all the contending parties. (For a comprehensive list of UN peacekeeping operations, see Appendix 2.) For this reason, the term "UN peacekeeping operations" is used here to include all of the missions in the UN list, whether or not they meet the traditional definitions of peacekeeping.

Later chapters will explore different aspects of UN action in connection with conflict situations. Chapter 5 will deal with the use of force, both by UN peacekeeping forces and by non-UN forces operating under UN authority. Chapter 6 will examine various UN technical commissions created to deal with the results of conflict (including the commissions concerned with compensation, disarmament, and boundary demarcation). Chapter 7 will address the international criminal tribunals.

Legal Authority

International peacekeeping was not invented by the United Nations. For example, peacekeeping missions were deployed under the authority of the League of Nations to assist in the international administration of an area on the border between Peru and Colombia, and the conduct of a plebiscite in the Saar.[5] In spite of this prior experience and the predictable need for peacekeeping operations in the UN system, no reference to such missions is made in the Charter, although Chapter VI recites many alternatives for the peaceful resolution of disputes and Chapter VII provides in some detail for the coercive use of force in enforcement actions under the authority of the Security Council.

During the Cold War period, when mandatory actions under Chapter VII were rarely taken, various theories were put forward for the legal basis under the UN Charter for peacekeeping operations. With respect to the Security Council, which authorized most UN peacekeeping missions, UN actors and commentators referred to several possible sources of authority, including the general grant by Article 24 of primary responsibility to the Council for the maintenance of international peace and security; the authority of the Council under Chapter VI and Article 39 to make recommendations to states for the peaceful resolution of their disputes; the authority of the Council under Article 29 to establish subsidiary organs to carry out its functions; and the authority of the Council under Article 98 to delegate functions to the secretary-general.[6] Secretary-General Dag Hammarskjöld referred to peacekeeping as "Chapter Six and a Half."[7] Whatever the specific theory for it, the Security Council's authority to create peacekeeping and similar missions came to be accepted over the years and was specifically confirmed by the International Court of Justice.[8]

With the end of the Cold War, the Council began freely to use its powers under Chapter VII, which include the very broad categories of "measures not involving the use of armed force" under Article 41 and "action by air, sea, or land forces" under Article 42. When applied to the authorization of peacekeeping operations, this broad scope of Chapter VII authority removed any residual doubts about the Council's authority to create peacekeeping missions with wide-ranging functions.

The involvement of the General Assembly in peacekeeping has been more controversial. Although the Security Council clearly has the "primary" responsibility under the Charter for the maintenance of peace and security, the General Assembly has some secondary authority. Under Articles 11 and 14, the Assembly may discuss any questions relating to peace and security and may make recommendations on such questions to the states concerned or to the Council; and under Article 22, the Assembly may establish subsidiary organs to carry out its functions. But Article 12 prohibits the Assembly from acting in any situation where the Council is exercising its functions under the Charter.[9]

These issues came to the fore in 1950 with the North Korean invasion of South Korea. The Council was briefly able to act because of a temporary absence of the Soviet delegation, and it recommended that states contribute forces to a unified command under the United States to resist the North Korean advance, but the Council was again immobilized when the Soviet delegation returned.[10] The General Assembly thereupon took up the matter and adopted the so-called Uniting for Peace Resolution, which asserted that:

> . . . if the Security Council, because of lack of unanimity of the permanent members, fails to exercise its primary responsibility for the maintenance of international peace and security in any case where there appears to be a threat to the peace, breach of peace, or act of aggression, the General Assembly shall consider the matter immediately with a view to making appropriate recommendations to Members for collective measures, including in the case of a breach of the peace or act of aggression the use of armed force when necessary, to maintain or restore international peace and security.

The Assembly also created a Peace Observation Commission and a Collective Measures Committee to make recommendations to the Assembly on possible conflict situations.[11]

This assertion of authority was tested in 1956, when Israeli, UK, and French forces invaded the Sinai and occupied the Suez Canal in response to the Egyptian nationalization of the canal.[12] The Security Council was unable to act because of British and French vetoes, and the matter was then taken up by the Assembly under the Uniting for Peace Resolution. The Assembly adopted a resolution calling for a cease-fire, withdrawal of forces, and the reopening of the canal.[13] It then established an emergency force under UN command— the United Nations Emergency Force (UNEF I)—to deploy into the Sinai to monitor and assist in the implementation of the cease-fire.[14] This action was remarkable not only for its use of the Uniting for Peace authority, but also for its bold deployment of UN forces into a highly dangerous situation where a resumption of serious armed conflict was always a possibility (and did in fact later occur).

Four years later, when the newly independent Congo was on the brink of collapse into anarchy and foreign intervention, the Council created a peacekeeping force—the United Nations Operation in the Congo (ONUC)—to assist the Congolese government.[15] However, when a constitutional crisis subsequently arose within the Congolese government and the Security Council was unable to decide how to respond, the General Assembly acted under Uniting for Peace, deciding (among other things) on the apportionment of expenses for the peacekeeping operation.[16]

The Soviet Union objected strongly to this use of Uniting for Peace, taking the view that the Assembly had no authority to create a peacekeeping force or to make decisions on the mandate or financing of such a force, on the grounds that these matters were within the exclusive authority of the Council under the Charter. Consequently, the Soviet Union (among others, including France) refused to pay its share of the expenses of UNEF I and ONUC. In an attempt to resolve the matter, the Assembly requested the ICJ to give an advisory opinion as to whether the expenses of UNEF I and ONUC, as decided by the Assembly, were legitimate expenses of the United Nations. The court decided that they were, on the grounds that the Assembly had the authority to create subordinate bodies (in this case, peacekeeping forces) and to recommend that states contribute forces to them.[17]

However, this validation by the ICJ of the Assembly's authority to create peacekeeping forces did not, in the long run, have much practical significance. The end of the Cold War substantially decreased the likelihood of impasses among the permanent members in the Council, and the shift of political power in the Assembly to the Third World discouraged the Western powers from resorting to the Assembly or seeking to enhance its authority. From a legal standpoint, the Assembly's authority was far from satisfactory as a substitute for the Council's authority, because the Assembly could only make recommendations to states; it could not authorize a UN force to act without the consent of the state or states involved, to initiate the use of force, or to take enforcement action. (As noted later, these became matters of significant concern during the post–Cold War period.) As a result, every UN peacekeeping operation after the Cold War has been conducted under the authority of the Council rather than the Assembly.

Therefore, post–Cold War UN peacekeeping forces have been subsidiary organs of the Security Council, which defines their mandates and authority; but the Council has also made them subordinate to the secretary-general, who appoints and supervises the force commanders and special representatives who direct their operations. At the same time, UN peacekeeping forces are composed largely of national contingents voluntarily made available to the United Nations by contributing states, which typically retain certain forms of authority over them, such as disciplinary power and criminal jurisdiction. These national contingents are under UN command, though national authorities have sometimes attempted to control their operations.[18]

SCOPE OF UN PEACEKEEPING OPERATIONS

A substantial number of UN peacekeeping missions were conducted during the Cold War, and in some cases (such as the Congo and the Arab-Israeli conflicts) these missions were of considerable importance. Even so, with the end of the Cold War, the number and size of such missions increased substantially.

Four waves of post–Cold War peacekeeping operations can be identified. (Of course, these "waves" were not strictly sequential and have overlapped over time.) First, by 1988, the incipient end of the Cold War could be seen in the gradual winding down of regional conflicts in Latin America, Africa, and Asia that had, to one degree or another, been involved in the strategic competition between the United States and the Soviet Union. UN peacekeeping missions played an important role in the implementation of the agreements that ended these conflicts—for example, in Afghanistan (UNGOMAP), Namibia (UNTAG), Central America (ONUCA), El Salvador (ONUSAL), and Cambodia (UNTAC).[19] (For a translation of all the cryptic UN peacekeeping acronyms, see Appendix 2.) This involvement of UN peacekeeping missions in the resolution of Cold War conflicts was, on the whole, a great success.

Second, UN peacekeeping missions became involved in the series of new conflicts that resulted from the collapse of the Soviet Union and the Yugoslav communist regime at the end of the Cold War. Some prominent examples were the UN missions in the former Yugoslavia (UNPROFOR), Croatia (UNCRO and UNTAES), Macedonia (UNPREDEP), Bosnia (UNMIBH), Georgia (UNOMIG), Tajikistan (UNMOT), and Kosovo (UNMIK).[20]

Third, the immediate post–Cold War period was marked by a series of internal conflicts—particularly in Africa—in which UN missions became heavily involved. They included peacekeeping missions in Angola (UNAVEM), Somalia (UNOSOM), Rwanda (UNAMIR), Liberia (UNOMIL), and Haiti (UNMIH).[21] Later there were similar missions in Sierra Leone (UNOMSIL), the Central African Republic (MINURCA), the Congo (MONUC), Côte d'Ivoire (UNOCI), and Burundi (ONUB).[22] The creation of these missions was part of the general readiness of the Security Council and the international community in the post–Cold War period to intervene in internal conflicts to preserve regional peace, to respond to humanitarian concerns, and to preserve new democratic governments.

Fourth, the post–Cold War period was marked by international conflicts that required the involvement of UN missions to implement cease-fires and similar agreements. This included missions in Iraq (UNIKOM), East Timor (UNTAET), and Eritrea-Ethiopia

(UNMEE).[23] At the same time, several UN missions that had been created to address interstate conflicts during the Cold War era continued to operate during the post–Cold War period, including those in the Golan (UNDOF), Lebanon (UNIFIL), India and Pakistan (UNMOGIP), and Cyprus (UNFICYP).[24]

These four waves of post–Cold War peacekeeping resulted in a substantial increase in the number and size of UN peacekeeping operations. Fewer than fifteen peacekeeping operations were created from 1948 through 1987, while more than twenty were created from 1988 through 1994 alone.[25] At the beginning of 1988, fewer than 12,000 personnel were deployed in UN peacekeeping operations; by the end of 1994, more than 75,000 were deployed.[26] In 1988, the annual UN peacekeeping budget was less than $250 million; by 1994, it had grown to more than $3.5 billion.[27] The active use of the Council's authority to create peacekeeping operations has continued to the present: by late 2004, more than fifty-five operations had been created, more than 60,000 personnel were deployed, and the annual budget stood at about $3 billion.[28] (A complete list is in Appendix 2.)

PEACEKEEPING MANDATES

First-generation peacekeeping

UN peacekeeping during the Cold War consisted primarily of "traditional" or "first-generation" peacekeeping operations—that is, lightly armed military personnel sent to an area of recent interstate conflict with the consent of the states involved, carrying out relatively limited tasks aimed at discouraging any resumption of fighting. These tasks might include observing activities in the conflict zone; patrolling borders or cease-fire lines; deterring infiltration; serving as a buffer between opposing forces; monitoring and helping to implement agreements on force withdrawal, demobilization, disarmament, and prisoner exchange; clearing mines; providing humanitarian relief; and maintaining order in limited areas under their temporary control. Typical of such operations were UNEF in the Sinai, UNDOF in the Golan, UNIFIL in Lebanon, UNMOGIP in Kashmir, and UNFICYP in Cyprus.[29]

Some peacekeeping operations in the post–Cold War period have also had "first-generation" mandates: for example, ONUCA in Central America, UNOMIG in Georgia, UNGOMAP in Afghanistan, and UNIKOM in Iraq.[30] UNPREDEP in Macedonia, a "preventive deployment force" designed to anticipate and prevent any outbreak of conflict, also operated essentially as a traditional peacekeeping force.[31] Most other forces with more expanded mandates also performed such "traditional" functions.

Second-generation peacekeeping

As the United Nations became involved in internal conflicts that presented more complicated problems and more "complex emergencies," its peacekeeping missions had to take on a "second generation" of political, economic, and humanitarian functions that went well beyond the relatively straightforward tasks of first-generation peacekeeping. One conspicuous example of this circumstance was the ONUC operation in the Congo. ONUC was originally established in 1960 after Belgium granted independence to the Congo, which was followed by mutinies among Congolese soldiers, internal disorder, intervention by Belgian troops and foreign mercenaries, and the secession of the mineral-rich Katanga province. At the request of the Congolese government, the Security Council created ONUC and gave it a mandate of assisting Congolese forces in maintaining law and order and of bringing about the withdrawal of Belgian forces. As disorder, constitutional crisis, and civil war spread, ONUC acted to protect political leaders, expel mercenaries, and retake areas held by secessionist forces. ONUC also had to carry out a variety of civilian functions that Congolese authorities were unable to handle, including restoring public services, managing the economy and monetary system, providing relief, and recruiting and training Congolese nationals for civil administration and police functions. It was not until 1963 that the secession of Katanga was brought to an end and civil administration began to be returned to Congolese authorities.[32]

At the time, the experience of ONUC was widely regarded as an unpleasant aberration for UN peacekeeping. It produced a severe political crisis in the United Nations, including extreme tension between the Soviet Union and the secretary-general, and a serious financial crisis caused by the withholding of contributions. But in fact, the Congo experience illustrated many of the problems to be faced by the UN forces that were introduced into internal conflicts in the post–Cold War period and the functions that these "second-generation" peacekeeping forces would have to perform.

Second-generation UN peacekeeping resumed in 1989, after the conclusion of an agreement for the independence of Namibia, when the Security Council authorized the deployment of a UN force (UNTAG) to supervise the transition to independence. UNTAG had many of the traditional first-generation peacekeeping functions— including the monitoring of a cease-fire and the withdrawal of South African forces—but it was also charged with ensuring free and fair elections for a new independent government, which involved the revision of electoral laws, the supervision of registration and voting, the maintenance of law and order during the election period, the creation of public information systems, and the return of refugees.[33]

Similar functions relating to political transitions were later given to a number of other peacekeeping operations, including UNAVEM in Angola, ONUMOZ in Mozambique, UNOMIL in Liberia, ONUSAL in El Salvador, UNTAC in Cambodia, UNMIBH in Bosnia, UNTAES in Croatia, and UNMIH in Haiti.[34] These operations required not only the deployment of military personnel to ensure security and prevent armed interference with the election process, but also the use of election specialists, administrators, and large numbers of police and police monitors.

International involvement in civil conflicts also led to the inclusion in the mandates of UN forces of extensive responsibilities for dealing with humanitarian emergencies. The most prominent early example was the case of Somalia,[35] where a traditional UN peacekeeping force (UNOSOM I) was unable to cope with the severe humanitarian crisis caused by drought, famine, civil chaos, and obstruction by local warlords. As will be discussed in the next chapter, UNOSOM I had to be superseded by a multinational force (the Unified Task Force, or UNITAF), which had much greater armed power and was able to provide temporary security for humanitarian efforts.[36]

Four months later, the Security Council created a new UN peacekeeping force (UNOSOM II) to replace UNITAF, with a broad mandate to create the conditions necessary to address the humanitarian catastrophe. UNOSOM II was given general responsibility "for the consolidation, expansion and maintenance of a secure environment throughout Somalia," including the enforcement of the arms embargo, the provision of security for the resettlement of refugees, and the protection of UN and other international personnel; at the same time, the secretary-general was charged with providing humanitarian relief, rebuilding essential Somali institutions, and resurrecting the Somali economy.[37] The mandate of UNOSOM II specifically included protecting ports, airports, lines of communication, and other infrastructure essential to providing humanitarian relief and assistance in reconstruction.[38] The effort to restore order and bring about national economic and political reconstruction was abandoned after the force began to take casualties in fighting with Somali warlords, but hundreds of thousands of lives were nonetheless apparently saved through humanitarian relief efforts protected by these operations.[39]

Providing and protecting humanitarian relief and refugee efforts became a frequent part of UN peacekeeping. Examples included UNAVEM III in Angola, ONUMOZ in Mozambique, UNAMIR in Rwanda, UNOMIL and UNMIL in Liberia, UNTAC in Cambodia, UNCRO in Croatia, UNAMSIL in Sierra Leone, UNMIK in Kosovo, UNTAET in East Timor, and MONUC in the Congo.[40] In the case of Bosnia, the Council authorized the deployment of UNPROFOR troops to ensure the security and functioning of the Sarajevo airport to facilitate the delivery of humanitarian relief and to protect relief convoys.[41]

Protecting the civilian population from attack has also emerged as an important function of UN peacekeeping. It was not unusual for UN forces engaged in traditional peacekeeping to intervene on an ad hoc basis on behalf of civilians if their areas of deployment happened to come under attack.[42] However, the conditions of civil conflict into which UN peacekeeping forces were deployed during the post–Cold War period soon led to mandates from the Security Council that made the protection of civilian populations and civilian areas a primary part of their responsibilities.

This responsibility was direct and specific in the cases of Rwanda and the former Yugoslavia, where the civilian populations were seriously threatened by campaigns of ethnic cleansing and genocide. In the case of Rwanda, the belated response of the Security Council to the 1994 genocide included a direction to UNAMIR to "contribute to the security and protection of displaced persons, refugees, and civilians at risk, including through the establishment and maintenance, where feasible, of secure humanitarian areas."[43] (The Council also authorized France to establish a temporary zone in southwestern Rwanda where French forces would protect the civilian population, as will be discussed in the next chapter.[44])

In the case of the former Yugoslavia,[45] the Council created an elaborate system of "safe areas" in which UN peacekeeping forces were to protect threatened civilians from attack. In 1992, the Council authorized UNPROFOR to deploy into a series of United Nations Protected Areas in Croatia populated by Serb civilians, and to ensure their demilitarization and protection. It also authorized UNPRO-FOR to monitor the actions of Croatian authorities in a series of "pink zones" where significant numbers of Serbs lived.[46] In 1993, the Council designated the Srebrenica area in Bosnia as a "safe area" from which Bosnian Serb forces were to be withdrawn and UNPROFOR troops to be strengthened to prevent hostile actions and ethnic cleansing.[47] The "safe area" concept was then expanded to include Sarajevo and a series of other towns in Bosnia.[48] The Council also authorized UNPROFOR to protect convoys of released civilian detainees.[49]

Protecting civilians from attack was also an important function of a number of later peacekeeping forces, such as KFOR/UNMIK in Kosovo, UNTAET in East Timor, UNAMSIL in Sierra Leone, MONUC in the Congo, and UNMIL in Liberia.[50] On the whole, UN peacekeeping forces have had mixed success in carrying out this responsibility, saving many civilian lives but also experiencing tragic failures where military strength, robust rules of engagement, or the political will to take the risk of serious fighting and casualties were lacking.

Finally, UN peacekeeping forces were given a variety of other functions in the post–Cold War period as part of their mandate to restore and keep the peace in various internal conflicts. A number of these forces were given the task of training and assisting the police and security personnel of host governments. For example, the functions of UNAMIR included the establishment and training of a new, integrated Rwandan national police force; UNMIBH's responsibilities under the framework of the Dayton Peace Agreement included training, advising, and accompanying Bosnian law enforcement personnel; and UNMIH was charged with assisting in the creation and training of a separate Haitian police force.[51] Several UN peacekeeping forces assisted in monitoring human rights compliance and investigating and apprehending war criminals (a matter which will be discussed in detail in chapter 7).

Third-generation peacekeeping

The phrase "third-generation peacekeeping" has been used to describe the mandates given to UN operations in Kosovo and East Timor. Unlike first- and second-generation peacekeeping, these missions involved the assumption by the United Nations of all the functions of governing the territories in question, pending the creation of local institutions capable of such governance.[52]

Before the United Nations was established, there were various cases of temporary international administration of small enclaves, such as Danzig and the Saar.[53] During the Cold War period, the United Nations had frequently been involved in the conduct or monitoring of elections, but had relatively little experience in the actual governance of territories. Chapter XII of the Charter created an international trusteeship system that applied to territories previously placed under League of Nations mandate, detached from "enemy states" as a result of World War II, or voluntarily committed to the system by "states responsible for their administration." They included island groups in the South Pacific that had been heavily affected by combat operations in World War II.[54] However, the UN role with respect to such territories was prescribed by agreement with the states involved, and typically amounted only to very general supervision, as actual governance was carried out by the state granted the trusteeship.[55]

The United Nations did administer Irian Jaya (western New Guinea) for a brief period (1962–1963) during the transition from Dutch colonial rule to Indonesian control, under agreement between Indonesia and the Netherlands.[56] The United Nations also asserted the right to govern the territory of Namibia after the General Assembly terminated the trusteeship that South Africa had first acquired under the League of Nations, but it never exercised governance functions because of South Africa's refusal to yield the territory to UN administration. When South Africa finally agreed to withdraw, the United Nations Transition Assistance Group (UNTAG) was created to monitor the agreed cease-fire and withdrawal of forces, as well as the election process, but the United Nations did not engage in actual governance of the territory.[57]

The first major UN exercise in governance came in 1991, when the contending factions in Cambodia agreed to delegate various governmental functions to a UN Transitional Authority in Cambodia (UNTAC) that was to be created by the Security Council. UNTAC was given direct control over Cambodian agencies in the areas of foreign affairs, national defense, finance, public security, and information. UNTAC was also charged with supervising other agencies that could influence the outcome of elections and was given the right to investigate various other government organs to determine whether they were undermining the accords, and, if so, to take corrective measures.[58]

The United Nations was also involved in some international governance functions in connection with the resolution of the conflicts in Bosnia and Croatia in the mid-1990s. In accordance with a November 1995 agreement providing for the reintegration of Eastern Slavonia (which had been occupied by Serb forces) into Croatia, the Council created a United Nations Transitional Administration (UNTAES) with military and civilian components charged with implementing the agreement.[59] The "transitional administration" provided by the United Nations essentially involved supervising the return of local governing institutions to Croatian authority and providing security for the process. UNTAES retained "authority and the ability to intervene and overrule decisions should the situation deteriorate."[60] After two years, the secretary-general reported that "UNTAES has successfully achieved the basic objectives for which it was established" and the transitional administration was terminated.[61]

The 1995 Dayton Peace Agreement likewise relied on local institutions to govern Bosnia but also provided for the designation of a "High Representative" to monitor and coordinate the implementation of the civilian aspects of the agreement.[62] The High Representative was to "respect the autonomy" of local organizations but was also given "final authority" regarding the interpretation of the agreement.[63] This authority has been interpreted as including the power to make binding decisions to resolve any difficulties in implementation, including the removal from office of officials who were found by the High Representative to have violated the peace agreement and the imposition of measures having the force of law if Bosnian legislative authorities failed to carry out their obligations under the agreement.[64] The High Representative also received certain temporary governance functions for the disputed Brcko enclave from the arbitral tribunal created by the peace agreement to determine its status.[65] The High Representative is neither a UN official nor selected by the organization, but these representatives' designation and powers are, respectively, approved and confirmed by the UN Security Council.

Successive High Representatives have made frequent use of these authorities to enforce compliance with the peace agreement and to suppress opposition to its provisions. Many public officials have been suspended or removed for obstruction of the agreement or incitement of ethnic tensions, from mayors and municipal administrators to the president of the Republika Srpska himself.[66] On numerous occasions, existing laws have been amended or repealed and new laws imposed on subjects ranging from property disposition, citizenship, and the judicial structure, to the national anthem and design of the national coat of arms.[67] In short, the High Representative does not directly govern Bosnia but has had very significant influence on the governing process.

The 1999 Kosovo conflict presented a radically different situation in which there were no local authorities to rely on, and it became necessary for the United Nations to assume all governance functions directly. By the conclusion of the NATO air campaign, most of the Kosovar population had been driven from their homes by Serb repression. Economic activity had come to a halt, Serb officials and technical personnel had departed, social services were essentially shut down, and there was no functioning law enforcement system.[68]

In response, the Security Council created an international security presence in the form of a multilateral Kosovo Force (KFOR) consisting primarily of NATO forces and an international civil presence known as the United Nations Interim Administration Mission in Kosovo (UNMIK). UNMIK, directed by a Special Representative of the Secretary-General (SRSG), was empowered to provide "transitional administration while establishing and overseeing the development of provisional democratic self-governing institutions."[69] The special representative promptly assumed "all . . . executive authority with respect to Kosovo," including the appointment and removal of all civil servants and judges and the administration of all public funds and property.[70] He created a four-part structure for the governance of Kosovo that relied heavily on the leadership and resources of various states and international organizations: (1) a civil administration component, led by the United Nations itself, to revive health, education, police, the courts, and other public services; (2) an institution-building component, led by the Organization for Security and Cooperation in Europe, to promote democratization, the training of local administrators, and the creation of independent media and professional organizations; (3) a humanitarian component, led by the UN High Commissioner for Refugees, to provide humanitarian relief and clear mines; and (4) a reconstruction component, led by the European Union, to rebuild key infrastructure and a market-based economic system.[71]

The performance of these functions required that UNMIK identify the laws that would govern in Kosovo and make new law as needed, which was done through the promulgation of a series of regulations. At first, the SRSG applied the laws imposed by the Federal Republic of Yugoslavia prior to its withdrawal from Kosovo, but later, in response to strong complaints from Albanian Kosovars, resurrected the laws that had been in force before the FRY revoked the autonomy of Kosovo in 1989.[72] Further, the SRSG immediately set about to make new law by regulation where existing law appeared inadequate, in such areas as customs, currency regulation, import and sale of petroleum and other products, telecommunications, and bank operations.[73] There has also been a substantial revision of the criminal laws and court structures of Kosovo to assist in the vital task of controlling interethnic crime, restoring general law and order, and prosecuting atrocities committed during the conflict.[74]

In addition, UNMIK's mandate from the Security Council included "the establishment, pending a final settlement, of substantial autonomy and self-government."[75] For this purpose, a constitutional framework and "Provisional Institutions of Self-Government" have been created and have tentatively begun to function, elections have been conducted, the "Kosovarization" of municipal governments has begun, and efforts have been made to create a multi-ethnic civil service and judicial structure.[76] Efforts at reconstruction suffered a serious setback as a result of widespread violence by Albanian Kosovars against Serb Kosovars in March 2004.[77] The difficult task of deciding Kosovo's political status is just now getting started.

Within months of assuming the task of governing Kosovo, the United Nations faced a task of comparable scope and complexity in East Timor. That territory had been under Portuguese control until 1975, when Indonesian forces occupied it over the protest of the Security Council.[78] In 1999, after many years of negotiation, Portugal and Indonesia agreed to ask the UN secretary-general to conduct a "popular consultation" of the East Timorese population on the question of independence or autonomy within Indonesia, and the East Timorese rejected autonomy.[79] This rejection was followed by an intense campaign of violence and intimidation by anti-independence militias that resulted in heavy destruction of buildings and infrastructure and the displacement of hundreds of thousands of civilians.[80]

In response, the Security Council established a United Nations Transitional Administration in East Timor (UNTAET), which was given "overall responsibility for the administration of East Timor" and empowered "to exercise all legislative and executive authority, including the administration of justice." UNTAET was to be headed by an SRSG with the power "to enact new laws and regulations and to amend, suspend, or repeal existing ones."[81] An extensive set of regulations modeled on and similar to those adopted for Kosovo were promptly issued, covering such matters as the repeal of Indonesian security laws, the regulation of fiscal and budgetary matters, and the appointment of judges and prosecutors.[82]

In contrast to Kosovo, however, this administration was designed from the start to be of short duration, leading as quickly as possible to full independence for East Timor. This goal was accomplished in relatively rapid order. In August 2001, elections took place for a Constituent Assembly, which adopted a constitution in March 2002 that provided for an elected president, an elected national parliament, and an independent judiciary. In April 2002, presidential elections were held; and in May 2002, the new government was sworn in and the United Nations formally transferred power to an independent East Timor.[83] To sustain the still-fragile new state (now officially known as Timor-Leste), the Council created a United Nations Mission of Support in East Timor (UNMISET) to replace UNTAET and to carry out more traditional peacekeeping tasks.[84]

The experience of UN governance in Kosovo and East Timor, while certainly not without significant problems, suggests that third-generation peacekeeping can be a viable option for "failed states" or societies devastated by conflict. Nonetheless, it is apparent that the Security Council will not automatically resort to third-generation mandates in every such case. The clearest proof is in the recent conflicts in Afghanistan and Iraq, where little of the body of post–Cold War precedent for ambitious UN peacekeeping efforts has been applied.

The prolonged conflict in Afghanistan had, by the time of the defeat of the Taliban regime at the end of 2001, left Afghan institutions in a state of serious collapse. But rather than imposing a UN governance regime along the lines of the Kosovo–East Timor model, or even a second-generation peacekeeping force with a mandate to restore order and begin the reconstruction of local institutions, the Council opted for a relatively modest UN mission (UNAMA), with a mandate only to provide various forms of secondary support for the Afghan Interim Authority created by the 2001 Bonn Agreement.[85] Instead of authorizing a second- or third-generation UN peacekeeping operation, the Council (as will be described in the next chapter) authorized the establishment of a multinational security force under Western command (the International Security Assistance Force, or ISAF) to assist in providing security, and welcomed the presence of separate coalition forces led by the United States that were fighting the remnants of Taliban and al Qaeda forces.[86]

To date, the UN secretary-general has reported significant accomplishments by the Interim Authority in advancing the political process (which produced the presidential elections of October 2004), returning refugees to their homes, and re-establishing financial institutions and reforming the judicial system. But at the same time, the secretary-general has reported that the difficult security situation and the slow pace of extending national authority to areas outside Kabul remain serious problems that must be resolved if the transition process is to succeed.[87]

Not even this degree of UN involvement has to date occurred in Iraq. Rather, the United States and United Kingdom assumed all the functions and burdens of governing Iraq as occupying powers after removing the existing government. In May 2003, the Security Council essentially acquiesced in this situation, recognizing the authority of the two governments as occupying powers and calling on them to govern the country during the transition to a permanent Iraqi government. The Council turned over to the occupation authority funds collected by the United Nations under previous Council resolutions, and limited the UN role to the completion of the Oil-for-Food Program and the appointment of a Special Representative with a mandate to coordinate international support and assistance for the occupation authority.[88]

In October 2003, the Council resolved to strengthen its role in Iraq by providing humanitarian relief, promoting economic reconstruction, and assisting in the restoration of government institutions. To date, this role remains essentially unfulfilled, in part because of the serious security situation in the country and in part because of disagreement over the proper extent of the UN role.[89] At the same time, the Council recognized the new Iraqi Governing Council created by the coalition as the interim administration that would embody the sovereignty of Iraq until an internationally recognized government could be established, and authorized the creation of a non-UN multinational force to take all necessary measures to provide security for the process.[90] In 2004, the Council endorsed the formation of the "sovereign Interim Government of Iraq" and the timetable for elections and the drafting of a permanent constitution in 2005.[91]

These actions by the Council gave some measure of international recognition and legitimacy to the new Iraqi government created by the coalition. They were also useful to the coalition from a legal standpoint in that they effectively approved political and institutional changes that might well have been beyond the normal authority of an occupying power. Specifically, an occupying power has traditionally been regarded as only a "de facto administrator" that may not change the basic form of government or legal structure of the occupied territory.[92]

However, the Council has not assumed any of the responsibilities and burdens of governing Iraq during the transition process. It remains to be seen whether that transition can be effectively completed without a stronger UN role.

In short, while the Kosovo and East Timor experiences have provided the Council with a full box of legal tools to deal with societies affected by conflict, they have not established any uniform solution. The third-generation peacekeeping model will not necessarily be appropriate for all situations—even for all cases of failed states or devastated societies. But UN involvement in governance has many advantages in mobilizing international resources and in creating legal and political legitimacy, and the precedents and possibilities of the Kosovo and East Timor experiences should not be forgotten. The Iraqi experience in particular demonstrates that much can be lost when the Council is unable or unwilling to exercise the authority and techniques that it has developed during the past decade.

Finally, proposals have been made to create new structures and capabilities to facilitate peacekeeping and peacebuilding. In particular, the World Summit resolution adopted by the General Assembly in September 2005 included the following:

* Support for efforts by the European Union, the African Union, and other regional entities to develop capabilities for rapid deployment and reinforcement of peacekeeping forces in crisis situations.[93]
* Support for the creation of an initial operating capability for a "standing police capacity" to strengthen police components of UN peacekeeping forces.[94]

❖ A decision to establish a "Peacebuilding Commission" to "bring together all relevant actors to marshal resources and to advise on and propose integrated strategies for postconflict peacebuilding and recovery."[95]

Constraints on Peacekeeping

There has been considerable debate over the years regarding the inherent constraints on the role and actions of UN peacekeepers in carrying out their mandates. During peacekeeping operations in the Cold War era, the UN Secretariat articulated certain "essential characteristics" of peacekeeping: (1) that peacekeeping operations would be initiated only "with the consent of the parties to the conflict in question," (2) that peacekeeping missions must be "impartial" and "must not in any way favour one party against another," (3) that peacekeeping operations "must not interfere in the internal affairs of the host countries," and (4) that the use of force by peacekeepers must be "limited to self-defence, as a last resort."[96] To some extent, these "essential characteristics" reflected the fact that peacekeeping missions during the Cold War were typically Chapter VI operations, which did not benefit from the Council's authority under Chapter VII to impose mandatory obligations, authorize the use of force, and intervene in matters within the domestic jurisdiction of states.

But in fact, even for Chapter VI peacekeeping operations during the Cold War, these "essential characteristics" were never as clear and immutable as they may have seemed, and were stretched or ignored in various cases. During the post–Cold War period, the involvement of the United Nations in internal conflicts made strict adherence to these characteristics less feasible and less compatible with the Council's objectives in a number of situations. In any event, the new willingness of the Council to use its considerable Chapter VII authority has, as a legal matter, given the Council a full measure of discretion to decide, on policy grounds, whether or not to take the risks of more aggressive peacekeeping. The first three of these "essential characteristics"—consent, impartiality, and noninterference in internal affairs are considered here. The fourth—use of force—will be examined in the next chapter.

Consent

UN officials have consistently stressed over the years that "peace-keeping operations are set up only with the consent of the parties to the conflict in question" and that "the consent and cooperation of all the parties concerned is a *sine qua non* of peacekeeping."[97] There are indeed good reasons to secure such consent and cooperation from all elements that may pose a threat to peacekeepers and their mission, whenever that is possible. However, as a legal matter, the requirement is not absolute, and, as a practical matter, it may not always be achievable or consistent with the objectives of the mission.

It is correct that a peacekeeping mission created by the Security Council solely under Chapter VI (or, hypothetically, created by the General Assembly under the Uniting for Peace precedent) may deploy into the territory of a state only with that state's consent. Even in the context of a non–Chapter VII operation, however, this leaves open a number of questions.

First, if a state gives its consent to the entry of a non–Chapter VII UN peacekeeping operation, can it later withdraw that consent and insist on the departure of the UN force, or insist on changes in the force's mandate or restrictions on its activities as a condition for allowing it to stay? In the case of UNEF I, which was deployed into Egyptian territory in the Sinai at the end of the 1956 Arab-Israeli War with the authorization of the General Assembly (under Uniting for Peace), Egypt gave its consent. But while the Egyptian government took the position that the UN force must withdraw if Egypt should later withdraw its consent, Secretary-General Hammarskjöld argued that Egypt had consented to the presence of the force for certain tasks set out by the General Assembly and could not withdraw its consent before the completion of those tasks. In fact, Egypt did withdraw its consent nine years later and insisted on the departure of UNEF I, at which point the secretary-general (then U Thant) acquiesced, and war immediately broke out with Israel.[98]

In the case of ONUC, which was deployed into Congolese territory in 1960, differences soon arose between the United Nations and the Congolese government as to the proper scope of the UN mandate. The Congo attempted to compel the United Nations to accept its view of the matter by restricting the movement of UN forces. Secretary-General Hammarskjöld insisted that the Congolese government had no right to do so, on the grounds that a host country could not unilaterally discontinue a force authorized by the Council or dictate the terms of its mandate.[99]

The Council was well aware of these problems in the post–Cold War period and responded to them with the use of its Chapter VII authority. In the case of UNIKOM in 1991, the Council invoked Chapter VII to give mandatory force to its decision to deploy peace-keepers into the area along the Iraq-Kuwait border and specifically noted that the mission "can be terminated only by a further decision of the Council."[100]

In 1992, when the Council decided to establish UNPROFOR to protect Serb civilians in Croatia, Secretary-General Boutros-Ghali recommended that the Council's resolution make clear that the force could be withdrawn before the expiration of its specified term only if the Council made a decision to that effect.[101] In fact, the Council's resolution did state that the force was to be deployed "for an initial period of twelve months unless the Council subsequently decides otherwise," but the resolution did not invoke Chapter VII to give its provisions express mandatory force.[102] However, a year later, after UNPROFOR had experienced considerable difficulty in obtaining compliance from Croatian forces, the Council did invoke Chapter VII and demand that UNPROFOR's mandate and freedom of movement be respected.[103]

Thereafter the Council frequently invoked Chapter VII for peacekeeping forces, which insulated those operations—as a legal matter—from any withdrawal of consent or restrictions on the forces' activities. For example, Chapter VII was invoked with respect to UNPROFOR in Bosnia, UNOSOM II in Somalia, UNCRO and UNTAES in Croatia, MONUA in Angola, UNMIK in Kosovo, UNAMSIL in Sierra Leone, UNTAET in East Timor, MONUC in the Congo, MINUSTAH in Haiti, and ONUB in Burundi.[104] Of course, the withdrawal of consent or the imposition of restrictions by these governments might have made the continued presence of the UN force impractical; yet even so, it would have been very damaging for the United Nations to have accepted the proposition that host governments were entitled to take such action—for example, that

Iraq had a right to expel or restrict UNIKOM, or Croatia to expel or restrict UNTAES.

Second, if the state into whose territory a Chapter VI force is being deployed gives consent, is it necessary to obtain the consent of other parties to the conflict—whether states or nonstate entities? The legal answer is that such consent is not necessary, since only the government of the state in question has a sovereign right to object to the entry of UN forces.

Once again, the ONUC operation in the Congo is instructive. Three important elements of the ONUC mandate were the withdrawal of Belgian troops, the removal of foreign mercenaries, and the restoration of the authority of the Congolese government in areas controlled by secessionist forces. Yet the Council acted to deploy ONUC to the Congo without waiting for the consent of the Belgian government, the foreign mercenaries, or the secessionist elements in Katanga; nor would the operation have been feasible if the prior consent of these parties had been necessary.[105]

By the early 1990s (as noted above), the Council was regularly invoking Chapter VII with respect to peacekeeping forces deployed into situations of active internal conflict. In such cases, the secretary-general would usually, for obvious practical reasons, seek the consent of any forces that might obstruct the operations of UN forces or cause casualties among UN peacekeepers. Nonetheless, the secretary-general was now confident in denying that such consent was required; this was, for example, his position with respect to Serb consent for UNPROFOR protection of the Tuzla airport in Bosnia.[106] Once again, it would have been very damaging for the United Nations, for example, to have accepted that its peacekeeping forces were legally unable to continue their operations in the face of opposition by the *genocidaires* in Rwanda, or the various warlords in Somalia, or the rebels in Sierra Leone.

Third, if there is no functioning legitimate government in the territory in question, or if there are a number of contenders for that status, what consent is required for a Chapter VI operation? Consistent with the preceding analysis, one might argue that the requirement of consent can simply be dispensed with for such a "failed state" on the theory that there can be no intrusion into the sovereignty of a state that has no functioning government. However, for practical as well as theoretical reasons, the United Nations has chosen to handle the matter differently.

In the case of Cambodia, where there were several contenders for power and United Nations did not recognize the de facto regime in control in Phnom Penh, a Supreme National Council was created by agreement among the factions, and the UN treated that council as the embodiment of Cambodian sovereignty from which consent to the Chapter VI UN operation could flow.[107] In the case of Somalia, the Council noted the "absence of a government in Somalia," but acted under Chapter VII and also sought ad hoc arrangements with factional leaders in areas in which international forces deployed from time to time.[108]

Impartiality

The criterion of "impartiality" is frequently cited as essential for peacekeeping, but its meaning and application are not clear. In 1990, the UN review of peacekeeping operations stated that, "It is a key principle that the [peacekeeping] operation must not . . . in any way favor one party against another. This requirement of impartiality is fundamental, not only on grounds of principle but also to ensure that the operation is effective. A United Nations operation cannot take sides without becoming a part of the conflict which it has been set up to control or resolve."[109] This concept may have been feasible for first-generation peacekeeping efforts in interstate conflicts where the United Nations was in fact neutral and essentially wanted only to end the conflict. Whenever the United Nations can accomplish its objectives without "taking sides," it is clearly preferable to do so.

However, there have been a number of conflicts in the post–Cold War period in which the United Nations did favor one party over another, or at least strenuously opposed some fundamental aspect of the policies and actions of one of the parties. For example, in the cases of Haiti and Sierra Leone, it was the avowed objective of the Security Council to remove a military junta from power and to restore a democratically elected government. In the cases of Angola, Bosnia, and Sierra Leone, the Council imposed sanctions on one of the sides. In the cases of Rwanda, Somalia, and the Federal Republic of Yugoslavia, the Council (or its subordinate bodies) openly sought the arrest and prosecution of the leaders of one party to the conflict. In the cases of Bosnia and Croatia, the Council sought to prevent one side from conducting military operations in key areas. In the cases of Iraq and Bosnia, the Council authorized the use of substantial military force to compel one side of the conflict to conform to its demands.

It is true that in most of these cases, the UN peacekeeping missions were not themselves expected to accomplish these objectives of the Council; typically the Council turned to economic sanctions and to non-UN forces to compel the recalcitrant governments or factions to relent or depart. But in some cases, such as Bosnia and Somalia, UN peacekeepers were directly involved in implementing these objectives, and it would not be realistic to expect that the government or faction against which the Council was acting to regard the United Nations and its peacekeeping missions as "impartial." In such situations, UN peacekeeping missions must be provided with the resources—human and physical—as well as the support and freedom of action necessary to carry out their mandates, even if they are not "impartial" in the traditional sense or are not accepted by all sides as being impartial.

The 2000 Report of the Panel on United Nations Peace Operations (the "Brahimi Report") articulated a different concept of "impartiality," recognizing that it could not, for these purposes, mean "neutrality or equal treatment of all parties in all cases for all time, which can amount to a policy of appeasement." Rather, impartiality must "mean adherence to the principles of the Charter and to the objectives of the mandate that is rooted in these Charter principles. . . . In some cases, local parties consist not of moral equals but of obvious aggressors and victims," and peacekeepers must be prepared to act accordingly.[110] This is not the traditional concept of impartiality, but a more realistic notion that UN missions must carry out principled mandates, even if doing so means opposing one or more of the parties to a conflict.[111]

If the Council acts under Chapter VII, there is no legal requirement to avoid "taking sides." There may, of course, be compelling policy reasons to avoid doing so, but the events of the past fifteen years suggest that it is not always possible to do so.

Another aspect of the UN's original concept of impartiality relates to the composition of its peacekeeping forces. In the case of the "traditional" peacekeeping forces of the Cold War era, the secretary-general deliberately excluded military units from the permanent members of the Council or other states seen as having a direct interest in the situation in question.[112] With the end of the Cold War, this policy was soon abandoned for a number of reasons, including the lessening of political competition among the permanent members, the urgent need for larger numbers of capable personnel to meet the much greater peacekeeping demands of the period, and the desirability of great-power involvement to demonstrate the serious intent of the United Nations and the consequences of opposing its peacekeeping operations.

In particular, military personnel from the permanent members became a frequent part of UN peacekeeping operations: for example, French and Russian military observers and British troops in UNAVEM III in Angola; French and U.S. troops in UNOSOM II in Somalia; Russian military observers and British troops in UNAMIR in Rwanda; French, Chinese, U.S., British, and Russian troops in UNTAC in Cambodia; French, British, Russian, and U.S. troops in UNPROFOR in the former Yugoslavia; and French and U.S. troops in UNMIH in Haiti.[113] It was even considered acceptable to deploy military units of a permanent member into an area it had occupied in the past, such as U.S. troops in Haiti and Russian troops in Georgia.[114]

Internal affairs

The assertion that peacekeeping missions may not intervene in the internal affairs of the host country is belied by the activities of those missions over the years. To be sure, the concept of a state's internal affairs has been rapidly changing in recent decades, and some matters—such as the commission of gross violations of human rights—are increasingly seen as issues of international concern that are not shielded by state sovereignty. But as shown by the previous discussion of the expanding mandates of UN missions, it is very common for UN peacekeeping operations to become heavily involved in matters that are commonly accepted as being within the domestic jurisdiction of states—the conduct of elections, the restructuring of judicial institutions and police forces, the amendment or repeal of domestic laws, even the question of what authorities should govern.

A state may, of course, consent to such international involvement. But the Council's Chapter VII authority obviates the objection of interference in internal affairs—at least as a legal matter. The prohibition in Article 2(7) of the Charter on UN intervention "in matters which are essentially within the domestic jurisdiction of any state" expressly excludes enforcement measures under Chapter VII. In adhering to the UN Charter, member states accept the authority of the Council under Chapter VII, and this is not a derogation from their sovereignty but an exercise of it.

A more difficult question is whether there are limits to the Council's authority with respect to the most central aspects of state sovereignty—issues that especially may arise with respect to third-generation missions. In particular, may the Council change the political status of a territory—for example, by recognizing its independence, transferring it from one state to another, or giving it autonomy? May the Council make basic changes in the legal system of a territory—for example, by promulgating a new constitution? May the Council decline to give autonomy or independence to a territory that claims it is entitled to such status as a matter of "self-determination"? Such issues would have been directly posed by the situation in East Timor if Indonesia had not relinquished its claim of sovereignty, and they will be directly posed by the situation in Kosovo if it proves impossible to reach agreement with Serbia and with Kosovar representatives on the territory's final status.[115] Such changes go well beyond the traditional authority of occupying powers.

Yet there may in fact be situations in which the Council would be justified in directing under Chapter VII a change in some aspect of the status, boundaries, political structure, or legal system of territory within a state, if the Council determines that doing so is necessary to restore and maintain international peace and security. To suggest some hypothetical examples: the Council may find that a change in the boundaries of a state is necessary to give its neighbors better security against a repetition of armed attack, or that a guarantee of autonomy to a particular part of a state's territory or population is necessary to avoid a repetition of civil conflict that would threaten the peace of the region, or that the nullification of discriminatory restrictions on one population group is necessary to bring a conflict to an end. Further, the Council would have authority to deny autonomy or independence to a territory if it believed that granting such status would reignite or exacerbate a conflict.

Even to the extent that such measures intrude into state sovereignty or assertions of self-determination, the Council would have legal authority under Chapter VII to take such action. As noted earlier, Article 24 of the Charter does require that the Council act in accordance with the "Purposes and Principles of the United Nations" in Articles 1–2, which include the principles of "self-determination of peoples" and the "sovereign equality" of UN members, as well as conformity with the principles of international law in the settlement of international disputes. But the content and interpretation of these principles—particularly that of self-determination—is far from self-evident, which gives the Council much practical latitude in their application. Further, in a situation in which any of these purposes and principles conflicts with the maintenance of peace and security, Article 24 does not say how this conflict is to be resolved. Logically, weighing conflicting purposes remains a matter for judgment and decision by the Council.

In contrast to this ambiguity, Articles 39–42 give the Council broad authority to decide what measures are to be taken to maintain or restore the peace, and Article 2(7) expressly permits the Council to intervene under Chapter VII in matters within the domestic jurisdiction of states. There must be room in the Council's broad Chapter VII authority for limited and reasonable intrusions on the territory or sovereign authority of states when the Council finds these intrusions necessary to maintain the peace. Of course, such a decision should never be lightly taken, and the Council would have to exercise good judgment, historical perspective, and common sense in deciding whether to take such a step.

ASSESSMENT

Peacekeeping has often been described as a process in which an impartial UN mission is sent into a situation in which all the contending parties have agreed to cease violent conflict and resolve their differences peacefully with the help and good offices of the United Nations. For example, the Argentine delegate in the Security Council stated in a 1995 debate on Bosnia:

> When the international community decides to establish a peacekeeping force, it does so on the understanding that the forces deployed are not there to fight, nor to take sides in a conflict, but, rather—with an entirely different logic—that of peace—to assist in creating conditions for the parties themselves to make progress in the search for a negotiated solution. This assumes, first, that the parties have decided that armed confrontation is no longer a valid option and, secondly, that they sincerely wish to engage in peaceful dialogue and to show mutual respect and tolerance.[116]

Unfortunately, this idyllic description bears little resemblance to the kind of situation that so many UN peacekeeping forces have had to face in the conflicts of the post–Cold War period. More often, they have found themselves in situations where one or more of the parties to the conflict have not given up on the use of armed force or the commission of atrocities as a means of accomplishing their objectives; where there is no commitment to peaceful dialogue and mutual tolerance; where they cannot avoid "taking sides" if they are to carry out their mandate, including protecting innocents and preserving the peace; where, indeed, there may not yet be a "peace" to keep.

The UN Security Council has developed a legal framework to enable UN peacekeeping missions to handle such situations, including a considerable expansion of their mandates and much greater use of the authority of Chapter VII. Some will argue that these developments are incompatible with the basic purpose of peacekeeping, in that they tend to transform UN missions from neutral facilitators of peace into parties to the conflict. These concerns are understandable. Unfortunately, conflict situations such as those of the past fifteen years often demand that the international community play both roles at the same time—mediating and implementing consensual solutions whenever possible, but also taking more direct action when necessary. In particular, it is not acceptable for the United Nations to tolerate ethnic cleansing or other atrocities in a conflict in which its peacekeepers are involved, and it would be irresponsible simply to pull out in such circumstances.

A valid legal framework is a necessary but not sufficient condition for ensuring that peacekeeping forces can carry out these added responsibilities safely and effectively. This fact was demonstrated by the repeated violation of the safe areas in Bosnia and Croatia, the taking of UN peacekeepers as hostages in Bosnia and Sierra Leone, and the collapse of UN operations in Somalia. Clearly, UN peacekeepers cannot carry out these expanded mandates in situations of internal conflict without adequate forces, robust rules of engagement, coherent and capable command, and the political will on the part of their governments and the Council to persevere, if necessary, in the face of armed opposition and casualties. Alternatively, UN peacekeepers must be protected and supported by non-UN military forces that are capable and ready to do the job. This is the subject of the next chapter.

In cases of the total collapse of political and legal authority in a state or territory, the Council has now asserted the power to govern that territory, at least for some interim period, and has accumulated practical experience in doing so. The experiences of Kosovo and East Timor show that this is a necessary and appropriate exercise of authority, and the experiences of Afghanistan and Iraq show that action by states on their own authority may not be an adequate substitute. Whether the Council's authority may properly extend to making changes in the status and institutions of such a territory is a question not yet resolved in the Council's practice, but this study has attempted to advance the view that it is legally credible, at least in some circumstances, and should be regarded as part of the Council's expanded range of potential authority.

5

THE USE OF FORCE

ERHAPS THE MOST IMPORTANT development in the practice of the Security Council in the post–Cold War period has been the extensive exercise of its power to authorize the use of force, by both UN peacekeeping missions and non-UN entities. The Council has used this power not only to defeat aggression but also to deal with a wide range of other circumstances considered to be threats to the peace, including the breakdown of internal order, massive human rights violations, severe humanitarian catastrophes, and the overthrow of democratic governments.

This chapter will consider the legal framework for the use of force, the great expansion in the authorization of the use of force by the Council during the post–Cold War period, and various issues presented by the Council's extensive reliance on non-UN forces. The delegation to states and regional organizations of the authority to use force has become an indispensable option for the prevention, control, and suppression of armed conflict, but the Council will also need the option of authorizing units under UN command to use force in appropriate circumstances—assuming they are given the necessary resources, a strong command structure, and a clear mandate.

LEGAL FRAMEWORK

The framers of the UN Charter clearly understood that the use of force would be necessary from time to time to restore and maintain international peace and security. A state may, of course, consent to the conduct of military operations in its territory by foreign forces, whether under UN authority or otherwise.[1] Apart from that, the Charter acknowledges three principal bases for the use of force: (1) individual and collective self-defense pursuant to Article 51, (2) enforcement measures adopted by the Security Council under Chapter VII, and (3) action by regional organizations under Chapter VIII.[2]

Self-defense

Article 51 of the United Nations Charter provides:

> Nothing in the present Charter shall impair the inherent right of individual or collective self-defense if an armed attack occurs against a Member of the United Nations, until the Security Council has taken measures necessary to maintain international peace and security. Measures taken by Members in the exercise of this right of self-defense shall be immediately reported to the Security Council and shall not in any way affect the authority and responsibility of the Security Council under the present Charter to take at any time such action as it deems necessary in order to maintain or restore international peace and security.

The authorization of the Council is not required for the exercise of individual or collective self-defense; indeed, this right serves as an essential safety net for the protection of states in the event that the Council is unable or unwilling to take action on its own to deal with armed attack. On the other hand, the exercise of that right is clearly subject to the authority of the Council under Chapter VII, and the Council may choose to restrict its exercise in a particular case. For example, this can be the effect of the imposition by the Council of a cease-fire or arms embargo on all parties to a conflict, to the extent that such measures prevent the victim of aggression from taking the full range of military actions to which it would otherwise be entitled under the right of self-defense.

Alternatively, the Council may choose to sanction and support the exercise of self-defense by states acting individually, through ad hoc coalitions or regional organizations, or as part of UN forces. It may do so in a number of ways: by affirming that an armed attack has occurred, by reaffirming the right of self-defense in a particular situation, by recommending that other states assist in the exercise of self-defense, or by allowing states to fly the UN flag. None of these steps has any direct legal effect as such, but they give powerful political support and legitimacy to the self-defense effort. The Council may also give support through actions under Chapter VII that have direct legal effect but do not amount to an independent authorization for the use of force, such as imposing sanctions on the aggressor or requiring other states to provide rights of transit, access, or overflight to the state or states exercising self-defense.

According to Article 51, the right of self-defense continues "until the Security Council has taken measures necessary to maintain international peace and security." It is sometimes asserted that the right of self-defense is curtailed as soon as the Council begins to act with respect to a particular situation. But the more reasonable interpretation of Article 51 is that self-defense is suspended only when the Council has taken actions that effectively restore and maintain international peace and security, or that are inconsistent with separate national military action. For example, where the Council authorizes major military operations under unified command, it would be reasonable to conclude that states may not conduct separate military operations that would interfere with or compromise those directed by the Council. On the other hand, the Council may take measures (such as the imposition and enforcement of sanctions) that are not intended to supersede the exercise of self-defense by states and are not inconsistent with it. It would not be sensible in such a case to conclude that the Council's partial measures to constrain or terminate the aggression preclude national military actions in pursuit of the same objective.[3]

As to the scope of the right of self-defense, the current U.S. administration has publicly articulated a doctrine of "pre-emptive" self-defense. In its September 2002 *National Security Strategy of the United States,* the administration announced that the threat of the use of weapons of mass destruction by terrorist groups and "rogue" states required that the United States not limit itself to responses in self-defense after an attack might occur: ". . . The greater the threat, the greater is the risk of inaction—and the more compelling the case for taking anticipatory action to defend ourselves, even if uncertainty remains as to the time and place of the enemy's attack. To forestall or prevent such hostile acts by our adversaries, the United States will, if necessary, act pre-emptively."[4]

This assertion has generated heated debate on the legality and wisdom of pre-emptive self-defense, which this chapter will not attempt to recapitulate.[5] The significance of this assertion will depend in large part on how this doctrine, which as yet has been stated only in general terms, is further articulated and applied. It is important to note that neither the U.S. military actions in Afghanistan after September 11, 2001, nor the invasion of Iraq in 2003 were justified on the basis of pre-emptive self-defense; the former was conventional self-defense in response to actual armed attack, and the latter was justified as authorized by the previous decisions of the Security Council on Iraq.[6] It is also important to note that the legal adviser to the State Department confirmed that the doctrine is limited to cases where "an armed attack . . . is legitimately deemed imminent," while noting that the threat of WMD use may require a concept of imminence that goes beyond "an advancing army or ships on the horizon."[7]

It would be one thing to advocate the use of force to forestall or prevent an attack that has already been initiated or is genuinely imminent (particularly if the consequences of the attack would be very serious), but quite another to advocate the use of force simply on the basis of what a potential adversary might do at some point in the future. The former is easier to square with the language of Article 51 and the practice of states; the latter would be a more radical assertion that could have serious precedent-setting implications (for example, if others used the doctrine to justify major pre-emptive military actions in the Arab-Israeli or India-Pakistan situations).[8] In any event, authorization of the use of force in such circumstances by the Security Council under Chapter VII would provide a much stronger basis, both legally and politically.

Finally, the question arises as to whether the right of self-defense is applicable when a state is attacked by nonstate actors such as international terrorists, or whether it is limited to attacks by other states.

The Security Council seems to have given the former answer in its Resolution 1638, in which it recognized the right of self-defense in connection with the September 11, 2001 attacks. This answer is correct: Article 51 applies by its terms to *any* armed attack against a member state, and it is difficult to imagine that states could accept any other result. There is language in the recent advisory opinion of the International Court of Justice in the case of the Israeli wall in Palestine that may be read to suggest a different answer;[9] but if that is really what the Court intended, it is wrong, and such a conclusion is not likely to be generally followed by states, particularly those that may be attacked by international terrorists.

UN enforcement action

The framers of the UN Charter understood that the right of self-defense would not be a sufficient guarantee of international peace and security, and that the Security Council needed broader authority for the use of force. Article 42 provides, "Should the Security Council consider that measures provided for in Article 41 would be inadequate or have proved to be inadequate, it may take such action by air, sea, or land forces as may be necessary to maintain or restore international peace and security. Such action may include demonstrations, blockade, and other operations by air, sea, or land forces of Members of the United Nations."

The initial plan was that such operations would be conducted under UN direction by national forces provided to the Council by member states.[10] According to Article 43, all UN members undertake to make available to the Council, "on its call and in accordance with a special agreement or agreements," armed forces, assistance, facilities, and rights of passage. The special agreements were to be negotiated "as soon as possible" and were to govern "the numbers and types of forces, their degree of readiness and general location, and the nature of the facilities and assistance to be provided." According to Article 46, "plans for the application of armed force shall be made by the Security Council with the assistance of the Military Staff Committee." That committee consists of the chiefs of staff of the permanent members of the Council (or their representatives) and is "to be responsible under the Security Council for the strategic direction of any armed forces placed at the disposal of the Security Council. Questions relating to the command of such forces shall be worked out subsequently."

The system contemplated by Articles 43 through 47 never came to fruition because of fundamental differences among the permanent members. The new Military Staff Committee attempted to reach agreement on the terms under which national forces would be provided to the Council, but there were disagreements on a number of points that reflected Cold War strategic differences, including the number and character of forces to be provided and where these forces would be stationed.[11]

Nevertheless, the authority given to the Council under Chapter VII is very broad and is not, by its terms, limited to the modalities set forth in Articles 43 through 47. Article 40 authorizes the Council to "call upon the parties concerned to comply with such provisional measures as it deems necessary or desirable." Article 42 provides for Council action through military operations by the forces of UN members—which might be carried out by states acting individually or through ad hoc coalitions, regional organizations, or forces under UN command. Article 48 provides that actions required to carry out the Council's decisions for the maintenance of international peace and security "shall be taken by all the Members of the United Nations or by some of them, as the Security Council may determine." Some commentators also take the view that the Council may authorize the use of force as a necessary result of Chapter VII taken as a whole, even apart from any specific authorization in any of its articles.[12] In any event, the International Court of Justice (in an advisory opinion) rejected the argument that the mechanism in Articles 43 through 47 was the exclusive means by which the Council could authorize the deployment of forces, stating that "it cannot be said that the Charter has left the Security Council impotent in the face of an emergency situation when agreements under Article 43 have not been concluded."[13]

The Council's authority to use force under Chapter VII is available to deal with any situation that the Council regards as a threat to the peace. As we have seen, in the post–Cold War period, the Council has taken a robust view of what might constitute such a threat, including armed aggression, the overthrow of democratically elected governments, genocide and other serious atrocities, internal disorder leading to humanitarian crises or massive refugee flows, and the possible acquisition of WMD by dangerous regimes or private actors.

This range of circumstances goes well beyond those in which the right of self-defense is available. There has been considerable debate over the extent to which the right of self-defense is limited to a response to armed attack that has already begun. But under any interpretation, the right of self-defense does not justify the use of force to deal with the wide range of general threats to peace that are encompassed by Chapter VII.

Even when action by states in self-defense without Council approval is justifiable, there may be significant advantages to authorization by the Council under Chapter VII as well. The first is the political benefit of authorization by the international community as a whole, which can greatly enhance the legitimacy of the operation and the readiness of states to support it. The Council's invocation of Chapter VII—which overrides any contrary legal obligations—may also help to deal with any hesitation by other states about giving assistance, access, overflight, and transit rights—hesitation that may stem from concerns about the traditional obligations of neutrals or any special treaty obligations (such as those governing passage through international canals or rivers). Further, a Chapter VII authorization may help to dispel any doubts about the scope of action available under the right of self-defense—particularly with respect to actions that some might argue to be unnecessary or disproportionate, such as invasion of the aggressor's heartland, strikes on targets in population centers, and removal of the aggressor regime.[14]

Needless to say, the Council should exercise its broad power to authorize the use of force only where it is necessary and prudent to do so, and where the likely advantages of the use of force will outweigh its often considerable costs. The 2004 report of the UN secretary-general's high-level panel suggested five criteria in this regard: (1) whether the threat to state or human security is sufficiently clear and serious; (2) whether the primary purpose for the use of force is to avert the threat in question, whatever other purposes may be involved; (3) whether there are reasonable grounds to believe that nonmilitary alternatives will not succeed; (4) whether the action proposed is the minimum necessary to meet the threat; and (5) whether there is a reasonable chance of success, with the consequences not likely to be worse than those of inaction.[15]

Action by regional authorities

As noted above, a regional organization might be an instrument for military action in collective self-defense or pursuant to enforcement action under Chapter VII. In addition, Article 53(1) of Chapter VIII of the Charter provides, "The Security Council shall, where appropriate, utilize . . . regional arrangements or agencies for enforcement action under its authority. But no enforcement action shall be taken under regional arrangements or by regional agencies without the authorization of the Security Council."

The requirement for Council authorization for regional enforcement action has been a source of considerable controversy over the years. Among the most important issues have been (1) whether a recommendation by a regional organization that its members use force constitutes "enforcement action"; (2) whether regional intervention in a civil war with the consent of the recognized government is "enforcement action"; (3) whether a particular entity constitutes a "regional agency" for the purpose of Chapter VIII; and (4) whether Council authorization for enforcement action may be given retroactively or by implication.[16] These issues were hotly debated during the Cold War in such cases as the Cuban missile crisis, the Dominican Republic, and Grenada.[17]

But none of this affects the ability of the Council to authorize the use of force by any regional body or coalition under Chapter VII or Chapter VIII. In fact, the Council has relied heavily on regional bodies and coalitions for these purposes during the post–Cold War period.

Humanitarian intervention

Finally, a number of commentators have argued that states have a right under customary international law—independent of self-defense or authorization by the Security Council—to intervene with force in another state to prevent or terminate massive violations of human rights, at least under some circumstances. This is still a minority view among states, although it is frequently recognized that such interventions may be morally and politically legitimate if no other alternative is available.[18] Without recapitulating this complex debate, a few basic points are worth noting.

There is no provision in the UN Charter for humanitarian intervention without the authorization of the Council. It has been argued that Article 2(4)—which prohibits the use of force "against the territorial integrity or political independence of any state, or in any other manner inconsistent with the Purposes of the United Nations"—does not preclude forcible intervention designed solely to stop the commission of mass atrocities.[19] However, this provision was apparently intended by the UN founders as a comprehensive prohibition on the use of force (other than as provided in Chapters VII and VIII), and it is difficult to see how bombardment or invasion of another state without its consent could fail to violate its territorial integrity.[20]

It has nonetheless been suggested that the actions of states in Kosovo and elsewhere are in practice bringing about (or have already brought about) either a revision of the meaning of Article 2(4) or the creation of new customary law that would permit humanitarian intervention without Council authorization. Yet it is difficult to see how such a fundamental provision of the Charter could in effect be revised or reinterpreted in this way when it remains a minority view among states and in particular has not been adopted by the United States and some of the other major powers.[21]

There will certainly be cases (such as Kosovo) where states will act in the absence of Council authorization to prevent severe humanitarian catastrophes, even though they do not necessarily have any clear legal basis for doing so. Nonetheless, the assertion by states or regional organizations of a *legal right* to carry out such "benign" uses of force on their own authority could create precedents for future interventions by others that might be destabilizing and dangerous. This is one of the main reasons the United States has never asserted the doctrine.

But there is a much stronger legal and political basis for forcible humanitarian intervention under Chapters VII or VIII. Virtually any massive campaign of atrocities is likely to have repercussions on other states that would justify a finding of a threat to the peace by the

Council. In acting under Chapters VII or VIII, the Council is not
limited to preventing or terminating atrocities, but can take action
(including the use of force) to deal with all other aspects of the situation that may threaten the peace, including the maintenance of internal order, the restoration of democratic government, and the resur-
rection of public institutions. The Council may maintain a long-term
military and governing presence to ensure future stability and recovery long after the immediate threat of atrocities has passed. And
action under the authority of the Council will have much stronger
international legitimacy and support (and present less of a dangerous
precedent for future abuse by others) than intervention by states or
regional bodies acting on their own authority.[22]

THE USE OF FORCE BY UN PEACEKEEPING MISSIONS

The "traditional" view of the use of force by UN peacekeepers in the
Cold War era was very restrictive.[23] According to the 1990 UN survey of UN peacekeeping operations, "The peacekeepers have no
rights of enforcement and their use of force is limited to self-defense,
as a last resort. This means that if a party chooses not to cooperate, it
can effectively defy a peacekeeping operation. . . . Those who serve in
peacekeeping forces are equipped with light defensive weapons but
are not authorized to use force except in self-defense. This right is
exercised only sparingly because of the obvious danger that if a United
Nations force uses its weapons its impartiality is, however unfairly,
called in question."[24] In fact, this assessment was already at variance
with the use of force authorized and exercised by peacekeeping forces
during the Cold War.

To begin with, UN peacekeeping forces are composed of
national military units, which retain the right of individual and collective self-defense under Article 51 in response to attacks against
them. However, as the mandates and circumstances of peacekeeping
missions became more demanding, the concept of self-defense by a
peacekeeping force began to expand beyond this traditional scope.
For example, the secretary-general's guidelines for UNEF II in the
Sinai in 1973 provided that the force's right of self-defense included
"resistance to attempts by forceful means to prevent it from discharg-

ing its duties under the Security Council's mandate."[25] The same formulation was approved by the Security Council in 1978 with respect to UNIFIL in Lebanon.[26]

Taken together with the freedom of movement insisted upon by the secretary-general and the Security Council, these formulations potentially constituted an authorization to use force well beyond traditional concepts of self-defense. For example, if a force's mandate authorized it to restore order or governmental control in a particular area, it could send military units into the area and then use force in "self-defense" to dispose of any armed resistance to its actions.

Further, the Council occasionally authorized the use of force without representing it as self-defense. In particular, as ONUC in the Congo faced ever more serious internal disorders and secessionist challenges, the Council authorized it to use force "if necessary, in the last resort" to "prevent the occurrence of civil war,"[27] and "to take vigorous action, including the use of the requisite measure of force, if necessary" for the apprehension and deportation of foreign military personnel and mercenaries.[28] In fact, the use of offensive force did prove to be necessary and ONUC took military action on a number of occasions to protect the civilian population, to round up and expel foreign mercenaries, and, in the end, to occupy areas held by secessionist forces.[29]

After the end of the Cold War, UN peacekeeping forces became increasingly involved in conflicts where it was necessary for them to use force to carry out their missions. At first, such authorizations were not welcomed by all Council members; in particular, China periodically voiced "reservations" about the use of Chapter VII and the use of force by peacekeepers.[30] However, express authorization for limited uses of force by peacekeeping missions soon became a frequent feature of Council resolutions—sometimes described as self-defense and sometimes not.

For example, in 1993, the Council authorized UNOSOM II to take "all necessary measures" (a term that was understood to include the use of force) to establish its effective authority throughout Somalia.[31] In the same year, the Council authorized UNPROFOR, "acting in self-defence, to take the necessary measures, including the use of force," to reply to bombardments against the safe areas in

Bosnia, to armed incursions into those areas, or to any obstruction to the freedom of movement of UNPROFOR or of humanitarian convoys.[32] In 1994, the Council recognized that UNAMIR in Rwanda "may be required to take action in self-defense against persons or groups who threaten protected sites and populations, United Nations and other humanitarian personnel, or the means of delivery and distribution of humanitarian relief."[33]

In 1998, the Council stated that MINURCA in the Central African Republic "may be required to take action to ensure security and freedom of movement of its personnel in the discharge of its mandate," which included assisting national security forces in maintaining law and order and in protecting key installations in the capital.[34] In 1999, UNAMSIL in Sierra Leone was authorized "to take the necessary action" to protect "civilians under imminent threat of physical violence."[35] In the same year, UNTAET in East Timor was authorized to take "all necessary measures" to fulfill its mandate, which included providing security, law, and order throughout the territory.[36]

However, UN peacekeeping missions frequently found themselves unable to deal effectively with the military threats they faced, whether because of a lack of sufficient military capabilities, an uncertain command structure, or a lack of will on the part of UN or national authorities. This was, for example, an acute problem in Somalia, Bosnia, Rwanda, the Congo, and Sierra Leone.

One occasional response to this problem has been the deployment, on an ad hoc basis, of more heavily armed national military units to operate under UN command as part of a threatened peacekeeping force—for example, the Rapid Reaction Force of troops from France, the Netherlands, and the United Kingdom that was authorized by the Council in 1995 to operate as part of UNPROFOR for the purpose of responding to threats to UN peacekeepers and to provide military muscle to carry out UNPROFOR's expanded mandate.[37] A second response has been the temporary deployment of national forces to protect and support UN peacekeepers on an ad hoc basis, but not under UN command—for example, when rebel forces in Sierra Leone seized hundreds of UN peacekeepers in May 2000, the United Kingdom deployed 700 combat troops (supported by warships and combat aircraft), which restored security in the Free-town area and led to the release of the peacekeepers.[38]

A third option was suggested in Secretary-General Boutros-Ghali's 1992 *Agenda for Peace,* which proposed the creation of regular "peace-enforcement units" to be deployed along with or in place of traditional peacekeeping forces. These units were to be composed of more heavily armed national units that would be made available by states for deployment under UN command on call of the Security Council.[39] As a legal matter, this would be a perfectly valid option, but in practice it has never materialized, presumably because of the reluctance of governments to commit their forces in advance to serious military action under UN command; or to doubts about the ability of the United Nations to organize, command, and support major military operations; or to an aversion in certain quarters to the appearance of creating a standing UN force.

In the alternative, the Council might entrust the use of force to governments or regional organizations, as will be discussed in the next section of this chapter. But this will not always be feasible or sensible, and may in some cases decrease the political acceptability and effectiveness of the overall effort. In the absence of such national deployments, UN peacekeepers cannot ignore atrocities and threats to innocent persons, and they may have to carry out limited uses of force to implement some aspect of their mandate from the Council. Therefore, the option of authorizing UN peacekeeping forces to engage in such limited use of force must be retained, and the Council needs to exercise its best judgment in deciding whether or not to do so in any particular situation. Needless to say, for such an option to be effective, the Council must ensure that the UN force has adequate resources and command, a strong and clear mandate, and robust rules of engagement.

USE OF FORCE BY NON-UN FORCES

Although limited use of force may be a realistic option for UN peace-keeping forces in some situations, it is widely recognized that it is not feasible to rely on UN forces to conduct major combat operations. In the words of Secretary-General Boutros-Ghali, "neither the Security

Council nor the secretary-general at present has the capacity to deploy, direct, command, and control operations for this purpose, except perhaps on a very limited scale."[40] On various occasions during the post–Cold War period—most notably in the cases of Somalia and Haiti—the secretary-general advised the Council that the United Nations would not be able to deploy and command the forces needed for a particular urgent purpose, or would not be able to do so in time.[41]

National military establishments have capabilities that the United Nations does not: the rapid deployment of combat units; the deployment and support of large, heavily equipped military formations; the provision of the full range of necessary combat support, including air forces, heavy logistics, and intelligence; integrated command and experience in common operations; the political and military resources of the major states that stand behind them; and the will to use these resources in the face of serious combat risk. Although the founders of the UN system may have assumed that the major powers would be willing to commit all these resources and capabilities to UN command, this has not proved to be the case.

The Cold War period

The Council's use during the Cold War of its power to authorize the use of force by states and regional organizations under Chapters VII and VIII was episodic and tentative. In the case of the North Korean invasion of South Korea in 1950, the Council did not expressly authorize the use of force. The Council was able (because of the temporary absence of the Soviet delegation on account of the dispute over the representation of China) to take certain actions—to confirm that the Republic of Korea had been the object of an armed attack, to recommend that UN members assist the Republic of Korea and provide military forces for this purpose to a unified command under the United States, and to authorize that command to use the UN flag in its operations.[42] Most legal commentators view these actions as the support by the Council of action in collective self-defense, although the authorization for a "UN" command can also be seen as an exercise of the Council's authority under Chapter VII.[43] In any event, the UN never played any serious role in the command of these operations.

More than fifteen years later, the Council acted to prevent the arrival at Beira (in the Portuguese colony of Mozambique) of tankers believed to be carrying oil for Southern Rhodesia. Specifically, the Council called on the United Kingdom (the recognized colonial administrator of Southern Rhodesia) "to prevent, by the use of force if necessary" the arrival of the tankers and "empowered" the United Kingdom to arrest and detain a particular tanker upon its departure from Beira in the event it had discharged its cargo there.[44] Although these steps could have been taken without Council authorization against the ships of consenting flag states, the Council's action can, on the whole, be seen as an exercise of its Chapter VII power to authorize the use of force.

The Council did not otherwise authorize the use of force during the entire Cold War era. This limited use of its powers under Chapters VII and VIII quickly gave way to vigorous and innovative uses of that authority after the end of the Cold War, when the political and strategic disagreements among the permanent members began to subside. The Council soon began authorizing the use of force by a variety of non-UN entities, including states, ad hoc coalitions, and regional organizations.

Iraq

In the case of the Iraqi invasion of Kuwait in 1990, the Council's initial reaction was to affirm that an armed attack had occurred and that the right of individual and collective self-defense applied in accordance with Article 51, while at the same time imposing comprehensive economic sanctions against Iraq.[45] It soon became apparent, however, that Iraq would make every effort to continue its maritime trade in violation of the sanctions and that armed interdiction of such seaborne traffic would be necessary to enforce the trade embargo. The United States was prepared to do so under the right of collective self-defense at the request of Kuwait without Council authorization, and in fact U.S. naval interdiction operations were initiated on that basis.[46]

However, a number of U.S. allies clearly preferred to have the affirmative authorization of the Council, and the United States quickly took the point. The Council thereupon adopted a resolution calling on "those Member States cooperating with the Government of Kuwait which are deploying maritime forces to the area to use such measures commensurate to the specific circumstances as may be necessary under the authority of the Security Council" to halt all inward and outward shipping for the purpose of inspecting cargos and enforcing the embargo.[47] The resolution was adopted by a vote of 13 to 0. Cuba and Yemen abstained on the grounds that the use of force was unwarranted and premature, and that it granted excessive and undefined authority to states outside the control of the Council.[48]

The United States announced during the Council debate that it would be "coordinating" the interdiction operations and thanked the Council for providing "an additional and most welcome basis under United Nations authority" beyond the existing right of self-defense.[49] The U.S. representative also stated that the United States was "ready to discuss an appropriate role in this process for the Military Staff Committee," but in fact the committee never played a significant role in the operation.[50]

Three months later, when neither the embargo nor the maritime interdiction had caused Iraq to withdraw from Kuwait, the United States and other members of the anti-Iraq coalition might in theory have decided to commence military operations to expel Iraqi forces from Kuwait entirely under the right of collective self-defense at the request of Kuwait. Instead, the coalition found it useful to seek the additional authorization of the Council under Chapter VII. In November 1990, the Council adopted Resolution 678, which gave Iraq a "pause of goodwill" to comply with the previous Council resolutions until January 15, 1991, and if Iraq failed to do so, the resolution authorized "Member States cooperating with the Government of Kuwait . . . to use all necessary means to uphold and implement" the Council's previous resolutions and "restore international peace and security in the area."[51]

This resolution was clearly understood by all Council members as authorizing the use of force by the coalition.[52] In fact, it was so broadly drafted that it provided a basis for coalition forces to enter Iraq, did not specify or restrict the command arrangements to be adopted by the coalition, and might have been interpreted on its face to permit the forcible removal of the Iraqi regime if that were deemed necessary to restore peace to the area—though this would have been contrary to the intentions of both the Council and the coalition members at the time. The resolution was generally understood to preclude the initiation of the military campaign during the "pause of goodwill," but the United States, the United Kingdom, the Soviet Union, and France all nonetheless reserved their right to act during that period in self-defense to protect their nationals if the Iraqi government were to harm them.[53]

From the point of view of the coalition partners, the Council's authorization had several important advantages, even though operations against Iraqi forces could in theory have been conducted as a matter of collective self-defense without the Council's authorization. It gave legitimacy to the operation and made it easier (domestically as well as internationally) for states to participate in the military campaign. It alleviated any concerns about the obligations of neutrality on the part of states that were asked to allow transit, overflight, and access to facilities by coalition forces in their territory. It eased concerns that might have arisen under the right of self-defense about the authority of coalition forces to enter Iraq and bomb the Iraqi heartland. Indeed, it gave the coalition an extra measure of authority to restore peace and security in the region that arguably went well beyond the requirements of self-defense.

After the successful conclusion of coalition operations against Iraq, the Security Council adopted Resolution 687—the "mother of all resolutions"—that set forth comprehensive requirements on Iraq, including the elimination of its WMD, the acceptance of UN inspectors to verify that elimination, and the renunciation of Iraqi support for terrorism. The Council affirmed that its previous resolutions (including the resolutions authorizing the use of force) would continue in force but declared that a formal cease-fire would be effective once Iraq had formally accepted these requirements—which did occur shortly thereafter.

The Council did not expressly authorize the use of force against Iraq after the cease-fire. However, on a number of subsequent occasions, the United States (sometimes in conjunction with the United Kingdom) used force against Iraq on the grounds that its "material breach" of the conditions of the 1991 cease-fire resurrected the

Council's original authorization for the use of force to restore peace and security in the region. In particular, in January 1993, the president of the Council stated, on behalf of the Council, that Iraqi violations concerning UN inspections and the demilitarized zone between Iraq and Kuwait constituted "material breaches of Resolution 687 (1991), which established the cease-fire and provided the conditions essential for the restoration of peace and security in the region" and warned Iraq of the "serious consequences that will flow" from these actions.[54] This was followed several days later by coalition air strikes against Iraqi targets, apparently with the approval of other Council members, and the UN secretary-general stated that coalition forces did indeed have a mandate for these actions under Resolutions 678 and 687.[55]

On the other hand, this apparent degree of acceptance within the Council of the use of force to address Iraqi violations was not present on later occasions. In November 1998, the Council condemned the Iraqi decision to end cooperation with UN inspectors as a "flagrant violation" of Resolution 687 but did not declare it to be a material breach of the cease-fire, for which there would be "serious consequences."[56] The United States and United Kingdom nonetheless took the view that Iraq's actions were such a material breach—whether or not officially declared to be such by the Council—and conducted extensive air strikes against Iraqi WMD-related targets on that basis.[57] This view was controversial and was disputed inside and outside of the Council.[58]

In November 2002, following strenuous efforts by the United States and the United Kingdom to convince the Council to take serious action to compel Iraq to end its violations concerning WMD, the Council adopted Resolution 1441, which (among other things) did the following:

* recognized that Iraqi actions constituted a threat to international peace and security, and recalled that Resolution 678 had authorized the use of all necessary means to restore peace in the area;
* recalled that the cease-fire adopted in Resolution 687 was based on Iraqi acceptance of the requirements of that resolution, which

included Iraq's obligations to eliminate WMD and give full access to UN inspectors;

❖ decided that Iraq "has been and remains in material breach" of Resolution 687;

❖ imposed additional requirements concerning declarations and inspections on Iraq, and declared that any Iraqi failure to comply with them would constitute a further material breach;

❖ directed the UN agencies charged to carry out the inspections to report any violations immediately to the Council, and decided that the Council would immediately convene to consider such a report; and

❖ recalled its previous warnings that Iraq "will face serious consequences" as a result of continued violations.

In effect, the Council had reiterated all the elements of its 1993 statements, but in this instance there clearly was no consensus within the Council that force could be used without further express Council authorization in the event of continued Iraqi noncompliance.[59] Nonetheless, the United States and its coalition partners launched military operations against Iraq (this time, a full-scale invasion to remove the regime of Saddam Hussein) and cited Resolutions 686, 687, and 1441 as the legal basis for their actions.[60] This decision has been, to say the least, the object of considerable debate, as to both its legal basis and policy justification.[61] Although it was based on essentially the same legal justification that the U.S. had relied upon since 1991, there were important differences, including the fact that Iraq apparently had eliminated its WMD stocks by 2003, that UN inspectors were still able to operate in Iraq, and that the coalition's use of force was not limited to the destruction of WMD-related capabilities but was aimed more broadly at the destruction and replacement of the existing government for a variety of reasons.

In October 2003, the Council and the U.S.-led coalition came closer together through the authorization by the Council of a multinational force under unified national command to "take all necessary measures" to maintain security and stability and to assist in the ongoing political transition.[62] This authorization was reaffirmed in June 2004, when the Council endorsed the formation of a sovereign Iraqi

Interim Government, subject to the understanding that Iraqi security forces would be responsible to the new government and would act in "full partnership" with the multinational force. This mandate was to expire upon completion of the transition to a permanent constitutionally elected government by December 2005, or earlier if requested by the Interim Government.[63]

To summarize, the Council's response to the Iraqi invasion of Kuwait established that it had the authority under Chapter VII to authorize the use of offensive force on a massive scale to deal with threats to the peace, notwithstanding the fact that the arrangements originally contemplated by the founders of the Charter for the use of force had never been brought into being. It also established that the Council may delegate the authority to use force to states and coalitions of states on such terms as it decides are appropriate and need not retain operational control over the operations it authorizes. As for the 2003 invasion of Iraq, the U.S. legal justification is heavily dependent on the interpretation of the specific Council resolutions on Iraq and is therefore less likely to be a significant legal precedent for the future. At the same time, however, the Iraqi experience shows that serious differences within the Council—particularly among the permanent members—on the legality and propriety of the use of force can undercut the political viability of such operations, whatever the technical merits of the legal arguments.

The Balkans

In the case of the dissolution of Yugoslavia and the resulting conflicts in Croatia and Bosnia, the Council came more gradually and reluctantly to the authorization of the use of force by non-UN entities. After months of agonizing about the inability of UNPROFOR to ensure the flow of humanitarian assistance to the civilian population of Bosnia, the Council acted in August 1992 under Chapter VII, calling on states to take "all measures necessary to facilitate" the delivery of humanitarian assistance.[64] This was understood by Council members as authorizing the use of military force by NATO members.[65] The resolution was adopted by a vote of 12-0; China, India, and Zimbabwe abstained—the latter two on the grounds that the Council should not have delegated to states its authority to use force.[66]

This resolution was followed by a series of other Council authorizations for the use of force by non-UN actors. In November 1992, the Council acted under both Chapters VII and VIII, calling on states "acting nationally or through regional agencies or arrangements" to use "such measures commensurate with the specific circumstances as may be necessary" to halt shipping bound to or from Yugoslavia to enforce the Council's arms and trade embargos.[67] In March 1993, the Council authorized states or regional organizations, "subject to close coordination with the Secretary-General and UNPROFOR," to take "all necessary measures" to ensure compliance with its ban on flights in Bosnian airspace.[68] In June 1993, the Council authorized "all necessary measures, through the use of air power," to support UNPROFOR's protection of the safe areas and the civilian population in Bosnia.[69] Similar authorizations were given with respect to the situation in Croatia.[70]

With the conclusion of the Dayton Accords for Bosnia and similar arrangements for Croatia, the Council gave states and regional organizations even broader authority to use force to enforce these peace agreements. The 1995 Dayton Peace Agreement requested the Security Council to authorize member states and regional organizations to establish a multinational military Implementation Force (IFOR) with broad power to ensure compliance with the agreement in Bosnia.[71] In response, the Council authorized member states, acting "through or in cooperation with" NATO, to establish the multinational force and to take "all necessary measures" to ensure compliance with the relevant parts of the agreement, as well as to defend IFOR and assist it in carrying out its mission.[72] This time, the vote was unanimous.[73] One year later, the Council authorized the creation of a multinational Stabilization Force (SFOR) as a follow-on to IFOR and authorized SFOR and the states "acting through or in cooperation with" NATO to take "all necessary measures" to ensure continued compliance with the peace agreement.[74] In the case of Croatia, following the conclusion of the 1995 Basic Agreement for Eastern Slavonia, the Council created a UN peacekeeping operation (UNTAES) to implement the agreement and authorized member states "acting nationally or through regional organizations or arrangements" to take "all necessary measures, including close air support" to defend UNTAES at its request.[75]

The Council was initially unable to take comparable action with respect to the situation in Kosovo because of intense disagreement among the permanent members on the appropriateness of forcible international intervention to restrain Serb actions against the non-Serb Kosovar population. The Council did direct the Belgrade regime to desist, determined that its actions constituted a threat to the peace, and imposed an arms embargo under Chapter VII.[76] However, the Council was unable—because of Russian and Chinese opposition—to authorize the use of force.[77] As a result, NATO forces carried out military operations against the Federal Republic of Yugoslavia without Council authorization—a decision strongly opposed by Russia and China as unlawful and improper.[78] Upon conclusion of the NATO air campaign and Serbian agreement to withdraw from Kosovo, the Council was able to authorize the deployment of an "international security presence"—essentially a NATO operation—with the responsibility of enforcing a cease-fire, preventing the return of Serb forces, demilitarizing Kosovar armed groups, protecting international personnel, and establishing a secure environment.[79]

Finally, the Council authorized a more limited operation in Albania, where Italy offered to lead a temporary force to address internal disorders that threatened to cause destabilizing refugee flows and exacerbate ethnic divisions in neighboring states. Acting under Chapter VII, the Council authorized the creation of a "multinational protection force to facilitate the safe and prompt delivery of humanitarian assistance, and to help create a secure environment for the missions of international organizations in Albania" and for this purpose authorized participating states to act to ensure the security and freedom of movement of the force.[80] The operation was initially limited to a three-month period but later extended for an additional forty-five days.[81] No delegation voted against this operation, but China abstained on the grounds that it improperly allowed interference in the internal affairs of a member state.[82]

An important aspect of the Council's authorizations for the use of force in the Balkans is that they encompassed not only the protection of a victim state from aggression by another (which was an element of the Council's actions in Bosnia), but also the protection of the civilian population from atrocities and armed attack, even in the context of civil conflict. In effect, the Council was expanding its Chapter VII authority for the use of force beyond the traditional bounds of collective security to include more general threats to peace and stability.

Africa

The use of the Council's authority under Chapters VII and VIII with respect to the conflicts in Kuwait and the former Yugoslavia soon became precedents for the authorization of force in the numerous internal conflicts in Africa in the 1990s. The first was the humanitarian crisis caused by the internal conflict and chaos in Somalia, which the small UN peacekeeping force (UNOSOM) was wholly unable to handle. In late 1992, as the UN peacekeepers found themselves cornered in the Mogadishu airport and relief organizations were unable to get substantial supplies to millions of threatened Somali civilians, the secretary-general decided that firm action, including the use of force, was necessary. He presented three options to the Council: (1) a show of force by UNOSOM troops in Mogadishu to deter further interference by local armed groups; (2) a country-wide enforcement operation by willing states under Council authorization; and (3) a country-wide enforcement operation under UN command. However, the first option was clearly inadequate and the secretary-general advised that the United Nations was simply unable to carry out the third option with the scale and promptness required.[83]

As a result, when the United States offered to lead a multinational operation and to contribute substantial U.S. forces, the Council welcomed the offer and authorized states to carry it out, using "all necessary means in order to establish as soon as possible a secure environment for humanitarian relief operations in Somalia."[84] This was understood to include the use of force if necessary. The multinational force (UNITAF) came ashore in December 1992, quickly established control over large areas of southern and central Somalia, and substantially alleviated the immediate humanitarian crisis; but the task of restoring security to the entirety of Somalia and disarming the local militias was not completed when the decision was taken to withdraw UNITAF in May 1993 in favor of a new UN force (UNOSOM II).[85] UNOSOM II was ultimately unable to prevail over the opposition of warlord Mohamed Farah Aideed, and following fighting in Mogadishu that caused a number of U.S. and Pakistani casualties, the Council decided to withdraw from Somalia, authorizing states to take any necessary action to carry out that withdrawal.[86]

In the years that followed, other multinational forces under national command were authorized to act under Chapter VII to manage humanitarian crises in connection with African civil wars. In 1994, a small UN peacekeeping mission in Rwanda (UNAMIR) found itself in the midst of a humanitarian disaster it could not cope with—the genocidal campaign by militant Hutus that began in May 1994. The secretary-general recommended a modest expansion of UNAMIR; but in June, recognizing that even the first phase of this deployment could not be completed until July, he recommended that the Council accept an offer by the French government to lead a multinational force into southwestern Rwanda (Operation Turquoise) to establish a "humanitarian protected zone."[87] The Council welcomed the French offer, agreed that a multinational operation could proceed in Rwanda "until UNAMIR is brought up to the necessary strength," and authorized member states participating in the operation to use "all necessary means" to carry it out.[88] The mission was limited to two months; accordingly, the French-led operation (with troops from six other African states) was launched in June and withdrew in August, although the expanded UNAMIR did not reach full strength until October.[89] This operation obviously did not stop the main carnage of the genocidal campaign, and the failure of the Council to act more promptly and forcefully was one of the worst in the post–Cold War period—a failure for which the United States was largely responsible. Nonetheless, France did take credit for protecting almost a million refugees and safely evacuating more than a thousand persons who were directly threatened.

In November 1996, the Council authorized a multinational force to enter eastern Zaire (now the Democratic Republic of the Congo) to use "all necessary means" to facilitate humanitarian relief for refugees of the Rwanda conflict and for the local civilian population.[90] In August 1997, in connection with the civil conflict in the Central African Republic, the Council authorized the states participating in the African multinational force that was charged with implementing the Bangui Agreements to take action to ensure the security and freedom of movement of its personnel.[91] In May 2003, after years of bloody civil war that understrength UN peacekeeping forces had been unable to control, the Council authorized the deployment of a small Interim Emergency Multinational Force (under French command) to the town of Bunia, where particularly serious fighting and atrocities had been occurring.[92]

In addition, the Council gave its approval and assistance on several occasions to the Economic Community of West African States in connection with its military operations. Troops from several western African countries, organized under the ECOWAS Monitoring Group (ECOMOG), intervened in the Liberian internal conflict in the early 1990s to impose a cease-fire, restore order, provide humanitarian relief, and bring about elections for a new government.[93] The Council never expressly authorized the intervention (as contemplated by Article 53 of Chapter VIII) but from time to time adopted resolutions and issued presidential statements (often referring to Chapter VIII) that commended the actions of ECOWAS, called on the parties to the conflict to comply with its cease-fire, determined that the situation constituted a threat to the peace, imposed an arms embargo on recipients other than ECOWAS, and created a peacekeeping mission (UNOMIL) to work with ECOMOG.[94]

Similarly, during the late 1990s, the Council adopted a series of resolutions giving various forms of support to the ECOWAS intervention in Sierra Leone, particularly in the effort to restore the democratically elected Kabbah government to power and to protect the civilian population from atrocities committed by opposition forces.[95] The steps taken by the Council included commending ECOWAS efforts; determining that the situation constituted a threat to the peace; imposing sanctions on the military junta that had overthrown Kabbah and on the illicit diamond trade that supported rebel groups; and creating peacekeeping missions (UNOMSIL and UNAMSIL) to work with ECOMOG and if necessary to use force to protect civilians and secure key installations.[96] Once again, the Council did not expressly authorize the armed intervention of ECOMOG forces but did authorize ECOWAS, pursuant to Article VIII, to implement the Council's sanctions through maritime interdiction operations.[97]

Even more than in the Balkans, the Council's authorizations for the use of force in Africa were not limited to addressing interstate aggression but were largely directed at restoring order and protecting the civilian population in internal conflicts (many of which involved ethnic conflicts that crossed state boundaries). In addition, the Council authorized the use of force for the restoration of democracy in Sierra Leone and for the protection of political and economic reconstruction throughout the region.

Other areas

Similar authorizations were given for the use of force by multinational and regional forces in other parts of the world. In the case of Haiti, when the military junta refused to honor its commitments to return power to the democratically elected Aristide government, the Council acted under Chapters VII and VIII in October 1993 to authorize member states, "acting nationally or through regional agencies or arrangements," to enforce the Council's economic sanctions, including through maritime interdiction operations.[98]

When these measures failed, the Council authorized member states in July 1994 "to form a multinational force under unified command and control and, in this framework, to use all necessary means" to bring about the departure of the junta, the restoration of the Aristide government, and the maintenance of a secure environment in Haiti.[99] It was understood that the United States would command and provide the bulk of the fighting forces for this operation.[100] Several delegates expressed serious reservations about giving such broad authority to such a force, particularly without any time limit.[101] However, delegates were well aware of the fact that the secretary-general had concluded that the United Nations would be unable to assemble and command the force that would be necessary to overcome serious military opposition, and certainly not in the time desired.[102] As a result, the resolution was adopted by a vote of 12 to 0, with Brazil and China abstaining.[103] In the end, the threat of U.S. military intervention, together with a last-minute U.S. diplomatic effort, persuaded the junta to leave, and the multinational force was able to carry out its mission without serious hostilities.[104]

Unfortunately, permanent stability in Haiti did not result, and in recent years, a period of repression and insurgent activity led to a general outbreak of armed conflict and Aristide's departure in February 2004.[105] At that point, the Council found it necessary once again to authorize the deployment of a Multinational Interim Force for a period of up to three months, with authority to use "all necessary means" to restore order and facilitate international assistance.[106] In April, the Council created a UN Stabilization Mission (MINUSTAH) to take over from the multinational force.[107]

In East Timor, when the situation had deteriorated into general chaos and unconstrained violence against civilians and international personnel, the Council authorized in September 1999 the establishment of an International Force for East Timor (INTERFET) under unified command, with authority to take "all necessary measures" to restore peace and security and to protect other international operations.[108] Australia had announced its readiness to lead the force, and the Council expressed its understanding that it would be replaced as soon as it was possible to deploy a UN peacekeeping mission. In fact, INTERFET was able to complete its mission and turn over responsibility to a UN peacekeeping force (UNTAET) by February 2000.[109]

In the case of the attacks against the World Trade Center and the Pentagon on September 11, 2001, the Council promptly confirmed that the right of individual and collective self-defense applied, but it did not find it necessary to add the authority of Chapter VII for the use of force against the Taliban and al Qaeda.[110] In December 2001, following the defeat of the Taliban by national forces led by the United States (Operation Enduring Freedom), the Council welcomed the developments in Afghanistan and authorized the establishment of an International Security Assistance Force (ISAF) under Western command to assist the new Afghan Interim Authority in maintaining security in the Kabul area; member states participating in the force were authorized to take "all necessary measures" to fulfill this mandate.[111]

These Council actions in various parts of the world were consistent with the trends established with respect to the conflicts in Africa and Europe. As in the case of Sierra Leone, the Council's action in Haiti in 1994 was an instance of the authorization of force to restore a democratic government overthrown by military coup. As in the case of Kosovo, the Council's action with respect to East Timor was an instance of authorizing force to make possible the political and economic reconstruction of a territory devastated by conflict. In both cases, the suppression of human rights violations and the protection of the civilian population were primary objectives of the Council's actions. Notwithstanding the earlier concerns of many governments about the delegation of the authority to use force to states and coalitions, this has now become a generally accepted tool at the Council's disposal to address a variety of political, humanitarian, and security problems that threaten the peace.

CONDITIONS ON COUNCIL AUTHORIZATIONS

A frequent issue in the Security Council's consideration of authorizations for the use of force by non-UN entities was the degree to which there should be conditions or limits on the actions of those entities. This issue arose with respect to Council actions designed to threaten the use of force but stopping short of actual authorization. It also arose in the case of actual authorization for the use of force with respect to the breadth of the mandate given, the time limit (if any) on the mandate, the arrangements (if any) for UN supervision or coordination, and the relationship between UN and non-UN forces.

Threats of force

The Council has often attempted to resolve situations short of the actual use of force by threatening such action if the miscreant party did not comply with the Council's requirements. Sometimes the Council has threatened the use of force (either expressly or by implication) without actually authorizing it, has conditioned an authorization for the use of force by offering a further opportunity for compliance, or has authorized a lesser use of force with the threat of more drastic force to follow.

The Council used all of these tactics with respect to Iraq. In taking various sanctions and other measures against Iraq in the summer and fall of 1990, the Council frequently threatened to take "further steps" to ensure compliance.[112] In late August 1990, the Council

authorized the use of force for the limited purpose of maritime interdiction of prohibited shipping to and from Iraq, while strongly reiterating its determination to bring the Iraqi occupation of Kuwait to an
end.[113] In November, the Council authorized the full use of force but
conditioned it on "one final opportunity, as a pause of goodwill" until
January 15, 1991, for Iraq to comply without war.[114] In the years after
the Gulf War, the Council did not expressly authorize the use of force
to compel Iraq to comply with Council requirements but from time
to time threatened "serious consequences" that were understood to
include the possible use of force.[115] In 2002, members who believed
that Resolution 1441 did not actually authorize the use of force evidently viewed it as another variation of this pattern, in which force
was implicitly threatened but would be resorted to only upon a further affirmative decision of the Council.

The Council used a similar range of threats and conditional
authorizations in the former Yugoslavia. The Council often took sanctions and other partial measures against Serbia and Serb factions, while
threatening "further steps" if necessary.[116] Limited uses of force were
authorized—for example, to interdict maritime shipments or to protect
safe areas—with the threat that "new and tougher" measures may follow.[117] The Council sometimes stated that such measures would be
reconsidered if Serb actors complied with its requirements.[118]

Such threats may sometimes have useful results but obviously
cannot necessarily be counted on to resolve the situation, as demonstrated by the UN experience with respect to Iraq, Yugoslavia, the
Congo, and elsewhere. Sometimes actual authorization of force without limits or conditions is enough by itself to produce compliance, as
was the case with respect to Haiti in 1994. But the Council cannot
give authorization for the use of force as a deterrent threat without
being prepared to accept the consequence that such force will actually be used, nor can it assume that such a threat will be credible if
force is not actually authorized. This was, of course, the dilemma the
Council faced regarding Iraq in 2002.

The scope of the authorization

As noted earlier, the Council can, if it chooses, give states extremely
broad scope for military action or narrowly restrict it. As described

previously, several members of the Council took strong issue with the breadth of some of the earlier mandates during the post–Cold War period, while others expressed concerns but accepted the necessity of the actions. The mandate to coalition forces in Iraq after the invasion of Kuwait was the broadest, including the authority "to use all necessary means . . . to restore international peace and security in the area."[119]

The mandates for Somalia and Rwanda, and the earliest mandates for Bosnia, focused somewhat more narrowly on providing a secure environment for humanitarian relief and protection of the civilian population, and the mandate in Haiti on restoring the democratically elected government. In several cases, special authorization was given for the enforcement of maritime embargos and no-fly zones. The mandates for Croatia, Albania, the Central African Republic, the Congo, and Afghanistan were yet narrower.

Nonetheless, the Council has continued to give broad mandates where it has felt them to be necessary. In particular, the mandate given to IFOR (and later SFOR) in Bosnia to implement the Dayton Peace Agreement was very broad, as were the mandates given to multinational forces in Kosovo and East Timor. If the Council should decide at some future time to authorize a major war against a serious opponent, the Council is unlikely to impose narrow limits on the mandate or to restrict the scope of military action needed to accomplish that mandate, even if it may not give as open-ended an authorization as that for Operation Desert Storm.

Time limits

An alternative device for retaining some measure of control has been the imposition of time periods on such authorizations. The mandates for the use of force by non-UN entities in Iraq, Haiti, and Somalia, as well as the initial mandates in Bosnia, were not limited in time— and this was a matter of concern for some Council members.[120] However, time periods became common thereafter: for example, one year for IFOR and SFOR in Bosnia, for UNTAES in Croatia, and for KFOR in Kosovo; six months in Afghanistan; three months in Albania and the Congo; and two months in Rwanda. In some cases, there was a genuine expectation that the operations authorized would end in the specified time frame (or soon thereafter), but in other cases the authorizations were regularly renewed (and, for example, continue to this day in Bosnia and Kosovo).

The effect of such periods depends in theory on how their provisions for renewal are structured. In the case of Kosovo, KFOR was authorized for an initial period of twelve months but continued thereafter "unless the Security Council decides otherwise"—which means in theory that any permanent member could by itself ensure its indefinite continuation. On the other hand, the other authorizations expired after the initial term unless affirmatively renewed by the Council (as was frequently done)—which means in theory that any permanent member could single-handedly ensure the termination of the authorization. In this sense, the effect of time limits is therefore not so much about the ability of the Council to control the duration of a mandate—because it can always terminate a mandate at any time—but, rather, whether a controlling veto is given to permanent members that might favor its continuation or those that might oppose it. The choice between these alternatives is a question of whether it is more important to ensure the continuity of the particular operation or to ensure that it ceases if it no longer enjoys general support in the Council. This is not a judgment that can be made sensibly in the abstract but depends on the circumstances of the particular situation.

UN supervision

As noted before, no UN supervision or coordination was required with respect to the military operations of the Desert Storm coalition.[121] This was a matter of considerable debate in the Council: Yemen objected that "the command of these forces will have nothing to do with the United Nations, although their actions will have been authorized by the Security Council. It is a classic example of authority without accountability."[122] Cuba argued that the resolution "is equivalent to giving the United States and its allies carte blanche to use their enormous sophisticated military capability."[123] Malaysia objected that states authorized to use force should be "fully accountable for their actions to the Council through a clear system of reporting and accountability," which was not provided.[124] Nonetheless, the coalition was not willing to accept UN supervision or control over the complex and difficult military operations that were about to start, and the Council was not about to require it.

In the case of Somalia, the Council provided that the secretary-general and the states participating in the multinational Unified Task Force (UNITAF) would "make the necessary arrangements for the unified command and control of the forces involved"—but in fact the United States, as commander of the force, retained control over its operations, notwithstanding significant disagreements with the Secretariat about the objectives to be pursued.[125]

In the case of Bosnia, the Council's 1993 authorizations for the use of force by NATO members were "subject to close coordination with the Secretary-General and UNPROFOR," and in this case, real UN control was established in the form of a "dual key" over the initiation of air strikes—that is, an arrangement requiring both UN and NATO approval in each instance. The inhibiting effect of this arrangement over the use of air power to defend the safe zones was a matter of considerable controversy, and in the end the United Nations had to be persuaded temporarily to relinquish its veto power so that NATO could decide on its own to proceed with the air strikes against Bosnian Serb targets that were one of the decisive factors leading to the Dayton Peace Agreement.[126]

This unhappy experience with UN control over non-UN military operations reinforced the reluctance of the United States and other leaders of military coalitions to accept such constraints, and the "dual key" system was not revived in subsequent authorizations. Indeed, in the case of the recent conflict in Afghanistan, where the Council authorized ISAF in the Kabul area under Western command, not only does the ISAF operate without UN control but the U.S. Central Command was acknowledged to have authority over ISAF to the extent necessary to ensure that ISAF activities and the independent U.S.-led military campaign against al Qaeda do not interfere with each other.[127]

It does not appear that UN control over the day-to-day military decisions of non-UN forces in such situations is feasible or desirable. On the other hand, there will usually be a need for some form of coordination or liaison with UN representatives in countries where such forces are operating, given the fact that UN and other international agencies typically are present in countries affected by conflict.[128]

In addition, the Council typically calls for regular reporting to the Council by the forces to which such authorizations are given: sometimes time periods are specified (in one case, within seven days), and sometimes not.[129] The Council also customarily requests the secretary-general to provide regular reports on the progress of such operations. In the case of Somalia, the Council created an "ad hoc commission" to report to the Council on implementation of its authorizing resolution.[130] By themselves, such arrangements do not constrain the states that report, but they are useful in offering reassurance to Council members and in providing a basis for the Council to modify or terminate a mandate if it chooses to do so.

The relationship between UN and non-UN forces

In a number of conflict situations in the post–Cold War period, both UN and non-UN forces have deployed, either simultaneously or sequentially. This practice has evolved as a means of exploiting the unique capabilities of both types of forces—non-UN forces for rapid entry and the conduct of serious military operations, and UN peacekeeping forces to facilitate long-term security and political transformation.

In some cases, a non-UN force was deployed with the Council's authorization to defeat military opposition and to restore order, and was then replaced by a UN peacekeeping mission to maintain security or to carry out other political and economic objectives. This was, for example, the case in Iraq (where coalition forces were replaced along the Iraq-Kuwait border by UNIKOM), in Somalia (where the U.S.-led UNITAF force was replaced by UNOSOM II), in Haiti (where the U.S.-led multinational force was replaced by UNMIH), in Rwanda (where the French-led Operation Turquoise was replaced by UNAMIR), and in East Timor (where the Australian-led INTERFET was replaced by UNTAET). In such cases, the Council needed to provide for the transition from non-UN to UN deployments, which sometimes involved the transfer of national military units from multinational to UN command.[131]

In other instances, non-UN and UN forces have operated simultaneously in the same country—for example, in Bosnia (UNPROFOR and NATO), in Georgia (UNOMIG and Russian-led forces of the Commonwealth of Independent States), in Sierra Leone (UNAMSIL and the Nigerian-led ECOMOG force), and in the Congo (MONUC and the French-led Interim Emergency Multinational Force). In each case, the Council needed to define the relationship between the mandates and responsibilities of the two forces. For example, the mandate of NATO in Bosnia was to provide direct military support for UNPROFOR operations under integrated command arrangements—to protect UNPROFOR and to enforce UN sanctions, safe areas, and no-fly zones.[132] In Sierra Leone, on the other hand, UNAMSIL and ECOMOG operated independently, and the Council set forth a separate mandate for UNAMSIL that was largely directed at support for the Sierra Leone government; ECOMOG and UNAMSIL were called on to maintain "close cooperation and coordination . . . in carrying out their respective tasks" but had no common command arrangement.[133]

ASSESSMENT

As a result of the experiences of the past decade, the Council has developed an extensive range of legal options for the use of force to deal with threats to the peace, and it has shown its willingness to make vigorous use of them. Ironically, these options do not include the system originally intended by the founders of the United Nations— that is, the use under the direction of the Military Staff Committee of forces made available by member states under standing agreements pursuant to Article 43. Nor has the Council developed any alternative system for major military operations under UN command.

Instead, the Council has developed a three-part system in which (1) UN peacekeeping forces may be given limited authority to use force—typically for the protection of international personnel and the civilian population, or to deal with any armed resistance to the accomplishment of their own missions; (2) the Council may, in appropriate cases, endorse and support the actions of states in individual or collective self-defense without giving them any additional authority to use force; or (3) the Council may delegate the authority to use force to states, acting individually, in ad hoc coalitions, or in regional organizations—particularly where there is a need for immediate deployment of substantial military forces, or where major use of force against serious opposition may be necessary. Often a combination of two or more of these options may be used in the same situation, either simultaneously or sequentially.

A number of states and commentators have lamented the necessity of delegating the right to use force to entities not under UN control. They point to the risk that doing so will lead to the pursuit by powerful states of their own parochial interests, reduce the chances of consensual resolution of conflicts, and bring disrepute on the United Nations. These are legitimate concerns and can be addressed to some extent by reporting and coordination, by care in crafting the Council's mandates, and by the sensible integration of non-UN forces with UN peacekeeping missions and other international operations. Nevertheless, the key to responsible and effective use of non-UN forces in the service of the Council will still primarily be a matter of good political preparation and accommodation, particularly among the states that typically play the key roles in both the Council and the forces deployed.

The Council could, as a legal matter, use its authority under Article 42 to assume directly more of the military missions currently being delegated to non-UN entities. In time, doing so could, for example, lead to the creation of something like the UN peace-enforcement units proposed earlier in the decade to make it possible for the United Nations to rapidly deploy forces capable of handling moderate military threats. But for practical and political reasons, it seems unlikely that the United Nations will be able to deploy forces capable of dealing with serious military opposition, let alone to conduct operations of the magnitude and risk of Operation Desert Storm.

On the other side of the equation, the fact that this system depends on decisions by the Security Council means that it cannot work effectively when there is a fundamental difference of political interest and perspective among the permanent members—as occurred with respect to Iraq in the years after the Gulf War and with respect to Kosovo prior to the conclusion of the NATO campaign. In such a situation, the international community is returned to the chaos of the Cold War system, where action by states on their own authority takes the place of international action, often at the risk of wider conflict and political stalemate. For the present, there is no effective remedy for such situations, except through the difficult and frequently unpleasant work of political accommodation and political pressure that is often necessary to restore agreement among the permanent members.

Taking all this into account, the striking facts about the experience of the past decade in this regard are not the limitations of the system that has emerged but its considerable potential. The international community has developed the legal authority to use force for its common purposes, rather than being limited to watching from the sidelines as states use force on their own authority and for their own ends. These common purposes now include—in addition to the traditional objective of preventing aggression—such basic international goals as maintaining democratic government, suppressing violations of human rights, and suppressing internal conflict when there is a threat to the peace. In a violent world, this is an essential step toward a coherent and effective system of international conduct.

6

UN TECHNICAL COMMISSIONS

THE SECURITY COUNCIL has created a new breed of institutions since the end of the Cold War to address conflict situations and to lessen the likelihood of a renewal of hostilities. These institutions include a series of important UN technical commissions (which are examined in this chapter) and international criminal tribunals (the subject of the next chapter).

The most important technical commissions created by the Council were designed to address three aspects of the 1990–91 Gulf War: (1) the UN Compensation Commission (UNCC), which adjudicates claims for injury and loss resulting from the Iraqi invasion and occupation of Kuwait; (2) the UN Iraq-Kuwait Boundary Demarcation Commission, which resolved the border dispute that was one of the ostensible causes of the war; and (3) the UN Special Commission (UNSCOM) and its successor, the UN Monitoring, Verification, and Inspection Commission (UNMOVIC), which were created to monitor the elimination of Iraqi weapons of mass destruction. In creating these commissions, the Security Council imposed significant obligations on Iraq, provided for the resolution of difficult legal issues, and tackled practical problems of considerable importance for Iraq and its neighbors.

For various practical reasons, these important institutional by-products of the Gulf War were not reproduced elsewhere during the ensuing decade. However, they stand as precedents for similar action should the need arise, and they have created an important body of legal principles for the resolution of similar issues in other forums. Together, they represent a significant new element of international law making and problem solving, and an important demonstration of the creative uses that can be made of the Council's extensive authority under Chapter VII.

COMPENSATION

Background

Almost from the very outset of the Iraqi invasion and occupation of Kuwait, it became clear that the conflict would cause immense damage and loss. Among other things, more than a million foreign workers were forced to leave Iraq and Kuwait; Iraqi forces removed or destroyed large amounts of Kuwaiti property; many Kuwaiti citizens and foreign nationals were imprisoned, killed, or injured; the Kuwaiti economy was largely brought to a standstill; a great volume of contractual relationships with foreign companies in Iraq and Kuwait were interrupted; and, in the final weeks of the war, Iraqi forces caused vast damage to Kuwaiti oil fields and reserves, as well as widespread environmental damage by burning oil wells and dumping oil into the Gulf. In all, the damage was reckoned in hundreds of billions of dollars.

By the end of the war, it had become clear that a program to compensate for these losses would be an essential part of the regime ending the war—to help in restoring stability to the region, in dealing with the most severe consequences of the war, and (it was hoped) in deterring any repetition of the Iraqi actions. Thus, while questions of international responsibility for acts of states do not normally fall within the category of threats to the peace (for which the Council may invoke Chapter VII of the Charter), in this case the urgent need for compensation was an integral part of a situation over which the Council already had Chapter VII jurisdiction. Restoring losses caused by the conflict was a legitimate part of the Council's authority to restore and maintain the peace.

The international community was determined that Iraq should pay for this damage to the full extent of its capacity to do so. In October 1990, the Security Council pointedly reminded Iraq "that under international law it is liable for any loss, damage, or injury arising in regard to Kuwait and third States, and their nationals and corporations, as a result of the invasion and illegal occupation of Kuwait by Iraq," and invited states to begin collecting information about these losses "with a view to such arrangements as may be established in accordance with international law."[1]

The Council was correct in its assertion that, under existing international law, Iraq was liable for losses suffered by other states and their nationals as a result of its unlawful use of force.[2] Further, there had been a number of past cases in which victorious powers had extracted reparations from the losing party in a conflict, sometimes in genuine compensation for the victims of unlawful actions and sometimes as punitive measures to benefit the victors. In other cases, states had voluntarily entered into agreements to resolve claims arising from conflicts or comparable situations, either though the operation of international arbitral tribunals or commissions, or by negotiating "lump-sum" payments that were distributed by claimant governments to their nationals.[3]

But none of these precedents provided an adequate basis for the resolution of the vast volume of claims and damage produced by the Gulf War. Nor did any of them offer any prospect of immediate relief for the hundreds of thousands of individuals who suffered serious loss or offer the kind of legitimacy that a UN-sanctioned program would provide.

The largest international claims program up to that point was the Iran-U.S. Claims Tribunal, created by the 1981 Algiers Accords, a series of international agreements that resolved the Iran hostage crisis.[4] Although that tribunal has resolved roughly a thousand large cases and awarded more than $3 billion,[5] the claims tribunal process has had a number of inherent drawbacks.

The tribunal is a bilateral arbitration mechanism in which (as in most arbitration proceedings) the contending parties have equal standing and participation, and in which all questions of law and fact have to be decided through a formal adversary process. Iran was able to delay and obstruct the proceedings, to harass non-Iranian arbitrators, and to interfere with the payment of awards. The tribunal was unable to deal with the thousands of "small" claims (under $250,000) that were resolved only in 1990 through the negotiation by Iran and the United States of a lump-sum payment to the U.S. government (which it distributed to U.S. nationals).[6] After more than twenty years, the largest claims are still unresolved, and the end of the process is not in sight.

Creation of the Compensation Commission

At the end of the Gulf War, the Security Council was well aware that the model of adversarial case-by-case arbitration represented by the Iran-U.S. Claims Tribunal would be wholly inadequate to handle the claims against Iraq, and it was determined to pursue an entirely different course. In its Resolution 686 of March 2, 1991 (when coalition forces had just completed their successful Desert Storm campaign), the Council demanded, as one of the conditions for an end of hostilities, that Iraq "accept in principle its liability under international law" for loss and damage resulting from the invasion and occupation of Kuwait—a demand with which Iraq was forced to comply.

One month later, the Council decided, in Resolution 687 (its comprehensive "mother of all resolutions" that ended the conflict) "that Iraq . . . is liable under international law for any direct loss, damage—including environmental damage and the depletion of natural resources—or injury to foreign governments, nationals, and corporations as a result of its unlawful invasion and occupation of Kuwait." The Council further decided to create a fund to pay for these claims and a commission to administer the fund, and decided that the fund would be constituted from the deduction of a percentage of the value of Iraq's future oil exports. The Council asked the secretary-general to provide recommendations for the structuring of these institutions, for the process of adjudicating and paying claims, and for the percentage to be deducted from Iraqi oil revenues.

In response, the secretary-general recommended that a United Nations Compensation Commission be created as a subsidiary organ of the Council, to be directed by a fifteen-member Governing Council. The Governing Council would have the same composition as the Security Council itself but could make decisions on almost all issues by majority vote and without regard to the veto. The Governing Council would be assisted by expert commissioners who would examine the specific claims and make recommendations on their validity and value, and by a secretariat headed by an executive secretary to administer the fund and the claims process. The final decisions on awards and payments would be made by the Governing Council itself.[7] The secretary-general then recommended that up to 30 percent of Iraq's oil export revenues be deposited into the fund, to both compensate claimants and pay for UNCC operations.[8]

Iraq immediately objected that under these proposals, the Council, as a political body, would exceed its Charter authority by making decisions on what Iraq considered to be "judicial matters" that would more properly be handled by the International Court of Justice. According to Iraq, the "absolute powers" to be given to the Governing Council "have never been given to any international organization in modern history."[9] The council was not at all persuaded by these objections and proceeded to accept the secretary-general's recommendations.[10]

Framework of the compensation process

It then fell to the Governing Council to make a series of decisions as to what claims would be eligible for compensation and how claims would be processed and paid. The Governing Council decided that its first priority would be the prompt provision of relief to the hundreds of thousands of individuals who were displaced or injured as a result of the Iraqi invasion. For this purpose, the Governing Council permitted persons who had departed from Iraq or Kuwait during the war; or who had suffered serious personal injury; or whose spouse, parent, or child had died to apply for a fixed sum of $2,500 without having to prove their actual loss. (If the loss was greater, the claimant could choose instead to prove the actual loss in a later stage of the process.[11]) Through this expedited mechanism, more than $3 billion was promptly awarded to resolve more than 900,000 claims.[12]

Next, the Governing Council established an expedited process
for considering other claims of individuals for losses of up to $100,000
as a result of death, personal injury, or departure during the war.
These claims had to be documented by "appropriate evidence" of the
circumstances and the amount of the loss, but only the "reasonable
minimum" of documentation "that is appropriate under the circumstances" had to be submitted.[13] Relying on modern techniques for
mass claims, such as sampling, statistical modeling, computerized
analysis, and standardized determinations for classes of similar claims,
the UNCC awarded more than $5 billion to resolve more than 1.7
million claims in this category.[14]

Next are the largest claims of individuals, corporations, governments, and international organizations—smaller in number (more
than 20,000) but much larger in claimed value (more than $300 bil-
lion).[15] They include such large and complex claims as the oil sector
claims, the claims for environmental destruction, and the large construction contract claims. For these categories, the Governing Council decided early on that it might "refer unusually large or complex
claims to panels of commissioners for detailed review, possibly
involving additional written submissions and oral proceedings" at
which the claimant would be allowed to present its case directly to
the panel.[16]

Nonetheless, even as the process began to look somewhat more
like case-by-case arbitration, the UNCC still used methods to expedite and simplify the resolution of these large claims through such
methods as grouping of similar claims, resolution of common issues
for the various categories, and standard valuation methods.[17] The
Governing Council has also issued detailed guidance concerning the
elements of loss that would be compensable. For example, in the case
of environmental claims, it specified that compensation may be
sought for losses or expenses resulting from abatement and prevention of environmental damage, measures to clean up and restore the
environment, monitoring and assessment of environmental damage,
monitoring of public health, and depletion or damage to natural
resources.[18] In the end, the UNCC awarded more than $45 billion to
resolve more than 20,000 claims in these categories.[19]

In June 2005, the UNCC completed its processing of claims in all categories, awarding a total of more than $52 billion.[20] This total far exceeds that of any other international claims process.

From the start, it was recognized that it would not be easy to find funds to pay such a large volume of awards. The Compensation Fund was to be financed by a 30 percent deduction from Iraqi oil exports, but Iraq failed to meet the Security Council's preconditions for resumption of commercial exports (particularly with respect to the elimination of WMD). The Council nonetheless decided in 1991, as an exception to the embargo, to allow Iraq to export substantial amounts of oil to pay for humanitarian imports, with 30 percent of the proceeds going to the Compensation Fund, but Iraq refused for years to do so.[21] To meet the operating expenses of the UNCC during these first few years, the Security Council provided for the liquidation and transfer to the Compensation Fund of certain of the proceeds of Iraqi oil shipments that had been in transit at the outset of the war, but this did not allow payment of any substantial portion of the outstanding claims.[22]

In 1995, Iraq finally agreed to begin exports under the Council's Oil-for-Food Program, and from that time forward (with periodic interruptions by Iraq to make political points) substantial amounts began to flow into the Compensation Fund.[23] The initial amount of exports allowed in 1995 ($4 billion per year) was raised in 1998 to more than $10 billion; in 1999, the ceiling on allowable exports for these purposes was lifted altogether.[24] Following the 2003 invasion of Iraq and the removal of the Saddam Hussein regime, the Security Council decided that the Oil-for-Food Program would be terminated and that all proceeds from future Iraqi oil exports would be deposited into the Development Fund administered by the United States and United Kingdom until such time as an internationally recognized Iraqi government would be constituted, with a percentage of these proceeds to be deposited into the Compensation Fund. The obligation to contribute to the Compensation Fund will continue to be binding on the Iraqi government unless that government and the UNCC decide otherwise at some future date.[25] However, one political result of Saddam Hussein's removal was the reduction in the percentage for the Compensation Fund to 5 percent.[26]

Because of these limitations on available funds, from time to time the Governing Council has had to make decisions on the priority of payment of awards. Consistent with its basic priorities, the Governing Council decided at an early point that the small individual claims would be paid before payments would begin for other categories.[27] In the second phase of payments, the Governing Council decided that up to $100,000 would be paid for approved claims in all categories.[28] In the third phase, claimants in the larger categories were to receive payments of up to $5 million each, and then $10 million, with priority given to environmental monitoring and assessment claims.[29] However, the reduction in the percentage for the Compensation Fund will necessitate slower payment to claimants.

As a result, full payment of all the largest claims—particularly those of governments—is unlikely in the foreseeable future. However, the UNCC has already, as of mid-2005, paid more than $19 billion to claimants, and the decisions on priority for adjudication and payment of claims have ensured that virtually all of the highest-priority categories of awards, particularly the individual claimants who most needed compensation, have been paid on a reasonably prompt basis.[30] These achievements go far beyond those of any previous international claims process.

Policy decisions behind the process

The UNCC program has been the product of certain fundamental decisions by the Security Council and its "alter ego," the Governing Council, to carry out the Security Council's basic policy priorities in restoring the damage done by the war and in putting the burden for that restoration on the aggressor. These decisions were not simply a mirror of existing law or practice but, rather, were based on a unique calculation of policy priorities in the specific context of the Gulf War and a judgment about what the program might feasibly attempt to do, given the enormity of the loss and the limited resources likely to be available. The result has been a claims program that has differed in fundamental ways from international arbitral programs like the Iran-U.S. Claims Tribunal.

First of all, the Security Council determined from the start that the Iraqi invasion and occupation was illegal and that Iraq was liable for the consequences. This decision dispensed with the need for litigation before the commission on the legality of Iraqi actions, which would have been both politically undesirable and potentially time-consuming, and it eliminated one of the possible arguments for giving Iraq a co-equal adversarial role in the process, which might have substantially complicated and prolonged it. Some questioned the appropriateness of a political body rendering such legal judgments, but in fact the determination that a state has committed aggression is an explicit part of the Council's authority under Chapter VII, and international law is clear that an aggressor is liable for damage caused by its aggression.[31]

The second major difference in the UNCC regards the scope of losses to be compensated, which was defined in a way that addressed both the need for expeditious action and the limited resources available. The Security Council offered compensation for "direct" loss or damage resulting from the Iraqi invasion and occupation of Kuwait, which the Governing Council defined as including losses resulting from (1) military operations or the threat of military action by either side; (2) departure from or inability to leave Iraq or Kuwait during the war; (3) actions by Iraqi officials, employees, or controlled entities in connection with the invasion or occupation; (4) the breakdown of civil order in Kuwait or Iraq during the war; and (5) hostage taking or other illegal detention.[32] This definition eliminated from the outset issues that had complicated other arbitral proceedings (such as the liability of a government for civil disorder and voluntary departures) and avoided potentially distracting issues about the reasonableness and lawfulness of coalition military actions.[33]

On the other hand, certain categories of losses were excluded from compensation from the fund, even though they would not have occurred if Iraq had not invaded Kuwait. In particular, the Governing Council excluded losses suffered as a result of the trade embargo and related measures taken by the Council against Iraq; the ostensible reason was that the "causal link" between the Iraqi invasion and the embargo losses was "not sufficiently direct," but a compelling factor was obviously the fact that the sheer magnitude and open-ended character of such claims would have severely depleted the fund's resources.[34] For much the same reason, the Governing Council declined to give compensation based simply on the generally chaotic economic situation that followed the Iraqi invasion (including a sharp rise in oil prices and reduction in tourism and other business activity in the region).[35]

The Governing Council likewise refused to give compensation for the cost to coalition members of conducting the Desert Shield and Desert Storm military operations, and denied compensation for loss or injury to members of coalition military forces (with the exception of the unlawful treatment of coalition prisoners of war).[36] These costs and losses were arguably very direct, and injured coalition troops and the families of those killed in action were clearly deserving of compensation; but the majority of the Governing Council had no desire to pay for military operations and expected coalition governments to take care of their own military personnel.

The Security Council also decided that it would not attempt to bring Iraq's prewar debts into this scheme, partly because they were obviously not a result of the invasion and occupation of Kuwait, partly because they were so large as to deplete the resources of the Compensation Fund, and partly because traditional mechanisms already existed for servicing and paying such debts. The Council therefore limited itself to demanding that Iraq "adhere scrupulously to all of its obligations concerning servicing and repayment of its foreign debt," noting that these matters would "be addressed through the normal mechanisms" and requiring that the secretary-general take into account the amounts needed for external debt service when deciding on the size of the deduction to be made from Iraqi oil proceeds for the Compensation Fund.[37]

These various exclusions were not based on the conclusion that Iraq was not liable for the losses excluded, and in fact states were free to pursue such claims against Iraq in whatever forum they might find and against whatever Iraqi assets they might be able to locate.[38] Rather, they were pragmatic and policy judgments that the limited resources of the Compensation Fund should not be used for these claims.

A third difference in the UNCC's new approach was that the Security Council, with its responsibility to the international community as a whole, did not limit compensation to the nationals and governments of particular states (a common aspect of international arbitral agreements) but offered compensation to the nationals of all states, and also to persons who were not represented by any state— namely, the large numbers of Palestinian workers who had to leave Iraq and Kuwait during the war. (This required the adoption of special arrangements with international organizations to process and submit Palestinian claims.[39]) The only exception was the exclusion of Iraqi nationals, although an Iraqi with genuine dual nationality could submit a claim through his or her other state of nationality.[40] Also, as already noted, the Governing Council decided from the outset that, unlike the Iran-U.S. Claims Tribunal and other arbitral bodies, it would give strict priority in both processing and payment to the claims of the hundreds of thousands of individuals displaced or injured by the Iraqi invasion and occupation. One practical effect was that the dominant members of the Security Council gave priority to the nationals of South Asian and Middle Eastern countries over their own nationals and corporations.

In addition, the Governing Council abandoned the traditional formal adversary procedures of international arbitration in favor of expedited administrative procedures and methods that reduced the process to its simplest terms. This was a matter of necessity in that the UNCC could not conceivably have processed even a small fraction of its claims within the lifetime of any living person under traditional arbitral procedures.

Another difference in the UNCC's approach concerns procedural matters. The Governing Council gave Iraq a relatively minimal role in the proceedings of the UNCC in comparison with that normally afforded to the contending governments in international arbitral proceedings. Iraq was given the right to address the Governing Council, to give comments on claims filed, and to make such additional submissions as it chose, but it did not have the rights of a party to arbitral proceedings—such as an equal voice in determining the composition of arbitral panels and the right to formal hearings in which it could present at length its views on all claims.[41] Arbitrating parties have sometimes used these rights to obstruct or delay proceedings against them—as Iran did in the Iran-U.S. Claims Tribunal—and the Security Council was determined not to give Iraq the same opportunity in the UNCC. Iraq complained repeatedly about this aspect of the UNCC process, but the Governing Council did not find merit in those objections in light of the administrative and non-adversarial character of the commission.

Last, the method adopted by the Security Council for obtaining the very large amounts of money required to provide the compensation being awarded by the UNCC was designed specifically for the Iraqi situation. Iraqi oil exports provide a large source of revenue with an unusually high margin of surplus over production cost, and these exports can, for all practical purposes, continue indefinitely. Maritime shipment of oil is, by and large, controllable by naval forces (although considerable leakage and evasion is of course possible and did occur). Since oil export was almost the exclusive source of Iraqi export earnings, Iraq had a considerable incentive to ship oil and to accept the deduction of compensation as a condition of doing so.

The UNCC as precedent

When measured against the purposes the Council intended it to serve, the UNCC has been a considerable success. It has provided monetary relief and a sense of redress to dozens of governments and hundreds of thousands of individuals. It has provided another means by which the international community can impose real consequences on aggressor states and thereby perhaps have some deterrent effect on potential aggressors in the future, as well as restore the victim states and lessen their vulnerability to renewed aggression. The United States was the key proponent and player in the creation and operation of the UNCC.[42]

It is also important to note, in light of the recent exposure of the serious flaws in the structure and administration of the UN Oil-for-Food Program (as described in chapter 3), that the UNCC experience shows that a complex program on the same order of magnitude as the Oil-for-Food Program can be run effectively within the UN structure under the authority of the Security Council. The UNCC operated under a clear line of authority to the Governing Council, which gave definite policy guidance and exercised continuing oversight throughout the process. The commission had a large, dedicated, and expert staff and sufficient financial resources. It made decisions based on legal and technical criteria, supported by detailed analysis.

Iraq was not allowed to impede or corrupt the process, and political intrusion by other governments into the process does not appear to have been any significant problem.

Much of the work of the UNCC could provide important precedents for future international claims programs. This is particularly true of its administrative structure and methods (as opposed to the formal adversarial process typical of international arbitral tribunals), the modern expedited procedures it adopted to deal with mass claims, and the development of substantive law in the consideration of different theories of relief and measures of compensation.

However, there have been no clones of the UNCC in the decade since its creation, and it would be unrealistic to think that the UNCC model will be routinely replicated in future conflict situations where there is a need for compensation for massive amounts of war damage. The UNCC model was based on several circumstances that will infrequently occur together: (1) a conflict in which one side is clearly the aggressor; (2) the readiness of the Security Council to condemn that side and to impose continuing liability on it for the consequences of the war; (3) the decisive defeat of the condemned side, which was accordingly compelled to acquiesce in the transfer of massive amounts of resources to its victims; (4) the ability of that defeated state—notwithstanding its own severe losses—to generate a large volume of revenues that might be used for compensation; and (5) the availability of a source of revenue that can be substantially controlled and exploited by the international community without having to occupy the defeated country for a prolonged period. This combination of circumstances was not present in the cases of Bosnia, Kosovo, Rwanda, Somalia, Sierra Leone, Angola, East Timor, Afghanistan, or any of the other conflicts of the post–Cold War period in which there were large numbers of victims and considerable damage.

Nonetheless, the UNCC experience does demonstrate once again the scope of the Security Council's authority to address the consequences of conflict and in particular its ability to combine creative legal mechanisms with its coercive powers under Chapter VII. Where there is the political will to do so, the Council could draw elements from the UNCC model to create compensation programs uniquely suitable for future conflict situations, even if none is a precise copy of the UNCC. The same might be done with respect to victims of international terrorism, if adequate funding could be found for the purpose.

Other compensation models

Although no other situation has yet arisen that would lend itself to the full scope of the UNCC model, other approaches have been taken with the authority or support of the Council to compensate for damage caused by armed conflict or terrorism.

In the case of the destruction of Pan American Flight 103 by Libyan agents, one of the Council's principal demands was that Libya provide adequate compensation to the families of the victims.[43] It enforced this demand by imposing economic and political sanctions that would not be lifted until Libya complied.[44] In September 2003, following a long process of negotiation between the Libyan government and the Pan Am 103 families on arrangements for compensation, the Council indicated its satisfaction by lifting the sanctions.[45]

Libya had argued, among other things, that the Council, as a political body, had no authority to decide in effect that Libya was legally responsible for the incident, and that such a decision should have been left to the International Court of Justice or some other juridical body. However, the Gulf War precedent shows that the Council does have the authority under Chapter VII to confirm or impose liability on the perpetrators of unlawful acts of force as part of its general authority to restore and maintain international peace and security. Where the provision of compensation is deemed necessary to avert the use of force or to reduce its chances of recurrence in the future, it is well within the Council's Chapter VII authority to require compensation and to specify the means for providing it.

The Libyan case could provide a model for action in any situation in which the Council is prepared to impose a duty of compensation on a state (or other entity) and to enforce it through the use of Chapter VII sanctions, but is not prepared to specify the basis for the awarding and payment of compensation or to create institutional machinery for the purpose. This gives flexibility to the parties affected to determine the modalities, which could include agreement on a lump-sum payment to the victims, submission of claims to a national court or international tribunal, or even the creation of a new tribunal or commission for the purpose. On the other hand, the negotiation of such a solution between perpetrator and victim could be difficult, and the Council's imposition of sanctions may not provide sufficient incentive for a prompt and effective solution. It is a model that may be better suited for discrete incidents like the Pan Am 103 case rather than situations of massive destruction and chaos like the Gulf War.

Other mechanisms for compensation were created in the case of the ad hoc international criminal tribunals for Rwanda and the former Yugoslavia, and the hybrid court for Sierra Leone (which are discussed in the next chapter)—each of which were sanctioned by the Security Council. The statute of the Yugoslav tribunal provides that a trial chamber, in sentencing a convicted defendant, may order the return of any property and proceeds acquired by criminal conduct to their rightful owners.[46] The rules of the tribunal provide that the competent authorities of the state concerned are to be informed of the conviction of any accused for a crime that has caused injury, that the victim may bring action in national court (or other competent body) for compensation, and that for this purpose the tribunal's judgment shall be final and binding as to the criminal responsibility of the convicted defendant.[47] Similar provisions were adopted in the case of the Rwanda tribunal and the special court for Sierra Leone.[48]

Such provisions may be useful in particular cases, assuming that a defendant can be found who has possession of illegally acquired property or otherwise has assets that can be attached for use in suits brought by his or her victim. Apart from the compensation actually provided, such remedies also reinforce the responsibility of the convicted defendant and the sense of redress for the victim. However, such remedies are limited in their application to the individual perpetrators and victims of successfully prosecuted crimes and to the assets in the hands of those perpetrators. They would provide little or no relief to the great majority of those suffering injury or loss in conflict situations.

Another compensation program of limited scope was established for Bosnia by Annex 7 to the Dayton Peace Agreement, which gives refugees and displaced persons the right either to have restored to them property of which they were deprived in the course of the hostilities or to be compensated for any property that cannot be restored.[49] A commission was created to implement these rights—now known as the Commission for Real Property Claims of Displaced Persons and Refugees. Compensation for any unrestored property was to be paid from a Refugees and Displaced Persons Property Fund, which was to receive the proceeds of property transactions by the commission and contributions from Bosnian authorities or international donors.[50]

In December 2000, at the end of the two-year war between Ethiopia and Eritrea, the two sides signed an agreement providing for a termination of hostilities and, among other things, creating an Ethiopia-Eritrea Claims Commission to decide all claims related to the conflict by one government against the other, or by the nationals of one against the government of the other. The commission was to be a more traditional claims exercise: each government appointed two of its five members, with a president selected by the others. Claims were to be submitted by each government for itself and its nationals; these claims were to be decided through binding arbitration. The agreement provided that claims would be submitted within one year and that the commission would endeavor to complete its work within a further three years.[51] In 2003, the process of deciding claims began with a series of partial awards concerning the treatment of prisoners of war by the two sides, followed in 2004 with partial awards concerning other governmental actions.[52]

This claims process was the product of bilateral agreement and not authorization by the Security Council. However, it is operating in the context of a conflict in which (as described later) the Council has been involved in various important ways, including the creation of a peacekeeping mission to monitor the separation of the forces of the two sides and various forms of support for a boundary commission to resolve the border dispute underlying the conflict. It is an illustration of how traditional claims settlement methods can be used in a conflict situation in which the Security Council is otherwise exercising its Chapter VII authorities to end the conflict and deal with its consequences.

Territorial Disputes

Background

Disputes concerning boundaries and sovereignty over territory have long been one of the classic subjects of international law and litigation. Such disputes (if not settled by war) have traditionally been resolved by negotiation, arbitration, or submission to international tribunals. Roughly a third of the cases decided by the International Court of Justice have involved such disputes, including a number in which the dispute had led to (or resulted from) armed conflict.[53] During the Cold War, the Security Council became involved in such disputes only where there was an immediate threat of conflict, and even then typically did not attempt to dictate the solution to the underlying dispute. However, in the case of the Iraqi invasion of Kuwait, it became essential for the Council to address the boundary issue directly as a means of restoring and maintaining the peace.

One of the ostensible causes of the war was the ongoing dispute between Iraq and Kuwait over their mutual land and maritime boundary. (Of course, Iraq's ultimate position was that Kuwait was merely a province of Iraq and its ultimate objective was the permanent occupation and annexation of all of Kuwait.) One of the primary objectives of the Security Council at the end of the Gulf conflict was to confirm the sovereignty and independence of Kuwait and to resolve, once and for all, the location of the boundary.

After World War I and the collapse of the Ottoman Empire, the United Kingdom administered Kuwait as a self-governing protectorate. When Iraq became independent in 1932, the Iraqi and Kuwaiti authorities confirmed their acceptance of the boundary as it had been defined by Britain and the Ottoman Empire prior to the war. In 1961, the United Kingdom recognized the full independence of Kuwait, but Iraq contested its independence and objected to the continuing presence of British troops. Because the Soviet Union supported the Iraqi position, it was initially impossible for the Security Council to resolve the matter. However, in 1963, following the withdrawal of British forces and their replacement by Arab League forces, a set of Agreed Minutes was signed in which Iraq accepted the independence of Kuwait and the boundary that had been confirmed in 1932.[54]

After the end of the Iran-Iraq War, Saddam Hussein began to press various claims against Kuwait, including the allegation that Kuwait was illegally occupying certain Iraqi islands and blocking Iraq's maritime access to the Gulf. On August 2, 1990, Iraq began its invasion of Kuwait, claiming in the Security Council that it would withdraw "as soon as order has been restored." However, on August 7, Iraq announced its "comprehensive, eternal, and inseparable merger" with Kuwait.[55] The Security Council reacted strongly to the invasion and annexation, demanding immediate Iraqi withdrawal and deciding on August 9 "that annexation of Kuwait by Iraq under any form and whatever pretext has no legal validity, and is considered null and void."[56]

The creation of the Boundary Commission

At the conclusion of Operation Desert Storm, the Council included, as one of its preconditions for a definitive end of the hostilities, a demand that Iraq rescind its purported annexation—and Iraq was forced to accept the Council's demands.[57] Then, in the omnibus Resolution 687, the Council noted Iraq's acceptance in 1963 of Kuwaiti independence and the previously established boundary, called on the secretary-general to make arrangements with Iraq and Kuwait to demarcate it, and decided to "guarantee the inviolability" of the boundary that would be so demarcated.[58] In support of these decisions, the Council created a demilitarized zone on either side of that boundary and authorized a UN observer unit (UNIKOM) to monitor the zone.[59]

Resolution 687 declared that a formal cease-fire would be effective upon official notification by Iraq of its acceptance of the resolution. Three days later, the Iraqi foreign minister sent the president of the Council a letter complaining that "the Security Council has determined in advance the boundary between Iraq and Kuwait. And yet it is well known, from the juridical and practical standpoint, that in international relations boundary issues must be the subject of an agreement between states, since this is the only basis capable of guaranteeing the stability of frontiers." Iraq further asserted that the 1963

Agreed Minutes confirming the boundary had never been properly ratified by Iraq, "thus leaving the question of the boundary pending and unresolved." Yet the letter stated that Iraq had "no choice but to accept this resolution."[60] After consultation with the Iraqi representative, the president of the Security Council took this communication as Iraq's acceptance of Resolution 687—"irrevocable and without qualifying conditions"—and the Council agreed that the formal cease-fire was therefore effective.[61]

Two months later, the secretary-general submitted his report to the Council on the arrangements for the demarcation of the boundary. He stated that an Iraq-Kuwait Boundary Demarcation Commission would be established, to be composed of one representative each of Iraq and Kuwait and three independent experts to be appointed by him (with decisions to be taken by majority vote). The task of the commission was to demarcate in geographical coordinates the international boundary set out in general terms in the 1963 Agreed Minutes, and then to arrange for the erection of pillars to mark that boundary on the ground.[62]

Kuwait readily accepted these terms. Iraq, on the other hand, reiterated its objections to the process and to the 1963 Agreed Minutes but indicated that it would appoint a representative to take part in the commission "because the circumstances forcing our acceptance persist."[63] The Iraqi appointee did in fact participate in the commission during its first year of work but then absented himself during its second year.[64]

Both the Security Council and the commission insisted that the commission was "not reallocating territory between Kuwait and Iraq," because that matter had already been resolved by the 1963 Agreed Minutes, which the Council had confirmed and Iraq had again accepted at the end of the Gulf War. Rather, the commission was "simply carrying out the technical task necessary to demarcate the precise coordinates of the boundary."[65] For this purpose, the commission used aerial photography, satellite observations, physical surveys, and searches of the historical record, and it produced a detailed list of coordinates, a map depicting the demarcation, and an array of physical markers along the boundary. Apart from these technical tasks, the commission also had to interpret the 1963 agreement on a number of points and make decisions about rights of maritime navigation and access.[66]

The commission's final report was submitted to the Council in May 1993, and the Council promptly acted under Chapter VII to reaffirm that the commission's decisions were final, to demand that Iraq and Kuwait respect the inviolability of the boundary as demarcated by the commission, and to "guarantee" its inviolability and "to take as appropriate all necessary measures to that end."[67] Kuwait welcomed the report and agreed to abide by it.[68] Iraq reiterated its objections and denounced the commission's work as "one link in the chain of Western imperialist games which began after the First World War and which have always been the subject of indignation and rejection on the part of the Arab Nation."[69] But in due course, as part of an effort to gather international support for a lifting of sanctions, Iraq notified the United Nations that its National Assembly had formally declared its recognition of the independence of Kuwait and its acceptance of the boundary as demarcated by the commission.[70]

The Council's authority

The Council obviously did not give credence to the Iraqi objection that it did not have the authority to resolve the issues of Kuwait's sovereignty and boundaries. UN officials stressed that Iraq had agreed to Kuwaiti sovereignty and the location of the boundary long before the war and reconfirmed that agreement at the end of the war. One may ask whether Iraq's acceptance of Resolution 687 at the end of the Gulf War was binding in light of the fact that it was obviously the product of irresistible military force. The technical answer is that only the threat or use of force in violation of international law voids such consent, which of course would not apply to the use of force with the Council's authorization under Chapter VII.[71] The practical answer is that it would be impossible to conclude binding cease-fire, armistice, and peace agreements if the losing party were then able to renounce them because its consent was the product of its military defeat.

In any event, when Iraq invaded, the Council had to decide the question of Kuwaiti sovereignty to determine if the Iraqi actions constituted aggression; it had to determine where the boundary was located to establish a cease-fire, a demilitarized zone, and a peacekeeping force to patrol it; and it needed a definitive and final confirmation and demarcation of the boundary in order to restore a lasting peace. In theory, these matters could have been decided on an interim basis, pending decisions by some authoritative body like the International Court of Justice. However, the reopening of these questions in the aftermath of the war—in the context of a judicial process that could be expected to take years to conclude—would not have been conducive to restoring peace and stability in the region, and the Council was not about to give any credence to Iraq's highly dangerous territorial claims. This stance was perfectly reasonable and well within the scope of the Council's authority under Chapter VII.[72] (Indeed, as argued earlier, in an extreme case the Council might even direct a change in national boundaries if necessary to deter or help prevent future aggression.)

The Boundary Commission as a precedent

In the decade since the end of the Gulf War, the Security Council has been involved in the resolution of a number of disputes over territory and sovereignty. In some cases, the Council intervened directly. When civil war broke out in Yugoslavia in the early 1990s, the Council had to take a position on the sovereignty and territorial integrity of its constituent republics—treating the Socialist Federal Republic as a single state until the spring of 1992, but in May 1992 voting to admit Bosnia, Croatia, and Slovenia as UN members, and from that point forward insisting on respect for the territory of the new states within their boundaries as former Yugoslav republics.[73] Seven years later, the Council reaffirmed the sovereignty of the Federal Republic of Yugoslavia (that is, Serbia and Montenegro) over Kosovo, while providing an international "interim administration" for the province that would give it "substantial autonomy." In both cases, the Council authorized the deployment of international forces to ensure that its decisions were respected.

In other cases, the Council supported the resolution of such issues by other bodies. In 1990, Chad and Libya submitted their dispute over the Aouzou Strip to the International Court of Justice, which decided on the location of the boundary in 1994 (in accordance with the position of Chad). The two governments then requested the Security Council to deploy a team of observers to monitor and confirm the withdrawal of Libyan forces to the boundary established by the court, and in response, the Council created the UN Aouzou Strip Observer Group (UNASOG), which successfully did so.[74]

In 1998, after Ethiopia and Eritrea resorted to war to resolve their long-standing border dispute, the Council asked the secretary-general to provide technical support to the parties to assist in the eventual delimitation and demarcation of the border and established a trust fund for the purpose.[75] After two years of bloody hostilities, the two sides reached an Agreement on Cessation of Hostilities, which, among other things, established a "temporary security zone" from which the opposing forces would withdraw, asked the United Nations to establish a peacekeeping force to patrol it, and committed themselves to a peaceful resolution of the border dispute through arbitration.[76] The Security Council responded by deploying a UN Mission in Ethiopia and Eritrea (UNMEE) to monitor the separation process and the security zone, and to clear land mines in the affected areas.[77]

Then in December 2000, the two sides concluded a more comprehensive agreement (already noted previously in the context of claims), which provided for the establishment of a commission to delimit and demarcate the boundary—with two members appointed by each side and a president to be selected by them—operating with the assistance of the UN cartographer and financed by the Council's 1998 trust fund and by contributions from the parties.[78] The Boundary Commission received submissions from the parties and issued its decision in April 2002.[79] In the next phase of the project—the demarcation of the boundary on the ground—the UN force has provided or is prepared to provide various essential services, including the clearance of land mines from the demarcation sites and access routes to them, administrative and logistical support to the demarcation teams, and monitoring of the transfer of national control over border areas to comply with the newly established boundary.[80] However, even though both sides had initially accepted the commission's delimitation decision, Ethiopia later expressed serious concerns and held up demarcation of important parts of the boundary unless its objections were resolved in its favor, which led to an impasse in the entire process.[81]

Where there is no immediate threat to the peace, territorial disputes are often resolved by arbitration or submission to the International Court of Justice, without any particular involvement by the Security Council. This is the case, for example, of a dozen or so territorial disputes brought to the court during the past decade, typically by agreement between the parties. In none of these cases did the Council authorize the creation of a UN technical commission to resolve a territorial dispute, as it did in the Iraq-Kuwait case.

Where the parties to a dispute have created their own means for resolution of territorial questions—whether through an ad hoc arbitration process or by submission to the International Court of Justice—there is no need for the Council to take matters into its own hands. Rather, it can support the solution chosen by the parties by deploying peacekeepers to preserve the peace while the boundary is resolved or by assisting in the implementation of the boundary decision. However, should there again be a need for Council action to resolve a dangerous territorial dispute where the matter cannot be safely left to the parties, the Iraq-Kuwait solution provides a very useful precedent.

Control of Arms

Background

For the most part, the control of arms during the Cold War era was accomplished through agreements among states, either bilateral (such as the U.S.-Soviet strategic arms treaties) or multilateral (such as the treaties on nuclear nonproliferation and biological weapons).[82] Some of these agreements gave theoretical roles to the Security Council in their enforcement. For example, the 1972 Biological Weapons Convention provided that a party may lodge a complaint with the Security Council of alleged noncompliance by any other party, that all parties undertake to cooperate with any Council investigation of such a complaint, and that every party undertake to assist any other party that the Council decided had been exposed to danger as a result of a violation.[83] Some multilateral agreements also provided that advance notices of withdrawal be sent to the Security Council, presumably to give the Council the opportunity to act if a withdrawal threatened the peace.[84] Of course, the Council did not need such provisions to deal under Chapter VII with any violations or withdrawals that might threaten the peace, but Cold War divisions on the Council precluded any possibility of Council action on allegations affecting the permanent members.

Further, as described in chapter 3, the sanctions imposed on Southern Rhodesia and South Africa prohibited the supply of arms of all kinds, as well as related equipment, technical data, and training. And as noted in chapter 4, the mandates of "first-generation" peacekeeping missions during the Cold War era often included monitoring and enforcing agreements on force withdrawals, demobilization, disarmament, and mine clearance. These actions inhibited the acquisition of dangerous weapons but in no case amounted to a comprehensive prohibition on their development, acquisition, or retention by the state or faction in question, nor a comprehensive scheme for the enforcement of such a prohibition.

Measures against Iraq

By the conclusion of the Gulf War, it had become evident that a comprehensive regime was needed to eliminate Iraq's WMD and long-range delivery systems, and to prevent Iraq from reacquiring them in the future. Resolution 687—the Council's "mother of all resolutions" that set forth the terms of the permanent cease-fire—took several steps toward this end.

First, it "invited" Iraq to "reaffirm unconditionally" its obligations as a party to the multilateral agreements that prohibited it from using chemical and biological weapons, acquiring or retaining biological weapons, and acquiring nuclear weapons.[85] Second, it "decided that Iraq shall unconditionally accept" the destruction of all chemical and biological weapons, all nuclear-weapon-usable materials, all ballistic missiles with a range greater than 150 kilometers, and all related equipment and facilities, and that it "shall unconditionally undertake" not to use, develop, or acquire these items.[86] Third, it decided that "Iraq shall submit" comprehensive declarations of the location, amounts, and types of all such items in its possession and agree to international on-site inspection to verify Iraqi compliance with its obligations.[87] Fourth, it assigned the task of international inspection to the International Atomic Energy Agency (IAEA) regarding nuclear items, and to a special commission to be created regarding the other items.[88] Fifth, it conditioned the lifting of the embargo on imports of Iraqi goods on compliance with these weapons-related obligations and provided for the indefinite continuation of the embargo on the exports to Iraq of all arms and related material.[89]

As with other aspects of Resolution 687, the conclusion of a formal cease-fire was conditional on Iraqi acceptance of all these provisions. As noted earlier, the Iraqi foreign minister informed the president of the Council that Iraq had no choice but to accept the resolution, and the Council and the secretary-general insisted that Iraq was obligated to carry out these requirements unconditionally.

At the Council's request, the secretary-general and the IAEA submitted plans for carrying out these inspections. In particular, the secretary-general proposed—and the Council approved—the creation of a special commission (UNSCOM) with an executive chairman who would supervise the operation of five groups of international experts, to be assisted by a large number of inspectors, disposal teams, and field support officers.[90]

Thus began a long, painful, and well-documented process in which the commission achieved considerable successes in finding and eliminating Iraqi weapons and facilities, but in which Iraq also regularly concealed prohibited items, falsified declarations, and obstructed commission inspections.[91] In response, the Council repeatedly demanded that Iraq allow the UNSCOM and IAEA inspectors "immediate, unconditional, and unrestricted access to any and all areas, facilities, equipment, records, and means of transportation which they wish to inspect" and cease all attempts at concealment.[92] As described in chapter 5, the Council determined on a number of occasions that Iraq's actions constituted "a material breach" of its obligations under the cease-fire resolution, and coalition forces carried out a series of air strikes against suspect WMD sites and the Iraqi forces that protected them, culminating in missile and air strikes in December 1998 following Iraq's halting of cooperation with UNSCOM.[93]

One year later, in an effort to restart UN inspections, the Council replaced UNSCOM with a UN Monitoring, Verification, and

Inspection Commission, which assumed UNSCOM's functions and, like UNSCOM, would have "immediate, unconditional, and unrestricted access" to all areas and facilities it might wish to inspect in Iraq. UNMOVIC had an executive chairman and a College of Commissioners that was to meet regularly to provide "advice and guidance" to the executive chairman including in his submission of reports on Iraqi compliance.[94] In November 2002, the Council determined that Iraq remained in material breach and decided to give Iraq a "final opportunity" to comply, setting up an "enhanced inspection regime" that involved, among other things, a requirement for another full and complete declaration and a set of enhanced powers for UNMOVIC and the IAEA.[95]

Although Iraq then permitted these agencies to conduct their inspections, the results were still unsatisfactory to the U.S.-led coalition, which in 2003 abandoned the reliance on international inspections and occupied Iraq by force. In Resolution 1483—the comprehensive resolution that set the framework for postconflict cooperation between the UN and the occupying powers—the Council reaffirmed that Iraq must meet its disarmament obligations but stated its intention to "revisit" the mandates of UNMOVIC and the IAEA and lifted the sanctions (except for the arms embargo) that had served until then as the guarantee of Iraqi disarmament.

These events gave rise to a vigorous debate as to whether UN inspections were essentially a success that the coalition aborted for larger political objectives or a failure that had to be remedied through the use of force, though as time has passed there have been increasing indications that the inspections process and the related UN sanctions were in fact more successful in deterring Iraqi reacquisition of WMD stocks than had widely been assumed.[96] In any case, for the purpose of this chapter, the Council had clear authority to both require the elimination of these weapons and use inspections or sanctions or armed force to achieve that objective.

Broader action against arms proliferation

Thus far the Council has not created a body similar to UNSCOM/UNMOVIC in any other situation. Most other efforts by the Council in the post–Cold War period to control dangerous arms stocks and capabilities with respect to particular countries have followed the patterns established during the Cold War era. As described in chapter 3, the Council imposed restrictions or prohibitions on the supply of arms to a number of sanctioned countries under Chapter VII, including Yugoslavia, Somalia, Libya, Liberia, Haiti, Rwanda, Ethiopia, and Eritrea. As described in chapter 4, the Council's "first-," "second-," and "third-generation" peacekeeping missions often included extensive efforts to disarm local forces and eliminate dangerous stocks of weapons, including missions in Angola, Mozambique, Liberia, Cambodia, the former Yugoslavia, and Sierra Leone. No doubt these traditional means of controlling arms will continue to be an important tool for the Council in sanctions and peacekeeping situations.

The precedents established by the Council in creating UNSCOM could, however, be of considerable importance in the future, notwithstanding the difficulties it encountered in the face of Iraqi intransigence. The obligations imposed on Iraq to eliminate WMD and delivery systems went well beyond what it had accepted by treaty, and similar obligations could be imposed with respect to proliferation threats in other countries. For example, the Council could require states to refrain from acquiring nuclear weapons (or other WMD) or to eliminate existing stocks where their possession is judged to be a threat to the peace, even if the states in question had not ratified the relevant treaties. This requirement could be enforced by sanctions or even by the use of force to eliminate stockpiles and facilities for their manufacture.

Likewise, the obligations imposed on Iraq to permit international inspection to confirm the elimination of the prohibited items went well beyond what it was required to accept under treaties it had ratified, and the same sort of obligations could be imposed on other states that appear to present proliferation threats. For example, the Council could establish a commission to verify and assist in the elimination of nuclear weapons (or other WMD) in a regional situation where their possession by particular states is a threat to the peace, and to confirm over time that they are not reacquired. Such a UN commission might prove to be a vital means of giving regional states the confidence to give up the option of developing or retaining indigenous weapons capabilities. Obviously, this is much easier where the states in question are prepared in principle to give up such weapons (provided their regional rivals do likewise) than where the states are determined to resist and evade inspections. In the latter event, the Council must be prepared to consider the possibility of sanctions or other measures.

Beyond the imposition of limits on particular states, the Council has now taken an important step toward the control of proliferation problems on a generic basis. As examined previously, in April 2004 the Council determined in Resolution 1540 that the proliferation generally of WMD and their means of delivery constitutes a threat to the peace and acted under Chapter VII to impose obligations on all states to prevent the acquisition of such items and capabilities by nonstate actors. Specifically, the Council decided that all states shall refrain from providing any form of support to nonstate actors that attempt to acquire WMD, and that all states shall adopt national laws and domestic controls to prohibit and prevent such acquisition, including requirements for accounting, physical security, and export controls. The Council created a committee consisting of all Council members to review the steps taken by states to implement the resolution.

There was intense debate during the consideration of Resolution 1540 concerning the propriety of imposing these obligations, both among Council members and other UN members who participated in a series of open meetings of the Council. It was argued that the Council was improperly acting as a "global legislature" in requiring such a comprehensive program of domestic measures by all states, that the creation of such obligations should more properly be left to the negotiation of multilateral treaties that states could accept or reject, and that the resolution might be used as a pretext by certain states for the use of force (obviously referring to the U.S. use of force against Iraq to enforce previous Council decisions).[97] To assuage these objections, the resolution was explained as an exceptional measure urgently needed to deal with a serious gap in the existing structure of nonproliferation treaties,[98] and language was inserted into the resolution to say that nothing in it shall be interpreted as altering the rights and obligations of parties to the major nonproliferation treaties.[99] Assurances were made that the resolution did not authorize unilateral enforcement action against states alleged to be in violation of their obligations.[100] With these assurances, the resolution was adopted unanimously.

In the end, Resolution 1540 was an important step that was well within the Council's legal authority. It addressed a clear threat to the peace, and the practice of Council action during the post–Cold War period demonstrates that the Council may impose legal obligations on member states (including requirements to take domestic measures) to address such threats. Nothing in the Charter or the Council's practice suggests that it may not take such action against generic threats to the peace. Nonetheless, the debate over Resolution 1540 shows that many states would resist the exercise of "legislative" power by the Council to impose nonproliferation obligations on states generally, outside the context of a specific situation, at least where there is not a demonstrable need for urgent action that could not wait for the lengthy process of treaty negotiation and ratification. The Council will have to take these reservations seriously and avoid using its broad legal authority in ways that might appear designed to supersede the normal treaty process.

Assessment

In the three areas covered by this chapter—compensation, territorial disputes, and control of arms—the actions taken by the Council in the post–Cold War period have provided important new tools for dealing with the results of conflict in ways that can reduce the likelihood of its recurrence. Providing fair compensation to the victims of loss and injury conveys a sense of redress that makes recrimination and reprisal less likely, helps to restore the economic and political health of victimized societies so as to reduce the likelihood that they will be easy victims of future aggression or internal unrest, and adds an element of deterrence, to the extent that the aggressor bears the burden of compensation. Resolving territorial disputes in a fair and final manner reduces the risk that these disputes will recur and provoke renewed conflict, and helps to ensure security and access to resources for each party to the dispute. Eliminating dangerous arms capabilities can lessen the chances of future hostilities and the destructiveness of conflict if it does recur, and can provide important protection against catastrophic terrorist attacks.

Of course, these same processes can exacerbate tension and contribute to a renewal of conflict if undertaken unfairly or unwisely. The agreements concluding World War I are often cited as an example of measures in all three of these areas that contributed to a renewal of conflict—partly because they created a sense of retribution and injustice, and partly because they did not create sufficient barriers to rearmament and renewal of aggression. Obviously, a compensation regime should not preclude the economic recovery of the defeated state or cause unnecessary suffering to its people, a territorial settlement should not punitively divest it of territory in disregard of the desires of the affected population, and a disarmament regime should not deprive it of a reasonable ability to defend itself from future aggression.

The Council's efforts in the post–Cold War period cannot be faulted on these grounds. The Iraqi compensation regime cannot reasonably be criticized as being retributive or as preventing Iraqi economic recovery. The resolution of the Iraq-Kuwait boundary question was fair and complete, and it cannot reasonably be seen as punitive. There is continuing debate on the extent to which the UN program for the elimination of Iraqi WMD accomplished its objectives, but it cannot be dismissed as mere retribution or military hegemony.

In fact, the Council's use of technical commissions has created a very useful set of new methods and precedents for addressing these and other problem areas. By creating new institutions with broad and flexible powers designed specifically for the particular situations with which they were faced, the Council has made it possible to resolve very difficult problems much more quickly than would otherwise have been possible, and with much greater conformance to the Council's policy priorities. In each of these cases, the Council did not hesitate to use its considerable Chapter VII authority to innovate and act decisively—to draw on existing legal mechanisms and principles where they were useful but to modify or add to them where necessary to reach the appropriate results.

There is no reason the Council should not be able to deal with many kinds of problems that arise from conflict situations through the innovative and flexible use of technical commissions. To name a few possibilities, technical commissions might be created to resolve the future status of a territory involved in internal conflict, to work out a system for reducing and controlling military confrontations between neighboring states with a history of violent encounters, or to assist in managing the economic or environmental recovery of a state or province damaged by conflict.[101] Among the keys to the success of such operations would be the willingness of the Council to give the commission sufficient authority to carry out its task, including the authority to create obligations and resolve legal disputes; a readiness to adapt the structure, procedures, and personnel of the commission to the task at hand and not be unnecessarily limited by past methods and precedents; and a determination to produce results rather than simply to satisfy political constituencies.

In this way, the Council's use of technical commissions to date can be a springboard to the creative solution of ongoing problems and needs—many of which we probably cannot even foresee— rather than simply a new set of templates to be used again and again. There is no need to reinvent the wheel on every occasion, nor any value in abandoning traditional methods that still have utility. On the other hand, the Council should not hesitate to innovate as necessary to use this new form of institutional action to its maximum potential.

7   Prosecution of Crimes

O NE OF THE MORE SIGNIFICANT international legal developments of the past decade has been the revival of prosecutions, by or with the assistance of the international community, for crimes associated with armed conflict or international
terrorism. The Security Council created two ad hoc international tribunals, and this in turn stimulated consideration of a permanent
International Criminal Court (ICC) and hybrid prosecutions of a
mixed national and international character. This chapter will consider
the international legal basis for the Council's actions and the role the
Council might play with respect to such prosecutions in the future.
The availability of such international criminal tribunals serves important policy and legal purposes, and both the United States and the
proponents of the ICC—however much they are currently at odds—
have serious long-term common interests in effective cooperation
between the Council and the court that can be achieved only by pragmatic action and mutual accommodation.

THE AD HOC TRIBUNALS

Previous international prosecutions

The only criminal prosecutions by international tribunals between the end of World War II and the end of the Cold War were those of the Nuremberg and Tokyo tribunals, created for the trial of Axis leaders.[1] These tribunals were created by agreement among the Allied states and were based on their success as belligerent powers in occupying Axis territory and in securing custody over Axis nationals.[2] The Nuremberg and Tokyo trials affirmed in a dramatic way the personal responsibility of all individuals—including military commanders and political leaders—for the commission of war crimes and crimes against humanity, and their liability to trial and punishment by international tribunals.

Yet in spite of the extensive war crimes and other atrocities committed during the Cold War period in Korea, Vietnam, Cambodia, Central America, Iran and Iraq, Bangladesh, southern Africa, and elsewhere, no serious international effort was made to prosecute those responsible. In several of these conflicts, the superpowers had fought for or backed opposing sides; in others, they felt no compelling need for further involvement where their national interests did not require it; and there was neither a ready institutional means for international prosecution nor the will to create it.

In the months following the Iraqi invasion of Kuwait in 1990, the Security Council pointedly reminded Iraq of the liability of individuals for the commission of war crimes.[3] Coalition forces made intensive efforts to document Iraqi crimes, and (as discussed in the previous chapter) the Council imposed financial responsibility on Iraq for war crimes committed by its forces. Nonetheless, no war criminals were discovered among Iraqis taken prisoner by coalition forces, and no effort was made at that time to institute international prosecutions—partly because of a perception that doing so might inhibit a successful coup against Saddam Hussein by Iraqi military commanders who might themselves be subject to such charges.

Creation of the Yugoslav tribunal

By the second half of 1992, however, the international community had become so appalled by the widespread atrocities being committed in the former Yugoslavia and so frustrated by its inability to effectively deal with the conflict through other means that a consensus began to develop in favor of some form of international prosecution of those responsible.[4] Among the reasons were (1) the need for emphatic international opposition to these atrocities, which were severely exacerbating the conflict and obstructing the possibilities for peace; (2) the hope that such action would deter the further commission of such crimes, both in Yugoslavia and elsewhere; (3) the desire to reduce the urge for vengeance among the victimized ethnic groups by providing some form of accountability and justice; (4) the hope that international action would have the effect of politically isolating the persons indicted and removing them from positions of power, even if they could not be brought immediately into custody; and (5) the desire of many to begin creating structures and precedents for the international prosecution of such crimes in other situations in the future.

For these reasons, the Council began reminding the parties to the conflict of their obligation to comply with international humanitarian law and the individual liability of persons committing such crimes. It also threatened "further measures" if those crimes did not stop.[5] In October 1992, the Council asked the secretary-general to establish a Commission of Experts to investigate reports of atrocities.[6] The commission soon confirmed that widespread atrocities had been committed.[7] The Council then decided that an international tribunal would be established and requested the secretary-general to propose how this could be done.[8]

It was not clear what the legal and institutional basis for such an international tribunal would be. The model of the Nuremberg and Tokyo tribunals—trial by victorious belligerent powers of enemy nationals who were in their custody—was not applicable to the situation in the former Yugoslavia, where the conflict was far from over, the major international powers were not party to the conflict, and the perpetrators of crimes had not been defeated or apprehended. Hence, it was proposed that an international tribunal be created by agreement among the states involved in the conflict and others that would support and cooperate in the prosecutions. In particular, a panel of rapporteurs appointed by the Conference on Security and Cooperation in Europe proposed the creation by treaty of an ad hoc tribunal for the former Yugoslavia under which the former Yugoslav republics and other states would "cede" to the tribunal their jurisdiction over crimes committed in their territory or by their nationals.[9] However, the concept of creating a tribunal by treaty had several serious drawbacks: it probably would have taken years to negotiate and implement such a multilateral agreement; there might have been a long delay in obtaining the ratification of various key states (such as the United States and Russia); the tribunal would have had jurisdiction only over the territory and nationals of states that ratified the treaty (which would in all likelihood exclude the former Yugoslav republics that were the object of the exercise); and states not ratifying the treaty would have had no obligation to surrender indicted persons or provide evidence to the tribunal.

To overcome these drawbacks, the United States and others proposed that the tribunal be created by a decision of the Security Council under Chapter VII, based on the Council's judgment that international prosecutions would contribute to the restoration and maintenance of the peace.[10] This proposal offered a number of important advantages: (1) the tribunal would be created immediately (at least as a formal matter); (2) it would have jurisdiction from the start over crimes committed in any of the former Yugoslav republics, whether or not they consented to that jurisdiction; (3) all states would immediately be bound to cooperate with the tribunal, including by surrendering indicted persons and producing evidence; (4) the mandatory powers of the Council under Chapter VII, including the possible threat or imposition of sanctions on states that failed to cooperate, would more readily be available to support the tribunal; and (5) action by the Council would encourage participation and support by its members, which included those with the political, economic, and military resources that would eventually be needed.

This was in fact the option ultimately recommended by the secretary-general. His report concluded that it was within the Council's authority under Chapter VII to establish such a tribunal as a subsidiary organ, although of course it would function as an independent judicial body.[11] During the Council's consideration of the proposal, Brazil and China took the position that the tribunal should instead be created by an international convention ratified by states.[12] China argued that it was inappropriate for the Council to create the tribunal and that its displacement of national jurisdiction was "not in compliance with the principle of state judicial sovereignty."[13] However, in the end, the Council accepted the advice of the secretary-general that it had sufficient authority for this purpose and approved his recommendation for the creation of the tribunal by action under Chapter VII.[14]

The tribunal proposed by the secretary-general and approved by the Council was very similar to that proposed by the United States.[15] The International Criminal Tribunal for the Former Yugoslavia (ICTY) had trial and appeals chambers and an independent prosecutor. It had an adversarial system of trial characteristic of common-law jurisdictions. It had the authority to require states to surrender indicted persons and to produce evidence. It had primacy over national courts and could require them to defer to it in the prosecution of any person indicted by the tribunal. It had jurisdiction over war crimes, crimes against humanity, and genocide committed in the former Yugoslavia since January 1, 1991.[16] It had jurisdiction over all persons committing such crimes, including nationals of all sides to the conflict (as well as nationals of other states),[17] including even heads of state and government.[18]

Unlike the Nuremberg tribunal, the ICTY did not have jurisdiction over "crimes against peace"—that is, aggression. A number of factors went into this decision, including (1) a general desire to focus on the atrocities being committed in the conduct of the war, (2) a desire to avoid trespassing by the tribunal on the Security Council's responsibility for determining that acts of aggression had occurred, (3) a general desire to avoid having the tribunal drawn into a highly political process of judging the rights and wrongs of the resort to force by the states and factions of the former Yugoslavia, and (4) a desire on the part of some to avoid setting a precedent for future prosecutions based on national policy decisions about war and peace.

As would be expected, the legality of the creation of the tribunal was challenged by the first defendant to be tried (Dusko Tadic), who argued (among other things) that the establishment of a tribunal did not in fact respond to a threat to the peace for purposes of Chapter VII of the Charter; that it was never intended by the Charter that the Security Council should, under Chapter VII, establish a judicial body, let alone a criminal tribunal; and that the Council had no authority to take primacy over national courts.[19] The Appeals Chamber found that the defendant's challenges to the legality of the tribunal's creation were without merit.

To begin with, the Appeals Chamber held that the Council was clearly justified in determining that the situation in the former Yugoslavia constituted a threat to the peace, in light of the common UN understanding and practice that internal armed conflicts could constitute such a threat.[20] It held that the Council has a "very wide margin of discretion" to decide what measures to apply under Chapter VII in response to such a threat, and that the list in Article 41 of nonforcible measures available to the Council was only exemplary and did not exclude other steps, including the creation of a tribunal.[21] It held that the fact that the Council was not a judicial organ did not preclude it from creating judicial organs for the purpose of dealing with a threat to the peace.[22] Finally, it held that taking primacy over national courts was within the Council's authority, given the international character of the crimes in question and the fact that Article 2(7) of the Charter expressly exempts Chapter VII enforcement actions from the prohibition on UN intervention in the domestic affairs of states.[23] To be sure, the Appeals Chamber was correct on all these points.

Creation of the Rwanda tribunal

Long before this challenge to the legality of the Yugoslav tribunal had been disposed of, the Council was faced with another situation of mass atrocities that led to the creation of a second ad hoc criminal tribunal under the Council's Chapter VII authority. In the wake of genocide on a vast scale in Rwanda, the Council in July 1994 requested the secretary-general to establish a Commission of Experts to investigate the situation and provide recommendations for action.[24] But before the commission could even begin its work, it became apparent that some form of international prosecution would be necessary to give any prospect for impartial justice and thereby help to forestall further waves of revenge killings and encourage the return of the large numbers of Rwandans who had fled the country during the conflict.

The United States proposed that the Security Council act to expand the jurisdiction of the existing ad hoc Yugoslav tribunal to include the Rwandan genocide rather than create a new tribunal, and that new trial chambers and substantial prosecutorial staff be added for this purpose.[25] The proposal was justified on the grounds that it would encourage consistent prosecutorial policies and legal results and minimize the time and effort of creating a whole new institutional structure from the ground up. Such an expansion of the jurisdiction of the existing tribunal might have led, in time, to the practical equivalent of a permanent criminal tribunal that would from time to time acquire jurisdiction over new situations that the Council might decide were suitable for international prosecution.

However, the Council as a whole was not prepared to take such a step and decided instead to create a separate tribunal for Rwanda.[26] The structure for the tribunal was largely the same as that of the ICTY, except that certain elements of the Yugoslav tribunal were used for Rwanda as well. Specifically, the Rwanda tribunal had its own Trial Chamber, which sat in Arusha, Tanzania, while the judges of the Appeals Chamber of the Yugoslav tribunal in The Hague served as the Appeals Chamber for Rwanda as well.[27] Similarly, the Rwanda tribunal had its own staff of prosecutors and investigators who worked in Kigali and Arusha, but the chief prosecutor for the Yugoslav tribunal served the same function for the Rwanda tribunal as well.[28] The substantive jurisdiction and powers of the tribunals were essentially the same.[29]

Nearly all of the Council members voted in favor of the creation of the Rwanda tribunal, but there was significant dissent in some quarters. As in the case of Yugoslavia, Brazil and China expressed doubts about the authority of the Council to create such a tribunal.[30] Rwanda voted against the resolution (even though it had requested such a tribunal and did not contest the Council's authority to create it), citing a variety of objections to the tribunal's jurisdiction, its structure, and its provisions for punishment.[31]

Operation of the two ad hoc tribunals

There has been a considerable body of commentary on the operations of the two ad hoc tribunals.[32] This chapter will not attempt to cover that ground here, except with respect to the ongoing involvement of the Security Council. The original proposal of the United States for the Yugoslav tribunal contemplated the creation of a subordinate body of the Council that would exercise general administrative control over the staffing and operations of the tribunal and its prosecutor.[33] Although this proposal was not designed to establish Council control over substantive decisions of the tribunal, but only to ensure that it would have adequate resources and be run efficiently, other Council members nonetheless thought it was inappropriate, and it was not adopted. (The proposal was not repeated in the case of the Rwanda tribunal.)

As it turned out, both tribunals encountered considerable delays and difficulties in getting off the ground. In particular, the Rwanda tribunal experienced serious inefficiencies and irregularities in its early years, and the task of creating a whole new judicial system was complicated by the lack of any suitable physical and institutional infrastructure in Arusha.[34] The process was obstructed in both cases by the circumstances in which the tribunals had to operate: by the ongoing conflict in Yugoslavia and the initial refusal of Serb and Croat authorities to cooperate, by the chaotic conditions and continuing ethnic tensions in Rwanda, and by the difficulty of operating far from the crime scenes and without functioning law enforcement systems and basic infrastructure. Because of the scope and character of the crimes committed, the multilingual character of the proceedings, and the logistics involved, investigations and trials were inevitably more complex, expensive, and time consuming than ordinary criminal proceedings.

The Council attempted to accelerate and improve the process over the years by authorizing the appointment of a separate chief prosecutor for Rwanda[35] and of a large number of *ad litem* judges to perform pretrial and other functions.[36] It called on both tribunals to take "all possible measures" to complete investigations by the end of 2004, to complete all trials by the end of 2008, and to complete all work in 2010.[37] To meet these targets, the tribunals have taken a number of steps to simplify and streamline their work, including consolidating cases, exercising greater control over the scope of the cases presented, transferring cases involving mid- and lower-level offenders to national authorities, and placing a greater reliance on plea bargaining.[38]

At the time the two tribunals were created, there was considerable skepticism as to their prospects, particularly in light of the facts that the Yugoslav conflict was far from over, the major suspects were apparently safe within their own lines, and many of the major Rwandan perpetrators had fled the country. Even the most optimistic comments focused only on the possibility that the tribunals would establish a public historical record of the responsibility for the atrocities and isolate the main perpetrators internationally, rather than predict that they would actually be brought to justice.[39] In retrospect, although both tribunals have had considerable difficulties, on the whole they have been more successful than originally predicted and have become reasonably credible institutions that have produced some important results.

By mid-2005, more than fifty defendants had been tried by the Yugoslav tribunal and more than fifty indicted persons were in custody, including a number of high-ranking Serb and Croat political and military leaders, most notably the former president of Serbia, Slobodan Milosevic.[40] More than twenty defendants had been tried by the Rwanda tribunal and more than forty indicted persons were in custody, among them the major military and political leaders of the Rwandan genocide, including persons who had been prime minister, cabinet ministers, and high-ranking military commanders at the time.[41]

Equally important, the two tribunals have contributed substantially to the exposure and delegitimization of the campaigns in which atrocities were committed, as well as the loss of political power and international status by a number of the major accused perpetrators (such as Radovan Karadzic, Ratko Mladic, and Milosevic). They seem to have had a positive effect in giving victim groups some sense of justice and in discouraging mass reprisals. Further, the tribunals have made a major contribution to the creation of a new jurisprudence for international criminal prosecution, as well as an extensive body of valuable experience in how to conduct international investigations and prosecutions (and how not to).

It is very difficult to judge how much the tribunals may have contributed to deterring or preventing actual atrocities, and prosecutions can never take the place of effective political and military action to stop their commission. Obviously, the existence of the tribunals did not end the atrocities in Central Africa and the former Yugoslavia, as the experiences of Srebrenica, Kosovo, Burundi, and the Congo demonstrate, and some important accused perpetrators are still at large, most notably the former military and political leaders of the Bosnian Serb republic. Nonetheless, we must hope and assume that the tribunals have contributed, to some important degree, to curbing the sense of impunity that perpetrators may have had in the past.

It is important to note that the success achieved by the tribunals has largely been the result of the support and authority given by the Security Council and its permanent members. For example, the Council used its Chapter VII authority to impose obligations on all states to surrender indicted persons, provide evidence, and otherwise cooperate with the tribunals and their investigators.[42] It confirmed that these obligations override anything to the contrary in domestic law (such as prohibitions on the surrender of a state's nationals).[43] The authority given by the Council to the UN peacekeeping force in Croatia and to the multilateral forces in Bosnia and Kosovo provided the legal basis for arrests of suspects by those forces and ultimately resulted in many detentions.[44]

Further, both the Council and its Western permanent members maintained a strong linkage between financial assistance to states of the former Yugoslavia and cooperation with the Yugoslav tribunal, which in the end was a critical factor in obtaining the surrender of various political and military leaders.[45] The Western permanent members—in particular the United States—provided essential voluntary contributions of money, personnel, and equipment to both tribunals. Without this support, the tribunals would have been dead in the water.

THE INTERNATIONAL CRIMINAL COURT

Creation of the court

The concept of a permanent international criminal court of general jurisdiction has been pursued intermittently within the UN system since the early days of the United Nations—in the International Law Commission and in special committees created by the General Assembly.[46] Momentum for the creation of such a court began to pick up in the mid-1990s in the wake of the establishment of the ad hoc tribunals as it became apparent that a single standing court would be more efficient than separate ad hoc structures for each conflict situation in which international prosecution seemed desirable.

Because the permanent court was to be established by treaty and not pursuant to a Chapter VII decision of the Council, it took considerable time and effort to bring it formally into existence. The Council could have established a permanent tribunal under Chapter VII, adding specific situations to its jurisdiction from time to time as it found appropriate; however, the prevailing view was that creation of a permanent tribunal was more appropriately done by a multilateral treaty to which there was wide adherence, presumably on the theory that this would provide a broader political and legal basis. After many years of debate, detailed proposals were produced in 1994 by the International Law Commission, in 1995 by an ad hoc committee of the General Assembly, and in 1996 by a Preparatory Committee created by the Assembly. In 1998, a diplomatic conference convened by the Assembly adopted the Rome Statute of the International Criminal Court.[47] The statute provided that it would enter into force after sixty states had ratified, and entry into force finally occurred on July 1, 2002.[48] (A list of parties to the statute is in Appendix 3.)

The types of crimes over which the ICC will have jurisdiction are broadly similar to those of the ad hoc tribunals (genocide, crimes against humanity, and war crimes), except that the Rome Statute contemplates the addition of "the crime of aggression" if and when an amendment is adopted defining the crime and the conditions under which the court would exercise jurisdiction over it.[49] The structure of the court is also broadly similar to that of the ad hoc tribunals, with an independent prosecutor and a series of judicial chambers.[50]

A great debate has occurred in the United States as to whether the U.S. government should join and support the ICC or deny U.S. adherence and support and exert pressure on others to do likewise.[51] The United States voted against the adoption of the ICC statute for a variety of reasons, including its potential negative effect on U.S.

participation in peace operations abroad if U.S. military personnel and political leaders were subject to the possibility of prosecution without authorization by the Security Council.[52] In December 2000, President Clinton authorized U.S. signature of the statute, while at the same time stating that he would not recommend U.S. ratification until these concerns were satisfied.[53]

In May 2002, the Bush administration formally notified the secretary-general that the United States did not intend to become a party to the statute and accordingly had no further obligations as a result of its earlier signature.[54] The administration also began an energetic campaign to shield U.S. personnel from the jurisdiction of the court. This campaign has included the negotiation of bilateral agreements precluding the surrender of various categories of U.S. persons to the court.[55] (Article 98 of the ICC statute prevents the court from proceeding with a request for any surrender that would be inconsistent with international agreements prohibiting surrender of a person without the consent of the sending state.[56])

In addition, the United States insisted that the Security Council use its Chapter VII authority to immunize from ICC prosecution any U.S. personnel participating in UN peace operations. (Article 16 of the ICC statute provides that no prosecution may proceed for a period of twelve months after the Council makes a request to that effect in a Chapter VII resolution.) In July 2002, under a U.S. threat to veto peacekeeping authorizations if such action were not taken, the Council made such a request under Chapter VII to preclude for twelve months any investigation or prosecution of "current or former officials or personnel from a contributing state not a party to the Rome Statute over acts or omissions relating to a United Nations established or authorized operation."[57] At the same time, the Council expressed its intention to renew this request every year "for as long as may be necessary," and one year later the Council did so.[58] However, this request was not renewed in 2004, in the wake of disclosures of the mistreatment of Iraqi prisoners in U.S. custody.[59]

During the same period, the U.S. Congress also acted to shield U.S. personnel from ICC prosecution. It adopted the "American Servicemembers' Protection Act of 2002,"[60] that prohibits, among other things, U.S. cooperation with the court, investigations by ICC personnel in U.S. territory, assistance to governments that are party to the statute (with various exceptions), and the participation of U.S. military personnel in peace operations under UN command where they have not been exempted from ICC jurisdiction. It also authorizes the president to use "all means necessary" to bring about the "release from captivity" of U.S. or allied persons under detention by or on behalf of the court.

On the other hand, the act does include certain waiver provisions that could permit significant cooperation with the court, at least to the extent that U.S. personnel are not involved. In particular, one section permits the rendering of assistance to international efforts to bring to justice foreign nationals accused of genocide, war crimes, or crimes against humanity, which presumably would include cooperation with the court in the investigation, arrest, and prosecution of foreign nationals. Another section provides that the prohibitions on cooperation with the court do not apply to actions taken by the president in the exercise of his executive power under the U.S. Constitution, which presumably would include voting in the Security Council for measures in support of the court in particular cases, such as the reference of situations to the court not currently within its jurisdiction.

Whether or not the United States ever becomes party to the ICC statute or modifies its efforts to shield its personnel from the court's jurisdiction, it will obviously play a key role in decisions by the Council affecting the court. The ICC was not created by the Council but, rather, by the states that have ratified its statute. Nonetheless, the scope of its authority and its future prospects will depend in various ways on the authority and support of the Council. At present, the United States is at serious odds with most of the Council concerning the court, but as time passes there will likely be situations in which Council members have common interests with respect to possible ICC prosecutions. With this in mind, it is important to understand the role that the Council may play, either in expanding or restricting the ICC's authority.

The role of the Council under the ICC statute

The role to be played by the Security Council in the operation of the court was one of the more hotly debated issues during the long ICC negotiations. The draft statute proposed by the International Law Commission (ILC) in 1994 assigned a prominent role to the Council. Under that proposal, the Council would have the authority to refer matters to the court that would otherwise not fall within its jurisdiction; for example, a complaint of aggression could not be brought unless the Council had first determined that aggression had occurred, and no prosecution could be commenced with respect to a situation being addressed by the Council under Chapter VII unless the Council decided otherwise.[61]

This part of the ILC proposal became a matter of considerable controversy, particularly among nonaligned delegations. Some argued that giving such authority to a political body would compromise the judicial independence of the ICC and that it would violate the sovereign equality of states by giving the limited membership of the Council a special voice. Others answered that the proposal took proper account of the unique role of the Council under the Charter and would not impair the independence of the court because its prosecutor would not be compelled to bring prosecutions for cases referred by the Council.[62]

In the end, a different version of the ILC provision was adopted. Under the final text of the statute, the court has jurisdiction only over crimes committed in the territory of a state that has accepted its jurisdiction or by a national of such a state, but this restriction is lifted if the situation is referred to the ICC prosecutor by the Council under Chapter VII.[63] As already noted, the Council may also defer or interrupt any investigation or prosecution for a period of twelve months (which may be repeated).[64] Unlike the ILC proposal, however, this provision requires an affirmative decision of the Council and is not simply the consequence of the fact that the matter is under consideration by the Council. No provision was made for the Council's role in prosecutions for aggression.

Expanding the court's authority

The ICC statute limits the court's jurisdiction in ways that could effectively exclude it from trying many serious crimes. However, action by the Security Council could expand the court's jurisdiction in important ways.

First, as indicated above, the ICC statute itself provides that the Council may refer certain situations to the court that would otherwise not be within the court's jurisdiction—that is, where the crimes in question were not committed in the territory of a state that has accepted its jurisdiction or by a national of such a state. (In the case of the ad hoc tribunals, the Council gave jurisdiction without regard to whether the states in question accepted that jurisdiction.) Particularly since the states that commit such crimes may be less likely to accept the court's jurisdiction, the court may be a helpless onlooker with respect to significant atrocities in future conflicts—particularly those that are internal in character—unless the Council authorizes prosecution.

Second, there is an important range of other circumstances in which the court would not have jurisdiction and where the statute does not provide that the Council may authorize it to exercise jurisdiction. In particular, the court does not have jurisdiction over crimes committed before its statute entered into force (July 1, 2002) or, with respect to a state ratifying after that date, before that state ratifies;[65] or over offenses that do not appear in the statute's enumeration of crimes, which are defined in a detailed and restrictive way.[66] (In contrast, the Council gave the ad hoc tribunals jurisdiction over crimes that occurred before their creation and over broadly defined categories of crimes.)

Acting under Chapter VII, the Council would have authority to confer jurisdiction on the court in such situations where it was determined to be necessary to restore and maintain the peace. Again, the Charter gives priority to Chapter VII decisions over any inconsistent provisions of other treaties, and the Council's authority to impose criminal responsibility and to create criminal jurisdiction is now a recognized part of its Chapter VII power. Accordingly, the Council could give the ICC the authority in a particular situation to exercise jurisdiction over crimes committed before a state's ratification of the statute or over crimes (such as international terrorism) not currently within the statute.[67] This could be a far more efficient and practical option than creating a new tribunal with the same jurisdiction, which is clearly within the Council's Chapter VII authority. On the other hand, it is not clear that the ICC would find it appropriate to exercise such jurisdiction or that parties to the statute would accept such an exercise. No doubt, many would take the view that the court's independence and legitimacy would be compromised by additions to its jurisdiction that are not contemplated by its statute.

Third, the ICC statute requires the court to treat a case as inadmissible where it is being (or has been) investigated or prosecuted by a state or where the state has decided not to prosecute, unless that state is found to be "unwilling or unable genuinely to carry out the investigation or prosecution."[68] (In contrast to this "principle of complementarity," each of the ad hoc tribunals has primacy over national courts and may at any time require a national court to defer to it in prosecuting a suspect. [69] An ad hoc tribunal may choose to do so for various reasons, even in cases where national courts are ready and willing to prosecute—for example, where national prosecutions might exacerbate tensions, or where international prosecution would be more credible or more widely acceptable.)

If, in such a case, the Security Council were to adopt a Chapter VII decision requiring national authorities to refrain from prosecution and giving jurisdiction to the ICC, it could reasonably be argued that this would take precedence over the provisions of the statute. Alternatively, the Council's decision would mean, for the purpose of the ICC statute, that national authorities would be unable to prosecute, with the result that the statute by its own terms would no longer preclude ICC proceedings. Again, although such an option would be legally available, there would still be the question as to whether the court would find it appropriate to exercise jurisdiction in such a case and whether the state in question would in fact refrain from its own proceedings.

Restricting the ICC's authority

On the other hand, there are likely to be circumstances in which international prosecution will not be desirable, for reasons of policy or practical considerations, even if authorized by the ICC statute. Although proponents of the ICC have often argued that such factors should be removed from consideration in the international prosecution of crimes, such a perspective is not always useful or realistic.

Prosecution can indeed play an important role in many conflicts in helping to bring about peace, national reconciliation, and democratic transition. Prosecution can have the effect of isolating the principal offenders and helping to exclude them from political power, lessening the desire for revenge among victim groups, and discouraging a repetition of crimes. Nonetheless, there may be situations in which the resolution of a conflict or a transition to democracy are better served by alternative means, such as amnesty or truth and reconciliation arrangements, as has arguably been the case in internal conflicts in South Africa and Latin America during the post–Cold War period.[70] Likewise, where a decision is taken in favor of prosecution in such a case, a judgment must be made as to whether to accept or encourage prosecution by national authorities, to insist on international prosecution (most likely in combination with national efforts), or to create some hybrid system drawing on both national and international elements.

Further, there may be cases where ICC prosecution would, for other reasons, not be productive or sensible. As noted earlier, the Council has already acted to give immunity from ICC prosecution to the personnel of states not party to the ICC who participate in Council-authorized peace operations. There may be specific future cases in which it would be desirable to defer ICC prosecutions that might otherwise disrupt ongoing peace negotiations aimed at ending a particular conflict. There may even be cases in which it would be futile, or destructive of the long-term prospects for the court and the international system as a whole, to attempt ICC prosecution of the leaders of a particular government. Any of these situations may require such a pragmatic judgment in the longer-term interests of peace or justice.

In the case of the ad hoc tribunals, these judgments are made by the Security Council regarding whether to mandate prosecution with respect to a particular conflict, and, if so, whether to entrust that prosecution to an international tribunal, to national authorities, or to some hybrid system. If prosecution is entrusted to an international tribunal, judgments would be made on the scope of its jurisdiction regarding the persons, offenses, and period of time covered, and the Council is the logical international body to make judgments of this kind.

If the Council were not to perform this role with respect to ICC prosecutions, the decision on whether to institute prosecution in a particular situation would be left to the prosecutor, with review by judges. But it is not clear to what extent it would be consistent with the ICC system for prosecutors and judges to refrain from prosecution on the basis of the factors just described.[71] It is, in any event, questionable whether they would have either the inclination or the political standing to make such decisions. For example, it is not easy to imagine an international prosecutor deciding that a proposed amnesty arrangement is or is not necessary or justified as a means of facilitating the end of a conflict or the transition to democracy in a particular country; nor is it likely that such a decision could be separated sensibly from the overall political and practical context of the situation or from the desires of the parties to the conflict or the major powers involved.

As already indicated, the ICC statute recognizes this fact in part by giving the Security Council the power to prevent an investigation or prosecution from proceeding for one or more twelve-month periods.[72] In effect, this was an acknowledgment that ICC prosecution might interfere with the Council's handling of a conflict situation and that the Council should at least be able, in such circumstances, to defer such a prosecution.

The Council may also refer situations for prosecution—and in doing so, the Council presumably would be entitled to restrict the time period, types of offenses, or classes of persons that might be prosecuted.[73] Further, because obligations under Council decisions under Chapter VII take precedence over other international agreements (such as the ICC statute), the Council in theory could limit ICC prosecution of particular classes of persons or in particular situations, even beyond that which is specifically provided for in the ICC statute.[74] (Of course, as a practical matter, the Council may be unlikely to take such action, given the fact that two of its permanent members are parties to the statute.)

Support for ICC prosecutions

Even if the ICC has jurisdiction to prosecute in a particular case, it cannot effectively do so unless it has the authority to compel the relevant states to surrender suspects, provide evidence, and cooperate in investigations. As noted earlier, one of the critical aspects of the Council's authority under Chapter VII in connection with the ad hoc tribunals has been its ability to impose such obligations on all states.

Because it was established by treaty, the ICC statute can bind only states that have ratified it and cannot give the court the power to impose such obligations on nonparty states. This could be a significant limitation, because suspects would likely seek refuge in such states, and the governments of those states may be reluctant to proceed against them in the absence of an international obligation to do so. But there should be no doubt about the authority of the Council under Chapter VII to require all states to cooperate with the ICC in a particular case if it determines that this would further the restoration or maintenance of the peace.

As noted earlier, the Security Council and its permanent members have provided important support to the ad hoc tribunals in various other ways, and such support may be equally important for the court. The threat or imposition of economic sanctions may well be needed to compel recalcitrant states to surrender suspects and otherwise to cooperate in investigations and prosecutions, and such sanctions are unlikely to be effective in most cases without action by the Council or at least the support of the Western permanent members. It may be necessary to authorize the use of force for these purposes, by either UN peacekeeping missions that are deployed in the area or states acting individually, in coalitions, or in regional organizations; doing so will typically require Council action. In a more general sense, criminal prosecutions will always be difficult or impossible as long as a conflict continues, and Council action will often be the most effective means of ending the conflict.

The U.S. role

The United States and the court (and ICC supporters) have strong mutual interests in maintaining a cooperative rather than an antagonistic relationship, regardless of whether or not the United States becomes a party to the statute. The court cannot realize the very great benefits of the authority and support of the Council if the United States is opposed, and U.S. antagonism will inevitably inhibit the court in many other respects, including access to resources and the ability to obtain the cooperation of other states. Thus it is prudent for the court to act with moderation and to give due regard to U.S. interests and sensibilities. ICC supporters should not automatically reject alternative means of prosecution or reasonable exemptions in particular cases simply out of loyalty to the court.

From the point of view of the United States, the Council can serve as a bridge across which the United States can advance its policy objectives and protect its interests in the court, even if it does not adhere to the ICC statute or agree to expose its personnel to ICC jurisdiction. In theory, the Council may still create additional ad hoc tribunals; in practice, the Council may be reluctant to do so, given the cost and effort involved and the political support for the court within the Council. Thus, in some circumstances, the court may be the only effective means of prosecuting persons whom the United States may strongly desire to see prosecuted—in particular, where the state with jurisdiction or custody is unable or unwilling to prosecute. Further, if in appropriate cases the United States supports the referral of situations by the Council to the court, or agrees to put the weight and authority of the Council behind the court's efforts to prosecute, the court will be more likely to respect U.S. interests. Also, a reasonably cooperative relationship with the ICC will better serve U.S. relationships with key allies that are ICC parties than will open antagonism.

For these reasons, the United States should keep open the option of cooperating with the court in cases where international prosecution is consistent with U.S. interests, assuming that the court proves in practice to be a reasonably fair and effective judicial institution.[75] The United States can do this even while refusing to allow ICC prosecution of its own personnel (which might never actually occur). The United States should not adopt an uncompromisingly hostile attitude toward the court or damage other U.S. interests by trying to defeat or minimize it. In particular, it should not sacrifice military assistance relationships or terminate peacekeeping operations that are otherwise in its interests simply to display its opposition to the ICC.

The practical benefits of such a posture have already become clear in the case of the egregious crimes committed in the Darfur region of Sudan. In that case, the United States strongly favored international prosecution, given the obvious unwillingness of Sudanese authorities to deal with the matter adequately, but it resisted referral of the situation by the Security Council to the ICC, proposing instead that an ad hoc tribunal be set up in Arusha for the purpose.[76] But in the end, the United States accepted the fact that the Council as a whole would not agree to this alternative and decided not to exercise its veto to prevent a referral to the ICC. Accordingly, in March 2005, by a vote of 11-0, with abstentions by Algeria, Brazil, China, and the United States, the Council decided to refer the situation in Darfur since July 1, 2002, to the ICC, with a proviso demanded by the United States that "nationals, current or former officials or personnel from a contributing state outside Sudan which is not a party to the Rome Statute . . . shall be subject to the exclusive jurisdiction of that contributing state" with respect to operations authorized by the Council or the African Union.[77]

The United States should likewise be prepared to assist the ICC in its investigation and prosecution of the crimes committed in Darfur, for example by providing intelligence and applying political and economic pressure on the Sudanese government to comply. If such collaboration between the United States and the ICC goes well, it may demonstrate the benefits of a more general cooperative relationship. If the court develops into a respectable judicial institution and gives due regard to U.S. interests, there is no reason why such a cooperative relationship should not be possible, at least with respect to prosecution of persons who are not U.S. personnel.

HYBRID PROSECUTIONS

Situations may arise in which it is desirable to have some combination of national and international elements in the system of prosecution—for example, where national courts are not capable of or suitable for prosecuting crimes committed during an armed conflict, and yet a full-fledged international tribunal is considered unnecessary or excessive. To this end, during the post–Cold War period, the Security Council has authorized new hybrid forms of prosecution that may involve both national and international personnel, national and international crimes, and national and international procedures.[78]

Sierra Leone

In light of the egregious atrocities committed during the conflict in Sierra Leone (particularly in the late 1990s) and the general collapse of the country's national legal system, it became apparent that a new judicial institution had to be created with international assistance to bring justice and deter further atrocities that would harm chances for peace and reconciliation. But the "tribunal fatigue" experienced by the Council in the second half of the decade made the creation of another full-fledged ad hoc international criminal tribunal unlikely.

As a result, in August 2000, the Council requested the UN secretary-general to negotiate an agreement with the government of Sierra Leone to create "an independent special court," with jurisdiction over violations of both international humanitarian law and crimes under the law of Sierra Leone.[79] The Secretariat promptly conducted those negotiations and reached agreement with Sierra Leone on the statute of a Special Court.[80] Following approval by the Security Council and the enactment by the Sierra Leonean parliament of implementing legislation, the process of setting up the Special Court and appointing its personnel began.[81] By the beginning of 2004, the prosecutor had announced a series of indictments, including several notorious rebel leaders and Liberian president Charles Taylor, and had begun hearing appeals to those indictments.[82]

The Special Court is an interesting hybrid of national and international elements—or as the secretary-general described it, "a treaty-based sui generis court of mixed jurisdiction and composition."[83] It has three chambers: two Trial Chambers, each consisting of one judge appointed by Sierra Leone and two by the secretary-general; and one Appeals Chamber, consisting of two judges appointed by Sierra Leone and three by the secretary-general.[84] There is a prosecutor appointed by the secretary-general and a Sierra Leonean deputy prosecutor.[85]

The jurisdiction of the Special Court was specifically designed to encompass the particular types of offenses that were committed during the conflict in Sierra Leone. It has jurisdiction over certain categories of international crimes—crimes against humanity and war crimes committed during internal armed conflict—and these crimes may be prosecuted notwithstanding the amnesty provided for in the 1999 Lome Peace Agreement.[86] In addition, it has jurisdiction over a series of crimes under Sierra Leonean law relating to abuse of children and destruction of property.[87] The Special Court has primacy over the courts of Sierra Leone but not over other national courts.[88]

The Special Court will draw on the work and expertise of the ad hoc tribunals in several ways. The Rules of Procedure and Evidence of the Rwanda tribunal apply to proceedings before the Special Court.[89] In sentencing persons convicted, the Trial Chambers will "have recourse to the practice regarding prison sentences" of the Rwanda tribunal.[90] The judges of the Appeals Chamber "shall be guided" by the decisions of the Appeals Chambers of the ad hoc tribunals.[91] (On the other hand, the Appeals Chamber is to be guided by the decisions of the Supreme Court of Sierra Leone with respect to Sierra Leonean law.) Finally, the two ad hoc tribunals have indicated their willingness to share their expertise with the Special Court in various ways, including consultations among judges, training of prosecutors and investigators, and sharing of legal materials.[92] In effect, although the Special Court will have a more national character than the ad hoc tribunals, it will still be strongly integrated with their law and practice.[93]

Cambodia

While the creation of the Special Court for Sierra Leone was a relatively straightforward process, the creation of a similar court for Cambodia has involved years of contentious negotiations between the UN Secretariat and the Cambodian government. In June 1997, the Cambodian government requested UN assistance in bringing to justice those responsible for the appalling crimes committed by the Khmer Rouge during the 1970s. The secretary-general created a Group of Experts, which in due course recommended the creation of an international tribunal for this purpose, but that proposal was rejected by the Cambodian government, which proposed instead that a special national court be created in which foreign judges and prosecutors would participate. Two and a half years of negotiations between the United Nations and the Cambodian government followed, which ended without agreement because of, among other things, disputes over the composition of the organs of the special court and the relative power of the national and international members of those organs.[94]

In December 2002, the UN General Assembly requested the secretary-general to resume negotiations,[95] and this time agreement was soon reached. Although the UN negotiators proposed a simplified set of organs in which the prosecutor, investigating judge, and a majority of judges would be international personnel, the Cambodian government refused. In the end, the UN team accepted a more complex structure in which international personnel do not have clear predominance.[96] A draft agreement embodying the new structure was referred to the General Assembly and approved in May 2003.[97]

Under the agreed framework, two national Cambodian courts called the Extraordinary Chambers will be created under Cambodian law. There will be a Trial Chamber, composed of three Cambodian judges and two international judges, which will take decisions by the affirmative vote of at least four judges. There will be a Supreme Court Chamber to hear appeals, composed of four Cambodian judges and three international judges, which will take decisions by an affirmative vote of at least five judges.[98] In other words, the international judges cannot produce a decision by themselves, but the vote of at least one of the international judges is needed for a decision.

There will then be one Cambodian and one international investigating judge responsible for the conduct of investigations. If they are unable to agree on whether to proceed with an investigation, it will proceed unless one of the investigating judges appeals the matter to a Pre-Trial Chamber, composed of three Cambodian and two international judges, which can terminate an investigation by the affirmative vote of at least four of the judges. Likewise, there will be one Cambodian prosecutor and one international prosecutor, responsible for the conduct of prosecutions. If they are unable to agree on whether to proceed with a prosecution, the matter is also referred to the Pre-Trial Chamber under the same procedure.[99]

The chambers will have jurisdiction over both international crimes (including genocide, crimes against humanity, and grave breaches of the 1949 Geneva Conventions) and over a set of national crimes (including homicide and torture). They will have jurisdiction over crimes committed during the period from April 17, 1975, to January 6, 1979, and over "senior leaders of Democratic Kampuchea and those who were most responsible" for those crimes.[100] The Cambodian government promises not to request any amnesty or pardon for any persons who may be investigated or convicted, but a pardon had already been granted in 1996 to one prominent Khmer Rouge leader and that matter is to be decided by the Extraordinary Chambers.[101]

This complicated hybrid system represents an uneasy compromise which the secretary-general obviously entered into with some considerable reluctance. In his report to the General Assembly, he stated that he "would very much have preferred" that the chambers have majorities of international judges who could take decisions by their own votes, and stated that "doubts might therefore still remain" as to whether the agreement reached would ensure a credible process "given the precarious state of the judiciary in Cambodia."[102] Unlike the international criminal tribunals for the former Yugoslavia and Rwanda, which were created by the Security Council under Chapter VII notwithstanding objections by the governments in question, the General Assembly had no authority to impose a judicial structure on Cambodia and had to accept the results of the negotiation if it wanted to proceed.

Territories under UN governance

As examined earlier in this work, "third-generation peacekeeping" operations—involving direct UN governance of territories affected by conflict—must include efforts to resurrect and maintain judicial and law enforcement operations. In the cases of Kosovo and East Timor, these operations took on a hybrid character for at least a transitional period, involving both national and international personnel, as well as national and international law.

In Kosovo, the UN Special Representative of the Secretary-General, as head of the UN operation in Kosovo (UNMIK), took immediate action to fill the judicial vacuum that existed at the end of the NATO bombing campaign, concluding that there was "an urgent need to build genuine rule of law in Kosovo, including through the immediate re-establishment of an independent, impartial, and multiethnic judiciary."[103] The SRSG promptly created ad hoc courts and prosecutors.[104] He asserted the authority to appoint and remove all judges and prosecutors in the province and created a commission of local and independent experts to advise him on their appointment.[105] He authorized the appointment and assignment of international judges and prosecutors "where this is considered necessary to ensure the independence and impartiality of the judiciary or the proper administration of justice," and in due course a number of such international judges and prosecutors were appointed.[106] In addition to crimes under the applicable national law, international crimes (such as war crimes and genocide) may be prosecuted by these authorities, although the International Criminal Tribunal for the Former Yugoslavia also has jurisdiction over Kosovo and may exercise its primacy over Kosovar courts at any time.[107] A significant number of these trials have now been completed with the assistance of international prosecutors and judges.[108]

Similar measures were taken in East Timor. The UN SRSG, as head of the UN operation in East Timor (UNTAET), assumed the authority to appoint and remove judges and prosecutors and created a commission composed of local and independent experts to advise him on their appointment.[109] In due course, a number of international judges and prosecutors were appointed.[110] Although the creation of an international tribunal for the prosecution of war crimes in East Timor was at one time proposed by special rapporteurs appointed by the UN High Commissioner for Human Rights, no such action was taken.[111] Indonesia created its own Ad Hoc Human Rights Tribunal for the same purpose, but the secretary-general periodically expressed frustration at both the slow pace and limited scope of those proceedings and the overturning of convictions by Indonesian appeals courts.[112] Yet a considerable number of verdicts have been rendered by special panels created under UN auspices in East Timor for "serious crimes" committed during the worst periods of violence.[113]

Iraq

As already mentioned, no international tribunal was created for the prosecution of the many crimes committed by the Saddam Hussein regime before, during, and after the 1990–91 Gulf War. Following the removal of that regime in 2003, the Security Council affirmed the need for accountability for these crimes and appealed to UN members to deny safe haven to the perpetrators, but it took no action to create any judicial structure to conduct prosecutions.[114] Instead, in December 2003, the American administrator of the Coalition Provisional Authority, acting as the occupying power under the laws of war, authorized the establishment of an Iraqi Special Tribunal by the

Iraqi Governing Council that had earlier been created by the coalition.[115] The Governing Council immediately promulgated a statute for the special tribunal. [116] As of late 2005, Saddam Hussein's trial had begun and a number of other Iraqis were awaiting indictment.[117]

The tribunal is an Iraqi court, and it is unclear whether it will have any meaningful hybrid aspects. It has jurisdiction over international crimes (genocide, crimes against humanity, and war crimes) defined in terms similar to those of the International Criminal Court, and also over a specific list of Iraqi national crimes.[118] Its statute provides that the Iraqi Governing Council can, if it deems necessary, appoint non-Iraqi judges to the Trial and Appellate Chambers and also requires that non-Iraqi nationals be appointed to act as advisers or observers to the chambers, the investigative judges, and the prosecution staff. The statute provides that, in appointing these advisers, the tribunal is entitled to request assistance from the international community, including the United Nations.[119] However, as of late 2005, no announcement had been made of the appointment of any non-Iraqi personnel to the tribunal.[120]

These provisions would make it possible for the special tribunal to function as a hybrid tribunal if international judges and other personnel do in fact play significant roles in the tribunal's operations. If the Security Council is satisfied with the arrangements for the tribunal and with the permanent Iraqi government taking shape, it might give formal sanction to the process or take other steps to support it (for example, by requiring other states to surrender suspects and evidence in their custody). Such steps would give important legitimacy to the process, but the ultimate test of its legitimacy will be the degree to which it actually operates as an impartial and efficient tribunal that complies with international standards of justice.

Future hybrid arrangements

The creation of the ICC should not preclude the creation of further hybrid courts in appropriate circumstances. Hybrid courts are an alternative to a purely international prosecution, where it seems desirable to retain national authority and participation, as well as international authority and involvement. ICC prosecutions—and for that matter, additional ad hoc international tribunals—would not necessarily serve the same ends, nor would they necessarily be acceptable to the states involved. Thus the authority of the Council to authorize hybrid courts—whether as part of a UN governance effort or otherwise—continues to be an important option for the future.

The examples discussed above show that a hybrid arrangement may be created under the aegis of either the Security Council, the General Assembly, or national authorities. However, authorization by the Council (or at least action by the Council in support of a tribunal created under other auspices) would have a number of potential advantages. For example, the Council can obligate all states to support the arrangement, including by surrendering accused persons found in their territories. The Council can authorize national or international forces to arrest accused persons or to protect the tribunal and its operations. The Council can apply sanctions to uncooperative states. And, if necessary, the Council can create hybrid tribunals in situations where the cooperation of the nominal sovereign is not readily available. Only the Council has this range of authority.

SUPPORT FOR NATIONAL PROSECUTIONS

International and hybrid prosecutions are useful means of addressing crimes that occur in the context of armed conflict and that national authorities cannot handle on their own. However, the international system has limited resources for such prosecutions and, of necessity, places primary reliance on national authorities for the prosecution of the great majority of such crimes pursuant to normal domestic procedures. For example, a number of international agreements obligate states to arrest and try or extradite persons who have committed war crimes and international terrorist crimes.[121] The ad hoc international tribunals have concurrent jurisdiction with national courts in the relevant countries, and although the tribunals may exercise priority over them, in fact they rely on national authorities for prosecution of the vast majority of offenders. As already noted, the ICC does not have primacy as such over national courts and is bound by the "principle of complementarity," under which it must defer to national prosecution unless it finds that national authorities are unable or unwilling to prosecute.

Further, the international community has supported and assisted national authorities in various ways in their prosecution of such crimes. As detailed in chapter 4, the mandates of many UN peacekeeping operations have included assistance in the rebuilding of national courts and prosecutorial authorities, with special priority on dealing with crimes committed in the context of recent or ongoing conflicts. On several occasions during the post–Cold War period, the Security Council has decided that national prosecution of crimes was necessary to address a threat to the peace and has acted under Chapter VII to require states to arrest, try, or extradite the perpetrators, or to assist them in doing so.

Lockerbie

In the wake of the terrorist bombing of Pan Am Flight 103 over Lockerbie, Scotland in December 1988, the president of the Council, speaking on the Council's behalf, called on all states to assist in the apprehension and prosecution of those responsible.[122] Nearly two years later, after U.S. and British investigators had determined that Libyan agents were responsible for the bombing and had secured indictments in domestic courts against them, the United States and the United Kingdom demanded, among other things, that Libya surrender them for trial and disclose all it knew about the crime, including full access to witnesses, documents, and other material evidence.[123]

In January 1992, the Security Council urged Libya to provide a "full and effective response" to the U.S.–British demands and also to similar demands by France concerning the bombing of a French airliner.[124] Two months later, in the absence of any meaningful Libyan response, the Council determined that the situation constituted a threat to the peace, acted under Chapter VII to decide that Libya "must now comply without any further delay" with the Council's previous demands, and imposed a series of economic and diplomatic sanctions that would apply until the Council decided that Libya had complied.[125] In effect, the Council used its authority under Chapter VII to attempt to compel Libya to assist U.S. and British domestic courts in the prosecution of a crime that had threatened the peace, including the surrender of two of its nationals for trial.

During the Council's debates on these resolutions, several delegations expressed concern about this use of the Council's power. Among other things, they argued that the dispute was essentially of a legal character that should be decided by the International Court of Justice and not a political body like the Council.[126] In the end, however, the Council rejected these arguments and acted under Chapter VII by a vote of 10-0, with five abstentions.[127]

In the meantime, Libya had taken its case to the ICJ under the 1971 Montreal Convention for Suppression of Unlawful Acts Against the Safety of Civil Aviation. Libya argued that the convention recognized the right of Libya, as the state in which the alleged offenders were found, to submit the case to its own authorities for the purpose of prosecution and obligated all other parties (including the United States and United Kingdom) to assist it in that effort, including by providing the evidence in their possession—which the U.S. and British governments had not done. Libya therefore asked the court, at the initial "provisional measures" phase of the case, to enjoin the two governments from taking any action (including resort to the Council) to compel Libya to surrender the accused to any jurisdiction outside of Libya.[128] The United States and United Kingdom responded, among other things, that the convention did not require parties to provide sensitive information concerning the investigation of such a crime to the party accused of perpetrating it, and that in any event, the court could not and should not issue any provisional measures that would interfere with the Council's exercise of its functions under Chapter VII.[129]

The court refused the Libyan requests, holding that decisions of the Council under Chapter VII prevail (under Article 103 of the UN Charter) over any contrary obligations in international agreements like the Montreal Convention; that this applied, prima facie, to the Council's decision requiring the surrender of the accused for trial by the United States or United Kingdom; and that the court therefore could not grant the relief requested by Libya, which would be contrary to the Council's decision.[130] Since the court was ruling only at a preliminary phase of the case on a request for provisional measures, its holdings did not represent a final resolution of the issues presented by Libya—and, in fact, the court never did rule definitively on these

questions. Nonetheless, the court's rejection of the Libyan preliminary requests amounted to a clear indication that the court accepted
the right of the Council to take such action under Chapter VII, notwithstanding anything to the contrary in national law or in other
international agreements.

After enduring years of sanctions, Libya finally agreed to surrender the two accused Libyans for trial by a Scottish court, pursuant to
a special arrangement under which the surrender and trial occurred in
the Netherlands (in a small enclave under the temporary control of
British authorities created specifically for the purpose of the trial).[131] In
approving the arrangement, the Council stated that its sanctions
would be suspended once the secretary-general reported that the two
accused had arrived in the Netherlands for trial, as finally occurred in
April 1999.[132] That court convicted one of the two Libyan agents of
murder as a result of having planted a bomb aboard the aircraft, and
he is currently serving his sentence in the United Kingdom.[133] (As
already noted, the ICJ case was terminated by agreement between the
parties after Libya agreed to meet the Council's requirements.)

The trial in the Netherlands was a national prosecution: a trial
for Scottish criminal offenses by a Scottish court under Scottish law
and procedure; only the site of the trial was outside the United Kingdom. However, the Council—and, at the Council's request, the
secretary-general—provided essential assistance, including (1) sanctions to compel Libya to surrender the accused; (2) mediation in
negotiating the arrangements for the trial; (3) assistance in the transfer and custody of the accused; (4) protection from unwanted outside
involvement; and (5) political cover and legitimacy for the surrender
and trial. Although it was an expensive and cumbersome way of conducting a national trial, these arrangements might be a precedent to
consider in future cases where some form of international aegis and
support is needed for a national prosecution.

Other transnational crimes

The Council reacted sharply to an attempted assassination of Egyptian president Hosni Mubarak in Ethiopia in June 1995 by persons
who took refuge in Sudan, calling on Sudan to take immediate action
to extradite them for trial in Ethiopia.[134] When Sudan failed to do so,

the Council determined that the situation constituted a threat to the peace and acted under Chapter VII to impose a series of sanctions on Sudan that were to apply until it did comply.[135] Those sanctions were maintained until September 2001, when Egypt and Ethiopia finally expressed their satisfaction with Sudanese efforts to control terrorism, and the Council thereupon lifted the sanctions.[136]

Similarly, in the wake of the al Qaeda attacks on the U.S. embassies in Kenya and Tanzania, and the U.S. indictment of Osama bin Laden for those crimes, the Security Council acted under Chapter VII in October 1999 to require the Taliban regime in Afghanistan to turn over bin Laden to the appropriate authorities in any country where he would then be prosecuted or extradited. To enforce this demand, limited sanctions were imposed against the Taliban that were to remain in effect until it complied.[137] A year later, when the Taliban had still not complied, the Council imposed more comprehensive sanctions against the Taliban and its senior officials, and later adopted a series of arrangements for monitoring and enforcing those sanctions.[138] After the defeat of the Taliban in Afghanistan, the Council adopted further Chapter VII sanctions against remaining al Qaeda and Taliban personnel and activities.[139]

In the aftermath of the September 11, 2001 attacks on the United States, the Council adopted a more comprehensive Chapter VII resolution applying generally to terrorist acts. Among other things, it required all states to (1) establish as "serious criminal offenses" any participation in the financing, planning, preparation, perpetration, or support of terrorist acts; (2) ensure that all persons who commit such offenses are brought to justice; and (3) afford one another "the greatest measure of assistance" in criminal investigations and prosecutions for such offenses.[140] Further, the resolution created a committee of the Council to monitor its implementation, which focused on exchanging information and reports on antiterrorist efforts among states and international organizations.[141]

It is likely that this sort of Council support for national law enforcement and prosecution will become even more important in the future as international cooperation against terrorist threats matures and gains wider acceptance. Council action under Chapter VII provides an important foundation for such cooperation, particularly in cases where economic or military sanctions are necessary to compel recalcitrant states to comply.

Assessment

Over the past decade, a variety of new options have been developed for handling crimes that arise from armed conflict or international terrorism. Several have been the direct result of action under Chapter VII by the Security Council, such as the two ad hoc tribunals, the hybrid Special Court for Sierra Leone, the courts in Kosovo and East Timor, and the *Lockerbie* prosecution. The statute of the International Criminal Court, which drew heavily on the precedent and experience of the ad hoc tribunals, gives an important role to the Security Council in its operation. On the whole, these developments have made prosecution of crimes an important tool for the international community in resolving conflicts and discouraging their resumption.

The United States has played a critical role—arguably *the* critical role—in most of these developments. U.S. leadership and support were essential in the case of the ad hoc tribunals, the Sierra Leone court, the "third-generation" arrangements in Kosovo and East Timor, and the *Lockerbie* prosecution. A number of Americans have occupied key positions in these institutions—including three judges and two presidents of the ICTY, the prosecutor for the Sierra Leone Special Court, and many prosecutors and investigators for the ad hoc tribunals. Yet this critical U.S. contribution has been endangered by the ongoing dispute over the ICC, which could make it more difficult for the court to operate effectively and, at the same time, discourage the creation of alternative mechanisms, as well as interfere with other essential forms of international action.

Again, it is in the interest of both the United States and the ICC to find some basis for future cooperation, even in the absence of U.S. adherence. Doing so would require each side to abstain from ideological or political reactions and to make reasonable accommodation for the interests of the other. Specifically, the United States should not embark on a campaign to destroy or cripple the ICC and should be prepared to assist it—directly and through action by the Security

Council—in cases where ICC prosecution serves mutual interests. At the same time, the ICC should be careful not to make imprudent use of its authority against U.S. interests. The U.S. decision to permit the referral of the crimes in Darfur to the ICC—in return for an exemption for the personnel of states that have not adhered to the court—suggests that such a course of cooperative action is possible and desirable. Any other course of action could amount to a serious reversal for the important efforts that have already been made during the post–Cold War period toward the use of criminal prosecution as a tool for addressing conflict situations.

CONCLUSION

I N THE POST–COLD WAR PERIOD, the United Nations Security Council has developed what is in many ways an entirely new system of legal authority for managing threats to peace and security. It has asserted the right to use its considerable Chapter VII powers with respect to any problem that might, in its judgment, "threaten the peace," including internal conflicts, widespread deprivations of human rights, humanitarian disasters, and serious threats to democratic government. It has used a variety of tools to deal with such problems, including economic and diplomatic sanctions, the creation of commissions and other organs with the power to make binding decisions, the prosecution of individuals, the disposition of the assets of states and individuals, the governance of territories, and armed force. It has made decisions on issues that go to the heart of state sovereignty, including statehood, territorial boundaries, and the political and economic structures of states and territories. The Council and the bodies it has created have exercised powers that are sometimes legislative, sometimes executive, and sometimes judicial in character. There are several ways to look at this new exercise of authority.

THE COUNCIL AS A SOURCE OF LEGAL AUTHORITY

In the U.S. State Department, the Council was seen as a source of legal authority to help solve a wide range of difficult foreign policy problems with myriad possibilities for international action. In the early post–Cold War period, some of these possibilities were relatively straightforward in a legal sense, such as the imposition of sanctions and the authorization of the use of force in such crises as the Gulf War and the former Yugoslavia. Some required the innovative use of Chapter VII to create new institutions, such as the two ad hoc criminal tribunals, the UN Compensation Commission, and the governing structures for Kosovo and East Timor. Some required a robust assertion of the Council's right to consider internal situations to be "a threat to the peace." In all these cases, the use of the Council's authority was more effective and expeditious than other alternatives. Indeed, it is difficult to see how many of these efforts could have been effectively accomplished in any other way.

None of the other elements of the current international system offers the same possibilities for rapid, decisive, flexible, and authoritative action. With some exceptions, the General Assembly cannot act with binding force and is not well suited to act decisively. Although the Assembly has in the past taken decisive action under the Uniting for Peace Resolution, that precedent has fallen into disuse and, in any event, could only be a basis for recommendations having no binding effect.

It is also true that regional organizations have the potential for rapid and decisive action, as has been demonstrated on occasion by NATO, ECOWAS, and other Chapter VIII entities. But the legal authority and capabilities of these organizations vary widely and are typically much weaker than those at the disposal of the Council. Under the Charter, they cannot take enforcement action without the authorization of the Council, and they have often operated as instrumentalities of the Council rather than as independent actors with respect to threats to the peace. As regional bodies, they are not effective vehicles for solving problems that go beyond a regional context.

It is also true that most international legal obligations are created through the negotiation of treaties and the operation of bodies they have created. This process allows full participation by all states in the formulation of and adherence to obligations, and, as a result, they can provide a more secure basis for acceptance and compliance than if the same obligations were simply imposed by the Council. But the negotiation and ratification of a treaty is typically a prolonged process, and a treaty cannot bind states that choose not to adhere to it. Thus a treaty is not usually a suitable vehicle for rapid and decisive action, nor for situations in which it is necessary to impose solutions on recalcitrant governments.

In the absence of authoritative international action, states will often resort to action on their own authority—either unilaterally or in "coalitions of the willing." Such action can of course be prompt and decisive, and in some situations is supported by international law and custom—for example, in the exercise of the right of self-defense or the rights of an occupying power. But such action is usually limited to ad hoc measures and is unsuitable for the creation of international institutions and legal regimes. Because it lacks the broader legal authority and political legitimacy that can derive from Council action, it may have difficulty in attracting broad international support and participation. Also, excessive reliance on such action can be dangerous for world order and stability, particularly where it involves the use of force or other coercive action, and it tends to subordinate legitimacy and the rule of law to the simple exercise of power.

From this perspective, it would be most unfortunate if the international community or its most powerful members were to turn away from the Council as a source of authority for the solution of critical problems. Over the years, one common criticism of the international system has been that its institutions are weak and have insufficient authority to create and enforce obligations that national governments and others are bound to obey. In particular, advocates of a stronger international system have always deplored the relative lack of authority of the international community as a whole to deal effectively with breaches of the peace and with underlying problems that threaten the peace. In the post–Cold War period, the Security Council has become a powerful new source of such authority.

None of this means that the Council can or should act as a "global legislature." In fact, the Council does exercise functions that are normally thought of as "legislative" in character, such as imposing legal obligations and creating subordinate bodies with legal authority. But the Council's jurisdiction is limited to actual threats to the peace, and while such threats can be generic in character rather than limited to specific situations, the Council does not have a mandate to address the broad range of international problems that do not pose such a threat. Nor would states accept that the Council should supersede the treaty-making process as the primary creator of legal obligations, as the debate over the Council's actions on WMD proliferation has shown. States will assent to the imposition of obligations where peace and security requires it, but they will otherwise insist on retaining the right to accept or reject such obligations and to participate in their formulation. But within these parameters, the Council's newfound authority is an essential legal basis for international action.

The Council as an Institution

Given the fact that the Council is a political body whose structure and method of work deliberately reflects the realities of power among states, one may ask whether it is an appropriate institution to create and exercise legal authority. (Indeed, in many ways the Council functions more as a forum for the interaction of its member states than as a single unified legal entity.) There has been much commentary by legal scholars in recent years on the "legitimacy" of the Council, the possibility of reform of its structure and rules, and the question of constraints or checks on its actions.

It has been argued from time to time that the Council, as a political body of state representatives, should not make legal decisions but should defer to judicial bodies like the International Court of Justice. Of course, neither the court nor any other judicial body in the current international system has the authority to make the legal decisions the Council has made under Chapter VII. But political bodies—particularly national legislatures—routinely make decisions on legal standards and obligations, create courts and other legal institutions, and decide how those obligations are to be enforced. There is no reason why the Council should not make such decisions as well, which implicate both policy and legal issues.

However, the Council itself may not be a suitable body to make specific kinds of decisions that may require the application of legal standards to complex factual situations (such as specific claims and the details of boundaries), or that require strict impartiality and separation from political influence (such as criminal proceedings). Generally, it would be appropriate for the Council to delegate such decisions to subordinate bodies that are composed of legal or other experts, and whose rules and methods of work are deliberative, transparent, and based on consistent standards. The Council did so with respect to the ad hoc criminal tribunals and the UN Compensation Commission, but may be faulted for failing to do so adequately in the case of some of the sanctions regimes, for example with respect to the identification of sanctioned persons and entities. No doubt, a person or entity affected by such a decision should have reasonable opportunity for input or appeal, and reasonable notice of the governing standards.

Further, during the post–Cold War period, the Council has used its newfound legal authority to create programs of great size and complexity, involving large sums of money and large numbers of transactions. As the allegations of fraud and abuse in the Iraqi Oil-for-Food Program clearly show, such programs must be administered by competent professionals with adequate authority and resources, and cannot be governed by special political interests. Administration must include auditing, monitoring, and (where necessary) inspection procedures that ensure the integrity and transparency of the process. Without such procedures in place, Council action might do as much harm as good. In cases where the UN Secretariat is unable to do so, the Council must establish special structures to do it, as was the case with the Compensation Commission and the governing bodies in East Timor and Kosovo.

As for the basic structure and operation of the Council, this matter has been extensively debated in the General Assembly and the Council itself.[1] Among other things, there has been criticism of the small and limited membership of the Council, the special status and influence of the five permanent members, the lack of openness and transparency in the Council's operations, and the predominant representation and influence of the developed states over the developing world. (To be more precise, Europe is heavily overrepresented and Asia heavily underrepresented.[2]) Quite apart from their political implications, one may ask whether these factors detract from the legitimacy of the Council in imposing and enforcing legal obligations.

In fact, other legal institutions in the international system share some of these characteristics. For example, the five permanent members of the Council effectively (if not formally) have permanent representation in the International Court of Justice and the International Law Commission. The membership of the court is as limited as the Council's and as weighted toward Europe and away from Asia. Although the members of these bodies are not representatives of their governments, nonetheless they are nominated by governments and it is fair to say that their basic orientation and perspectives reflect that fact.

This is not to say that the Council's current structure is ideal. Many states, including the United States, have indicated a willingness to consider moderate expansion of the Council and the inclusion of new permanent members—some of the prominent candidates being Japan, Germany, Brazil, and India.[3] As previously noted, the 2004 report of the secretary-general's high-level panel recommended an expansion in membership involving either new permanent members, a new class of semipermanent members, or additional nonpermanent members—none of whom would have the right of veto.[4] Such expansion would encourage more effective involvement and a greater sense of participation in the Council's work by non-European states and by important governments that can be expected to make unusual financial, military, and political contributions to the Council's efforts. Quite apart from its political benefits, expansion would offer a greater sense of legitimacy in the Council's creation of legal obligations that apply to all states.

As for the voting structure of the Council, although the permanent members are not about to give up or dilute their veto, it is possible for the Council to create subordinate bodies with different decision-making systems and to delegate important authority to these bodies. This has been done, for example, with the UN Compensation Commission, the ad hoc tribunals, and the governing authorities of territories administered pursuant to Chapter VII.

With respect to decisions taken directly by the Council itself, there is obviously room for improvement in the working methods of the Council to give greater transparency to its decisions and more effective input from all UN members. Some improvements have been made in recent years, including regular consultations with troop-contributing states, meetings open to all UN members, open briefing by Secretariat and other officials, and input from nongovernmental organizations.[5] Further efforts along these lines would be useful.

THE COUNCIL AND THE UNITED STATES

Two aspects of the relationship between the Council and its most powerful member have been much debated in policy circles during the post–Cold War period: the degree to which the United States should depend on the Council (or instead proceed unilaterally or through like-minded "coalitions of the willing") and the perceived dominance of the United States over the Council and its use to achieve U.S. ends. Without attempting here to resolve these larger policy issues, it may be useful to look at them briefly in light of the legal issues considered in this work.

As to the first aspect, there is no doubt that the effective expansion in the legal authority of the Council during this period has offered important possibilities for advancing U.S. interests and policy objectives. To take only a few prominent examples, the imposition of sanctions on Iraq and Serbia, the authorization for the use of force in the Gulf War, the creation of the ad hoc criminal tribunals and the UN Compensation Commission, the imposition of obligations concerning international terrorism and WMD proliferation—all were, to some degree, initiatives of the United States seeking to fulfill U.S. policy goals. In the absence of the exercise of legal authority by the Council, these U.S. initiatives would at the very least have been more difficult, less effective, less timely, or less likely to attract wide support. Furthermore, because the United States can prevent any adverse action by the Council, there is much less reason to fear that resort to the Council would create legal precedents for future action against U.S. interests—in contrast to unilateral action, which can be asserted as precedent for such action by others.

There will be situations in which the Council cannot be persuaded to support U.S. objectives, and in other cases it may be necessary for the United States to accept some constraints or limitations as the price for securing Council authorization. However, the events of the post–Cold War period show that in the great majority of cases, effective diplomacy, resolve, patience, and reasonable compromise have a good chance to produce Council action that is far better than unilateral options.

From the U.S. point of view, in virtually every case involving threats to the peace, there is every reason to look to the Council's legal authority and to exert every effort to make creative use of it. There are many reasons unilateral action, or action by "coalitions of the willing" without international mandate, is not a satisfactory substitute for action under the Council's authority, and among them are the legal tools and legal mandate provided by the exercise of Chapter VII. U.S. interests are plainly disserved by forgetting or ignoring the precedents set by Council action over the past fifteen years, or by bypassing the Council and thereby weakening its authority.

As to the second aspect, it is obvious that the United States has exercised considerable—in some ways, predominant—influence over the decisions of the Council (as have the other permanent members, though to a lesser degree). This is both inevitable and necessary, because effective action against threats to the peace will always depend on the leadership or acquiescence of states with predominant political, financial, and military power, and that would be true whatever the legal structure of the Council.

On the other hand, while the United States can prevent the Council from acting, it cannot compel it to act without the support of the other members of the Council, and this will be the case all the more if the Council's membership is expanded. To be sure, the United States has the advantage of continuity on the Council (as do the other permanent members), but this is also effectively the case in many other international bodies (such as the ICJ) where these states do not necessarily predominate. The interests of the permanent members do not always coincide, and even where they do, nothing in the structure or rules of the Council prevents other Council members from acting in concert to assert their own interests or to prevent action they consider to be inappropriate. If nonpermanent members refrain from doing so because they do not have the confidence or resources to pursue a different policy or because they wish to maintain good relations with powerful states, this is basically a reflection of underlying political and power realities and not of the structure and rules of the Council. (In fact, nearly all Council decisions are taken by unanimous or nearly unanimous votes, and changing the voting rules of the Council in this respect would not likely have much effect on the ability of the permanent members to secure adoption of their proposals.)

There are a number of ways in which the structure and operating methods of the Council can be improved, from moderate expansion in permanent and nonpermanent members, to greater transparency and inclusiveness in its decision making, to more effective and professional administration of its programs. But the interests of the less powerful states would not be served by weakening the Council, nor is it realistic to think that the Council can be effective in the area of peace and security if the more powerful states are not fully involved and do not exercise commensurate influence.

The United States and other UN members have a common interest in a strong Council, equipped with the expanded legal authority that it has developed in the post–Cold War period. It is in their common interest to have an authoritative international institution that can impose legal obligations, create institutions with legal authority, govern territories in chaos, and use force to deal with threats to the peace. Where the Council has failed during this period, typically it has not been because of excessive use of this authority but because of neglect, irresolution, or delay in using it. The United States largely was responsible for some of these failures—most notably the failure of the United Nations to take effective action on the Rwanda genocide—and U.S. interests are not well served by such inaction.

In the end, of course, no amount of legal authority can solve any serious problem in the international sphere without wise policy decisions, the will to exercise power when necessary, the commitment of adequate human and material resources, and the willingness to make genuine concessions in the interests of building consensus. The Council will never be able to exercise its inherently broad authority without a constant process of accommodation and compromise, together with vigorous leadership by governments that have the ability to exercise it. But the legal foundation for such a process has now been laid, if the international community is sufficiently wise and resolved to use it.

Appendix 1

Excerpts from the United Nations Charter

Chapter I
Purposes and Principles

Article 1

The Purposes of the United Nations are:

1. To maintain international peace and security, and to that end: to take effective collective measures for the prevention and removal of threats to the peace, and for the suppression of acts of aggression or other breaches of the peace, and to bring about by peaceful means, and in conformity with the principles of justice and international law, adjustment or settlement of international disputes or situations which might lead to a breach of the peace;

2. To develop friendly relations among nations based on respect for the principle of equal rights and self-determination of peoples, and to take other appropriate measures to strengthen universal peace;

3. To achieve international cooperation in solving international problems of an economic, social, cultural, or humanitarian character, and in promoting and encouraging respect for human rights and for fundamental freedoms for all without distinction as to race, sex, language, or religion; and

4. To be a center for harmonizing the actions of nations in the attainment of these common ends.

Article 2

The Organization and its Members, in pursuit of the Purposes stated in Article 1, shall act in accordance with the following Principles:

1. The Organization is based on the principle of the sovereign equality of all its Members.

2. All Members, in order to ensure to all of them the rights and benefits resulting from membership, shall fulfill in good faith the obligations assumed by them in accordance with the present Charter.

3. All Members shall settle their international disputes by peaceful means in such a manner that international peace and security, and justice, are not endangered.

4. All Members shall refrain in their international relations from the threat or use of force against the territorial integrity or political independence of any state, or in any other manner inconsistent with the Purposes of the United Nations.

5. All Members shall give the United Nations every assistance in any action it takes in accordance with the present Charter, and shall refrain from giving assistance to any state against which the United Nations is taking preventive or enforcement action.

6. The Organization shall ensure that states which are not Members of the United Nations act in accordance with these Principles so far as may be necessary for the maintenance of international peace and security.

7. Nothing contained in the present Charter shall authorize the United Nations to intervene in matters which are essentially within the domestic jurisdiction of any state or shall require the Members to submit such matters to settlement under the present Charter; but this principle shall not prejudice the application of enforcement measures under Chapter VII.

Chapter II
Membership

* * * * *

Article 5

A Member of the United Nations against which preventive or enforce-ment action has been taken by the Security Council may be sus-pended from the exercise of the rights and privileges of membership by the General Assembly upon the recommendation of the Security Council. The exercise of these rights and privileges may be restored by the Security Council.

Article 6

A Member of the United Nations which has persistently violated the Principles contained in the present Charter may be expelled from the Organization by the General Assembly upon the recommendation of the Security Council.

* * * * *

Chapter IV
The General Assembly

Article 11

1. The General Assembly may consider the general principles of co-operation in the maintenance of international peace and security, including the principles governing disarmament and the regulation of armaments, and may make recommendations with regard to such principles to the Members or to the Security Council or to both.

2. The General Assembly may discuss any questions relating to the maintenance of international peace and security brought before it by any Member of the United Nations, or by the Security Council, or by a state which is not a Member of the United Nations in accor-dance with Article 35, paragraph 2, and, except as provided in Arti-cle 12, may make recommendations with regard to any such ques-tions to the state or states concerned or to the Security Council or to both. Any such question on which action is necessary shall be

referred to the Security Council by the General Assembly either before or after discussion.

3. The General Assembly may call the attention of the Security Council to situations which are likely to endanger international peace and security.

4. The powers of the General Assembly set forth in this Article shall not limit the general scope of Article 10.

Article 12

1. While the Security Council is exercising in respect of any dispute or situation the functions assigned to it in the present Charter, the General Assembly shall not make any recommendation with regard to that dispute or situation unless the Security Council so requests.

* * * * *

CHAPTER V
THE SECURITY COUNCIL

Article 23

1. The Security Council shall consist of fifteen Members of the United Nations. The Republic of China, France, the Union of Soviet Socialist Republics, the United Kingdom of Great Britain and Northern Ireland, and the United States of America shall be permanent members of the Security Council. The General Assembly shall elect ten other Members of the United Nations to be non-permanent members of the Security Council, due regard being specially paid, in the first instance to the contribution of Members of the United Nations to the maintenance of international peace and security and to the other Purposes of the Organization, and also to equitable geographical distribution.

* * * * *

Article 24

1. In order to ensure prompt and effective action by the United Nations, its Members confer on the Security Council primary responsibility for the maintenance of international peace and security, and agree that in carrying out its duties under this responsibility the Security Council acts on their behalf.

2. In discharging these duties the Security Council shall act in accordance with the Purposes and Principles of the United Nations. The specific powers granted to the Security Council for the discharge of these duties are laid down in Chapters VI, VII, VIII, and XII.

3. The Security Council shall submit annual and, when necessary, special reports to the General Assembly for its consideration.

* * * * *

Article 25

The Members of the United Nations agree to accept and carry out the decisions of the Security Council in accordance with the present Charter.

Article 26

In order to promote the establishment and maintenance of international peace and security with the least diversion for armaments of the world's human and economic resources, the Security Council shall be responsible for formulating, with the assistance of the Military Staff Committee referred to in Article 47, plans to be submitted to the Members of the United Nations for the establishment of a system for the regulation of armaments.

Article 27

1. Each member of the Security Council shall have one vote.

2. Decisions of the Security Council on procedural matters shall be made by an affirmative vote of nine members.

3. Decisions of the Security Council on all other matters shall be made by an affirmative vote of nine members including the concurring votes of the permanent members; provided that, in decisions under Chapter VI, and under paragraph 3 of Article 52, a party to a dispute shall abstain from voting.

* * * * *

Article 29

The Security Council may establish such subsidiary organs as it deems necessary for the performance of its functions.

* * * * *

CHAPTER VI
PACIFIC SETTLEMENT OF DISPUTES

Article 33

1. The parties to any dispute, the continuance of which is likely to endanger the maintenance of international peace and security, shall, first of all, seek a solution by negotiation, enquiry, mediation, conciliation, arbitration, judicial settlement, resort to regional agencies or arrangements, or other peaceful means of their own choice.

2. The Security Council shall, when it deems necessary, call upon the parties to settle their dispute by such means.

Article 34

The Security Council may investigate any dispute, or any situation which might lead to international friction or give rise to a dispute, in order to determine whether the continuance of the dispute or situation is likely to endanger the maintenance of international peace and security.

* * * * *

Article 36

1. The Security Council may, at any stage of a dispute of the nature referred to in Article 33 or of a situation of like nature, recommend appropriate procedures or methods of adjustment.

2. The Security Council should take into consideration any procedures for the settlement of the dispute which have already been adopted by the parties.

3. In making recommendations under this Article the Security Council should also take into consideration that legal disputes should as a general rule be referred by the parties to the International Court of Justice in accordance with the provisions of the Statute of the Court.

Article 37

1. Should the parties to a dispute of the nature referred to in Article 33 fail to settle it by the means indicated in that Article, they shall refer it to the Security Council.

2. If the Security Council deems that the continuance of the dispute is in fact likely to endanger the maintenance of international peace and security, it shall decide whether to take action under Article 36 or to recommend such terms of settlement as it may consider appropriate.

Article 38

Without prejudice to the provisions of Articles 33 to 37, the Security Council may, if all the parties to any dispute so request, make recommendations to the parties with a view to a pacific settlement of the dispute.

Chapter VII
Action With Respect to Threats to the Peace, Breaches of the Peace, and Acts of Aggression

Article 39

The Security Council shall determine the existence of any threat to the peace, breach of the peace, or act of aggression and shall make recommendations, or decide what measures shall be taken in accordance with Articles 41 and 42, to maintain or restore international peace and security.

Article 40

In order to prevent an aggravation of the situation, the Security Council may, before making the recommendations or deciding upon the measures provided for in Article 39, call upon the parties concerned to comply with such provisional measures as it deems necessary or desirable. Such provisional measures shall be without prejudice to the rights, claims, or position of the parties concerned. The Security Council shall duly take account of failure to comply with such provisional measures.

Article 41

The Security Council may decide what measures not involving the use of armed force are to be employed to give effect to its decisions, and it may call upon the Members of the United Nations to apply such measures. These may include complete or partial interruption of economic relations and of rail, sea, air, postal, telegraphic, radio, and other means of communication, and the severance of diplomatic relations.

Article 42

Should the Security Council consider that measures provided for in Article 41 would be inadequate or have proved to be inadequate, it may take such action by air, sea, or land forces as may be necessary to maintain or restore international peace and security. Such action may include demonstrations, blockade, and other operations by air, sea, or land forces of Members of the United Nations.

Article 43

1. All Members of the United Nations, in order to contribute to the maintenance of international peace and security, undertake to make available to the Security Council, on its call and in accordance with a special agreement or agreements, armed forces, assistance, and facilities, including rights of passage, necessary for the purpose of maintaining international peace and security.

2. Such agreement or agreements shall govern the numbers and types of forces, their degree of readiness and general location, and the nature of the facilities and assistance to be provided.

3. The agreement or agreements shall be negotiated as soon as possible on the initiative of the Security Council. They shall be concluded between the Security Council and Members or between the Security Council and groups of Members and shall be subject to ratification by the signatory states in accordance with their respective constitutional processes.

* * * * *

Article 45

In order to enable the United Nations to take urgent military measures, Members shall hold immediately available national air-force contingents for combined international enforcement action. The strength and degree of readiness of these contingents and plans for their combined action shall be determined, within the limits laid down in the special agreement or agreements referred to in Article 43, by the Security Council with the assistance of the Military Staff Committee.

Article 46

Plans for the application of armed force shall be made by the Security Council with the assistance of the Military Staff Committee.

Article 47

1. There shall be established a Military Staff Committee to advise and assist the Security Council on all questions relating to the Security Council's military requirements for the maintenance of international peace and security, the employment and command of forces placed at its disposal, the regulation of armaments, and possible disarmament.

2. The Military Staff Committee shall consist of the Chiefs of Staff of the permanent members of the Security Council or their representatives. Any Member of the United Nations not permanently represented on the Committee shall be invited by the Committee to be associated with it when the efficient discharge of the Committee's responsibilities requires the participation of that Member in its work.

3. The Military Staff Committee shall be responsible under the Security Council for the strategic direction of any armed forces placed at the disposal of the Security Council. Questions relating to the command of such forces shall be worked out subsequently.

4. The Military Staff Committee, with the authorization of the security council and after consultation with the appropriate regional agencies, may establish regional subcommittees.

Article 48

1. The action required to carry out the decisions of the Security Council for the maintenance of international peace and security shall be taken by all the Members of the United Nations or by some of them, as the Security Council may determine.

2. Such decisions shall be carried out by the Members of the United Nations directly and through their action in the appropriate international agencies of which they are members.

Article 49

The Members of the United Nations shall join in affording mutual assistance in carrying out the measures decided upon by the Security Council.

Article 50

If preventive or enforcement measures against any state are taken by the Security Council, any other state, whether a Member of the United Nations or not, which finds itself confronted with special economic problems arising from the carrying out of those measures shall have the right to consult the Security Council with regard to a solution of those problems.

Article 51

Nothing in the present Charter shall impair the inherent right of individual or collective self-defense if an armed attack occurs against a Member of the United Nations, until the Security Council has taken measures necessary to maintain international peace and security. Measures taken by Members in the exercise of this right of self-defense shall be immediately reported to the Security Council and shall not in any way affect the authority and responsibility of the Security Council under the present Charter to take at any time such action as it deems necessary in order to maintain or restore international peace and security.

CHAPTER VIII
REGIONAL ARRANGEMENTS

Article 52

1. Nothing in the present Charter precludes the existence of regional arrangements or agencies for dealing with such matters relating to the maintenance of international peace and security as are appropriate for regional action, provided that such arrangements or agencies and their activities are consistent with the Purposes and Principles of the United Nations.

2. The Members of the United Nations entering into such arrangements or constituting such agencies shall make every effort to

achieve pacific settlement of local disputes through such regional arrangements or by such regional agencies before referring them to the Security Council.

3. The Security Council shall encourage the development of pacific settlement of local disputes through such regional arrangements or by such regional agencies either on the initiative of the states concerned or by reference from the Security Council.

4. This article in no way impairs the application of Articles 34 and 35.

Article 53

1. The Security Council shall, where appropriate, utilize such regional arrangements or agencies for enforcement action under its authority. But no enforcement action shall be taken under regional arrangements or by regional agencies without the authorization of the Security Council. . . .

* * * * *

Chapter XIV
The International Court of Justice

Article 92

The International Court of Justice shall be the principal judicial organ of the United Nations. . . .

* * * * *

Article 94

1. Each Member of the United Nations undertakes to comply with the decision of the International Court of Justice in any case to which it is a party.

2. If any party to a case fails to perform the obligations incumbent upon it under a judgment rendered by the Court, the other party may have recourse to the Security Council, which may, if it deems necessary, make recommendations or decide upon measures to be taken to give effect to the judgment.

* * * * *

Chapter XV
The Secretariat

Article 97

The Secretariat shall comprise a Secretary-General and such staff as the Organization may require. The Secretary-General shall be appointed by the General Assembly upon the recommendation of the Security Council. He shall be the chief administrative officer of the Organization.

* * * * *

Article 99

The Secretary-General may bring to the attention of the Security Council any matter which in his opinion may threaten the maintenance of international peace and security.

* * * * *

Chapter XVI
Miscellaneous Provisions

Article 103

In the event of a conflict between the obligations of the Members of the United Nations under the present Charter and their obligations under any other international agreement, their obligations under the present Charter shall prevail.

* * * * *

Chapter XVII
Transitional Security Arrangements

Article 106

Pending the coming into force of such special agreements referred to in Article 43 as in the opinion of the Security Council enable it to begin the exercise of its responsibilities under Article 42, the parties to the Four-Nation Declaration, signed at Moscow, October 30, 1943, and France, shall, in accordance with the provisions of paragraph 5 of that Declaration, consult with one another and as occasion requires with other Members of the United Nations with a view to such joint action on behalf of the Organization as may be necessary for the purpose of maintaining international peace and security.

* * * * *

APPENDIX 2

UN PEACEKEEPING OPERATIONS
(as listed by the UN Department of Peacekeeping Operations)

AFRICA

Angola:
— **UNAVEM I:** UN Angola Verification Mission I
  (December 1988–May 1991)
— **UNAVEM II:** UN Angola Verification Mission II
  (May 1991–February 1995)
— **UNAVEM III:** UN Angola Verification Mission III
  (February 1995–June 1997)
— **MONUA:** UN Observation Mission in Angola
  (June 1997–February 1999)

Burundi:
— **ONUB:** UN Operation in Burundi
  (May 2004–present)

Central African Republic:
— **MINURCA:** UN Mission in the Central African Republic
  (April 1998–February 2000)

Chad:
— **UNASOG:** UN Aouzou Strip Observer Group
  (May–June 1994)

Congo:
— **ONUC:** UN Operation in the Congo (July 1960–June 1964)
— **MONUC:** UN Organization Mission in the Democratic Republic of the Congo (November 1999–present)

Côte d'Ivoire:
— **UNOCI:** UN Operation in Côte d'Ivoire (April 2004–present)

Ethiopia-Eritrea:
— **UNMEE:** UN Mission in Ethiopia and Eritrea (July 2000–present)

Liberia:
— **UNOMIL:** UN Observer Mission in Liberia (September 1993–September 1997)
— **UNMIL**: UN Mission in Liberia (September 2003–present)

Mozambique:
— **ONUMOZ:** UN Operation in Mozambique (December 1992–December 1994)

Namibia:
— **UNTAG:** UN Transition Assistance Group (April 1989–March 1990)

Rwanda:
— **UNOMUR:** UN Observer Mission Uganda-Rwanda (June 1993–September 1994)
— **UNAMIR:** UN Assistance Mission for Rwanda (October 1993–March 1996)

Sierra Leone:
— **UNOMSIL:** UN Observer Mission in Sierra Leone (July 1998–October 1999)
— **UNAMSIL:** UN Mission in Sierra Leone (October 1999–present)

Somalia:
— **UNOSOM I:** UN Operation in Somalia I (April 1992–March 1993)

— **UNOSOM II:** UN Operation in Somalia II
(March 1993–March 1995)

Sudan:
— **UNMIS:** UN Mission in the Sudan (March 2005–present)

Western Sahara:
— **MINURSO:** UN Mission for the Referendum in Western
Sahara (April 1991–present)

AMERICAS

Central America:
— **ONUCA:** UN Observer Group in Central America
(November 1989–January 1992)

Dominican Republic:
— **DOMREP:** Mission of the Special Representative in the
Dominican Republic (May 1965–October 1966)

El Salvador:
— **ONUSAL:** UN Observer Mission in El Salvador
(July 1991–April 1995)

Guatemala:
— **MINUGUA:** UN Verification Mission in Guatemala
(January–May 1997)

Haiti:
— **UNMIH:** UN Mission in Haiti (September 1993–June 1996)
— **UNSMIH:** UN Support Mission in Haiti
(July 1996–June 1997)
— **UNTMIH:** UN Transition Mission in Haiti
(August–November 1997)
— **MIPONUH:** UN Civilian Police Mission in Haiti
(December 1997–March 2000)
— **MINUSTAH:** UN Stabilization Mission in Haiti
(April 2004–present)

ASIA

Afghanistan-Pakistan:
— **UNGOMAP:** UN Good Offices Mission in Afghanistan and
   Pakistan (May 1988–March 1990)

Cambodia:
— **UNAMIC:** UN Advance Mission in Cambodia
   (October 1991–March 1992)
— **UNTAC:** UN Transitional Authority in Cambodia
   (March 1992–September 1993)

East Timor:
— **UNTAET:** UN Transitional Administration in East Timor
   (October 1999–May 2002)
— **UNMISET:** UN Mission of Support in East Timor
   (May 2002–May 2005)

India-Pakistan:
— **UNIPOM:** UN India-Pakistan Observation Mission
   (September 1965–March 1966)
— **UNMOGIP:** UN Military Observer Group in India and
   Pakistan (January 1949–present)

Indonesia:
— **UNSF:** UN Security Force in West New Guinea
   (October 1962–April 1963)

Tajikistan:
— **UNMOT:** UN Mission of Observers in Tajikistan
   (December 1994–May 2000)

EUROPE

Cyprus:
— **UNFICYP:** UN Peacekeeping Force in Cyprus
   (March 1964–present)

Former Yugoslavia:
— **UNPROFOR:** UN Protection Force
   (February 1992–March 1995)

— **UNPREDEP:** UN Preventive Deployment Force
   (March 1995–February 1999)
— **UNCRO:** UN Confidence Restoration Operation
   (March 1995–January 1996)
— **UNMIBH:** UN Mission in Bosnia and Herzegovina
   (December 1995–December 2002)
— **UNTAES:** UN Transitional Authority in Eastern Slavonia,
   Baranja, and Western Sirmium (January 1996–January 1998)
— **UNMOP:** UN Mission of Observers in Prevlaka
   (February 1996–December 2002)
— **UNPSG:** UN Civilian Police Support Group
   (January–October 1998)
— **UNMIK:** UN Interim Administration in Kosovo
   (June 1999–present)

Georgia:
— **UNOMIG:** UN Observer Mission in Georgia
   (August 1993–present)

MIDDLE EAST

Golan Heights:
— **UNDOF:** UN Disengagement Observer Force
   (May 1974–present)

Iran-Iraq:
— **UNIIMOG:** UN Iran-Iraq Military Observer Group
   (August 1988–February 1991)

Iraq-Kuwait:
— **UNIKOM:** UN Iraq-Kuwait Observation Mission
   (April 1991–October 2003)

Lebanon:
— **UNOGIL:** UN Observation Group in Lebanon
   (June–December 1958)
— **UNIFIL:** UN Interim Force in Lebanon
   (March 1978–present)

Middle East:
— **UNTSO:** UN Truce Supervision Organization
   (May 1948–present)
— **UNEF I:** First UN Emergency Force
   (November 1956–June 1967)
— **UNEF II:** Second UN Emergency Force
   (October 1973–July 1979)

Yemen:
— **UNYOM:** UN Yemen Observation Mission
   (July 1963–September 1964)

APPENDIX 3

PARTIES TO THE STATUTE OF THE INTERNATIONAL CRIMINAL COURT
(as of December 2005*)

Adopted July 17, 1998 at Rome. Entered into force July 1, 2002.

Afghanistan (February 10, 2003)
Albania (January 31, 2003)
Andorra (April 30, 2001)
Antigua and Barbuda (June 18, 2001)
Argentina (February 8, 2001)
Australia (July 1, 2002)
Austria (December 28, 2000)
Barbados (December 10, 2002)
Belgium (June 28, 2000)
Belize (April 5, 2000)
Benin (January 22, 2002)
Bolivia (June 27, 2002)
Bosnia and Herzegovina (April 11, 2002)
Botswana (September 8, 2000)
Brazil (June 20, 2002)

---

* Ratification Status of the Rome Statute of the International Criminal Court, www.untreaty.un.org.

Bulgaria (April 11, 2002)
Burkina Faso (April 16, 2004)
Burundi (September 21, 2004)
Cambodia (April 11, 2002)
Canada (July 7, 2000)
Central African Republic (October 3, 2001)
Colombia (August 5, 2002) **
Congo, Democratic Republic of the (April 11, 2002)
Congo, Republic of the (May 3, 2004)
Costa Rica (June 7, 2001)
Croatia (May 21, 2001)
Cyprus (March 7, 2002)
Denmark (June 21, 2001)
Djibouti (November 5, 2002)
Dominica (February 12, 2001)
Dominican Republic (May 12, 2005)
Ecuador (February 5, 2002)
Estonia (January 30, 2002)
Fiji (November 29, 1999)
Finland (December 29, 2000)
France (June 9, 2000) **
Gabon (September 20, 2000)
Gambia (June 28, 2002)
Georgia (September 5, 2003)
Germany (December 11, 2000)
Ghana (December 20, 1999)
Greece (May 15, 2002)
Guinea (July 14, 2003)
Guyana (September 24, 2004)
Honduras (July 1, 2002)
Hungary (November 30, 2001)
Iceland (May 25, 2000)
Ireland (April 11, 2002)

** With a declaration under Article 124 of the Statute that it does not accept
the jurisdiction of the Court for a period of seven years with respect to war
crimes committed by its nationals or on its territory.

Italy (July 26, 1999)
Jordan (April 11, 2002)
Kenya (March 15, 2005)
Korea, Republic of (November 13, 2002)
Latvia (June 28, 2002)
Lesotho (September 6, 2000)
Liberia (September 22, 2004)
Liechtenstein (October 2, 2001)
Lithuania (May 12, 2003)
Luxembourg (September 8, 2000)
Macedonia (March 6, 2002)
Malawi (September 19, 2002)
Mali (August 18, 2000)
Malta (November 29, 2002)
Marshall Islands (December 7, 2000)
Mauritius (March 5, 2002)
Mexico (October 28, 2005)
Mongolia (April 11, 2002)
Namibia (June 25, 2002)
Nauru (November 12, 2001)
Netherlands (July 17, 2001)
New Zealand (September 7, 2000)
Niger (April 11, 2002)
Nigeria (September 27, 2001)
Norway (February 16, 2000)
Panama (March 21, 2002)
Paraguay (May 14, 2001)
Peru (November 10, 2001)
Poland (November 12, 2001)
Portugal (February 5, 2002)
Romania (April 11, 2002)
Saint Vincent and the Grenadines (December 3, 2002)
Samoa (September 16, 2002)
San Marino (May 13, 1999)
Senegal (February 2, 1999)
Serbia and Montenegro (September 6, 2001)
Sierra Leone (September 15, 2000)

Slovakia (April 11, 2002)
Slovenia (December 31, 2001)
South Africa (November 27, 2000)
Spain (October 24, 2000)
Sweden (June 28, 2001)
Switzerland (October 12, 2001)
Tajikistan (May 5, 2000)
Tanzania (August 20, 2002)
Timor-Leste (September 6, 2002)
Trinidad and Tobago (April 6, 1999)
Uganda (June 14, 2002)
United Kingdom (October 4, 2001)
Uruguay (June 28, 2002)
Venezuela (June 7, 2000)
Zambia (November 13, 2002)

APPENDIX 4

EXCERPTS FROM THE STATUTES OF THE INTERNATIONAL CRIMINAL TRIBUNALS

I. THE INTERNATIONAL CRIMINAL TRIBUNAL FOR THE FORMER YUGOSLAVIA
Adopted by UN Security Council Resolution 827 (May 25, 1993)

Article 1. Competence of the International Tribunal

The International Tribunal shall have the power to prosecute persons responsible for serious violations of international humanitarian law committed in the territory of the former Yugoslavia since 1991 in accordance with the provisions of the present Statute.*

* * * * *

Article 9. Concurrent jurisdiction

1. The International Tribunal and national courts shall have concurrent jurisdiction to prosecute persons for serious violations of international humanitarian law committed in the territory of the former Yugoslavia since January 1, 1991.

---

* Articles 2–5 provide that the serious violations over which the tribunal has jurisdiction are: (1) grave breaches of the 1949 Geneva Conventions; (2) violations of the laws or customs of war; (3) genocide; and (4) crimes against humanity.

2. The International Tribunal shall have primacy over national courts. At any stage of the procedure, the International Tribunal may formally request national courts to defer to the competence of the International Tribunal in accordance with the present Statute and the Rules of Procedure and Evidence of the International Tribunal.

* * * * *

Article 29. Cooperation and judicial assistance

1. States shall cooperate with the International Tribunal in the investigation and prosecution of persons accused of committing serious violations of international humanitarian law.

2. States shall comply without undue delay with any request for assistance or an order issued by a Trial Chamber, including, but not limited to:

   (a) the identification and location of persons;

   (b) the taking of testimony and the production of evidence;

   (c) the service of documents;

   (d) the arrest or detention of persons;

   (e) the surrender or the transfer of the accused to the International Tribunal.

II. THE INTERNATIONAL CRIMINAL TRIBUNAL FOR RWANDA
Adopted by UN Security Council Resolution 955 (November 8, 1994)

Article 1. Competence of the International Tribunal for Rwanda

The International Tribunal for Rwanda shall have the power to prosecute persons responsible for serious violations of international humanitarian law committed in the territory of Rwanda and Rwandan citizens responsible for such violations committed in the territory of neighboring States between January 1, 1994 and December 31, 1994, in accordance with the provisions of the present Statute.*

* * * * *

---

* Articles 2–4 provide that the serious violations over which the tribunal has jurisdiction are: (1) genocide; (2) crimes against humanity; and (3) violations of Article 3 and Additional Protocol II to 1949 Geneva Conventions.

Article 8. Concurrent jurisdiction

1. The International Tribunal for Rwanda and national courts shall have concurrent jurisdiction to prosecute persons for serious violations of international humanitarian law committed in the territory of Rwanda and Rwandan citizens for such violations committed in the territory of the neighboring States, between 1 January 1994 and 31 December 1994.

2. The International Tribunal for Rwanda shall have primacy over national courts of all States. At any stage of the procedure, the International Tribunal for Rwanda may formally request national courts to defer to its competence in accordance with the present Statute and the Rules of Procedure and Evidence of the International Tribunal for Rwanda.

* * * * *

Article 28. Cooperation and judicial assistance

1. States shall cooperate with the International Tribunal for Rwanda in the investigation and prosecution of persons accused of committing serious violations of international humanitarian law.

2. States shall comply without undue delay with any request for assistance or an order issued by a Trial Chamber, including, but not limited to:

    (a) the identification and location of persons;

    (b) the taking of testimony and the production of evidence;

    (c) the service of documents;

    (d) the arrest or detention of persons;

    (e) the surrender or the transfer of the accused to the International Tribunal for Rwanda.

III. The International Criminal Court

Adopted July 17, 1998 at Rome
Entered into force July 1, 2002

Article 1. The Court

An International Criminal Court ("the Court") is hereby established. It shall be a permanent institution and shall have the power to exercise its jurisdiction over persons for the most serious crimes of international concern, as referred to in this Statute, and shall be complementary to national criminal jurisdictions. The jurisdiction and functioning of the Court shall be governed by the provisions of this Statute.

* * * * *

Article 5. Crimes within the jurisdiction of the Court

1. The jurisdiction of the Court shall be limited to the most serious crimes of concern to the international community as a whole. The Court has jurisdiction in accordance with this Statute with respect to the following crimes:

   (a) The crime of genocide;

   (b) Crimes against humanity;

   (c) War crimes;

   (d) The crime of aggression.

2. The Court shall exercise jurisdiction over the crime of aggression once a provision is adopted in accordance with Articles 121 and 123 defining the crime and setting out the conditions under which the Court shall exercise jurisdiction with respect to this crime. Such a provision shall be consistent with the relevant provisions of the Charter of the United Nations.

* * * * *

Article 11. Jurisdiction ratione temporis

1. The Court has jurisdiction only with respect to crimes committed after the entry into force of this Statute.

2. If a State becomes a Party to this Statute after its entry into force, the Court may exercise its jurisdiction only with respect to crimes committed after the entry into force of this Statute for that State, unless that State has made a declaration under Article 12, paragraph 3.

Article 12. Preconditions to the exercise of jurisdiction

1. A State which becomes a Party to this Statute thereby accepts the jurisdiction of the Court with respect to the crimes referred to in Article 5.

2. In the case of Article 13, paragraph (a) or (c), the Court may exercise its jurisdiction if one or more of the following States are Parties to this Statute or have accepted the jurisdiction of the Court in accordance with paragraph 3:

   (a) The State on the territory of which the conduct in question occurred or, if the crime was committed on board a vessel or aircraft, the State of registration of that vessel or aircraft;

   (b) The State of which the person accused of the crime is a national.

3. If the acceptance of a State which is not a Party to this Statute is required under paragraph 2, that State may, by declaration lodged with the Registrar, accept the exercise of jurisdiction by the Court with respect to the crime in question. The accepting State shall cooperate with the Court without any delay or exception in accordance with Part 9.

Article 13. Exercise of jurisdiction

The Court may exercise its jurisdiction with respect to a crime referred to in Article 5 in accordance with the provisions of this Statute if:

   (a) A situation in which one or more of such crimes appears to have been committed is referred to the Prosecutor by a State Party in accordance with Article 14;

   (b) A situation in which one or more of such crimes appears to have been committed is referred to the Prosecutor by the Security Council acting under Chapter VII of the United Nations; or

   (c) The Prosecutor has initiated an investigation in respect of such a crime in accordance with Article 15.

* * * * *

Article 16. Deferral of investigation or prosecution

No investigation or prosecution may be commenced or proceeded with under this Statute for a period of twelve months after the Security Council, in a resolution adopted under Chapter VII of the Charter of the United Nations, has requested the Court to that effect; that request may be renewed by the Council under the same conditions.

Article 17. Issues of admissibility

1. Having regard to paragraph 10 of the Preamble and Article 1, the Court shall determine that a case is inadmissible where:

    (a) The case is being investigated or prosecuted by a State which has jurisdiction over it, unless the State is unwilling or unable genuinely to carry out the investigation or prosecution;

    (b) The case has been investigated by a State which has jurisdiction over it and the State has decided not to prosecute the person concerned, unless the decision resulted from the unwillingness or inability of the State genuinely to prosecute;

    (c) The person concerned has already been tried for conduct which is the subject of the complaint, and a trial by the Court is not permitted under Article 20, paragraph 3;

    (d) The case is not of sufficient gravity to justify further action by the Court.

* * * * *

Article 89. Surrender of persons to the Court

1. The Court may transmit a request for the arrest and surrender of a person, together with the material supporting the request outlined in Article 91, to any State on the territory of which that person may be found and shall request the cooperation of that State in the arrest and surrender of such a person. States Parties shall, in accordance with the provisions of this Part and the procedure under their national law, comply with requests for arrest and surrender.

* * * * *

Article 93. Other forms of cooperation

1. States Parties shall, in accordance with the provisions of this Part and under procedures of national law, comply with requests by the Court to provide the following assistance in relation to investigations or prosecutions:

    (a) The identification and whereabouts of persons or the location of items;

(b) The taking of evidence, including testimony under oath, and the production of evidence, including expert opinions and reports necessary to the Court;

(c) The questioning of any person being investigated or prosecuted;

(d) The service of documents, including judicial documents;

(e) Facilitating the voluntary appearance of persons as witnesses or experts before the Court;

(f) The temporary transfer of persons as provided in paragraph 7;

(g) The examination of places or sites, including the exhumation and examination of grave sites;

(h) The execution of searches and seizures;

(i) The provision of records and documents, including official records and documents;

(j) The protection of victims and witnesses and the preservation of evidence;

(k) The identification, tracing and freezing or seizure of proceeds, property and assets and instrumentalities of crimes for the purpose of eventual forfeiture, without prejudice to the rights of bona fide third parties; and

(l) Any other type of assistance which is not prohibited by the law of the requested State, with a view to facilitating the investigation and prosecution of crimes within the jurisdiction of the Court.

* * * * *

Article 98. Cooperation with respect to waiver of immunity and consent to surrender

1. The Court may not proceed with a request for surrender or assistance which would require the requested State to act inconsistently with its obligations under international law with respect to the State or diplomatic immunity of a person or property of a third State, unless the Court can first obtain the cooperation of that third State for the waiver of the immunity.

2. The Court may not proceed with a request for surrender which would require the requested State to act inconsistently with its

obligations under international agreements pursuant to which the consent of a sending State is required to surrender a person of that State to the Court, unless the Court can first obtain the cooperation of the sending State for the giving of consent for the surrender.

* * * * *

Article 124. Transitional Provision

Notwithstanding Article 12, paragraphs 1 and 2, a State, on becoming a party to this Statute, may declare that, for a period of seven years after the entry into force of this Statute for the State concerned, it does not accept the jurisdiction of the Court with respect to the category of crimes referred to in Article 8 when a crime is alleged to have been committed by its nationals or on its territory.* A declaration under this article may be withdrawn at any time. . . .

* * * * *

---

*Article 8 deals with war crimes.

Appendix 5

Excerpts from Significant Decisions of the Security Council in the Post–Cold War Period

Resolution 660
(August 2, 1990)

The Security Council,

Alarmed by the invasion of Kuwait on August 2, 1990 by the military forces of Iraq,

Determining that there exists a breach of international peace and security as regards the Iraqi invasion of Kuwait,

Acting under Articles 39 and 40 of the Charter of the United Nations,

1. *Condemns* the Iraqi invasion of Kuwait;

2. *Demands* that Iraq withdraw immediately and unconditionally all its forces to the positions in which they were located on August 1, 1990;

3. *Calls upon* Iraq and Kuwait to begin immediately intensive negotiations for the resolution of their differences and supports all efforts in this regard, and especially those of the League of Arab States;

4. *Decides* to meet again as necessary to consider further steps to ensure compliance with the present resolution.

RESOLUTION 661
(August 6, 1990)

The Security Council, . . .

Determined to bring the invasion and occupation of Kuwait by Iraq to an end and to restore the sovereignty, independence, and territorial integrity of Kuwait, . . .

Affirming the inherent right of individual or collective self-defense, in response to armed attack by Iraq against Kuwait, in accordance with Article 51 of the Charter,

Acting under Chapter VII of the Charter,

1. *Determines* that Iraq so far has failed to comply with paragraph 2 of Resolution 660 (1990) and has usurped the authority of the legitimate Government of Kuwait;

2. *Decides,* as a consequence, to take the following measures to secure compliance of Iraq with paragraph 2 of Resolution 660 (1990) and to restore the authority of the legitimate Government of Kuwait;

3. *Decides* that all States shall prevent:

    (a) The import into their territories of all commodities and products originating in Iraq or Kuwait exported therefrom after the date of the present resolution;

    (b) Any activities by their nationals or in their territories which would promote or are calculated to promote the export or trans-shipment of any commodities or products from Iraq or Kuwait; and any dealings by their nationals or their flag vessels or in their territories in any commodities or products originating in Iraq or Kuwait for the purposes of such activities or dealings;

    (c) The sale or supply by their nationals or from their territories or using their flag vessels of any commodities or products, including weapons or any other military equipment, whether or not originating in their territories but not including supplies intended strictly for medical purposes, and, in humanitarian circumstances, foodstuffs, to any person or body in Iraq or Kuwait or to any person or body for the purposes of any business carried on in or operated from Iraq or Kuwait, and any activities by their nationals or in their territories which promote or are calculated to promote such sale or supply of such commodities or products;

4. *Decides* that all States shall not make available to the Government of Iraq, or to any commercial, industrial, or public utility undertaking in Iraq or Kuwait, any funds or any other financial or economic resources and shall prevent their nationals and any persons within their territories from removing from their territories or otherwise making available to that Government or to any such undertaking any such funds to persons or bodies within Iraq or Kuwait, except payments exclusively for strictly medical or humanitarian purposes and, in humanitarian circumstances, foodstuffs;

5. *Calls upon* all States, including States nonmembers of the United Nations, to act strictly in accordance with the provisions of the present resolution notwithstanding any contract entered into or license granted before the date of the present resolution;

6. *Decides* to establish, in accordance with rule 28 of the provisional rules of procedure, a Committee of the Security Council consisting of all the members of the Council, to undertake the following tasks and to report on its work to the Council with its observations and recommendations:

   (a) To examine the reports on the progress of the implementation of the present resolution which will be submitted to the Secretary-General;

   (b) To seek from all States further information regarding the action taken by them concerning the effective implementation of the provisions laid down in the present resolution. . . .

Resolution 678
(November 29, 1990)

The Security Council, . . .
Acting under Chapter VII of the Charter,

1. *Demands* that Iraq comply fully with Resolution 660 (1990) and all subsequent relevant resolutions, and decides, while maintaining all

its decisions, to allow Iraq one final opportunity, as a pause of good-will, to do so;

2. *Authorizes* Member States cooperating with the Government of Kuwait, unless Iraq on or before January 15, 1991 fully implements, as set forth in paragraph 1 above, the above-mentioned resolutions, to use all necessary means to uphold and implement Resolution 660 (1990) and all subsequent relevant resolutions and to restore international peace and security in the area;

3. *Requests* all States to provide appropriate support for the actions undertaken in pursuance of paragraph 2 above;

4. *Requests* the States concerned to keep the Security Council regularly informed on the progress of actions undertaken pursuant to paragraphs 2 and 3 above;

5. *Decides* to remain seized of the matter.

RESOLUTION 687
(April 3, 1991)

The Security Council, . . .
Conscious of the need to take the following measures acting under Chapter VII of the Charter,

1. *Affirms* all thirteen resolutions noted above, except as expressly changed below to achieve the goals of the present resolution, including a formal cease-fire:

A

2. *Demands* that Iraq and Kuwait respect the inviolability of the international boundary and the allocations of islands set out in the "Agreed Minutes between the State of Kuwait and the Republic of Iraq regarding the restoration of friendly relations, recognition, and related matters," signed by them in the exercise of their sovereignty at Baghdad on October 4, 1963 and registered with the United Nations;

3. *Calls upon* the Secretary-General to lend his assistance to make arrangements with Iraq and Kuwait to demarcate the boundary between Iraq and Kuwait . . . ;

4. *Decides* to guarantee the inviolability of the above-mentioned international boundary and to take, as appropriate, all necessary measures to that end in accordance with the Charter of the United Nations;

B

5. *Requests* the Secretary-General, after consulting with Iraq and Kuwait, to submit within three days to the Council for its approval a plan for the immediate deployment of a United Nations observer unit to monitor the Khawr 'Abd Allah and a demilitarized zone, which is hereby established, extending ten kilometers into Iraq and five kilometers into Kuwait from the boundary referred to in the "Agreed Minutes between the State of Kuwait and the Republic of Iraq regarding the restoration of friendly relations, recognition, and related matters"; to deter violations of the boundary through its presence in and surveillance of the demilitarized zone and to observe any hostile or potentially hostile action mounted from the territory of one State against the other . . . ;

C

. . . 8. *Decides* that Iraq shall unconditionally accept the destruction, removal, or rendering harmless, under international supervision, of:

   (a) All chemical and biological weapons and all stocks of agents and all related subsystems and components and all research, development, support, and manufacturing facilities related thereto;

   (b) All ballistic missiles with a range greater than one hundred and fifty kilometers, and related major parts and repair and production facilities;

9. *Decides also,* for the implementation of paragraph 8, the following:

   (a) Iraq shall submit to the Secretary-General, within fifteen days of the adoption of the present resolution, a declaration on the locations, amounts, and types of all items specified in paragraph 8 and agree to urgent, on-site inspection as specified below;

   (b) The Secretary-General . . . within forty-five days of the adoption of the present resolution shall develop and submit to the

Council for approval a plan calling for the completion of the following acts within forty-five days of such approval:

(i)   The forming of a special commission which shall carry out immediate on-site inspection of Iraq's biological, chemical, and missile capabilities . . . ;

(ii) The yielding by Iraq of possession to the Special Commission for destruction, removal, or rendering harmless, taking into account the requirements of public safety, of all items specified under paragraph 8(a) . . . ;

10. *Decides further* that Iraq shall unconditionally undertake not to use, develop, construct, or acquire any of the items specified in paragraphs 8 and 9, and requests the Secretary-General, in consultation with the Special Commission, to develop a plan for the future ongoing monitoring and verification of Iraq's compliance with the present paragraph . . . ;

12. *Decides* that Iraq shall unconditionally agree not to acquire or develop nuclear weapons or nuclear-weapon-usable material or any subsystems or components or any research, development, support, or manufacturing facilities related to the above; to submit to the Secretary-General and the Director General of the International Atomic Energy Agency within fifteen days of the adoption of the present resolution a declaration of the locations, amounts, and types of all items specified above; to place all of its nuclear-weapon-usable materials under the exclusive control, for custody and removal, of the Agency, with the assistance and cooperation of the Special Commission . . . ; to accept, in accordance with the arrangements provided for in paragraph 13, urgent on-site inspection and the destruction, removal, or rendering harmless as appropriate of all items specified above; and to accept the plan discussed in paragraph 13 for the future monitoring and verification of its compliance with these undertakings;

13. *Requests* the Director General of the International Atomic Energy Agency . . . to carry out immediate on-site inspection of Iraq's nuclear capabilities based on Iraq's declarations and the designation of any additional locations by the Special Commission; to develop a plan for submission to the Council within forty-five days calling

for the destruction, removal, or rendering harmless as appropriate of all items listed in paragraph 12; . . . and to develop a plan . . . for the future ongoing monitoring and verification of Iraq's compliance with paragraph 12 . . . to be submitted to the Council for approval within one hundred and twenty days of the adoption of the present resolution; . . .

E

16. *Reaffirms* that Iraq, without prejudice to its debts and obligations arising prior to August 2, 1990, which will be addressed through the normal international mechanisms, is liable under international law for any direct loss, damage—including environmental damage and the depletion of natural resources—or injury to foreign Governments, nationals, and corporations as a result of its unlawful invasion and occupation of Kuwait; . . .

18. *Decides also* to create a fund to pay compensation for claims that fall within paragraph 16 and to establish a commission that will administer the fund;

19. *Directs* the Secretary-General to develop and present to the Council for decision, no later than thirty days following the adoption of the present resolution, recommendations for the Fund to be established in accordance with paragraph 18 and for a program to implement the decisions in paragraphs 16 to 18, including the following: administration of the Fund; mechanisms for determining the appropriate level of Iraq's contribution to the Fund, based on a percentage of the value of its exports of petroleum and petroleum products, not to exceed a figure to be suggested to the Council by the Secretary-General, taking into account the requirements of the people of Iraq, Iraq's payment capacity as assessed in conjunction with the international financial institutions taking into consideration external debt service, and the needs of the Iraqi economy; arrangements for ensuring that payments are made to the Fund; the process by which funds will be allocated and claims paid; appropriate procedures for evaluating losses, listing claims and verifying their validity, and resolving disputed claims in respect of Iraq's liability as specified in paragraph 16; and the composition of the Commission designated above;

F

20. *Decides*, effective immediately, that the prohibitions against the sale or supply to Iraq of commodities or products other than medicine and health supplies, and prohibitions against financial transactions related thereto contained in Resolution 661 (1990) concerning the situation between Iraq and Kuwait or, with the approval of the Committee, under the simplified and accelerated "no-objection" procedure, to materials and supplies for essential civilian needs as identified in the report to the Secretary-General dated March 20, 1991, and in any further findings of humanitarian need by the Committee;

21. *Decides* to review the provisions of paragraph 20 every sixty days in the light of the policies and practices of the Government of Iraq, including the implementation of all relevant resolutions of the Council, for the purpose of determining whether to reduce or lift the prohibitions referred to therein;

22. *Decides also* that upon the approval by the Council of the program called for in paragraph 19 and upon Council agreement that Iraq has completed all actions contemplated in paragraphs 8 to 13, the prohibitions against the import of commodities and products originating in Iraq and the prohibitions against financial transactions related thereto contained in Resolution 661 (1990) shall have no further force or effect;

23. *Decides further* that, pending action by the Council under paragraph 22, the Security Council Committee established by Resolution 661 (1990) concerning the situation between Iraq and Kuwait shall be empowered to approve, when required to assure adequate financial resources on the part of Iraq to carry out the activities under paragraph 20, exceptions to the prohibition against the import of commodities and products originating in Iraq;

24. *Decides* that . . . all States shall continue to prevent the sale or supply to Iraq, or the promotion or facilitation of such sale or supply, by their nationals or from their territories or using their flag vessels or aircraft, of:

(a) Arms and related materiel of all types . . . ;

(b) Items specified and defined in paragraphs 8 and 12 not otherwise covered above;

(c) Technology under licensing or other transfer arrangements used in the production, utilization or stockpiling of items specified in paragraphs (a) and (b);

(d) Personnel or materials for training or technical support services relating to the design, development, manufacture, use, maintenance or support of items specified in paragraphs (a) and (b); . . .

H

32. *Requires* Iraq to inform the Council that it will not commit or support any act of international terrorism or allow any organization directed towards commission of such acts to operate within its territory and to condemn unequivocally and renounce all such acts, methods, and practices of terrorism.

I

33. *Declares* that, upon official notification by Iraq to the Secretary-General and to the Security Council of its acceptance of the above provisions, a formal cease-fire is effective between Iraq and Kuwait and the Member States cooperating with Kuwait in accordance with Resolution 678 (1990) . . . .

RESOLUTION 688
(April 5, 1991)

The Security Council, . . .

1. *Condemns* the repression of the Iraqi civilian population in many parts of Iraq, including most recently in Kurdish-populated areas, the consequences of which threaten international peace and security in the region;

2. *Demands* that Iraq, as a contribution to removing the threat to international peace and security in the region, immediately end this repression . . . ;

3. *Insists* that Iraq allow immediate access by international humanitarian organizations to all those in need of assistance in all parts of Iraq and make available all necessary facilities for their operations; . . . .

RESOLUTION 731
(January 21, 1992)

The Security Council, . . .
Deeply concerned over the results of investigations, which implicate officials of the Libyan Government and which are contained in Security Council documents that include the requests addressed to the Libyan authorities by France, the United Kingdom of Great Britain and Northern Ireland, and the United States of America in connection with the legal procedures related to the attacks carried out against Pan American flight 103 and Union de transports aerens flight 772; . . .

1. *Condemns* the destruction of Pan American flight 103 and Union de transports aerens flight 772 and the resultant loss of hundreds of lives;

2. *Strongly deplores* the fact that the Libyan Government has not yet responded effectively to the above requests to cooperate fully in establishing responsibility for the terrorist acts referred to above
   . . . .

RESOLUTION 748
(March 31, 1992)

The Security Council, . . .
Determining, in this context, that the failure by the Libyan Government to demonstrate by concrete actions its renunciation of terrorism and in particular it continued failure to respond fully and effectively to the requests in Resolution 731 (1992) constitute a threat to international peace and security, . . .
Acting under Chapter VII of the Charter,

1. *Decides* that the Libyan Government must now comply without any further delay with paragraph 3 of Resolution 731 (1992) . . . ;

2. *Decides also* that the Libyan Government must commit itself definitively to cease all forms of terrorist action and all assistance to terrorist groups and that it must promptly, by concrete actions, demonstrate its renunciation of terrorism;

3. *Decides* that, on April 15, 1992, all States shall adopt the measures set out below, which shall apply until the Security Council decides that the Libyan Government has complied with paragraphs 1 and 2 above;

4. *Decides* that all States shall:

   (a) Deny permission to any aircraft to take off from, land in, or overfly their territory if it is destined to land in or has taken off from the territory of Libya, unless the particular flight has been approved on grounds of significant humanitarian need by the Committee established by paragraph 9 below;

   (b) Prohibit, by their nationals or from their territory, the supply of any aircraft or aircraft components to Libya . . . ;

5. *Decides further* that all States shall:

   (a) Prohibit any provision to Libya by their nationals or from their territory of arms and related material of all types . . . ;

   (c) Withdraw any of their officials or agents present in Libya to advise the Libyan authorities on military matters;

6. *Decides* that all States shall:

   (a) Significantly reduce the number and the level of the staff at Libyan diplomatic missions and consular posts and restrict or control the movement within their territory of all such staff who remain . . . ;

   (b) Prevent the operation of all Libyan Arab Airlines offices; . . . .

RESOLUTION 770
(August 13, 1992)

The Security Council, . . .

Recognizing that the situation in Bosnia and Herzegovina constitutes a threat to international peace and security and that the provision of humanitarian assistance in Bosnia and Herzegovina is an important element in the Council's effort to restore international peace and security in the area; . . .

Acting under Chapter VII of the Charter of the United Nations,

1. *Reaffirms* its demand that all parties and others concerned in Bosnia and Herzegovina stop the fighting immediately;

2. *Calls upon* States to take nationally or through regional agencies or arrangements all measures necessary to facilitate in coordination with the United Nations the delivery by relevant United Nations humanitarian organizations and others of humanitarian assistance to Sarajevo and wherever needed in other parts of Bosnia and Herzegovina. . . .

RESOLUTION 777
(September 19, 1992)

The Security Council, . . .

1. *Considers* that the Federal Republic of Yugoslavia (Serbia and Montenegro) cannot continue automatically the membership of the former Socialist Federal Republic of Yugoslavia in the United Nations; and therefore *recommends* to the General Assembly that it decide that the Federal Republic of Yugoslavia (Serbia and Montenegro) should apply for membership in the United Nations and that it shall not participate in the work of the General Assembly. . . .

RESOLUTION 794
(December 3, 1992)

The Security Council, . . .

Determining that the magnitude of the human tragedy caused by the conflict in Somalia, further exacerbated by the obstacles being created to the distribution of humanitarian assistance, constitutes a threat to international peace and security, . . .

1. *Reaffirms* its demand that all parties, movements, and factions in Somalia immediately cease hostilities, maintain a cease-fire throughout the country, and cooperate with the Special Representative of the Secretary-General for Somalia as well as with the military forces to be established pursuant to the authorization given in paragraph 10 below in order to promote the process of relief distribution, reconciliation, and political settlement in Somalia; . . .

7. *Endorses* the recommendation by the Secretary-General in his letter of November 29, 1992 to the President of the Security Council that action under Chapter VII of the Charter of the United Nations be taken in order to establish a secure environment for humanitarian relief operations in Somalia as soon as possible;

8. *Welcomes* the offer by a Member State described in the Secretary-General's above-mentioned letter concerning the establishment of an operation to create such a secure environment;

9. *Welcomes also* offers by other Member States to participate in that operation;

10. Acting under Chapter VII of the Charter of the United Nations, *authorizes* the Secretary-General and Member States cooperating to implement the offer referred to in paragraph 8 above to use all necessary measures to establish as soon as possible a secure environment for humanitarian relief operations in Somalia;

11. *Calls on* all Member States which are in a position to do so to provide military forces and to make additional contributions, in case or in kind . . . ;

12. *Also authorizes* the Secretary-General and the Member States concerned to make the necessary arrangements for the unified command and control of the forces involved, which will reflect the offer referred to in paragraph 8 above . . . .

Resolution 808
(February 22, 1993)

The Security Council, . . .

Expressing once again its grave alarm at continuing reports of widespread violations of international humanitarian law occurring within the territory of the former Yugoslavia, including reports of mass killings and the continuance of the practice of "ethnic cleansing,"

Determining that this situation constitutes a threat to international peace and security,

Determined to put an end to such crimes and to take effective measures to bring to justice the persons who are responsible for them,

1. *Decides* that an international tribunal shall be established for the prosecution of persons responsible for serious violations of international humanitarian law committed in the territory of the former Yugoslavia since 1991;

2. *Requests* the Secretary-General to submit for consideration by the Council at the earliest possible date, and if possible no later than sixty days after the adoption of the present resolution, a report on all aspects of this matter, including specific proposals and where appropriate options for the effective and expeditious implementation of the decision contained in paragraph 1 above, taking into account suggestions put forward in this regard by Member States. . . .

RESOLUTION 824
(May 6, 1993)

The Security Council, . . .

Deeply concerned at the continuing armed hostilities by Bosnian Serb paramilitary units against several towns in the Republic of Bosnia and Herzegovina and determined to ensure peace and stability throughout the country . . .

Recalling the provisions of Resolution 815 (1993) on the mandate of UNPROFOR and in that context *acting* under Chapter VII of the Charter, . . .

2. *Demands* that any taking of territory by force cease immediately;

3. *Declares* that the capital city of the Republic of Bosnia and Herzegovina, Sarajevo, and other such threatened areas, in particular the towns of Tuzla, Zepa, Gorazde, Bihac, as well as Srebrenica, and their surroundings should be treated as safe areas by all the parties concerned and should be free from armed attacks and from any other hostile act. . . .

RESOLUTION 827
(May 25, 1993)

The Security Council, . . .

Having considered the report of the Secretary-General . . . pursuant to paragraph 2 of Resolution 808 (1993),

Expressing once again its grave alarm at continuing reports of widespread and flagrant violations of international humanitarian law occurring within the territory of the former Yugoslavia, and especially in the Republic of Bosnia and Herzegovina, including reports of mass killings, massive, organized, and systematic detention and rape of women, and the continuance of the practice of "ethnic cleansing," including for the acquisition and the holding of territory,

Determining that this situation continues to constitute a threat to international peace and security,

Determined to put an end to such crimes and to take effective measures to bring to justice the persons who are responsible for them,

Convinced that in the particular circumstances of the former Yugoslavia the establishment as an ad hoc measure by the Council of an international tribunal and the prosecution of persons responsible for serious violations of international humanitarian law would enable this aim to be achieved and would contribute to the restoration and maintenance of peace, . . .

Acting under Chapter VII of the Charter of the United Nations,

1. *Approves* the report of the Secretary-General;

2. *Decides* hereby to establish an international tribunal for the sole purpose of prosecuting persons responsible for serious violations of international humanitarian law committed in the territory of the former Yugoslavia between January 1, 1991 and a date to be determined by the Security Council upon the restoration of peace and to this end to adopt the Statute of the International Tribunal annexed to the above-mentioned report; . . .

3. *Decides* that all States shall cooperate fully with the International Tribunal and its organs in accordance with the present resolution and the Statute of the International Tribunal and that consequently all States shall take any measures necessary under their domestic law to implement the provisions of the present resolution and the Statute, including the obligation of States to comply with requests for assistance or orders issued by a Trial Chamber under Article 29 of the Statute. . . .

RESOLUTION 836
(June 4, 1993)

The Security Council, . . .

Determining that the situation in the Republic of Bosnia and Herzegovina continues to be a threat to international peace and security,

Acting under Chapter VII of the Charter of the United Nations, . . .

4. *Decides* to ensure full respect for the safe areas referred to in Resolution 824 (1993);

5. *Decides* to extend to that end the mandate of UNPROFOR in order to enable it, in the safe areas referred to in Resolution 824 (1993), to deter attacks against the safe areas, to monitor the cease-fire, to promote the withdrawal of military or paramilitary units other than those of the Government of the Republic of Bosnia and Herzegovina and to occupy some key points on the ground, in addition to participating in the delivery of humanitarian relief to the population as provided for in Resolution 776 (1992) of September 14, 1992; . . .

9. *Authorizes* UNPROFOR, . . . in carrying out the mandate defined in paragraph 5 above, acting in self-defense, to take the necessary measures, including the use of force, in reply to bombardments against the safe areas by any of the parties or to armed incursion into them or in the event of any deliberate obstruction in or around those areas to the freedom of movement of UNPROFOR or of protected humanitarian convoys;

10. *Decides* that . . . Member States, acting nationally or through regional organizations or arrangements, may take, under the authority of the Security Council and subject to close coordination with the Secretary-General and UNPROFOR, all necessary measures, through the use of air power, in and around the safe areas in the Republic of Bosnia and Herzegovina, to support UNPROFOR in the performance of its mandate set out in paragraphs 5 and 9 above. . . .

Resolution 841
(June 16, 1993)

The Security Council, . . .

Recognizing the urgent need for an early, comprehensive, and peaceful settlement of the crisis in Haiti in accordance with the provisions of the Charter of the United Nations and international law, . . .

Deploring the fact that, despite the efforts of the international community, the legitimate Government of President Jean-Bertrand Aristide has not been reinstated,

Concerned that the persistence of this situation contributes to a climate of fear of persecution and economic dislocation which could increase the number of Haitians seeking refuge in neighboring Member States and *convinced* that a reversal of this situation is needed to prevent its negative repercussions on the region, . . .

Determining that, in these unique and exceptional circumstances, the continuation of this situation threatens international peace and security in the region,

Acting, therefore, under Chapter VII of the Charter of the United Nations, . . .

3. *Decides* that the provisions set forth in paragraphs 5 to 14 below, which are consistent with the trade embargo recommended by the Organization of American States, shall come into force at 00.01 EST on June 23, 1993 unless the Secretary-General, having regard to the views of the Secretary-General of the Organization of American States, has reported to the Council that, in light of the results of the negotiations conducted by the Special Envoy for Haiti of the United Nations and Organization of American States Secretaries-General, the imposition of such measures is not warranted at that time; . . .

5. *Decides* that all States shall prevent the sale or supply, by their nationals or from their territories or using their flag vessels or aircraft, of petroleum or petroleum products or arms or related materiel of all types, including weapons and ammunition, military vehicles and equipment, police equipment, and spare parts for the aforementioned, whether or not originating in their territories, to any person or body in Haiti or to any person or body for the

purpose of any business carried on in or operated in Haiti, and any activities by their nationals or in their territories which promote or are calculated to promote such sale or supply; . . .

8. *Decides* that States in which there are funds, including any funds derived from property, (a) of the Government of Haiti or of the de facto authorities of Haiti, or (b) controlled directly or indirectly by such Government or authorities or by entities, wherever located or organized, owned or controlled by such Government or authorities, shall require all persons or entities within their own territories holding such funds to freeze them to ensure that they are not made available directly or indirectly to or for the benefit of the de facto authorities in Haiti . . . .

RESOLUTION 929
(June 22, 1994)

The Security Council, . . .
Deeply concerned by the continuation of systematic and widespread killings of the civilian population in Rwanda,
Recognizing that the current situation in Rwanda constitutes a unique case which demands an urgent response by the international community,
Determining that the magnitude of the humanitarian crisis in Rwanda constitutes a threat to peace and security in the region,

1. *Welcomes* the Secretary-General's letter dated June 19, 1994 . . . and *agrees* that a multinational operation may be set up for humanitarian purposes in Rwanda until UNAMIR is brought up to the necessary strength;

2. *Welcomes also* the offer by Member States . . . to cooperate with the Secretary-General in order to achieve the objectives of the United Nations in Rwanda through the establishment of a temporary operation under national command and control aimed at contributing, in an impartial way, to the security and protection of displaced persons, refugees, and civilians at risk in Rwanda, on the understanding that the costs of implementing the offer will be borne by the Member States concerned;

3. *Acting* under Chapter VII of the Charter of the United Nations, *authorizes* the Member States cooperating with the Secretary-General to conduct the operation referred to in paragraph 2 above using all necessary means to achieve the humanitarian objectives set out in subparagraphs 4(a) and (b) of Resolution 925 (1994);

4. *Decides* that the mission of Member States cooperating with the Secretary-General will be limited to a period of two months following the adoption of the present resolution, unless the Secretary-General determines at an earlier date that the expanded UNAMIR is able to carry out its mandate. . . .

RESOLUTION 940
(July 31, 1994)

The Security Council, . . .
Gravely concerned by the significant further deterioration of the humanitarian situation in Haiti, in particular the continuing escalation by the illegal de facto regime of systematic violations of civil liberties, the desperate plight of Haitian refugees, and the recent expulsion of the staff of the International Civilian Mission . . .
Determining that the situation in Haiti continues to constitute a threat to peace and security in the region, . . .

2. *Recognizes* the unique character of the present situation in Haiti and its deteriorating, complex, and extraordinary nature, requiring an exceptional response;

3. *Determines* that the illegal de facto regime in Haiti has failed to comply with the Governors Island Agreement and is in breach of its obligations under the relevant resolutions of the Security Council;

4. *Acting* under Chapter VII of the Charter of the United Nations, *authorizes* Member States to form a multinational force under unified command and control and, in this framework, to use all necessary means to facilitate the departure from Haiti of the military leadership, consistent with the Governors Island Agreement, the prompt return of the legitimately elected President, and the restoration of the legitimate authorities of the Government of Haiti, and to establish and maintain a secure and stable environment that will

permit implementation of the Governors Island Agreement, on the understanding that the cost of implementing this temporary operation will be borne by the participating Member States; . . .

8. *Decides* that the multinational force will terminate its mission and UNMIH will assume the full range of its functions described in paragraph 9 below when a secure and stable environment has been established and UNMIH has adequate force capability and structure to assume the full range of its functions; the determination will be made by the Security Council, taking into account recommendations from the Member States of the multinational force, which are based on the assessment of the commander of the multinational force, and from the Secretary-General. . . .

RESOLUTION 955
(November 8, 1994)

The Security Council, . . .
Expressing once again its grave concern at the reports indicating that genocide and other systematic, widespread, and flagrant violations of international humanitarian law have been committed in Rwanda,
Determining that this situation continues to constitute a threat to international peace and security,
Determined to put an end to such crimes and to take effective measures to bring to justice the persons who are responsible for them,
Convinced that in the particular circumstances of Rwanda, the prosecution of persons responsible for serious violations of international humanitarian law would enable this aim to be achieved and would contribute to the process of national reconciliation and to the restoration and maintenance of peace, . . .
Acting under Chapter VII of the Charter of the United Nations,

1. *Decides* hereby, having received the request of the Government of Rwanda . . . , to establish an international tribunal for the sole purpose of prosecuting persons responsible for genocide and other serious violations of international humanitarian law committed in the territory of Rwanda and Rwandan citizens responsible for genocide and other such violations committed in the territory of neighboring

States, between January 1, 1994 and December 31, 1994 and to this end to adopt the Statute of the International Criminal Tribunal for Rwanda annexed hereto;

2. *Decides* that all States shall cooperate fully with the International Tribunal and its organs in accordance with the present resolution and the Statute of the International Criminal Tribunal and that consequently all States shall take any measures necessary under their domestic law to implement the provisions of the present resolution and the Statute, including the obligation of States to comply with requests for assistance or orders issued by a Trial Chamber under Article 28 of the Statute. . . .

RESOLUTION 986
(April 14, 1995)

The Security Council, . . .

Concerned by the serious nutritional and health situation of the Iraqi population, and by the risk of a further deterioration in this situation,

Convinced of the need as a temporary measure to provide for the humanitarian needs of the Iraqi people until the fulfillment by Iraq of the relevant Security Council resolutions, including notably Resolution 687 (1991) of April 3, 1991, allows the Council to take further action with regard to the prohibitions referred to in Resolution 661 (1990) of August 6, 1990, in accordance with the provisions of those resolutions,

Convinced also of the need for equitable distribution of humanitarian relief to all segments of the Iraqi population throughout the country, . . .

Acting under Chapter VII of the Charter of the United Nations,

1. *Authorizes* States, notwithstanding the provisions of paragraphs 3(a), 3(b) and 4 of Resolution 661 (1990) and subsequent relevant resolutions, to permit the import of petroleum and petroleum products originating in Iraq, including financial and other essential transactions directly relating thereto, sufficient to produce a sum not exceeding a total of one billion United States dollars every

ninety days for the purposes set out in this resolution and subject to the following conditions:

(a) Approval by the Committee established by Resolution 661 (1990), in order to ensure the transparency of each transaction and its conformity with the other provisions of this resolution . . . ;

(b) Payment of the full amount of each purchase of Iraqi petroleum and petroleum products directly by the purchaser in the State concerned into the escrow account to be established by the Secretary-General for the purposes of this resolution; . . .

8. *Decides* that the funds in the escrow account shall be used to meet the humanitarian needs of the Iraqi population and for the following other purposes, and *requests* the Secretary-General to use the funds deposited in the escrow account:

(a) To finance the export to Iraq, in accordance with the procedures of the Committee established by Resolution 661 (1990), of medicine, health supplies, foodstuffs, and materials and supplies for essential civilian needs, as referred to in paragraph 20 of Resolution 687 (1990) provided that:

   (i) Each export of goods is at the request of the Government of Iraq;

   (ii) Iraq effectively guarantees their equitable distribution, on the basis of a plan submitted to and approved by the Secretary-General, including a description of the goods to be purchased;

   (iii) The Secretary-General receives authenticated confirmation that the exported goods concerned have arrived in Iraq;

(b) To complement, in view of the exceptional circumstances prevailing in the Governorates mentioned below, the distribution by the Government of Iraq of goods imported under this resolution, in order to ensure an equitable distribution of humanitarian relief to all segments of the Iraqi population throughout the country, by providing between 130 million and 150 million United States dollars every ninty days to the United Nations Inter-Agency Humanitarian Program operating within the sovereign territory of Iraq in the three northern Governorates of Dihouk, Arbil, and Suleimaniyeh . . . ;

(c) To transfer to the Compensation Fund the same percentage of the funds deposited in the escrow account as that decided by the Council in paragraph 2 of Resolution 705 (1991) of August 15, 1991;

(d) To meet the costs to the United Nations of the independent inspection agents and the certified public accountants and the activities associated with implementation of this resolution;

(e) To meet the current operating costs of the Special Commission, pending subsequent payment in full of the costs of carrying out the tasks authorized by section C of Resolution 687 (1991). . . .

RESOLUTION 1031
(December 15, 1995)

The Security Council, . . .

Welcoming the signing on December 14, 1995 at the Paris Peace Conference of the General Framework Agreement for Peace in Bosnia and Herzegovina and the Annexes thereto (collectively the Peace Agreement . . .) by the Republic of Bosnia and Herzegovina, the Republic of Croatia, and the Federal Republic of Yugoslavia, and the other parties thereto, . . .

Determining that the situation in the region continues to constitute a threat to international peace and security, . . .

Acting under Chapter VII of the Charter of the United Nations,

1. *Welcomes and supports* the Peace Agreement and *calls upon* the parties to fulfill in good faith the commitments entered into in that Agreement;

12. *Welcomes* the willingness of the Member States acting through or in cooperation with the organization referred to in Annex 1-A of the Peace Agreement [the North Atlantic Treaty Organization] to assist the parties to the Peace Agreement by deploying a multinational implementation force; . . .

14. *Authorizes* the Member States acting through or in cooperation with the organization referred to in Annex 1-A of the Peace Agreement to establish a multinational implementation force (IFOR) under unified command and control in order to fulfill the role specified in Annex 1-A and Annex 2 of the Peace Agreement;

15. *Authorizes* the Member States acting under paragraph 14 above to take all necessary measures to effect the implementation of and to ensure compliance with Annex 1-A of the Peace Agreement, *stresses* that the parties shall be held equally responsible for compliance with that Annex, and shall be equally subject to such enforcement action by IFOR as may be necessary to ensure implementation of that Annex and the protection of IFOR, and *takes note* that the parties have consented to IFOR's taking such measures; . . .

17. *Authorizes* Member States to take all necessary measures, at the request of IFOR, either in defense of IFOR or to assist the force in carrying out its mission, and *recognizes* the right of the force to take all necessary measures to defend itself from attack or threat of attack; . . .

27. *Confirms* that the High Representative is the final authority in theatre regarding interpretation of Annex 10 on the civilian implementation of the Peace Agreement. . . .

RESOLUTION 1132
(October 8, 1997)

The Security Council, . . .

Recalling the statements of its President . . . condemning the military coup in Sierra Leone,

Deploring the fact that the military junta has not taken steps to allow the restoration of the democratically elected Government and a return to constitutional order,

Gravely concerned at the continued violence and loss of life in Sierra Leone following the military coup of May 25, 1997, the deteriorating humanitarian conditions in that country, and the consequences for neighboring countries,

Determining that the situation in Sierra Leone constitutes a threat to international peace and security in the region,

Acting under Chapter VII of the Charter of the United Nations,

1. *Demands* that the military junta take immediate steps to relinquish power in Sierra Leone and make way for the restoration of the democratically-elected Government and a return to constitutional order; . . .

5. *Decides* that all States shall prevent the entry into or transit through their territories of members of the military junta and adult members of their families . . . ;

6. *Decides* that all States shall prevent the sale or supply to Sierra Leone, by their nationals or from their territories, or using their flag vessels or aircraft, of petroleum and petroleum products and arms and related materiel of all types, including weapons and ammunition, military vehicles and equipment, and military equipment and spare parts for the aforementioned, whether or not originating in their territory; . . .

8. *Acting also* under Chapter VII of the Charter of the United Nations, *authorizes* ECOWAS, cooperating with the democratically elected Government of Sierra Leone, to ensure strict implementation of the provisions of this resolution relating to the supply of petroleum and petroleum products, and arms and related materiel of all types, including, where necessary and in conformity with applicable international standards, by halting inward maritime shipping in order to inspect and verify their cargoes and destinations, and *calls upon* all States to cooperate with ECOWAS in this regard. . . .

RESOLUTION 1192
(August 27, 1998)

The Security Council, . . .

Acting under Chapter VII of the Charter of the United Nations,

1. *Demands once again* that the Libyan Government immediately comply with the above-mentioned resolutions;

2. *Welcomes* the initiative for the trial of the two persons charged with
    the bombing of Pan Am flight 103 ("the two accused") before a
    Scottish court sitting in the Netherlands, as contained in the letter
    dated 24 August 1998 from the Acting Permanent Representatives
    of the United Kingdom of Great Britain and Northern Ireland and
    the United States of America ("the initiative") and its attachments,
    and the willingness of the Government of the Netherlands to coop-
    erate in the implementation of the initiative; . . .

4. *Decides* that all States shall cooperate to this end, and in particular
    that the Libyan Government shall ensure the appearance in the
    Netherlands of the two accused for the purpose of trial by the court
    described in paragraph 2, and the Libyan Government shall ensure
    that any evidence or witnesses in Libya are, upon the request of the
    court, promptly made available at the court in the Netherlands for
    the purpose of the trial; . . .

8. *Reaffirms* that the measures set forth in its Resolutions 748 (1992)
    and 883 (1993) remain in effect and binding on all Member States,
    and in this context reaffirms the provisions of paragraph 16 of Res-
    olution 883 (1993), and *decides* that the aforementioned measures
    shall be suspended immediately if the Secretary-General reports to
    the Council that the two accused have arrived in the Netherlands
    for the purpose of trial before the court described in paragraph 2 or
    have appeared for trial before an appropriate court in the United
    Kingdom or the United States, and that the Libyan Government
    has satisfied the French authorities with regard to the bombing of
    UTA 772. . . .

RESOLUTION 1199
(September 23, 1998)

The Security Council, . . .

Gravely concerned at the recent intense fighting in Kosovo and in particular the excessive and indiscriminate use of force by Serbian security
forces and the Yugoslav Army which have resulted in numerous civilian casualties and, according to the estimate of the Secretary-General,
the displacement of over 230,000 persons from their homes, . . .

Affirming that the deterioration of the situation in Kosovo, Federal Republic of Yugoslavia, constitutes a threat to peace and security in the region,

Acting under Chapter VII of the Charter of the United Nations,

1. *Demands* that all parties, groups, and individuals immediately cease hostilities and maintain a cease-fire in Kosovo . . . ;

2. *Demands also* that the authorities of the Federal Republic of Yugoslavia and the Kosovo Albanian leadership take immediate steps to improve the humanitarian situation and to avert the impending humanitarian catastrophe; . . .

4. *Demands further* that the Federal Republic of Yugoslavia, in addition to the measures called for under Resolution 1160 (1998), implement immediately the following concrete measures toward achieving a political solution to the situation in Kosovo as contained in the Contact Group statement of June 12, 1998:

    (a) cease all action by the security forces affecting the civilian population and order the withdrawal of security units used for civilian repression;

    (b) enable effective and continuous international monitoring in Kosovo by the European Community Monitoring Mission and diplomatic missions accredited to the Federal Republic of Yugoslavia, including access and complete freedom of movement of such monitors to, from, and within Kosovo unimpeded by government authorities . . . ;

    (c) facilitate, in agreement with the UNHCR and the International Committee of the Red Cross (ICRC), the safe return of refugees and displaced persons to their homes and allow free and unimpeded access for humanitarian organizations and supplies to Kosovo. . . .

RESOLUTION 1244
(June 10, 1999)

The Security Council, . . .

Determined to resolve the grave humanitarian situation in Kosovo, Federal Republic of Yugoslavia, and to provide for the safe and free return of all refugees and displaced persons to their homes, . . .

Determining that the situation in the region continues to constitute a threat to international peace and security,

Determined to ensure the safety and security of international personnel and the implementation by all concerned of their responsibilities under the present resolution, and *acting* for these purposes under Chapter VII of the Charter of the United Nations,

1. *Decides* that a political solution to the Kosovo crisis shall be based on the general principles in annex 1 and as further elaborated in the principles and other required elements in annex 2;

2. *Welcomes* the acceptance by the Federal Republic of Yugoslavia of the principles and other required elements referred to in paragraph 1 above, and *demands* the full cooperation of the Federal Republic of Yugoslavia in their rapid implementation;

3. *Demands* in particular that the Federal Republic of Yugoslavia put an immediate and verifiable end to violence and repression in Kosovo, and begin and complete verifiable phased withdrawal from Kosovo of all military, police, and paramilitary forces according to a rapid timetable, with which the deployment of the international security presence in Kosovo will be synchronized; . . .

5. *Decides* on the deployment in Kosovo, under United Nations auspices, of international civil and security presences, with appropriate equipment and personnel as required, and welcomes the agreement of the Federal Republic of Yugoslavia to such presences; . . .

7. *Authorizes* Member States and relevant international organizations to establish the international security presence in Kosovo as set out in point 4 of annex 2 with all necessary means to fulfill its responsibilities under paragraph 9 below; . . .

9. *Decides* that the responsibilities of the international security presence to be deployed and acting in Kosovo will include:

    (a) Deterring renewed hostilities, maintaining and where necessary enforcing a cease-fire, and ensuring the withdrawal and preventing the return into Kosovo of Federal and Republic military, police, and paramilitary forces, except as provided in point 6 of annex 2;

(b) Demilitarizing the Kosovo Liberation Army (KLA) and other armed Kosovo Albanian groups as required in paragraph 15 below;

(c) Establishing a secure environment in which refugees and displaced persons can return home in safety, the international civil presence can operate, a transitional administration can be established, and humanitarian aid can be delivered;

(d) Ensuring public safety and order until the international civil presence can take responsibility for this task;

(e) Supervising demining until the international civil presence can, as appropriate, take over responsibility for this task;

(f) Supporting, as appropriate, and coordinating closely with the work of the international civil presence;

(g) Conducting border monitoring duties as required;

(h) Ensuring the protection and freedom of movement of itself, the international civil presence, and other international organizations;

10. *Authorizes* the Secretary-General, with the assistance of relevant international organizations, to establish an international civil presence in Kosovo in order to provide an interim administration for Kosovo under which the people of Kosovo can enjoy substantial autonomy within the Federal Republic of Yugoslavia, and which will provide transitional administration while establishing and overseeing the development of provisional democratic self-governing institutions to ensure conditions for a peaceful and normal life for all inhabitants of Kosovo;

11. *Decides* that the main responsibilities of the international civil presence will include:

(a) Promoting the establishment, pending a final settlement, of substantial autonomy and self-government in Kosovo, taking full account of annex 2 and of the Rambouillet Accords . . . ;

(b) Performing basic civilian administration functions where and as long as required;

(c) Organizing and overseeing the development of provisional institutions for democratic and autonomous self-government pending a political settlement, including the holding of elections;

(d) Transferring, as these institutions are established, its administrative responsibilities while overseeing and supporting the consolidation of Kosovo's local provisional institutions and other peacebuilding activities;

(e) Facilitating a political process designed to determine Kosovo's future status, taking into account the Rambouillet Accords . . . ;

(f) In a final stage, overseeing the transfer of authority from Kosovo's provisional institutions to institutions established under a political settlement;

(g) Supporting the reconstruction of key infrastructure and other economic reconstruction;

(h) Supporting, in coordination with international humanitarian organizations, humanitarian and disaster relief aid;

(i) Maintaining civil law and order, including establishing local police forces and meanwhile through the deployment of international police personnel to serve in Kosovo;

(j) Protecting and promoting human rights;

(k) Assuring the safe and unimpeded return of all refugees and displaced persons to their homes in Kosovo; . . .

19. *Decides* that the international civil and security presences are established for an initial period of twelve months, to continue thereafter unless the Security Council decides otherwise. . . .

Resolution 1264
(September 15, 1999)

The Security Council, . . .

Deeply concerned by the deterioration in the security situation in East Timor, and in particular by the continuing violence against and large-scale displacement and relocation of East Timorese civilians, . . .

Appalled by the worsening humanitarian situation in East Timor, particularly as it affects women, children, and other vulnerable groups, . . .

Determining that the present situation in East Timor constitutes a threat to peace and security,

Acting under Chapter VII of the Charter of the United Nations,

1. *Condemns* all acts of violence in East Timor, *calls* for their immediate end and *demands* that those responsible for such acts be brought to justice; . . .

3. *Authorizes* the establishment of a multinational force under a unified command structure, pursuant to the request of the Government of Indonesia conveyed to the Secretary-General on September 12, 1999, with the following tasks: to restore peace and security in East Timor, to protect and support UNAMET in carrying out its tasks and, within force capabilities, to facilitate humanitarian assistance operations, and *authorizes* the States participating in the multinational force to take all necessary measures to fulfill this mandate . . . .

RESOLUTION 1267
(October 15, 1999)

The Security Council, . . .

Strongly condemning the continuing use of Afghan territory, especially areas controlled by the Taliban, for the sheltering and training of terrorists and planning of terrorist acts, and *reaffirming* its conviction that the suppression of international terrorism is essential for the maintenance of international peace and security,

Deploring the fact that the Taliban continues to provide safe haven to Osama bin Laden and to allow him and others associated with him to operate a network of terrorist training camps from Taliban-controlled territory and to use Afghanistan as a base from which to sponsor international terrorist operations,

Noting the indictment of Osama bin Laden and his associates by the United States of America for, *inter alia*, the August 7, 1998 bombings of the United States embassies in Nairobi, Kenya, and Dar es Salaam, Tanzania and for conspiring to kill American nationals outside the United States, and noting also the request of the United States of America to the Taliban to surrender them for trial . . . ;

Determining that the failure of the Taliban authorities to respond to the demands in paragraph 13 of resolution 1214 (1998) constitutes a threat to international peace and security, . . .

Acting under Chapter VII of the Charter of the United Nations,

1. *Insists* that the Afghan faction known as the Taliban, which also calls itself the Islamic Emirate of Afghanistan, comply promptly with its previous resolutions and in particular cease the provision of sanctuary and training for international terrorists and their organizations, take appropriate effective measures to ensure that the territory under its control is not used for terrorist installations and camps, or for the preparation or organization of terrorist acts against other States or their citizens, and cooperate with efforts to bring indicted terrorists to justice;

2. *Demands* that the Taliban turn over Osama bin Laden without further delay to appropriate authorities in a country where he has been indicted, or to appropriate authorities in a country where he will be returned to such a country, or to appropriate authorities in a country where he will be arrested and effectively brought to justice;

3. *Decides* that on November 14, 1999 all States shall impose the measures set out in paragraph 4 below, unless the Council has previously decided, on the basis of a report of the Secretary-General, that the Taliban has fully complied with the obligation set out in paragraph 2 above;

4. *Decides further* that, in order to enforce paragraph 2 above, all States shall:

   (a) Deny permission for any aircraft to take off or land in their territory if it is owned, leased, or operated by or on behalf of the Taliban as designated by the Committee established by paragraph 6 below, unless the particular flight has been approved in advance by the Committee on the grounds of humanitarian need, including religious obligation such as the performance of the Hajj;

   (b) Freeze funds and other financial resources, including funds derived or generated from property owned or controlled directly or indirectly by the Taliban, or by any undertaking owned or controlled by the Taliban, as designated by the Committee established by paragraph 6 below, and ensure that neither they nor any other funds or financial resources so designated are made available, by their nationals or by any persons within their territory, to or for the benefit of the Taliban or any undertaking owned or controlled, directly or indirectly, by the Taliban, except as may be authorized by the Committee on a case-by-case basis on the grounds of humanitarian need. . . .

RESOLUTION 1272
(October 25, 1999)

The Security Council, . . .
Deeply concerned by the grave humanitarian situation resulting from violence in East Timor and the large-scale displacement and relocation of East Timorese civilians, including large numbers of women and children, . . .
Determining that the continuing situation in East Timor constitutes a threat to peace and security,
Acting under Chapter VII of the Charter of the United Nations,

1. *Decides* to establish, in accordance with the report of the Secretary-General, a United Nations Transitional Administration in East Timor (UNTAET), which will be endowed with overall responsibility for the administration of East Timor and will be empowered to exercise all legislative and executive authority, including the administration of justice;

2. *Decides also* that the mandate of UNTAET shall consist of the following elements:

    (a) To provide security and maintain law and order throughout the territory of East Timor;

    (b) To establish an effective administration;

    (c) To assist in the development of civil and social structures;

    (d) To ensure the coordination and delivery of humanitarian assistance, rehabilitation and development assistance;

    (e) To support capacity-building for self-government;

(f) To assist in the establishment of conditions for sustainable development;

3. *Decides further* that UNTAET will have objectives and a structure along the lines set out in part IV of the report of the Secretary-General, and in particular that its main components will be:

  (a) A governance and public administration component, including an international police element with a strength of up to 1,640 officers;

  (b) A humanitarian assistance and emergency rehabilitation component;

  (c) A military component, with a strength of up to 8,950 troops and up to 200 military observers;

4. *Authorizes* UNTAET to take all necessary measures to fulfill its mandate. . . .

RESOLUTION 1306
(July 5, 2000)

The Security Council, . . .

Determining that the situation in Sierra Leone continues to constitute a threat to international peace and security in the region,

Acting under Chapter VII of the Charter of the United Nations, . . .

1. *Decides* that all States shall take the necessary measures to prohibit the direct or indirect import of all rough diamonds from Sierra Leone to their territory;

2. *Requests* the Government of Sierra Leone to ensure, as a matter of urgency, that an effective Certificate of Origin regime for trade in diamonds is in operation in Sierra Leone; . . .

5. *Decides* that rough diamonds controlled by the Government of Sierra Leone through the Certificate of Origin regime shall be exempt from the measures imposed in paragraph 1 above when the Committee has reported to the Council, taking into account expert advice obtained at the request of the Committee through the Secretary-General, that an effective regime is fully in operation. . . .

Resolution 1315
(August 14, 2000)

The Security Council, . . .

Deeply concerned at the very serious crimes committed within the territory of Sierra Leone against the people of Sierra Leone and United Nations and associated personnel and at the prevailing situation of impunity, . . .

Recalling that the Special Representative of the Secretary-General appended to his signature of the Lome Agreement a statement that the United Nations holds the understanding that the amnesty provisions of the Agreement shall not apply to international crimes of genocide, crimes against humanity, war crimes, and other serious violations of international humanitarian law, . . .

Recognizing that, in the particular circumstances of Sierra Leone, a credible system of justice and accountability for the very serious crimes committed there would end impunity and would contribute to the process of national reconciliation and to the restoration and maintenance of peace, . . .

Reiterating that the situation in Sierra Leone continues to constitute a threat to international peace and security in the region,

1. *Requests* the Secretary-General to negotiate an agreement with the Government of Sierra Leone to create an independent special court consistent with this resolution, and *expresses* its readiness to take further steps expeditiously upon receiving and reviewing the report of the Secretary-General referred to in paragraph 6 below;

2. *Recommends* that the subject matter of the special court should include notably crimes against humanity, war crimes, and other serious violations of international humanitarian law, as well as crimes under relevant Sierra Leonean law committed within the territory of Sierra Leone;

3. *Recommends further* that the special court should have personal jurisdiction over persons who bear the greatest responsibility for the commission of the crimes referred to in paragraph 2, including those leaders who, in committing such crimes, have threatened the establishment and implementation of the peace process in Sierra Leone; . . .

7. *Requests* the Secretary-General to address in his report the questions of the temporal jurisdiction of the special court, an appeals process including the advisability, feasibility, and appropriateness of an appeals chamber in the special court or of sharing the Appeals Chamber of the International Criminal Tribunals for the Former Yugoslavia and Rwanda or other effective options, and a possible alternative host State, should it be necessary to convene the special court outside the seat of the court in Sierra Leone, if circumstances so require. . . .

Resolution 1318
(September 7, 2000)

The Security Council,
Decides to adopt the attached declaration on ensuring an effective role for the Security Council in the maintenance of international peace and security, particularly in Africa.

Annex

The Security Council . . .
Affirms its determination to strengthen United Nations peacekeeping operations by:
— Adopting clearly defined, credible, achievable, and appropriate mandates,
— Including in those mandates effective measures for the security and safety of United Nations personnel and, wherever feasible, for the protection of the civilian population,
— Taking steps to assist the United Nations to obtain trained and properly equipped personnel for peacekeeping operations; . . .
Underlines the importance of enhancing the United Nations capacity for rapid deployment of peacekeeping operations and *urges* Member States to provide sufficient and timely resources; . . .
Stresses the critical importance of the disarmament, demobilization, and reintegration of ex-combatants, and emphasizes that such programs should normally be integrated into the mandates of peacekeeping operations. . . .

Resolution 1343
(March 7, 2001)

The Security Council, . . .

Determining that the active support provided by the Government of Liberia for armed rebel groups in neighboring countries, and in particular its support for the RUF [Revolutionary United Front] in Sierra Leone, constitutes a threat to international peace and security in the region,

Acting under Chapter VII of the Charter of the United Nations, . . .

2. *Demands* that the Government of Liberia immediately cease its support for the RUF in Sierra Leone and for other armed rebel groups in the region, and in particular take the following concrete steps:

   (a) expel all RUF members from Liberia . . . ;

   (b) cease all financial aid and, in accordance with Resolution 1171 (1998), military support to the RUF, including all transfers of arms and ammunition, all military training and the provision of logistical and communications support, and take steps to ensure that no such support is provided from the territory of Liberia or by its nationals;

   (c) cease all direct or indirect import of Sierra Leone rough diamonds which are not controlled through the Certificate of Origin regime of the Government of Sierra Leone, in accordance with Resolution 1306 (2000);

   (d) freeze funds or financial resources or assets that are made available by its nationals or within its territory directly or indirectly for the benefit of the RUF or entities owned or controlled directly or indirectly by the RUF; . . .

5. (a) *Decides* that all States shall take the necessary measures to prevent the sale or supply to Liberia, by their nationals or from their territories or using their flag vessels or aircraft, or arms or related materiel of all types . . . ;

6. *Decides further* that all States shall take the necessary measures to prevent the direct or indirect import of all rough diamonds from Liberia, whether or not such diamonds originated in Liberia; . . .

11. *Decides further* that the measures imposed by paragraphs 5 to 7 above shall be terminated immediately if the Council . . . determines that the Government of Liberia has complied with the demands in paragraph 2 above . . . ;

16. *Urges* all diamond exporting countries in West Africa to establish Certificate of Origin regimes for the trade in rough diamonds similar to that adopted by the Government of Sierra Leone. . . .

RESOLUTION 1373
(September 28, 2001)

The Security Council, . . .

Reaffirming . . . its unequivocal condemnation of the terrorist attacks which took place in New York, Washington, D.C., and Pennsylvania on September 11, 2001, and expressing its determination to prevent all such acts,

Reaffirming further that such acts, like any act of international terrorism, constitute a threat to international peace and security,

Reaffirming the inherent right of individual or collective self-defense as recognized by the Charter of the United Nations . . .

Acting under Chapter VII of the Charter of the United Nations,

1. *Decides* that all States shall:

    (a) Prevent and suppress the financing of terrorist acts;

    (b) Criminalize the willful provision or collection, by any means, directly or indirectly, of funds by their nationals or in their territories with the intention that the funds should be used, or in the knowledge that they are to be used, in order to carry out terrorist acts;

    (c) Freeze without delay funds and other financial assets or economic resources of persons who commit, or attempt to commit, terrorist acts or participate in or facilitate the commission of terrorist acts; of entities owned or controlled directly or indirectly by such persons; and of persons and entities acting on behalf of, or at the direction of such persons and entities . . . ;

    (d) Prohibit their nationals or any persons or entities within their territories from making any funds, financial assets, or economic resources or financial or other related services available, directly or indirectly, for the benefit of persons who commit or attempt to commit or facilitate or participate in the commission of terrorist acts, of entities owned or controlled, directly or indirectly, by such persons and of persons and entities acting on behalf of or at the direction of such persons;

2. *Decides also* that all States shall:

(a) Refrain from providing any form of support, active or passive, to entities or persons involved in terrorist acts, including by suppressing recruitment of members of terrorist groups and eliminating the supply of weapons to terrorists;

(b) Take the necessary steps to prevent the commission of terrorist acts, including by provision of early warning to other States by exchange of information;

(c) Deny safe haven to those who finance, plan, support, or commit terrorist acts, or provide safe havens;

(d) Prevent those who finance, plan, facilitate, or commit terrorist acts from using their respective territories for those purposes against other States or their citizens;

(e) Ensure that any person who participates in the financing, planning, preparation, or perpetration of terrorist acts or in supporting terrorist acts is brought to justice and ensure that, in addition to any other measures against them, such terrorist acts are established as serious criminal offences in domestic laws and regulations and that the punishment duly reflects the seriousness of such terrorist acts;

(f) Afford one another the greatest measure of assistance in connection with criminal investigations or criminal proceedings relating to the financing or support of terrorist acts, including assistance in obtaining evidence in their possession necessary for the proceedings;

(g) Prevent the movement of terrorists or terrorist groups by effective border controls and controls on issuance of identity papers and travel documents, and through measures for preventing counterfeiting, forgery, or fraudulent use of identity papers and travel documents. . . .

RESOLUTION 1386
(December 20, 2001)

The Security Council, . . .

Welcoming developments in Afghanistan that will allow for all Afghans to enjoy inalienable rights and freedom unfettered by oppression and terror, . . .

Reiterating its endorsement of the Agreement on provisional arrangements in Afghanistan pending the re-establishment of permanent government institutions, signed in Bonn on December 5, 2001 . . . ;

Welcoming the letter from the Secretary of State for Foreign and Commonwealth Affairs of the United Kingdom of Great Britain and Northern Ireland to the Secretary-General of December 19, 2001 . . . and *taking note* of the United Kingdom offer contained therein to take the lead in organizing and commanding an International Security Assistance Force, . . .

Determining that the situation in Afghanistan still constitutes a threat to international peace and security, . . .

Acting for these reasons under Chapter VII of the Charter of the United Nations,

1. *Authorizes,* as envisaged in Annex 1 to the Bonn Agreement, the establishment for six months of an International Security Assistance Force to assist the Afghan Interim Authority in the maintenance of security in Kabul and its surrounding areas, so that the Afghan Interim Authority as well as the personnel of the United Nations can operate in a secure environment;

2. *Calls upon* Member States to contribute personnel, equipment, and other resources to the International Security Assistance Force, and invites those Member States to inform the leadership of the Force and the Secretary-General;

3. *Authorizes* the Member States participating in the International Security Assistance Force to take all necessary measures to fulfill its mandate. . . .

Resolution 1422
(July 12, 2002)

The Security Council, . . .

Taking note of the entry into force on July 1, 2002, of the Statute of the International Criminal Court (ICC), . . .

Determining further that it is in the interests of international peace and security to facilitate Member States' ability to contribute to operations established or authorized by the United Nations Security Council,

Acting under Chapter VII of the Charter of the United Nations,

1. *Requests,* consistent with the provisions of Article 16 of the Rome Statute, that the ICC, if a case arises involving current or former officials or personnel from a contributing State not a Party to the Rome Statute over acts or omissions relating to a United Nations established or authorized operation, shall for a twelve-month period starting July 1, 2002 not commence or proceed with investigation or prosecution of any such case, unless the Security Council decides otherwise;

2. *Expresses* the intention to renew the request in paragraph 1 under the same conditions each July 1, for further twelve-month periods for as long as may be necessary;

3. *Decides* that Member States shall take no action inconsistent with paragraph 1 and with their international obligations. . . .

Resolution 1441
(November 8, 2002)

The Security Council, . . .

Recognizing the threat Iraq's noncompliance with Council resolutions and proliferation of weapons of mass destruction and long-range missiles poses to international peace and security,

Recalling that its Resolution 678 (1990) authorized Member States to use all necessary means to uphold and implement its Resolution 660 (1990) of August 2, 1990 and all relevant resolutions subsequent to

Resolution 660 (1990) and to restore international peace and security in the area,

Further recalling that its Resolution 687 (1991) imposed obligations on Iraq as a necessary step for achievement of its stated objectives of restoring international peace and security in the area,

Deploring the fact that Iraq has not provided an accurate, full, final, and complete disclosure, as required by Resolution 687 (1991), of all aspects of its programs to develop weapons of mass destruction . . . ,

Deploring further that Iraq repeatedly obstructed immediate, unconditional, and unrestricted access to sites designated by the United Nations Special Commission (UNSCOM) and the International Atomic Energy Agency (IAEA), failed to cooperate fully and unconditionally with UNSCOM and IAEA weapons inspectors, as required by Resolution 687 (1991), and ultimately ceased all cooperation with UNSCOM and IAEA in 1998, . . .

Deploring also that the Government of Iraq has failed to comply with its commitments pursuant to Resolution 687 (1991) with regard to terrorism, pursuant to Resolution 688 (1991) to end repression of its civilian population and to provide access by international humanitarian organizations to all those in need of assistance in Iraq, and pursuant to Resolutions 686 (1991), 687 (1991), and 1284 (1999) to return or cooperate in accounting for Kuwaiti and third country nationals wrongfully detained by Iraq, or to return Kuwaiti property wrongfully seized by Iraq,

Recalling that in its Resolution 687 (1991) the Council declared that a cease-fire would be based on acceptance by Iraq of the provisions of that resolution, including the obligations on Iraq contained therein, . . .

Acting under Chapter VII of the Charter of the United Nations,

1. *Decides* that Iraq has been and remains in material breach of its obligations under relevant resolutions, including Resolution 687 (1991), in particular through Iraq's failure to cooperate with United Nations inspectors and the IAEA, and to complete the actions required under paragraphs 8 to 13 of Resolution 687 (1991);

2. *Decides*, while acknowledging paragraph 1 above, to afford Iraq, by this Resolution, a final opportunity to comply with its disarmament

obligations under relevant resolutions of the Council; and accordingly decides to set up an enhanced inspection regime with the aim of bringing to full and verified completion the disarmament process established by Resolution 687 (1991) and subsequent resolutions of the Council;

3. *Decides* that, in order to begin to comply with its disarmament obligations, . . . the Government of Iraq shall provide to UNMOVIC, the IAEA, and the Council, not later that thirty days from the date of this resolution, a currently accurate, full, and complete declaration of all aspects of its programs to develop chemical, biological, and nuclear weapons, ballistic missiles, and other delivery systems such as unmanned aerial vehicles and dispersal systems designed for use on aircraft . . . ;

4. *Decides* that false statements or omissions in the declarations submitted by Iraq pursuant to this resolution and failure by Iraq at any time to comply with, and cooperate fully in the implementation of, this resolution shall constitute a further material breach of Iraq's obligations and will be reported to the Council for assessment in accordance with paragraphs 11 and 12 below;

5. *Decides* that Iraq shall provide UNMOVIC and the IAEA immediate, unimpeded, unconditional, and unrestricted access to any and all, including underground, areas, facilities, buildings, equipment, records, and means of transport which they wish to inspect, as well as immediate, unimpeded, unrestricted, and private access to all officials and other persons whom UNMOVIC or the IAEA wish to interview in the mode or location of UNMOVIC's or the IAEA's choice pursuant to any aspect of their mandates . . . ;

11. *Directs* the Executive Chairman of UNMOVIC and the Director-General of the IAEA to report immediately to the Council any interference by Iraq with inspection activities, as well as any failure by Iraq to comply with its disarmament obligations, including its obligations regarding inspections under this resolution;

12. *Decides* to convene immediately upon receipt of a report in accordance with paragraphs 4 or 11 above, in order to consider the situation and the need for full compliance with all of the relevant

Council resolutions in order to secure international peace and security;

13. *Recalls*, in that context, that the Council has repeatedly warned Iraq that it will face serious consequences as a result of its continued violations of its obligations. . . .

RESOLUTION 1483
(May 22, 2003)

The Security Council, . . .

Noting the letter of May 8, 2003 from the Permanent Representatives of the United States of America and the United Kingdom of Great Britain and Northern Ireland to the President of the Security Council . . . and recognizing the specific authorities, responsibilities, and obligations under applicable international law of these states as occupying powers under unified command (the "Authority"), . . .

Determining that the situation in Iraq, although improved, continues to constitute a threat to international peace and security,

Acting under Chapter VII of the Charter of the United Nations, . . .

4. *Calls upon* the Authority, consistent with the Charter of the United Nations and other relevant international law, to promote the welfare of the Iraqi people through the effective administration of the territory, including in particular working toward the restoration of conditions of security and stability and the creation of conditions in which the Iraqi people can freely determine their own political future;

5. *Calls upon* all concerned to comply fully with their obligations under international law including in particular the Geneva Conventions of 1949 and the Hague Regulations of 1907; . . .

8. *Requests* the Secretary-General to appoint a Special Representative for Iraq whose independent responsibilities shall involve reporting regularly to the Council on his activities under this resolution, coordinating activities of the United Nations in postconflict processes in Iraq, coordinating among United Nations and international agencies engaged in humanitarian assistance and reconstruction activi-

ties in Iraq, and, in coordination with the Authority, assisting the people of Iraq through:

(a) coordinating humanitarian and reconstruction assistance by United Nations agencies and between United Nations agencies and nongovernmental organizations;

(b) promoting the safe, orderly, and voluntary return of refugees and displaced persons;

(c) working intensively with the Authority, the people of Iraq, and others concerned to advance efforts to restore and establish national and local institutions for representative governance, including by working together to facilitate a process leading to an internationally recognized, representative government of Iraq;

(d) facilitating the reconstruction of key infrastructure, in cooperation with other international organizations;

(e) promoting economic reconstruction and the conditions for sustainable development, including though coordination with national and regional organizations, as appropriate, civil society, donors, and the international financial institutions;

(f) encouraging international efforts to contribute to basic civilian administration functions;

(g) promoting the protection of human rights;

(h) encouraging international efforts to rebuild the capacity of the Iraqi civilian police force; and

(i) encouraging international efforts to promote legal and judicial reform;

9. *Supports* the formation, by the people of Iraq with the help of the Authority and working with the Special Representative, of an Iraqi interim administration as a transitional administration run by Iraqis, until an internationally recognized, representative government is established by the people of Iraq and assumes the responsibilities of the Authority;

10. *Decides* that, with the exception of prohibitions related to the sale or supply to Iraq of arms and related materiel other than those arms and related materiel required by the Authority to serve the purposes

of this and other related resolutions, all prohibitions related to trade with Iraq and the provision of financial or economic resources to Iraq established by Resolution 661 (1990) and subsequent relevant resolutions, including Resolution 778 (1992) of October 2, 1992, shall no longer apply;

11. *Reaffirms* that Iraq must meet its disarmament obligations, *encourages* the United Kingdom of Great Britain and Northern Ireland and the United States of America to keep the Council informed of their activities in this regard, and *underlines* the intention of the Council to revisit the mandates of the United Nations Monitoring, Verification, and Inspection Commission and the International Atomic Energy Agency . . . ;

12. *Notes* the establishment of a Development Fund for Iraq to be held by the Central Bank of Iraq and to be audited by independent public accountants approved by the International Advisory and Monitoring Board of the Development Fund for Iraq . . . ;

13. *Notes further* that the funds in the Development Fund for Iraq shall be disbursed at the direction of the Authority, in consultation with the Iraqi interim administration, for the purposes set out in paragraph 14 below;

14. *Underlines* that the Development Fund for Iraq shall be used in a transparent manner to meet the humanitarian needs of the Iraqi people, for the economic reconstruction and repair of Iraq's infrastructure, for the continued disarmament of Iraq, and for the costs of Iraqi civilian administration, and for other purposes benefiting the people of Iraq; . . .

16. *Requests* also that the Secretary-General, in coordination with the Authority, continue the exercise of his responsibilities under Security Council Resolution 1472 (2003) of March 28, 2003 and 1476 (2003) of April 24, 2003, for a period of six months following the adoption of this resolution, and terminate within this time period, in the most cost effective manner, the ongoing operations of the "Oil-for-Food" Program (the "Program"), both at headquarters level and in the field, transferring responsibility for the administration of any remaining activity under the Program to the Authority . . . ;

17. *Further requests* that the Secretary-General transfer as soon as possible to the Development Fund for Iraq 1 billion United States dollars from unencumbered funds in the accounts established pursuant to paragraphs 8(a) and 8(b) of Resolution 986 (1995), . . . and *decides* that . . . all surplus funds in the escrow accounts established pursuant to paragraphs 8(a), 8(b), 8(d), and 8(f) of Resolution 986 (1995) shall be transferred at the earliest possible time to the Development Fund for Iraq; . . .

20. *Decides* that all export sales of petroleum, petroleum products, and natural gas from Iraq following the date of the adoption of this resolution shall be made consistent with prevailing international market best practices, . . . and *decides further* that, except as provided in paragraph 21 below, all proceeds from such sales shall be deposited into the Development Fund for Iraq until such time as an internationally recognized, representative government of Iraq is properly constituted;

21. *Decides further* that 5 percent of the proceeds referred to in paragraph 20 above shall be deposited into the Compensation Fund established in accordance with Resolution 687 (1991) and subsequent relevant resolutions and that, unless an internationally recognized, representative government of Iraq and the Governing Council of the United Nations Compensation Commission, in the exercise of its authority over methods of ensuring that payments are made into the Compensation Fund, decide otherwise, *this* requirement shall be binding on a properly constituted, internationally recognized, representative government of Iraq and any successor thereto. . . .

RESOLUTION 1511
(October 16, 2003)

The Security Council, . . .
Welcoming the decision of the Governing Council of Iraq to form a preparatory constitutional committee to prepare for a constitutional conference that will draft a constitution to embody the aspirations of the Iraqi people, and *urging* it to complete this process quickly, . . .

Determining that the situation in Iraq, although improved, continues to constitute a threat to international peace and security,

Acting under Chapter VII of the Charter of the United Nations,

1. *Reaffirms* the sovereignty and territorial integrity of Iraq, and *underscores*, in that context, the temporary nature of the exercise by the Coalition Provisional Authority (Authority) of the specific responsibilities, authorities, and obligations under applicable international law recognized and set forth in Resolution 1483 (2003), which will cease when an internationally recognized, representative government established by the people of Iraq is sworn in and assumes the responsibilities of the Authority, inter alia through steps envisaged in paragraphs 4 and through 7 and 10 below; . . .

4. *Determines* that the Governing Council and its ministers are the principal bodies of the Iraqi interim administration, which, without prejudice to its further evolution, embodies the sovereignty of the State of Iraq during the transitional period until an internationally recognized, representative government is established and assumes the responsibilities of the Authority; . . .

7. *Invites* the Governing Council to provide to the Security Council, for its review, no later than December 15, 2003, in cooperation with the Authority and, as circumstances permit, the Special Representative of the Secretary-General, a timetable and a program for the drafting of a new constitution for Iraq and for the holding of democratic elections under that constitution;

8. *Resolves* that the United Nations, acting through the Secretary-General, his Special Representative, and the United Nations Assistance Mission in Iraq, should strengthen its vital role in Iraq, including by providing humanitarian relief, promoting the economic reconstruction of and conditions for sustainable development in Iraq, and advancing efforts to restore and establish national and local institutions for representative government; . . .

10. *Takes note* of the intention of the Governing Council to hold a constitutional conference and, recognizing that the convening of the conference will be a milestone in the movement to the full exercise of sovereignty, *calls for* its preparation through national dialogue and consensus-building as soon as practicable and *requests* the

Special Representative of the Secretary-General, at the time of the convening of the conference or, as circumstances permit, to lend the unique expertise of the United Nations to the Iraqi people in this process of political transition, including the establishment of electoral processes; . . .

13. . . . *authorizes* a multinational force under unified command to take all necessary measures to contribute to the maintenance of security and stability in Iraq, including for the purpose of ensuring necessary conditions for the implementation of the timetable and program as well as to contribute to the security of the United Nations Assistance Mission for Iraq, the Governing Council of Iraq, and other institutions of the Iraqi interim administration, and key humanitarian and economic infrastructure; . . .

15. *Decides* that the Council shall review the requirements and mission of the multinational force referred to in paragraph 13 above not later than one year from the date of this resolution, and that in any case the mandate of the force shall expire upon the completion of the political process as described in paragraphs 4 through 7 and 10 above, and *expresses* readiness to consider on that occasion any future need for the continuation of the multinational force, taking into account the views of an internationally recognized, representative government of Iraq. . . .

Resolution 1540
(April 28, 2004)

The Security Council,

Affirming that proliferation of nuclear, chemical, and biological weapons, as well as their means of delivery, constitutes a threat to international peace and security, . . .

Acting under Chapter VII of the Charter of the United Nations,

1. *Decides* that all States shall refrain from providing any form of support to non-State actors that attempt to develop, acquire, manufacture, possess, transport, transfer, or use nuclear, chemical, or biological weapons and their means of delivery;

2. *Decides also* that all States, in accordance with their national procedures, shall adopt and enforce appropriate effective laws which prohibit any non-State actor to manufacture, acquire, possess, transport, transfer or use nuclear, chemical, or biological weapons and their means of delivery, in particular for terrorist purposes, as well as attempts to engage in any of the foregoing activities, participate in them as an accomplice, assist, or finance them;

3. *Decides also* that States shall take and enforce effective measures to establish domestic controls to prevent the proliferation of nuclear, chemical, or biological weapons and their means of delivery, including by establishing appropriate controls over related materials and to this end shall:

   (a) Develop and maintain appropriate effective measures to account for and secure such items in production, use, storage, or transport;

   (b) Develop and maintain appropriate effective physical protection measures;

   (c) Develop and maintain appropriate effective border controls and law enforcement efforts to detect, deter, prevent, and combat, including through international cooperation when necessary, the illicit trafficking and brokering in such items in accordance with their national legal authorities and legislation and consistent with international law;

   (d) Establish, develop, review, and maintain appropriate effective national export and transshipment controls over such items, including appropriate laws and regulations to control export, transit, transshipment, and re-export and controls on providing funds and services related to such export and transshipment such as financing, and transporting that would contribute to proliferation, as well as establishing end-user controls; and establishing and enforcing appropriate criminal or civil penalties for violations of such export control laws and regulations;

4. *Decides* to establish, . . . for a period of no longer than two years, a Committee of the Security Council, consisting of all members of the Council, which will . . . report to the Security Council for its examination, on the implementation of this resolution . . . ;

5. *Decides* that none of the obligations set forth in this resolution shall be interpreted so as to conflict with or alter the rights and obligations of State Parties to the Nuclear Nonproliferation Treaty, the Chemical Weapons Convention, and the Biological and Toxin Weapons Convention or alter the responsibilities of the International Atomic Energy Agency or the Organization for the Prohibition of Chemical Weapons; . . . .

RESOLUTION 1546
(June 8, 2004)

The Security Council, . . .
. . . *affirming* that the United Nations should play a leading role in assisting the Iraqi people and government in the formation of institutions for representative government, . . .
Determining that the situation in Iraq continues to constitute a threat to international peace and security,
Acting under Chapter VII of the Charter of the United Nations,

1. *Endorses* the formation of a sovereign Interim Government of Iraq, as presented on June 1, 2004, which will assume full responsibility and authority by June 30, 2004 for governing Iraq while refraining from taking any actions affecting Iraq's destiny beyond the limited interim period until an elected Transitional Government of Iraq assumes office as envisaged in paragraph four below;

2. *Welcomes* that, also by June 30, 2004, the occupation will end and the Coalition Provisional Authority will cease to exist, and that Iraq will reassert its full sovereignty;

3. *Reaffirms* the right of the Iraqi people freely to determine their own political future and to exercise full authority and control over their financial and natural resources;

4. *Endorses* the proposed timetable for Iraq's political transition to democratic government including:

    (a) formation of the sovereign Interim Government of Iraq that will assume governing responsibility and authority by June 30, 2004;

(b) convening of a national conference reflecting the diversity of Iraqi society; and

(c) holding of direct democratic elections by December 31, 2004 if possible, and in no case later that January 31, 2005, to a Transitional National Assembly, which will, inter alia, have responsibility for forming a Transitional Government of Iraq and drafting a permanent constitution for Iraq leading to a constitutionally elected government by December 31, 2005; . . .

7. *Decides* that in implementing, as circumstances permit, their mandate to assist the Iraqi people and government, the Special Representative of the Secretary-General and the United Nations Assistance Mission for Iraq (UNAMI), as requested by the Government of Iraq, shall:

(a) play a leading role to:

(i) assist in the convening, during the month of July 2004, of a national conference to select a Consultative Council;

(ii) advise and support the Independent Electoral Commission of Iraq, as well as the Interim Government of Iraq and the Transitional National Assembly, on the process for holding elections;

(iii) promote national dialogue and consensus-building on the drafting of a national constitution by the people of Iraq;

(b) and also:

(i) advise the Government of Iraq in the development of effective civil and social services;

(ii) contribute to the coordination and delivery of reconstruction, development, and humanitarian assistance;

(iii) promote the protection of human rights, national reconciliation, and judicial and legal reform in order to strengthen the rule of law in Iraq; and

(iv) advise and assist the Government of Iraq on initial planning for the eventual conduct of a comprehensive census; . . .

9. *Notes* that the presence of the multinational force in Iraq is at the request of the incoming Interim Government of Iraq and therefore

reaffirms the authorization for the multinational force under unified command established under Resolution 1511 (2003) . . . ;

10. *Decides* that the multinational force shall have the authority to take all necessary measures to contribute to the maintenance of security and stability in Iraq . . . ;

11. . . . *notes also* in this regard that Iraqi security forces are responsible to appropriate Iraqi ministers, that the Government of Iraq has authority to commit Iraqi security forces to the multinational force to engage in operations with it . . . ;

12. *Decides further* that the mandate for the multinational force . . . shall expire upon the completion of the political process set out in paragraph 4 above, and *declares* that it will terminate this mandate earlier if requested by the Government of Iraq. . . .

RESOLUTION **1593**
(March 31, 2005)

The Security Council, . . .

Determining that the situation in Sudan continues to constitute a threat to international peace and security,

Acting under Chapter VII of the Charter of the United Nations,

1. *Decides* to refer the situation in Darfur since July 1, 2002 to the Prosecutor of the International Criminal Court;

2. *Decides* that the Government of Sudan and all other parties to the conflict in Darfur, shall cooperate fully with and provide any necessary assistance to the Court and the Prosecutor pursuant to this resolution and, while recognizing that States not party to the Rome Statute have no obligation under the Statute, urges all States and concerned regional and other international organizations to cooperate fully; . . .

6. *Decides* that nationals, current or former officials, or personnel from a contributing State outside Sudan which is not a party to the Rome Statute of the International Criminal Court shall be subject to the exclusive jurisdiction of that contributing State for all alleged acts or omissions arising out of or related to operations in Sudan

established or authorized by the Council or the African Union, unless such exclusive jurisdiction has been expressly waived by the contributing State. . . .

NOTES

1. The following is a selection of some of the relevant treatises and casebooks covering this subject that have been published since the end of the Cold War: Barry E. Carter and Philip R. Trimble, *International Law,* 3d ed. (Boston: Little, Brown, 1999); Lori Fisler Damrosch et al., *International Law: Cases and Materials,* 4th ed. (St. Paul, Minn.: West Group, 2001); Yoram Dinstein, *War, Aggression, and Self-Defense,* 2d ed. (New York: Cambridge University Press, 1994); Thomas M. Franck, *Recourse to Force: State Action against Threats and Armed Attacks* (New York: Cambridge University Press, 2002); Hilaire McCoubrey and Nigel D. White, *International Law and Armed Conflict* (Brookfield, Vt.: Dartmouth Publishing Group, 1992); John Norton Moore, Frederick S. Tipson, and Robert F. Turner, eds., *National Security Law* (Durham, N.C.: Carolina Academic Press, 1990); Sean D. Murphy, *Humanitarian Intervention: The United Nations in an Evolving World Order* (Philadelphia: University of Pennsylvania Press, 1996); Oscar Schachter, *International Law in Theory and Practice* (Norwell, Mass.: Kluwer Academic Publishers, 1991); Malcolm N. Shaw, *International Law,* 4th ed. (New York: Cambridge University Press, 1997), chapters 19–20; Bruno Simma, ed., *The Charter of the United Nations: A Commentary,* 2d ed. (New York: Oxford University Press, 2002); and Jose E. Alvarez, *International Organizations as Law-Makers* (New York: Oxford University Press, 2005).

2. See Ian Brownlie, *International Law and the Use of Force by States* (New York: Oxford University Press, 1981), 14–50; Shaw, *International Law,* 778–80.

3. See Inis L. Claude, *Swords into Plowshares: The Problems and Progress of International Organization,* 4th ed. (New York: Random House, 1971), 28–34.

4. See Moore, Tipson, and Turner, eds., *National Security Law,* 62–65.

5. See ibid., 65–67.

6. See D. W. Bowett, *The Law of International Institutions,* 4th ed. (London: Stevens & Sons, 1982), 17–18; Moore, Tipson, and Turner, eds., *National Security Law,* 67–68.

7. General Treaty for the Renunciation of War (August 27, 1928), 46 *United States Statutes at Large* 2343; 94 *League of Nations Treaty Series* 57.

8. Judgment of the International Military Tribunal, September 30, 1946, in *American Journal of International Law* 41, no. 1 (January 1947): 186–218.

9. See Moore, Tipson, and Turner, eds., *National Security Law,* 68–71; Shaw, *International Law,* 780–81.

10. See Carter and Trimble, *International Law,* 1165–71; Moore, Tipson, and Turner, eds., *National Security Law,* 147–54; and Murphy, *Humanitarian Intervention,* 70–75.

11. For a general discussion of these issues, see Christine D. Gray, *International Law and the Use of Force* (New York: Oxford University Press, 2000), chapters 4–5; Damrosch et al., *International Law,* chapter 12; McCoubrey and White, *International Law and Armed Conflict,* chapter 6; Moore, Tipson, and Turner, eds., *National Security Law,* chapter 4; Schachter, *International Law in Theory and Practice,* 135–83.

12. As early as 1946, and consistently thereafter, abstentions were treated as "concurring votes"; see Simma, ed., *The Charter of the United Nations,* 493–99. In 1971, the International Court of Justice accepted the validity of this interpretation on the grounds that it was the consistent practice of the Council and had been generally accepted by UN members; Legal Consequences for States of the Continued Presence of South Africa in Namibia (South West Africa) Notwithstanding Security Council Resolution 276 (1970), Advisory Opinion of June 21, 1971, paras. 20–22. Absence and nonparticipation by permanent members were also treated from the beginning as equivalent to abstention; see Simma, ed., *The Charter of the United Nations,* 499–501.

13. For example, China abstained in the Council decisions authorizing the use of force against Iraq, UN Security Council Resolution 678 (1990); demanding an end to Iraqi repression of internal dissidents, UN Security Council Resolution 688 (1991); sanctioning Libya for its refusal to turn over the persons charged with destroying Pan Am Flight 103, UN Security Council Resolution 748 (1992); requiring the Federal Republic of Yugoslavia to halt its repression of the population of Kosovo, UN Security Council Resolution 1199 (1998); and authorizing international control and governance of Kosovo after the end of the NATO campaign, UN Security Council Resolution 1244 (1999).

14. See Leland M. Goodrich, Edvard Hambro, and Anne Patricia Simons, *Charter of the United Nations: Commentary and Documents* (New York: Columbia University Press, 1969), 216–21; Simma, ed., *The Charter of the United Nations,* 482–88.

15. See, for example, Bardo Fassbender, *UN Security Council Reform and the Right of Veto: A Constitutional Perspective* (Boston: Kluwer Law International, 1998), 234–55.

16. United Nations, *A More Secure World: Our Shared Responsibility*. Report of the Secretary-General's High-Level Panel on Threats, Challenges, and Change, UN Doc. A/59/565 (New York: United Nations, 2004), paras. 249–60.

17. A detailed account on the relative frequency of the use of the veto can be found in Peter Wallensteen and Patrik Johansson, "Security Council Decisions in Perspective," in *The UN Security Council: From the Cold War to the Twenty-First Century,* ed. John M. Malone (Boulder, Colo.: Lynne Rienner, 2004), 18–21. This account shows, for example, that the number of vetoes in the 1990s was the lowest for any decade in UN history.

18. For a summary of such proposals, see Bardo Fassbender, "Pressure for Security Council Reform," in Malone, ed., *The UN Security Council,* 351–52. A more detailed description can be found in Fassbender, *UN Security Council Reform and the Right of Veto,* 263–75.

19. Article 108 of the Charter provides that amendments come into force when adopted by two-thirds of the General Assembly and ratified by two-thirds of UN members, including all of the permanent members of the Council.

20. The 2004 UN High-Level Panel considered the veto to be "anachronistic" but saw no practical way of changing it; United Nations, *A More Secure World,* para. 256.

21. International Commission on Intervention and State Sovereignty, *The Responsibility to Protect* (Ottawa: International Development Center, 2001), 75.

22. United Nations, *A More Secure World,* para. 256.

23. See Goodrich, Hambro, and Simons, *Charter of the United Nations,* 221–22; Simma, ed., *The Charter of the United Nations,* 512–13.

24. For example, in 1994, eighty-two such statements were made, while only seventy-seven formal resolutions were adopted; in 1997, there were fifty-seven statements and fifty-four resolutions.

25. See Simma, ed., *The Charter of the United Nations,* 512–13.

26. For example, UN Docs. S/PRST/1996/36 and S/PRST/1998/1 (Iraqi refusal to give access to UN inspectors); S/PRST/1996/34 (Croatian refusal to surrender persons indicted by the International Criminal Tribunal for the Former Yugoslavia); S/PRST/1996/18 (Libyan flights in violation of sanctions); S/PRST/1998/13 (atrocities in Sierra Leone); S/PRST/2000/12 (Taliban violations of diplomatic immunities); and S/PRST/2000/15 (cease-fire violations by Congolese factions).

27. For example, UN Docs. S/PRST/1994/45 (deferral of sanctions against UNITA); S/PRST/1995/36 (no modification of sanctions against Libya); and S/PRST/1999/10 (suspension of Libyan sanctions).

28. For example, UN Docs. S/PRST/2002/16 (authority of Kosovo assembly) and S/PRST/2003/18 (authority of the International Criminal Tribunal for Rwanda).

29. See "Defensive Quarantine and the Law," *American Journal of International Law* 57, no. 3 (July 1963): 522, written by U.S. State Department deputy legal adviser Leonard Meeker.

30. For example, UN Security Council Resolution 788 (1992).

31. See Jules Lobel and Michael Ratner, "Bypassing the Security Council: Ambiguous Authorizations to Use Force, Cease-Fires, and the Iraqi Inspection Regime," *American Journal of International Law* 93, no. 1 (January 1999): 132; Lori F. Damrosch, "Concluding Reflections," in *Enforcing Restraint: Collective Intervention in Internal Conflicts,* ed. Lori F. Damrosch (New York: Council on Foreign Relations Press, 1993), 357.

32. UN Security Council Resolution 688 (1991).

33. See Jane Stromseth, "Iraq's Repression of Its Civilian Population," in Damrosch, ed., *Enforcing Restraint,* 77.

34. UN Security Council Resolutions 1199 (1998) and 1244 (1999).

35. See "Editorial Comments: NATO's Kosovo Intervention," *American Journal of International Law* 93, no. 2 (April 1999): 831–32.

36. For example, UN Security Council Resolutions 1021 (1995) (lifting of the arms embargo against Yugoslavia when the secretary-general reports that Bosnia, Croatia, and the Federal Republic of Yugoslavia have signed the Dayton Peace Agreement); 1192 (1998) (suspension of sanctions against Libya when the secretary-general reports that the Libyans accused of the destruction of Pan Am Flight 103 have arrived in the Netherlands for trial).

37. UN Security Council Resolution 841 (1993).

38. UN Security Council Resolution 864 (1993).

39. UN Security Council Resolution 687 (1991).

40. UN Doc. S/22480 (1991).

41. UN Security Council Resolution 833 (1993).

42. UN Security Council Resolutions 1244 (1999) and 1272 (1999).

43. UN Security Council Resolution 943 (1994).

44. Rule 28 of the Council's Provisional Rules of Procedure provides only that the Council "may appoint a commission or committee or a rapporteur for a specified question."

45. This may include standing bodies such as the Committee on Admission of New Members, established in 1946, or temporary bodies such as the various peacekeeping forces and the myriad of ad hoc advisory committees created from time to time. See Simma, ed., *The Charter of the United Nations,* 545–54.

46. For example, UN Security Council Resolutions 661 (1990), 700 (1991) (Iraq); 724 (1991) (Yugoslavia); 748 (1992) (Libya); 841 (1993) (Haiti); 864 (1993) (Angola); 985 (1995) (Liberia); 1132 (1997) (Sierra Leone); 1333 (2000) and 1363 (2001) (Afghanistan).

47. For example, UN Security Council Resolutions 670 (1990), 1210 (1998) (Iraq); 748 (1992) (Libya); 757, 760 (1992), 942 (1994) (Yugoslavia); 841 (1993), 917 (1994) (Haiti); 1132 (1997) (Sierra Leone); 1127 (1997), 1173 (1998) (Angola); 1267 (1999), 1333 (2000) (Afghanistan); 1298 (2000) (Eritrea-Ethiopia); and 1343 (2001) (Liberia).

48. For example, UN Security Council Resolutions 820 (1993) (Yugoslavia), 942 (1994) (Bosnia), and 1132 (Sierra Leone).

49. For example, UN Security Council Resolutions 757 (1992) and 829 (1993) (Yugoslavia).

50. For example, UN Security Council Resolutions 942 (1994) (Bosnia), 1132 (1997) and 1171 (1998) (Sierra Leone), 1137 (1997) (Iraq), 1343 (2001) (Liberia), and 1333 (Afghanistan).

51. For example, UN Security Council Resolutions 986 (1995) and 1175 (1998).

52. UN Security Council Resolutions 1284 (1999) and 1302 (2000).

53. UN Security Council Resolutions 687 and 692 (1991); UN Document S/22559 (1991).

54. UN Security Council Resolutions 827 (1993) (Yugoslavia) and 955 (1994) (Rwanda).

55. UN Doc. S/22559 (1991); see www.unog.ch/uncc.

56. UN Doc. S/22480 (1991).

57. Statute of the International Criminal Tribunal for the Former Yugoslavia, Articles 19, 23, and 25, in UN Doc. S/25704 (1993); Statute of the International Criminal Tribunal for Rwanda, Articles 18, 22, and 24, in annex to UN Security Council Resolution 955 (1994).

58. UN Security Council Resolution 232 (1966). Later, the Council decided that the sanctions would remain in force until the "aims and objectives" of its previous resolutions were "completely achieved"; UN Security Council Resolution 314 (1972).

59. UN Security Council Resolution 460 (1979).

60. For example, UN Security Council Resolutions 661 (1990) (initial economic sanctions against Iraq) and 733 (1992) (arms embargo against Somalia).

61. UN Security Council Resolution 713 (1991).

62. UN Security Council Resolution 687 (1991).

63. UN Security Council Resolution 788 (1992).

64. UN Security Council Resolutions 752 and 757 (1992).

65. UN Security Council Resolution 841 (1993).

66. UN Security Council Resolution 1160 (1998).

67. UN Security Council Resolution 1267 (1999).

68. The following had no time limits: UN Security Council Resolutions 665 (1990) (interdiction of maritime shipping to and from Iraq); 678 (1990) (expulsion of Iraqi forces from Kuwait); 770 (1992) (protection of humanitarian relief in Bosnia); 787 (1992) (interdiction of maritime shipping to and from Yugoslavia); 794 (1992) (relief operations in Somalia); 816 (1993) (enforcement of flight ban over Bosnia); 836 (1993) (support of UNPROFOR in Bosnia); 875 (1993) and 917 (1994) (interdiction of maritime shipments to Haiti); 908 (1994), 981 (1995), and 1037 (1996) (support of UN forces in Croatia); 940 (multinational force in Haiti); 958 (protection of safe areas in Bosnia and Croatia); 1031 (1995) (enforcement of Dayton Peace Agreement); 1080 (1996) (protection of humanitarian relief in Eastern Zaire); 1244 (1999) (international security presence in Kosovo); 1264 (1999) (multinational force in East Timor); and 1386 (2001) (International Security Assistance Force in Afghanistan). The following had time limits: UN Security Council Resolutions 929 (1994) (French operations in Rwanda); 1101 (1997) (multinational force in Albania); and 1125 (1997) (multinational force in the Central African Republic).

69. The arms embargo against Eritrea and Ethiopia in May 2000 was limited to an initial period of twelve months; UN Security Council Resolution 1298 (2000). The restrictions on trade in diamonds from Sierra Leone in July 2000 were limited to an initial period of eighteen months; UN Security Council Resolution 1306 (2000). The sanctions imposed against the Taliban in December 2000 had an initial time limit of twelve months; UN Security Council Resolution 1333 (2000). The sanctions imposed on Liberia in March 2001 had an initial period of twelve months; UN Security Council Resolution 1343 (2001).

70. For example, UN Security Council Resolutions 692 (1991) and 986 (1995).

71. See David Caron, "The Legitimacy of the Collective Authority of the Security Council," *American Journal of International Law* 87, no. 4 (October 1993); Simon Chesterman, *Just War or Just Peace: Humanitarian Intervention and International Law* (New York: Oxford University Press, 2001), 189–95.

72. Professor Caron has suggested the alternative of including a "modified voting clause" in sanctions decisions that would permit the adoption of a subsequent resolution terminating sanctions by a specified vote that would not include the veto; Caron, "The Legitimacy of the Collective Authority of the Security Council," 584–88. However, the Council may be unlikely to agree to a voting procedure for the Council itself that does not include the veto.

73. See, for example, Simma, ed., *The Charter of the United Nations,* 454–60.

74. See Case Concerning Questions of Interpretation and Application of the

1971 Montreal Convention Arising From the Aerial Incident at Lockerbie *(Libyan Arab Jamahariya v. United States of America),* Request for the Indication of Provisional Measures, Order of April 14, 1992, para. 42, 1992 *ICJ Reports* 114.

75. For example, in the debate about Council action to immunize UN peace-keepers from the jurisdiction of the International Criminal Court, several states argued that this would effectively modify the statute of the court (which took the form of a treaty) and was therefore beyond the authority of the Council. For example, UN Document S/PV.4568 (2002), p. 3 (Canada), pp. 5–6 (New Zealand), p. 11 (France), p. 15 (Costa Rica and Iran), p. 22 (Brazil), and pp. 26–27 (Mexico).

76. Geneva Conventions of August 12, 1949 on the Protection of War Victims, 75 *United Nations Treaty Series* 31–417.

77. For general descriptions of customary law, see, for example, Thomas Buergenthal and Sean D. Murphy, *Public International Law in a Nutshell* (St. Paul, Minn.: West Group, 2002), 21–23; Shaw, *International Law,* 56–73; and Carter and Trimble, *International Law,* 134–46.

78. See, for example, Erika de Wet, *The Chapter VII Powers of the United Nations Security Council* (Portland, Ore.: Hart, 2004), 182–83.

79. It has been argued that the Council may not override a special category of customary obligations known as *jus cogens* norms—that is, fundamental principles of universally accepted international law from which no derogation by states is permitted, such as the prohibitions on genocide and torture; for example, ibid., 187–91. However, there is considerable debate as to what norms should be treated as *jus cogens* and how such norms might affect the Council's authority under the Charter. For example, if the principle of nonuse of force were included in this category, it would nonetheless be clear that this principle does not override the clear authority of the Council under the Charter to authorize nondefensive uses of force. In general, it is unlikely that there has been universal state acceptance that any customary norm overrides authority granted by the Charter, which makes it difficult to accept that this could be part of a *jus cogens* principle.

80. For example, de Wet, *The Chapter VII Powers of the United Nations Security Council;* David Schweigman, *The Authority of the Security Council under Chapter VII of the UN Charter: Legal Limits and the Role of the International Court of Justice* (Boston: Kluwer Law International, 2001).

81. See Simma, ed., *The Charter of the United Nations,* 43.

82. UN Charter, Article 92. For general comment on the question of ICJ review of Council decisions, see, for example, W. Michael Reisman, "The Constitutional Crisis in the United Nations," *American Journal of International Law* 87, no. 1 (January 1993); Thomas M. Franck, "The 'Powers of Appreciation': Who Is the Ultimate Guardian of UN Legality?" *American Journal of International Law* 86, no. 3 (July 1992); Geoffrey R. Watson, "Constitutionalism, Judicial Review, and the World Court," *Harvard International Law Journal* 34, no. 1 (Winter 1993); de Wet, *The*

Chapter VII Powers of the UN Security Council, 69–132; Schweigman, *The Authority of the Security Council under Chapter VII of the UN Charter,* 210–86.

83. UN Charter, Article 96. Other organs of the United Nations and specialized agencies may be authorized by the General Assembly to request advisory opinions from the Court on legal questions arising within the scope of their activities.

84. Certain Expenses of the United Nations, Advisory Opinion of July 20, 1962, 1962 *ICJ Reports* 151.

85. Legal Consequences for States of the Continued Presence of South Africa in Namibia (South West Africa) Notwithstanding Security Council Resolution 276 (1970), Advisory Opinion of June 21, 1971, 1971 *ICJ Reports* 16.

86. In theory, the Assembly might ask the court for an advisory opinion on the legality of Council action in some regard. Article 12 of the Charter precludes the Assembly from making any recommendations with regard to a dispute or situation with respect to which the Council is exercising its functions unless the Council requested it to do so, but in its recent advisory opinion on the Israeli wall in Palestine, the court seems to have suggested that this would be no bar to an Assembly request for an advisory opinion; Legal Consequences of the Construction of a Wall in the Occupied Palestinian Territory, Advisory Opinion of July 9, 2004, paras. 25–28, 2004 *ICJ Reports* 136. Nonetheless, one may question whether the Assembly's use of the advisory-opinion mechanism to challenge the legal authority of the Council would be prudent or appropriate, and whether in such a case the court should exercise its discretion to decline to give such an opinion.

87. In the *Namibia* case, the court acknowledged that it "does not possess powers of judicial review or appeal in respect of decisions taken by the United Nations organs concerned"; Legal Consequences for States of the Continued Presence of South Africa in Namibia, Advisory Opinion of June 21, 1971, para. 89.

88. Another possible scenario for possible judicial review of Council actions is illustrated by the decision of the Appeals Chamber of the International Criminal Tribunal for the Former Yugoslavia in the *Tadic* case, in which the defendant argued that the case should be dismissed because the creation of the tribunal by the Council was beyond the Council's authority. The Appeals Chamber acknowledged that it had no authority as such to review the acts of the Council but nonetheless held that it could examine the legality of its own creation for the purpose of confirming that it had jurisdiction over the case before it; *Prosecutor v. Dusko Tadic,* Decision on the Defense Motion for Interlocutory Appeal on Jurisdiction, October 2, 1995, paras. 13–22, 35 *International Legal Materials* 32.

89. See Case Concerning Questions of Interpretation and Application of the 1971 Montreal Convention, Order of April 14, 1992.

90. See, for example, de Wet, *The Chapter VII Powers of the UN Security Council,* 69–132.

91. UN Security Council Resolution 748 (1992).

92. See Case Concerning Questions of Interpretation and Application of the 1971 Montreal Convention, Order of April 14, 1992, paras. 41–46.

93. In the *Lockerbie* case, there was still no decision on the merits when the case was finally dismissed by agreement of the parties more than a decade later; Case Concerning Questions of Interpretation and Application of the 1971 Montreal Convention, Order of September 10, 2003, 2003 *ICJ Reports* 152.

94. Article 39 says that the Council shall determine the existence of a threat to the peace, breach of the peace, or act of aggression, and decide what measures are to be taken as a result. Article 41 says that the Council may decide what measures short of the use of force are to be employed, and Article 42 says that the Council may take military measures if it considers that measures under Article 41 would be inadequate. Article 48 says that the Council may determine what states shall take such actions.

95. Legal Consequences for States of the Continued Presence of South Africa in Namibia, Advisory Opinion of June 21, 1971, para. 20.

96. *Prosecutor v. Dusko Tadic,* para. 28.

97. Ibid., para. 31.

CHAPTER 2: JURISDICTION AND MANDATE

1. See Simma, ed., *The United Nations Charter,* 719.

2. This occurred in 1948 during the debate on Palestine. The United Kingdom, which opposed a U.S. proposal to declare a threat to the peace under Chapter VII, argued that "the omission of the word 'international', in the first part of Article 39, may be due to an oversight." The United States responded that the language of Article 39 was chosen "with great care and a full understanding of its importance," and that a determination of a threat to the peace was therefore justified; *Official Records of the Security Council,* May 19, 1948, 6–7. In the end, the U.S. proposal was not adopted. In fact, a threat to international peace clearly existed at the time by any objective standard and was recognized soon thereafter by the Council in Resolution 54 (1948).

3. The Council referred to a threat to "the peace" in some resolutions on Southern Rhodesia, Bosnia, Somalia, and Ethiopia-Eritrea, but to "international peace and security," "peace and security in the region," or "regional peace and security" in other resolutions concerning the same situations. For example, Southern Rhodesia: UN Security Council Resolutions 221 and 232 (1966); Bosnia: UN Security Council Resolutions 757 and 787 (1992); Somalia: UN Security Council Resolutions 806 (1993) and 897 (1994); and Ethiopia-Eritrea: UN Security Council Resolutions 1297 and 1298 (2000). It used the "breach of the peace" formula in a resolution on the Iran-Iraq War in 1987, when there was no question about the serious international implications of the war, for both regional states and other neutrals; UN Security Council Resolution 598 (1987). It referred to a "threat to peace and security" in the case of East

Timor, which it did not consider to be an internal situation; UN Security Council Resolution 1264 (1999).

4. See, for example, Peter Malanczuk, *Akehurst's Modern Introduction to International Law,* 7th rev. ed. (New York: Routledge, 1997), 211–21; Shaw, *International Law,* 205–54; Alvarez, *International Organizations as Law-Makers,* 169–83; and Thomas Buergenthal, Dinah Shelton, and David P. Stewart, *International Human Rights in a Nutshell* (St. Paul, Minn.: West Group, 2002), 96–132.

5. See, respectively, UN Security Council Resolutions 54 (1948), 83 and 84 (1950), 502 (1982), and 598 (1987).

6. See, respectively, UN Security Council Resolutions 4 (1946) and 138 (1960). In the former, the Council took no action against Spain; in the latter, the Council asked Israel to make reparation for the violation of Argentine sovereignty.

7. UN Security Council Resolution 217 (1965).

8. UN Security Council Resolution 221 (1966).

9. UN Security Council Resolution 232 (1966).

10. UN Security Council Resolution 253 (1968).

11. *Department of State Bulletin,* March 6, 1967, 375–76.

12. Senate Foreign Relations Committee, Hearings on UN Sanctions Against Rhodesia, 92nd Cong., 1st Sess. (July 7, 1971), 37–38.

13. UN Security Council Resolution 134 (1960).

14. UN Security Council Resolution 181 (1963).

15. *Official Records of the Security Council,* August 7, 1963, 6–7.

16. UN Security Council Resolution 418 (1977).

17. For a useful quantitative analysis of the great expansion of Security Council activity in the post–Cold War period, see Wallensteen and Johansson, "Security Council Decisions in Perspective." See also Inger Osterdahl, *Threat to the Peace: The Interpretation by the Security Council of Article 39 of the UN Charter* (Uppsala, Sweden: Iustus Forlag, 1998).

18. UN Security Council Resolution 660 (1990).

19. UN Security Council Resolution 661 (1990).

20. See Murphy, *Humanitarian Intervention,* 165–69.

21. See Thomas G. Weiss, *Military-Civilian Interactions: Intervening in Humanitarian Crises* (Lanham, Md.: Rowman & Littlefield, 1999), 52–57.

22. UN Doc. S/PV.2932 (1991), pp. 27–30.

23. Ibid., p. 31.

24. Ibid., p. 46–47.

25. Ibid., pp. 3–4 (Turkey), 13–15 (Iran), 56 (Austria), 57–58 (United States),

59–60 (Soviet Union), 64–65 (United Kingdom).

26. Ibid., p. 6.

27. Ibid., p. 53.

28. Ibid., pp. 65–66.

29. See Mark Weller, "The International Response to the Dissolution of the Socialist Federal Republic of Yugoslavia," *American Journal of International Law* 86, no. 3 (July 1992).

30. UN Doc. S/PV.3009 (1991), p. 28 (Zimbabwe) and p. 49 (China).

31. Ibid., p. 31 (Zimbabwe) and p. 58 (United States).

32. Ibid., pp. 44–45 (India), p. 51 (Soviet Union), p. 57 (United Kingdom), and p. 58 (United States).

33. Ibid., p. 46.

34. Ibid., p. 50.

35. See Weiss, *Military-Civilian Interactions,* 69–78.

36. UN Doc. S/PV.3145 (1992), pp. 19–20 (Cape Verde) and p. 44 (Morocco).

37. Ibid., pp. 6–8 (Zimbabwe), pp. 12–14 (Ecuador), p. 17 (China), p. 30 (France), and p. 49 (India).

38. See Weiss, *Military-Civilian Interactions,* 167–75.

39. UN Doc. S/PV.3238 (1993), p. 9. Some members suggested that the situation was unique because the Council's action had been requested by Aristide, whom they considered to represent the legitimate government of Haiti, or because the Council's actions were in support of measures already recommended by a regional organization (the Organization of American States); UN Doc. S/PV.3238 (1993), p. 12 (Venezuela) and p. 17 (Brazil).

40. Ibid., p. 7 (Canada) and pp. 11–12 (Venezuela).

41. For example, Liberia: UN Security Council Resolution 788 (1992); Rwanda: UN Security Council Resolution 918 (1994); Central African Republic: UN Security Council Resolution 1125 (1997); and Angola: UN Security Council Resolution 1127 (1997).

42. UN Doc. S/PV.3822 (1997), p. 6 (France) and p. 8 (Korea).

43. Ibid., p. 11.

44. Ibid., p. 8.

45. Ibid., p. 14.

46. Ibid., p. 16.

47. UN Security Council Resolution 1474 (2003).

48. UN Security Council Resolution 1479 (2003).

49. UN Security Council Resolution 1484 (2003).

50. UN Security Council Resolution 1497 (2003).

51. UN Security Council Resolution 1529 (2004).

52. UN Security Council Resolution 1545 (2004).

53. UN Security Council Resolution 1556 (2004).

54. For a general account of the Council's actions in the post–Cold War period with respect to international terrorism, see Edward C. Luck, "Tackling Terrorism," in Malone, ed., *The UN Security Council.*

55. See UN Doc.S/PV.3063 (1992), p. 66 (United States), p. 76 (Hungary), p. 77 (Austria), and p. 79 (Russia).

56. Ibid., pp. 46–47 (Cape Verde), pp. 52–53 (Zimbabwe), p. 58 (India), p. 61 (China), and pp. 63–64 (Morocco).

57. UN Security Council Resolutions 1054 (1996) and 1070 (1996).

58. UN Security Council Resolutions 1189 and 1193 (1998).

59. UN Security Council Resolution 1267 (1999). Further sanctions were imposed in December 2000 under UN Security Council Resolution 1333 (2000).

60. UN Security Council Resolutions 1386 (2001), 1413 and 1444 (2002), and 1510 (2003).

61. For similar assessments of the significance of these generic uses of Chapter VII, see Paul Szasz, "The Security Council Starts Legislating," *American Journal of International Law* 96, no. 4 (October 2002); and Stefan Talmon, "The Security Council as World Legislature," *American Journal of International Law* 99, no. 1 (January 2005). See also Alvarez, *International Organizations as Law-Makers,* 195–98.

62. UN Security Council Resolution 1308 (2000).

63. UN Security Council Resolution 1325 (2000).

64. UN Document S/PV.4950 (2004), p. 15.

65. For general discussions of the Security Council's efforts to promote these objectives in the post–Cold War period, see the following chapters in Malone, ed., *The UN Security Council:* Thomas G. Weiss, "The Humanitarian Impulse"; Joanna Weschler, "Human Rights"; and Gregory H. Fox, "Democratization."

66. *Prosecutor v. Dusko Tadic,* Decision on the Defense Motion for Interlocutory Appeal on Jurisdiction, October 2, 1995, para. 28.

Chapter 3: Sanctions

1. There has been an extensive body of comment on the modern use of collective sanctions, including David Cortwright and George A. Lopez, *The Sanctions Decade: Assessing UN Strategies in the 1990s* (Boulder, Colo.: Lynne Rienner, 2000); Paul Conlon, *United Nations Sanctions Management: A Case Study of the Iraq Sanctions Committee* (Ardsley, N.Y.: Transnational Publishers, 2000); Thomas G. Weiss et al., eds., *Political Gain and Civilian Pain: Humanitarian Impacts of Economic Sanctions* (Lanham, Md.: Rowman & Littlefield, 1997); and Vera Gowlland-Debbas, ed., *United Nations Sanctions and International Law* (Boston: Kluwer Law International, 2001).

2. See Simma, ed., *The Charter of the United Nations,* 736–37; Christopher C. Joyner, "Sanctions, Compliance, and International Law," *Virginia Journal of International Law* 32, no. 1 (Fall 1991): 4–5; Kimberly Ann Elliott, "The Gulf War: The Law of International Sanctions," in *Proceedings of the 85th Annual Meeting of the American Society of International Law* (Washington, D.C.: ASIL, 1991), pp. 171–72.

3. UN Security Council Resolution 217 (1965).

4. UN Security Council Resolution 232 (1966).

5. UN Security Council Resolution 253 (1968).

6. For example, UN Security Council Resolutions 314 (1972), 320 (1972), 326 and 333 (1973), 388 (1976), 409 (1977), and 423 (1978).

7. See, for example, Joyner, "Sanctions, Compliance, and International Law," 7–8; M. Jennifer MacKay, "Economic Sanctions: Are They Actually Enforcing International Law in Serbia-Montenegro?" *Tulane Journal of International and Comparative Law* 3, no. 1/2 (December 1994): 212–16; Elliott, "The Gulf War," 171.

8. For example, UN Security Council Resolutions 181 (1963), 190 and 191 (1964), and 282 (1970).

9. UN Security Council Resolution 418 (1977). The resolution also required all states to refrain from any cooperation with South Africa in the manufacture and development of nuclear weapons.

10. UN Security Council Resolution 569 (1985).

11. UN Security Council Resolution 661 (1990).

12. Iraq and Kuwait: UN Security Council Resolutions 670 (1990), 687 (1991), and 1137 (1997); Yugoslavia: UN Security Council Resolutions 713 (1991), 757 and 787 (1992), 820 (1993), 970 (1995), and 1160 (1998); Somalia: UN Security Council Resolutions 733 (1992) and 1425 (2002); Libya: UN Security Council Resolutions 748 (1992) and 883 (1993); Liberia: UN Security Council Resolutions 788 (1992), 1343 (2001), and 1521 (2003); Haiti: UN Security Council Resolutions 841 (1993) and 917 (1994); Rwanda: UN Security Council Resolution 918 (1994); Bosnia: UN Security Council Resolution 942 (1994); Sudan: UN Security Council Resolutions 1054 and 1070 (1996); Angola: UN Security Council Resolution 1127 (1997); Afghanistan: UN Security Council Resolutions 1267 (1999), and 1388 and 1390 (2002); Ethiopia and Eritrea: UN Security Council Resolution 1298 (2000); Sierra Leone: UN Security Council Resolution 1306 (2000); Congo: UN Security Council Resolution 1493 (2003).

13. Southern Rhodesia: UN Security Council Resolutions 232 (1966) and 282 (1970); South Africa: UN Security Council Resolution 418 (1977); Yugoslavia: UN Security Council Resolutions 713 (1991) and 1160 (1998); Somalia: UN Security

Council Resolutions 733 (1992) and 1425 (2002); Libya: UN Security Council Resolution 748 (1992); Liberia: UN Security Council Resolution 788 (1992); Haiti: UN Security Council Resolution 841 (1993); Rwanda: UN Security Council Resolution 918 (1994); Eritrea-Ethiopia: UN Security Council Resolution 1298 (2000); Afghanistan: UN Security Council Resolution 1333 (2000).

14. UN Security Council Resolutions 661 (1990) and 687 (1991).

15. Yugoslavia: UN Security Council Resolution 713 (1991); Somalia: UN Security Council Resolution 733 (1992); Liberia: UN Security Council Resolution 788 (1992).

16. South Africa: UN Security Council Resolution 418 (1977); Libya: UN Security Council Resolution 748 (1992); Haiti: UN Security Council Resolution 841 (1993); Rwanda: UN Security Council Resolution 918 (1994); Eritrea-Ethiopia: UN Security Council Resolution 1298 (2000).

17. South Africa: UN Security Council Resolution 282 (1970); Libya: UN Security Council Resolution 748 (1992); Eritrea-Ethiopia: UN Security Council Resolution 1298 (2000).

18. South Africa: UN Security Council Resolutions 282 (1970) and 418 (1977); Libya: UN Security Council Resolution 748 (1992).

19. South Africa: UN Security Council Resolution 282 (1970).

20. UN Security Council Resolution 1425 (2002).

21. Iraq was already a party to the 1925 Geneva Protocol for the Prohibition of the Use in War of Asphyxiating, Poisonous, or Other Gases, and of Bacteriological Methods of Warfare (entered into force June 17, 1925), 26 *United States Treaties* 571, and had signed (but not ratified) the 1972 Convention on the Prohibition of the Development, Production, and Stockpiling of Bacteriological (Biological) and Toxin Weapons and on Their Destruction (entered into force April 10, 1977), 1015 *United Nations Treaty Series* 163. But in any event, these treaties did not include many of the obligations imposed by Resolution 687, including the requirement for destruction and non-acquisition of chemical weapons, long-range ballistic missiles, and facilities of various kinds, nor did they obligate Iraq to submit to the intrusive inspection regime mandated by the resolution.

22. UN Security Council Resolution 687 (1991).

23. See, for example, George A. Lopez and David Cortright, "Containing Iraq: Sanctions Worked," *Foreign Affairs,* July/August 2004; Central Intelligence Agency, *Comprehensive Report of the Special Adviser to the DCI on Iraq's WMD,* Washington, D.C., September 30, 2004, www.cia.gov/cia/reports/iraq_wmd_2004/index.html.

24. For example, UN Docs. S/PV.4950 (2004), p. 15 (Pakistan), p. 30 (Cuba), p. 31 (Indonesia), and p. 32 (Iran); S/PV.4950 (2004: Resumption 1), p. 5 (Mexico), p. 14 (Nepal), and p. 17 (Namibia).

25. For example, UN Docs. S/PV.4950, p. 3 (Philippines), p. 5 (Algeria), and p.

28 (Switzerland); S/PV.4950 (2004: Resumption 1), p. 2 (Egypt), p. 8 (Korea), p. 11 (Jordan), and pp. 3–4 (Pakistan).

26. For a similar assessment on this question, see Szasz, "The Security Council Starts Legislating," 901.

27. See Application of the Convention on the Prevention and Punishment of the Crime of Genocide *(Bosnia and Herzegovina v. Yugoslavia),* Application of Bosnia and Herzegovina, quoted in International Court of Justice, *Yearbook: 1996–97* (New York: United Nations Publications, 1997), 180–81.

28. For a contrary argument, see de Wet, *The Chapter VII Powers of the United Nations Security Council,* 248–50.

29. See, for example, Joyner, "Sanctions, Compliance, and International Law," 18–26; American Society of International Law, *Proceedings of the 85th Annual Meeting of the American Society of International Law,* 172–73.

30. UN Security Council Resolution 661 (1990).

31. The main U.S. statutory authorities for unilateral sanctions at the time of the Iraqi invasion were the Trading with the Enemy Act (50 U.S. Code App., sec. 1-5) and the International Emergency Economic Powers Act (50 U.S. Code App., sec. 1701–06). In addition, when the Council adopted Chapter VII sanctions, the UN Participation Act (22 U.S. Code, sec. 287) applied.

32. Executive Order 12722 (August 2, 1990), 55 *Federal Register* 31803.

33. UN Security Council Resolution 687 (1991).

34. UN Security Council Resolution 1483 (2003).

35. UN Security Council Resolution 713 (1991).

36. UN Security Council Resolution 757 (1992).

37. UN Security Council Resolution 820 (1993).

38. UN Security Council Resolution 942 (1994).

39. UN Security Council Resolution 943 (1994).

40. UN Security Council Resolutions 1021 and 1031 (1995).

41. UN Security Council Resolution 1160 (1998).

42. UN Security Council Resolution 1367 (2001).

43. UN Security Council Resolution 841 (1993).

44. UN Security Council Resolution 861 (1993).

45. UN Security Council Resolution 917 (1994).

46. The sanctions were then terminated; UN Security Council Resolution 944 (1994).

47. See, for example, Swiss Federal Office for Foreign Economic Affairs, *Expert Seminar on Targeting UN Financial Sanctions,* March 17–19, 1998; Gary C. Hufbauer and Barbara Oegg, "Targeted Sanctions: A Policy Alternative?" *Law and Policy in International Business* 32, no. 1 (Fall 2000).

48. UN Security Council Resolutions 748 (1992) and 883 (1993).

49. UN Security Council Resolution 1192 (1998).

50. UN Security Council Resolution 1506 (2003).

51. UN Security Council Resolution 1070 (1996).

52. UN Security Council Resolution 1372 (2001).

53. UN Security Council Resolution 1267 (1999). For a useful description of the efforts to enforce Resolution 1267, see Eric Rosand, "The Security Council's Efforts to Monitor the Implementation of al Queda/Taliban Sanctions," *American Journal of International Law* 98, no. 4 (October 2004).

54. UN Security Council Resolution 1399 (2002).

55. UN Security Council Resolution 1526 (2004).

56. UN Security Council Resolution 1127 (1997). For a description of the imposition of sanctions against UNITA, see David J. R. Angell, "The Angola Sanctions Committee," in Malone, ed., *The UN Security Council*, 195–204.

57. UN Security Council Resolutions 1412, 1432, 1439, and 1448 (2002).

58. UN Security Council Resolution 1306 (2000).

59. UN Security Council Resolution 1343 (2001).

60. UN Security Council Resolutions 1521 (2003) and 1532 (2004).

61. UN Security Council Resolution 1137 (1997).

62. UN Security Council Resolution 942 (1994).

63. UN Security Council Resolution 917 (1994).

64. United Nations, *A More Secure World,* para. 152. For an interesting description of due process issues encountered in the compilation and maintenance of the list of groups and individuals associated with the Taliban and al Qaeda, see Rosand, "The Security Council's Efforts to Monitor the Implementation of al Queda/Taliban Sanctions." See also Alvarez, *International Organizations as Law-Makers,* 174–76.

65. Case Concerning Questions of Interpretation and Application of the 1971 Montreal Convention, Order of April 14, 1992, paras. 42–44.

66. For example, UN Security Council Resolutions 661 and 670 (1990), 748 and 757 (1992), and 841 (1993).

67. For example, UN Security Council Resolutions 687 (1991) and 757 (1992).

68. UN Security Council Resolution 217 (1965).

69. UN Security Council Resolution 277 (1970).

70. UN Security Council Resolution 276 (1970).

71. Legal Consequences for States of the Continued Presence of South Africa in Namibia, Advisory Opinion of June 21, 1971.

72. UN Security Council Resolution 435 (1978).

73. UN Security Council Resolution 384 (1975).

74. UN Security Council Resolution 1272 (1999).

75. UN Security Council Resolution 662 (1990).

76. UN Security Council Resolution 664 (1990).

77. UN Security Council Resolution 713 (1991).

78. UN Security Council Resolution 752 (1992).

79. UN Security Council Resolutions 753, 754, and 755 (1992).

80. UN Security Council Resolution 757 (1992).

81. UN Security Council Resolution 777 (1992).

82. UN Security Council Resolution 1326 (2000).

83. UN Security Council Resolution 1244 (1999).

84. UN Security Council Resolution 1383 (2001).

85. UN Security Council Resolution 1453 (2002).

86. UN Security Council Resolution 1483 (2003).

87. UN Security Council Resolution 1500 (2003).

88. UN Security Council Resolution 1511 (2003).

89. UN Security Council Resolution 1546 (2004). The timetable endorsed by the Council provided for the holding of "direct democratic elections" no later than January 31, 2005, for a transitional national assembly that would have responsibility for forming a transitional government and drafting a permanent constitution leading to a "constitutionally elected government" by December 31, 2005.

90. UN Security Council Resolution 748 (1992).

91. UN Security Council Resolution 1054 (1996).

92. UN Security Council Resolution 661 (1990).

93. See, for example, Elliot, "The Gulf War"; William B. Hoffman, "Global Mandate, National Law," in *Proceedings of the 89th Annual Meeting of the American Society of International Law* (Washington, D.C.: ASIL, 1995).

94. UN Security Council Resolution 665 (1990).

95. UN Security Council Resolution 670 (1990). For a description of the application of flight controls by the Iraq Sanctions Committee, see Conlon, *United Nations Sanctions Management,* 87–98.

96. UN Security Council Resolution 661 (1990). For a description and critique of the handling of sanctions violations by the Iraq Sanctions Committee, see Conlon, *United Nations Sanctions Management,* 80–87.

97. UN Security Council Resolution 1306 (2000).

98. UN Security Council Resolution 1343 (2001).

99. UN Security Council Resolution 820 (1993).

100. UN Security Council Resolution 1132 (1997).

101. UN Security Council Resolution 1237 (1999).

102. Yugoslavia: UN Security Council Resolution 787 (1992); Haiti: UN Security Council Resolution 917 (1994).

103. UN Security Council Resolution 757 (1992).

104. UN Security Council Resolution 820 (1993).

105. UN Security Council Resolution 820 (1993).

106. See, for example, Conlon, *United Nations Sanctions Management;* David Cortright and George A. Lopez, "Reforming Sanctions," and Peter van Walsum, "The Iraq Sanctions Committee," in Malone, ed., *The UN Security Council;* G. L. Burci, "Interpreting the Humanitarian Exceptions Through the Sanctions Committees," in Gowlland-Debbas, ed., *United Nations Sanctions and International Law.*

107. See, for example, Eric Hoskins, "The Humanitarian Impacts of Economic Sanctions and War in Iraq," in Weiss et al., eds., *Political Gain and Civilian Pain;* Peggy Kozal, "Is the Continued Use of Sanctions as Implemented against Iraq a Violation of International Human Rights?" *Denver Journal of International Law and Policy* 28, no. 4 (Fall 2000).

108. See, for example, MacKay, "Economic Sanctions: Are They Actually Enforcing International Law in Serbia-Montenegro?" See also Julia Devin and Jaleh Dashti-Gibson, "Sanctions in the Former Yugoslavia: Convoluted Goals and Complicated Consequences," in Weiss et al., eds., *Political Gain and Civilian Pain.*

109. See, for example, Felicia Swindells, "UN Sanctions in Haiti: A Contradiction Under Articles 41 and 55 of the UN Charter," *Fordham International Law Journal* 20, no. 1 (June 1997).

110. UN Security Council Resolution 661 (1990).

111. UN Security Council Resolution 670 (1990).

112. UN Security Council Resolution 687 (1991).

113. For a description of the administration of humanitarian waivers by the Iraq Sanctions Committee, see Conlon, *United Nations Sanctions Management,* 59–80.

114. UN Security Council Resolutions 1284 (1999) and 1330 (2000).

115. UN Security Council Resolution 1330 (2000).

116. UN Security Council Resolution 1382 (2001).

117. UN Security Council Resolution 1454 (2002).

118. UN Security Council Resolution 706 and 712 (1991).

119. See Sarah Graham-Brown, *Sanctioning Saddam: The Politics of Intervention in Iraq* (New York: St. Martin's, 1999), 74–78.

120. UN Security Council Resolution 778 (1992).

121. Graham-Brown, *Sanctioning Saddam,* 77.

122. UN Security Council Resolution 986 (1995).

123. UN Security Council Resolution 1284 (1999).

124. UN Office of the Iraq Program, www.un.org/Depts/oip.

125. UN Security Council Resolution 1483 (2003).

126. UN Office of the Iraq Program, www.un.org/Depts/oip.

127. For example, Libya: UN Security Council Resolution 748 (1992); Yugoslavia: UN Security Council Resolutions 757 and 760 (1992), and 942 (1994); Haiti: UN Security Council Resolutions 841 (1993) and 917 (1994); Angola: UN Security Council Resolution 1127 (1997); Afghanistan: UN Security Council Resolution 1267 (1999).

128. For example, UN Security Council Resolutions 760 (1992), 841 (1993), and 917 (1994).

129. UN Security Council Resolution 1538 (2004).

130. Independent Inquiry Committee into the United Nations Oil-for-Food Program, *Interim Report* (New York, February 3, 2005), 4–6, 53–55, www.iic-offp.org.

131. Ibid., 16–18, 25–27.

132. Independent Inquiry Committee into the United Nations Oil-for-Food Program, *The Management of the United Nations Oil-for-Food Program,* vol. 1 (New York, September 7, 2005), www.iic-offp.org.

133. Ibid., 3–4.

134. Ibid., 1.

135. Ibid., 2.

136. United Nations, *A More Secure World,* para. 180.

137. See Simma, ed., *The Charter of the United Nations,* 784–88.

138. For example, Zambia: UN Security Council Resolutions 253 (1968) and 327 (1973); Botswana: UN Security Council Resolutions 403 and 406 (1977); Mozambique: UN Security Council Resolution 386 (1976).

139. UN Security Council Resolution 669 (1990).

140. See Paul Conlon, "Lessons From Iraq: The Functions of the Iraq Sanctions Committee as a Source of Sanctions Implementation Authority and Practice," *Virginia Journal of International Law* 35, no. 3 (Spring 1995), 653–54; Conlon, *United Nations Sanctions Management,* 98–110.

141. See Joyner, "Sanctions, Compliance, and International Law," 35; Conlon, *United Nations Sanctions Management*, 98–110.

142. See Graham-Brown, *Sanctioning Saddam*, 66–70; Conlon, *United Nations Sanctions Management*, 108; Independent Inquiry Committee into the United Nations Oil-for-Food Program, *Interim Report*, 42. Jordan, in particular, applied to the Sanctions Committee for permission to import Iraqi oil in repayment of Iraqi debts; the committee never formally agreed, but it was understood that the arrangement would continue.

143. Decision of the Governing Council of the UN Compensation Commission, "Propositions and Conclusions on Compensation for Business Losses: Types of Damages and Their Valuation," UN Doc. S/AC/26/1992/9 (1992), para. 6.

144. UN Security Council Resolution 757 (1992).

145. Ibid.

146. Michael P. Scharf and Joshua L. Dorosin, "Interpreting UN Sanctions: The Rulings and Role of the Yugoslavia Sanctions Committee," *Brooklyn Journal of International Law* 19, no. 3 (1993): 803–07.

147. UN Security Council Resolution 748 (1992).

148. UN Security Council Resolution 883 (1993).

149. UN Security Council Resolutions 53/107 (1998), 54/107 (2000), and 58/80 (2004).

150. United Nations, "Implementation of the Provisions of the Charter of the United Nations Related to Assistance to Third States Affected by the Application of Sanctions," Report of the Secretary-General, UN Doc. A/54/383 (1999).

151. For example, ibid., 3–8.

152. In the UN Special Committee on the Charter of the United Nations, the Russian Federation has proposed the adoption of a declaration on sanctions that would, among other things, state that "the creation of a situation in which the consequences of the introduction of sanctions would inflict considerable material and financial harm on third states or in which an innocent civilian population or neighboring countries would experience adverse consequences of international coercive measures is not permissible. The Secretariat must make an objective assessment of the consequences of sanctions for the target state and for third states, as far as possible, prior to their introduction in respect of the target state"; United Nations, "Report of the Special Committee on the Charter of the United Nations and on the Strengthening of the Role of the Organization," UN Doc. A/59/33 (2004), 11.

153. See, for example, de Wet, *The Chapter VII Powers of the United Nations Security Council*, 217–55; Kozal, "Is the Continued Use of Sanctions as Implemented against Iraq a Violation of International Human Rights?" 383; Swindells, "UN Sanctions in Haiti," 1878.

154. United Nations, Report of the Secretary-General on the Work of the Organization, 1998, UN Doc. A/53/1 (1998), para. 64.

155. See the Rome Statute of the International Criminal Court, July 17, 1998, Art. 8(2)(b)(xxv).

156. See W. Michael Reisman, "Assessing the Lawfulness of Nonmilitary Enforcement: The Case of Economic Sanctions," in *Proceedings of the 89th Annual Meeting of the American Society of International Law,* 350; Nicolas Angelet, "International Law Limits to the Security Council," in Gowlland-Debbas, ed., *United Nations Sanctions and International Law,* 72–74.

CHAPTER 4: UN PEACEKEEPING AND GOVERNANCE

1. For general background on UN peacekeeping activities in the post–Cold War period, see United Nations, *The Blue Helmets: A Review of United Nations Peace-keeping,* 3d ed. (New York: United Nations, 1996); William J. Durch, ed., *UN Peacekeeping, American Politics, and the Uncivil Wars of the 1990s* (New York: St. Martin's, 1996); Daniel Warner, ed., *New Dimensions of Peacekeeping* (Boston: Kluwer Academic Publishing, 1995); Frederic L. Kirgis, Jr., *International Organizations in Their Legal Setting* (St. Paul, Minn.: West Publishing, 1993), chapter 5.

2. Boutros Boutros-Ghali, *An Agenda for Peace: Preventive Diplomacy, Peace-making, and Peacekeeping.* Report of the Secretary-General Pursuant to the Statement Adopted by the Summit Meeting of the Security Council on January 31, 1992 (New York: United Nations, 1992), UN Doc. A/47/277–S/24111 (June 17, 1992), paras. 20, 21, 44, www.un.org/Docs/SG/agpeace.html. (Reprinted in 31 *International Legal Materials* 956.)

3. For example, the Clinton administration's 1994 Presidential Decision Directive on peacekeeping operations used the term "peace operations" to mean "the entire spectrum of activities from traditional peacekeeping to peace enforcement aimed at defusing and resolving international conflicts"; see 33 *International Legal Materials* 705.

4. The 2004 report of the UN High-Level Panel likewise criticized the tendency to distinguish between Chapter VI "peacekeeping" and Chapter VII "peace enforcement"; United Nations, *A More Secure World,* paras. 211–13.

5. See Simma, ed., *The Charter of the United Nations,* 664–65; Ralph Wilde, "From Danzig to East Timor and Beyond," *American Journal of International Law* 95, no. 3 (July 2001).

6. See, for example, D. W. Bowett, *United Nations Forces: A Legal Study* (New York: Praeger, 1964), 274–85; Simma, ed., *The Charter of the United Nations,* 684–86.

7. See, for example, chapter 1 ("An Evolving Technique") of the UN Department of Peacekeeping Operations' online *An Introduction to United Nations Peacekeeping,* www.un.org/Depts/dpko/dpko/intro/.

8. Certain Expenses of the United Nations, Advisory Opinion of July 20, 1962, *ICJ Reports 1962,* 166–67.

9. See Bowett, *United Nations Forces,* 285–90; Simma, ed., *The Charter of the United Nations,* 287–98.

10. UN Security Council Resolution 84 (1950). The Soviet Union was boycotting the Council over its refusal to seat the People's Republic of China in place of the Nationalist Chinese delegation, but the Soviets soon realized their mistake.

11. UN General Assembly Resolution 337A (1950).

12. See United Nations, *The Blue Helmets,* 3d. ed., 35–36.

13. UN General Assembly Resolution 997 (1956).

14. UN General Assembly Resolution 1000 (1956).

15. UN Security Council Resolution 143 (1960).

16. UN General Assembly Resolution 1474 (1960).

17. Certain Expenses of the United Nations, Advisory Opinion of July 20, 1962.

18. See Simma, ed., *The Charter of the United Nations,* 690–92.

19. See Stephen M. Hill and Shahin P. Malik, *Peacekeeping and the United Nations* (Brookfield, Vt.: Dartmouth Publishing Group, 1996), 59–85; United Nations, *The Blue Helmets,* 3d. ed., 203–29 (UNTAG), 415–21 (ONUCA), 425–44 (ONUSAL), 453–81 (UNTAC), 661–66 (UNGOMAP).

20. See United Nations, *The Blue Helmets,* 3d. ed., 513–41 and 556–63 (UNPROFOR), 548–56 (UNCRO), 564–66 (UNPREDEP), 561–62 (UNMIBH), 554–56 (UNTAES), 571–88 (UNOMIG), 591–607 (UNMOT).

21. See ibid., pp. 234–65 (UNAVEM), 291–94 and 298–318 (UNOSOM), 343–74 (UNAMIR), 377–98 (UNOMIL), 613–36 (UNMIH).

22. See the description of peacekeeping missions on the UN Department of Peacekeeping Operations' website, www.un.org/Depts/dpko.

23. See United Nations, *The Blue Helmets,* 3d. ed., 669–78 (UNIIMOG), 681–88 (UNIKOM), and ibid. for UNTAET. The conflict in East Timor is classified here as an international conflict in that Indonesian forces were heavily involved and the international community never recognized East Timor as a part of Indonesia.

24. See ibid., 71–80 (UNDOF), 81–112 (UNIFIL), 136–37 (UNMOGIP), 149–70 (UNFICYP).

25. See the overview of the UN Department of Peacekeeping Operations' website, www.un.org/Depts/dpko.

26. See United Nations, *The Blue Helmets,* 3d. ed., 4.

27. Ibid.

28. See the overview of the UN Department of Peacekeeping Operations' website, www.un.org/Depts/dpko.

29. See United Nations, *The Blue Helmets,* 3d. ed., 35–70 (UNEF I and II), 71–80 (UNDOF), 81–112 (UNIFIL), 136–37 (UNMOGIP), 149–70 (UNFICYP).

30. See ibid., 415–21 (ONUCA), 571–88 (UNOMIG), 661–66 (UNGOMAP), 681–88 (UNIKOM).

31. Ibid., 564–66.

32. Ibid., 175–99.

33. See ibid., 203–229; Cedric Thornberry, "Namibia," in Malone, ed., *The UN Security Council,* 407–22.

34. See United Nations, *The Blue Helmets,* 3d ed., 234–55 (UNAVEM I and II), 321–38 (ONUMOZ), 377–98 (UNOMIL), 425–44 (ONUSAL), 453–81 (UNTAC), 561–62 (UNMIBH), 554–56 (UNTAES), 613–36 (UNMIH).

35. For general background on UN peacekeeping in Somalia, see ibid., 285–318; Murphy, *Humanitarian Intervention,* 217–43; Durch, ed., *UN Peacekeeping,* 311–66; Weiss, *Military-Civilian Interactions,* 69–96.

36. See United Nations, *The Blue Helmets,* 3d. ed., 291–94; Murphy, *Humanitarian Intervention,* 217–28.

37. UN Security Council Resolution 814 (1993).

38. UN Security Council Resolution 897 (1994).

39. See United Nations, *The Blue Helmets,* 3d. ed., 315–16; Weiss, *Military-Civilian Interactions,* 91–96.

40. See United Nations, *The Blue Helmets,* 3d. ed., 255–65 (UNAVEM III), 321–38 (ONUMOZ), 343–74 (UNAMIR), 377–98 (UNOMIL), 453–81 (UNTAC), 548–56 (UNCRO); UN Security Council Resolutions 1244 (1999) (UNMIK); 1270 (1999) (UNAMSIL); 1272 (1999) (UNTAET); 1291 (2000) (MONUC); 1509 (2003) (UNMIL).

41. UN Security Council Resolution 761 (1992).

42. See, for example, United Nations, *The Blue Helmets,* 3d. ed., 158 with respect to UNFICYP protection of civilians in Cyprus, and 181–82 with respect to ONUC protection of civilians in the Congo.

43. UN Security Council Resolutions 925 and 965 (1994).

44. UN Security Council Resolution 929 (1994).

45. For general background on UN peacekeeping in the former Yugoslavia, see United Nations, *The Blue Helmets,* 3d. ed., 485–568; Murphy, *Humanitarian Intervention,* 198–217; Durch, ed., *UN Peacekeeping,* 193–274; Weiss, *Military-Civilian Interactions,* 97–135.

46. See United Nations, *The Blue Helmets,* 3d. ed., 513–14.

47. UN Security Council Resolution 819 (1993).

48. UN Security Council Resolution 824 (1993).

49. UN Security Council Resolution 776 (1992).

50. See UN Security Council Resolutions 1244 (1999) (UNMIK); 1272 (1999) (UNTAET); 1270 (1999) (UNAMSIL); 1291 (2000) (MONUC); 1509 (2003) (UNMIL).

51. See United Nations, *The Blue Helmets,* 3d. ed., 343–74 (UNAMIR), 561–562 (UNMIBH), 613–36 (Haiti).

52. This section is drawn largely from the author's contribution to a symposium in the January 2001 issue of the *American Journal of International Law,* for which it has kindly granted permission. See Michael J. Matheson, "United Nations Governance of Postconflict Societies," *American Journal of International Law* 95, no. 1 (January 2001).

53. See Wilde, "From Danzig to East Timor and Beyond."

54. The Marshall, Caroline, and Mariana Islands, formerly mandated to Japan, were placed under the UN trusteeship system in 1947 as a strategic trust territory, with the United States as administering authority. See the U.S. State Department's *Digest of International Law 1962,* 705–06.

55. See, for example, Simma, ed., *The Charter of the United Nations,* 1107–13.

56. Agreement Concerning West New Guinea (West Irian), August 15, 1962, 437 *United Nations Treaty Series* 274.

57. See *Digest of International Law 1978,* 38–54.

58. Agreement on a Comprehensive Political Settlement of the Cambodia Conflict, October 23, 1991, Article 6 and Annex 1; 31 *International Legal Materials* 184. For an excellent description and analysis, see Steven R. Ratner, "The Cambodia Settlement Agreements," *American Journal of International Law* 87, no. 1 (January 1993).

59. See Basic Agreement on the Region of Eastern Slavonia, Baranja and Western Sirmium, UN Doc. S/1995/951 (1995), annex; UN Security Council Resolution 1037 (1996).

60. UN Doc. S/1997/767 (1997).

61. UN Doc. S/1997/953 (1997).

62. The High Representative is nominated by the Steering Committee of the Peace Implementation Council, which comprises a large number of states and agencies involved in supporting the implementation of the Dayton Peace Agreement; see www.ohr.int.

63. Annex 10 to the General Framework Agreement for Peace, December 14, 1995; UN Security Council Resolution 1031 (1995), para. 27.

64. See the conclusions of the Peace Implementation Council, December 10, 1997, para. XI(2), http://www.ohr.int/pic/default.asp?content_id=5182#01.

65. See Dispute Over Inter-Ethnic Boundary in Brcko Area, February 14, 1997, in 36 *International Legal Materials* 396.

66. See the High Representative's decision of March 5, 1999, http://www.ohr. int/decisions/removalssdec/default.asp?content_id=267. Nikola Poplasen, the Republika Srpska president, was removed in March 1999 for (among other things) refusing to nominate as prime minister the candidate supported by a majority of the National Assembly. In removing one mayor for "creating a political atmosphere detrimental to the holding of free and fair elections," the High Representative reminded that "the international community is investing huge personnel and financial resources" to assist Bosnia and therefore would expect local officials to cooperate with the international effort or be replaced; High Representative's Decision of August 28, 1998, http://www. ohr.int/decisions/removalssdec/default.asp?content_id=258.

67. See High Representative's Decisions, www.ohr.int/decisions. The grounds for these actions have included the failure of local legislative assemblies to adopt on time the legislation required by the peace agreement and the inconsistency of such local legislation with the agreement.

68. See United Nations, Report of the Secretary-General on the United Nations Interim Administration Mission in Kosovo, UN Doc. S/1999/779 (1999).

69. UN Security Council Resolution 1244 (1999).

70. UNMIK Regulation 1999/1 on the Authority of the Interim Administration in Kosovo, July 25, 1999, http://www.unmikonline.org/regulations/1999/re99_01.pdf.

71. See United Nations, Report of the Secretary-General on the United Nations Interim Administration Mission in Kosovo, UN Doc. S/1999/779 (1999), paras. 54–78 (civil administration), 79–90 (institution-building), 91–100 (humanitarian), 101–09 (reconstruction).

72. See UNMIK Regulation 1999/1; UNMIK Regulation 1999/24 on the Law Applicable in Kosovo, December 12, 1999, http://www.unmikonline.org/regulations/1999/re1999_24.htm; United Nations, Report of the Secretary-General on the United Nations Interim Administration in Kosovo, UN Doc. S/1999/1250, para. 55.

73. For example, UNMIK Regulation 1999/3 on the Establishment of the Customs and Other Related Services in Kosovo, August 31, 1999, http://www. unmikonline.org/regulations/1999/re99_03.pdf; UNMIK Regulation 1999/4 on the Currency Permitted to be Used in Kosovo, September 2, 1999, http://www. unmikonline.org/regulations/1999/re99_04.pdf; UNMIK Regulation 1999/9 on the Importation, Transport, Distribution and Sale of Petroleum Products for and in Kosovo, September 20, 1999, http://www.unmikonline.org/regulations/1999/re99_09. pdf; UNMIK Regulation 1999/20 on the Banking and Payment Authority of Kosovo, November 15, 1999, http://www.unmikonline.org/regulations/1999/re99_20.pdf.

74. The new code bears the title of the Applicable Criminal Code of the Socialist Autonomous Province of Kosovo; see UNMIK Regulation 2003/1, January 6, 2003, http://www.unmikonline.org/regulations/2003/RE2003_01.pdf.

75. UN Security Council Resolution 1244 (1999).

76. See UN Docs. S/2003/421 (2003), S/2003/996 (2003), and S/2005/335 (2005).

77. See UN Doc. S/2004/613 (2004).

78. UN Security Council Resolution 384 (1975).

79. See UN Doc. S/1999/513, A/54/654 (1999).

80. See UN Doc. A/54/654 (1999).

81. UN Security Council Resolution 1272 (1999).

82. For example, UNTAET Regulation 1999/1 on the Authority of the Transitional Administration in East Timor, November 27, 1999, http://www.un.org/peace/etimor/untaetR/etreg1.htm; UNTAET Regulation 1999/3 on the Establishment of a Transitional Judicial Service Commission, December 3, 1999, http://www.un.org/peace/etimor/untaetR/etreg3.htm; UNTAET Regulation 2000/1 on the Establishment of the Central Fiscal Authority of East Timor, January 14, 2000, http://www.un.org/peace/etimor/untaetR/Reg001E.pdf.

83. See UN Doc. S/2002/432 (2002).

84. UN Security Council Resolution 1410 (2002); see UN Docs. S/2003/449 (2003) and S/2004/669 (2004).

85. UN Security Council Resolution 1401 (2002) and UN Doc. S/2002/278 (2002), paras. 94–115.

86. UN Security Council Resolutions 1386 (2001), 1413 and 1444 (2002), and 1510 (2003).

87. UN Docs. S/2003/333, S/2003/754, S/2003/1212 (2003); S/2004/634 (2004); and S/2005/525 (2005).

88. UN Security Council Resolutions 1483 (2003) and 1500 (2003).

89. See UN Doc. S/2004/625 (2004).

90. UN Security Council Resolution 1511 (2003).

91. UN Security Council Resolution 1546 (2004). A detailed account of the transitional process and the actions of coalition occupation authorities can be found in Sean D. Murphy, "Contemporary Practice of the United States Relating to International Law," *American Journal of International Law* 98, no. 3 (July 2004).

92. International Committee of the Red Cross, *Commentary on the Geneva Conventions of 12 August 1949*, vol. 4, *Geneva Convention Relative to the Protection of Civilian Persons in Time of War* (Geneva: ICRC, 1958), 273–74. See, for example, Jean-Philippe Lavoyer et al., "Jus in Bello: Occupation Law and the War in Iraq," in *Proceedings of the 98th Annual Meeting of the American Society of International Law* (Washington, D.C.: ASIL, 2004), 117–20. The Annex to the Fourth Hague Convention of 1907 ("Respecting the Laws and Customs of War on Land") requires an occupying power to respect the laws in force "unless absolutely prevented" and restricts the collection and expenditure of revenues; the Fourth Geneva Convention of 1949 requires the occupying power to observe the penal laws of the occupied territory except to the extent necessary to provide for its own security and to administer the territory.

93. 2005 World Summit Outcome, paras. 92–93, in UN General Assembly Resolution 60/1 (2005).

94. Ibid., para. 92.

95. Ibid., paras. 97–105.

96. United Nations, *The Blue Helmets: A Review of United Nations Peacekeeping,* 2d ed. (New York, United Nations, 1990), 4–9.

97. See, for example, ibid. For a discussion of the question of consent for UN peacekeeping forces, see Christine Gray, *International Law and the Use of Force* (New York: Oxford University Press, 2000), 183–87.

98. This sequence of events is described in detail in Kirgis, *International Organizations in Their Legal Setting,* 741–45, 764–72.

99. Ibid., 773–78.

100. UN Security Council Resolution 689 (1991).

101. UN Doc. S/23592 (1992).

102. UN Security Council Resolution 743 (1992).

103. UN Security Council Resolution 807 (1993).

104. UNPROFOR: UN Security Council Resolution 836 (1993); UNOSOM II: UN Security Council Resolution 897 (1994); UNCRO: UN Security Council Resolution 981 (1995); UNTAES: UN Security Council Resolution 1037 (1995); MONUA: UN Security Council Resolution 1135 (1997); UNMIK: UN Security Council Resolution 1244 (1999); UNAMSIL: UN Security Council Resolution 1270 (1999); UNTAET: UN Security Council Resolution 1272 (1999); MONUC: UN Security Council Resolution 1291 (2000); MINUSTAH: UN Security Council Resolution 1542 (2004); ONUB: UN Security Council Resolution 1545 (2004).

105. See United Nations, *The Blue Helmets,* 3d ed., 175–99.

106. Ibid., 528.

107. Ibid., 454–55.

108. See ibid., 287–97; UN Security Council Resolution 897 (1994).

109. United Nations, *The Blue Helmets,* 2d ed., 4–9.

110. United Nations, Report of the Panel on United Nations Peace Operations, UN Doc. A/55/305–S/2000/809 (2000), para. 50, http://www.un.org/peace/reports/peace_operations/.

111. A similar view was expressed by the Austrian delegate in a 1992 Security Council debate on the UNPROFOR deployment in Bosnia. He objected to "the attempt carefully to maintain impartiality towards all parties to the conflict" and asked, "Can we be equally distant from the victim and the victimizer? In its endeavor to display impartiality, the Security Council should not lose sight of what is causing the conflict." See UN Doc. S/PV.3106 (1992), 23–24.

112. See Lori F. Damrosch, "The Role of the Great Powers in United Nations Peacekeeping," *Yale Journal of International Law* 18, no. 1 (Winter 1993).

113. United Nations, *The Blue Helmets*, 3d ed., 716–17 (Angola), 722–23 (Somalia), 729–30 (Rwanda), 741–42 (Cambodia), 744–46 and 750–51 (former Yugoslavia), 767–68 (Haiti).

114. In the case of Georgia, a few members of the Council expressed serious misgivings about Russian participation in the peacekeeping forces authorized by the Council, particularly in the force deployed by the Commonwealth of Independent States.

115. For an extended discussion of these questions, see de Wet, *The Chapter VII Powers of the United Nations Security Council*, 311–37.

116. UN Doc. S/PV.3512 (1995), 26.

CHAPTER 5: THE USE OF FORCE

1. The entry of foreign forces on the basis of consent may raise various legal issues, including the legitimacy of the regime giving consent as the government of the state in question, the authority of the official giving consent to act on behalf of that government, the alleged violation by the intervening forces of the terms of that consent, and the right of foreign forces to intervene by consent in a civil war. For discussion of these issues, see, for example, Gray, *International Law and the Use of Force*, 51–83; Lori Fisler Damrosch and David J. Scheffer, *Law and Force in the New International Order* (Boulder, Colo.: Westview, 1991), 113–42.

2. In addition, Chapter XVII ("Transitional Security Arrangements") was included to make provision for the possible need to use force to deal with security threats in the immediate post–World War II environment while the permanent security structure contemplated by the Charter was being assembled. Article 106 provides that, pending the coming into force of arrangements necessary for the Security Council to begin the exercise of its responsibilities under Article 42, the states that were to become the permanent members were to consult with a view to joint action to maintain international peace and security pursuant to the 1943 Moscow Declaration of the major Allied powers. Because this provision depended on agreement among the permanent members, it was never put to use and never emerged as an alternative to Council action under Chapter VII. Article 107 provides that nothing in the Charter precludes action authorized as a result of World War II against any state that was an enemy of any UN signatory during that war. This provision lost practical significance as the Axis states were admitted to the United Nations and the state of war against them was terminated. See Simma, ed., *The Charter of the United Nations*, 1330–40.

3. This view is taken by many commentators. See, for example, Oscar Schachter, "United Nations Law in the Gulf Conflict," 458–59; and "Agora: The Gulf Crisis in International and Foreign Relations Law," *American Journal of International Law* 85, no. 3 (July 1991).

4. The White House, *The National Security Strategy of the United States* (Washington, D.C.: The White House, September 2002), 15, www.whitehouse.gov/nsc/nss.pdf.

5. See, for example, "Agora: Future Implications of the Iraq Conflict," *American Journal of International Law* 97, no. 3 (July 2003).

6. See the letter of March 20, 2003, from the permanent representative of the United States to the United Nations, UN Doc. S/2003/351.

7. William Howard Taft IV, "Pre-emptive Action in Self-Defense," in *Proceedings of the 98th Annual Meeting of the American Society of International Law*, 331–33.

8. In this regard, the 2004 report of the UN High-Level Panel affirmed the right to use force in self-defense "as long as the threatened attack is imminent, no other means would deflect it, and the action is proportionate." In the case of threats that are not imminent, the report argued that "if there are good arguments for preventive military action, with good evidence to support them, they should be put to the Security Council, which can authorize such action if it chooses to. . . . For those impatient with such a response, the risk to global order and the norm of nonintervention on which it continues to be based is simply too great for the legality of unilateral preventive action, as distinct from collectively endorsed action, to be accepted. Allowing one to so act is to allow all." United Nations, *A More Secure World,* paras. 189–91.

9. Specifically, the court rejected the Israeli government's argument that its construction of the wall was a lawful exercise of self-defense in response to terrorist attacks against it. The court seemed to say that because Israel did not claim that the terrorist attacks were imputable to a foreign state, its actions could not fall under Article 51. Legal Consequences of the Construction of a Wall in the Occupied Palestinian Territory, Advisory Opinion of July 9, 2004, paras. 138–39. Three of the judges expressly questioned this language. See Declaration of Judge Buergenthal, paras. 5–6; Separate Opinion of Judge Higgins, para. 33; Separate Opinion of Judge Kooijmans, para. 35.

10. See Simma, ed., *The Charter of the United Nations,* 760–71.

11. See ibid., 762–63.

12. See, for example, Sean D. Murphy, "De Jure War in the Gulf," *New York International Law Review* 5, no. 2 (Summer 1992).

13. Certain Expenses of the United Nations, Advisory Opinion, 151, 167.

14. On the doctrines of necessity and proportionality, see, for example, Gray, *International Law and the Use of Force,* 105–8; Moore, Tipson, and Turner, eds., *National Security Law,* 105–11.

15. United Nations, *A More Secure World,* para. 207.

16. See, for example, Moore, Tipson, and Turner, eds., *National Security Law,*

111–29. There were once serious debates on the qualifying characteristics of regional organizations for the purpose of Chapter VIII (for example, with respect to the Arab League), but in recent years the Council and the international community in general have tended to be more liberal in accepting the status of regional bodies under Chapter VIII. In particular, such status has been recognized for bodies that do not identify themselves as Chapter VIII organizations in their constituent documents or that are not open to all states in a region. See, for example, Gray, *International Law and the Use of Force*, 204–6; Simma, ed., *The Charter of the United Nations*, 828–35.

17. In the 1962 Cuban missile crisis, the issues included whether the Organization of American States recommendation to its members to carry out a "quarantine" of Cuba constituted enforcement action, and whether the Council's failure to condemn the quarantine amounted to implicit authorization. In the case of the Dominican Republic, the issues included whether OAS intervention in 1965 at the request of the recognized government was enforcement action. In the case of the 1983 Grenada intervention, the issues included whether the Organization of Eastern Caribbean States had the authority to act as a regional authority under Chapter VIII.

18. See, for example, Schachter, *International Law in Theory and Practice*, 126; Louis Henkin, "Kosovo and the Law of Humanitarian Intervention," *American Journal of International Law* 93, no. 4 (October 1999): 824–28; Thomas M. Franck, "Lessons of Kosovo," *American Journal of International Law* 93, no. 4 (October 1999): 857–60. On the general question of humanitarian intervention, see Murphy, *Humanitarian Intervention;* Peter Malanczuk, *Humanitarian Intervention and the Legitimacy of the Use of Force* (Hingham, Mass.: Nijhoff International, 1993); Gray, *International Law and the Use of Force*, 26–31.

19. See, for example, W. Michael Reisman, "Humanitarian Intervention to Protect the Ibos," in *Humanitarian Intervention and the United Nations,* ed. Richard B. Lillich (Charlottesville: University Press of Virginia, 1973).

20. See Murphy, *Humanitarian Intervention,* 70–75.

21. William Howard Taft IV, the legal adviser of the State Department during the first Bush administration, confirmed that the United States did not adopt a theory of humanitarian intervention independent of authorization by the Council; Taft, "Pre-Emptive Action in Self-Defense," 332–33.

22. The World Summit Outcome adopted by the General Assembly in September 2005 recognized that the international community has the responsibility to use various peaceful means to help protect populations from genocide, war crimes, ethnic cleansing, and crimes against humanity, and that it was prepared to take forcible action for this purpose "through the Security Council, in accordance with the Charter, including Chapter VII, on a case-by-case basis and in cooperation with relevant regional organizations as appropriate"; 2005 World Summit Outcome, para. 139, in UN General Assembly Resolution 60/1 (2005).

23. For general discussion of the question of the use of force by peacekeeping missions, see Gray, *International Law and the Use of Force*, 158–83; Oscar Schachter,

"Authorized Uses of Force by the United Nations and Regional Organizations," in Damrosch and Scheffer, eds., *Law and Force in the New International Order*, 79–86.

24. United Nations, *The Blue Helmets*, 2d ed., 4–9.

25. United Nations, *The Blue Helmets*, 3d ed., 60.

26. UN Security Council Resolution 426 (1978).

27. UN Security Council Resolution 161 (1961).

28. UN Security Council Resolution 169 (1961).

29. United Nations, *The Blue Helmets*, 3d ed., 184–96.

30. UN Docs. S/PV.3228 (1993), p. 49; S/PV.3356 (1994), p. 10; S/PV.3512 (1995), p. 28.

31. UN Security Council Resolution 837 (1993).

32. UN Security Council Resolution 836 (1993).

33. UN Security Council Resolution 918 (1994).

34. UN Security Council Resolution 1159 (1998).

35. UN Security Council Resolution 1270 (1999).

36. UN Security Council Resolution 1272 (1999).

37. See United Nations, *The Blue Helmets*, 3d ed., 558.

38. See John Hirsch, *Sierra Leone: Diamonds and the Struggle for Democracy* (Boulder, Colo.: Lynne Rienner, 2001), 87–88; UN Doc. S/2000/751 (2000).

39. The secretary-general characterized the use of such peace-enforcement units as a "provisional measure" under Article 40 of Chapter VII; Boutros-Ghali, *An Agenda for Peace.*

40. United Nations, *Supplement to an Agenda for Peace.* Report of the Secretary-General on the Work of the Organization, UN Doc. S/1995/1, www.un.org/Docs/SG.

41. See United Nations, *The Blue Helmets*, 3d ed., 293–94 (Somalia); UN Doc. S/1994/828, paras. 16–20 (Haiti).

42. UN Security Council Resolutions 83 and 84 (1950).

43. See, for example, Simma, ed., *The Charter of the United Nations*, 727–28; Gray, *International Law and the Use of Force*, 148–49.

44. UN Security Council Resolution 221 (1966).

45. UN Security Council Resolution 661 (1990).

46. The U.S. representative in the Council confirmed that the United States and other states had deployed naval forces for this purpose, before being authorized to act by the Council, at the request of the Kuwaiti government under the right of collective self-defense; UN Doc. S/PV.2938 (1990), pp. 29–30. The UK representative noted that there was sufficient authority to take action under Article 51 pursuant to the request already received from Kuwait; UN Doc. S/PV.2938 (1990), p. 48.

47. UN Security Council Resolution 665 (1990).

48. See UN Doc. S/PV.3106 (1992), pp. 11, 16–17.

49. UN Doc. S/PV.2938 (1990), pp. 29–31.

50. UN Doc. S/PV.2938 (1990), pp. 29–30.

51. In spite of the fact that this resolution invoked Chapter VII and "authorized" the coalition to use force, some commentators still preferred to see it as merely a confirmation of the right of collective self-defense. See "Agora: The Gulf Crisis in International and Foreign Relations Law," 508–09. One commentator observed that the resolution "may be read as consistent with both Article 51 and Article 42"; Schachter, "United Nations Law in the Gulf Conflict," 462.

52. UN Doc. S/PV.2963 (1990), p. 33 (Yemen), p. 62 (China), p. 71 (Canada), pp. 76–77 (Malaysia), pp. 81–82 (United Kingdom).

53. Ibid., p. 68 (France), p. 82 (United Kingdom), p. 96 (Soviet Union), p. 103 (United States).

54. UN Doc. S/25091 (1993).

55. Statement of January 14, 1993. See Murphy, *Humanitarian Intervention*, 180–82.

56. UN Security Council Resolution 1205 (1998).

57. See UN Doc. S/PV.3939 (1998), p. 10 (United Kingdom); "Legal Authority for the Possible Use of Force Against Iraq," in *Proceedings of the 92nd Annual Meeting of the American Society of International Law* (Washington, D.C.: ASIL: 1998), 136–50.

58. See, for example, UN Doc. S/PV.3858 (1998), p. 7 (Brazil), pp. 14–15 (China), p. 17 (Russia); Lobel and Ratner, "Bypassing the Security Council," 124.

59. See, for example, UN Doc. S/PV.4644 (2002), p. 5 (France), p. 8 (Russia), pp. 12–13 (China).

60. See, for example, UN Docs. S/PV.4726 (2003), p. 25 (United States); S/2003/51 (United States); S/2003/350 (United Kingdom); S/2003/352 (Australia).

61. On the legal issues, see, for example, "Agora: Future Implications of the Iraq Conflict"; Sean D. Murphy, "Assessing the Legality of Invading Iraq," *Georgetown Law Journal* 92, no. 2 (January 2004).

62. UN Security Council Resolution 1511 (2003).

63. UN Security Council Resolution 1546 (2004).

64. UN Security Council Resolution 770 (1992).

65. See, for example, UN Doc. S/PV.3106 (1992), p. 12 (India), p. 16 (Zimbabwe), p. 50 (China). China abstained for this reason.

66. UN Doc. S/PV.3106 (1992), pp. 13–17, 26.

67. UN Security Council Resolution 787 (1992).

68. UN Security Council Resolution 816 (1993).

69. UN Security Council Resolution 836 (1993).

70. UN Security Council Resolutions 908 (1994) and 958 (1994).

71. Annex 1A to the General Framework Agreement for Peace, Article I (1), www.ohr.int/dpa.

72. UN Security Council Resolution 1031 (1995).

73. UN Doc. S/PV.3607 (1995), p. 19.

74. UN Security Council Resolution 1088 (1996).

75. UN Security Council Resolution 1037 (1996).

76. UN Security Council Resolutions 1199 and 1203 (1998).

77. See UN Doc. S/PV.3937 (1998), pp. 14–15.

78. See UN Doc. S/PV.4011 (1999), pp. 7–9. However, the Council, by a vote of 12-3, refused to condemn the NATO operation.

79. UN Security Council Resolution 1244 (1999).

80. UN Security Council Resolution 1101 (1997).

81. UN Security Council Resolutions 1101 and 1114 (1997).

82. UN Docs. S/PV.3758 (1997), p. 3; S/PV.3791 (1997).

83. See United Nations, *The Blue Helmets,* 3d ed., 293–94.

84. UN Security Council Resolution 794 (1992).

85. See, for example, Weiss, *Military-Civilian Interactions,* 82–87; Murphy, *Humanitarian Intervention,* 223–28.

86. UN Security Council Resolution 954 (1994). See, for example, United Nations, *The Blue Helmets,* 3d ed., 311–18; Weiss, *Military-Civilian Interactions,* 87–91; Murphy, *Humanitarian Intervention,* 228–36.

87. See United Nations, *The Blue Helmets,* 3d ed., 350–52.

88. UN Security Council Resolution 929 (1994).

89. See Weiss, *Military-Civilian Interactions,* 149–54; Murphy, *Humanitarian Intervention,* 247–54.

90. UN Security Council Resolution 1080 (1996).

91. UN Security Council Resolution 1125 (1997).

92. UN Security Council Resolution 1484 (2003).

93. See United Nations, *The Blue Helmets,* 3d ed., 377; Murphy, *Humanitarian Intervention,* 145–58.

94. For example, UN Security Council Resolutions 788 (1992); 813 and 866 (1993).

95. For a general description of the conflict in Sierra Leone and the response of the international community, see Hirsch, *Sierra Leone.*

96. For example, UN Security Council Resolutions 1132 (1997); 1162 and 1181 (1998); 1260 and 1270 (1999); 1289 and 1306 (2000); 1389 (2002).

97. UN Security Council Resolution 1132 (1997).

98. UN Security Council Resolutions 875 (1993) and 917 (1994).

99. UN Security Council Resolution 940 (1994).

100. See UN Doc. S/PV.3413 (1994), p. 13.

101. UN Doc. S/PV.3413 (1994), p. 5 (Mexico), p. 6 (Cuba), p. 9 (Brazil), p. 10 (China).

102. UN Docs. S/PV.3413 (1994), p. 22; S/1994/828.

103. UN Doc. S/1994/828, p. 12.

104. See Murphy, *Humanitarian Intervention,* 260–75; Weiss, *Military-Civilian Interactions,* 175–89.

105. See UN Doc. S/2004/300.

106. UN Security Council Resolution 1529 (2004).

107. UN Security Council Resolution 1542 (2004).

108. UN Security Council Resolution 1264 (1999).

109. See UN Doc. S/2000/738, para. 51.

110. UN Security Council Resolutions 1368 and 1373 (2001).

111. UN Security Council Resolution 1386 (2001). During the years that followed, the Council periodically acted to extend this authorization and acknowledge the passing of command of ISAF within NATO; UN Security Council Resolutions 1413 and 1444 (2002), and 1510 (2003).

112. For example, UN Security Council Resolutions 660, 661, and 667 (1990).

113. UN Security Council Resolution 665 (1990).

114. UN Security Council Resolution 678 (1990).

115. For example, UN Doc. S/25091 (1993).

116. For example, UN Security Council Resolutions 757 (1992); 819 and 824 (1993).

117. UN Security Council Resolutions 770, 787 (1992); 816, 836 (1993).

118. For example, UN Security Council Resolution 820 (1993).

119. UN Security Council Resolution 678 (1990).

120. See, for example, UN Doc. S/PV.3413 (1994), p. 5 (Mexico), p. 6 (Cuba).

121. The Security Council resolution authorizing the maritime interdiction operation against Iraq called for coordination "using, as appropriate, mechanisms of the Military Staff Committee," but the committee did not play any significant role in the coordination of the operation; UN Security Council Resolution 665 (1990).

122. UN Doc. S/PV.2963 (1990), p. 33.

123. Ibid., 58.

124. Ibid., 76.

125. See Weiss, *Military-Civilian Interactions,* 85–86.

126. See Steven L. Burg and Paul S. Shoup, *The War in Bosnia-Herzegovina: Ethnic Conflict and International Intervention* (Armonk, N.Y.: M.E. Sharpe, 1999), 347–48; Richard C. Holbrooke, *To End a War* (New York: Random House, 1998), 63–65, 71–72, 99.

127. Letter from UK foreign minister Jack Straw to Secretary-General Annan, December 19, 2001, UN Doc. S/2001/1217.

128. For a description of such coordination and liaison relationships in various recent conflict situations, see United Nations, *The Blue Helmets,* 3d ed., and the reports of the secretary-general to the Council at www.un.org/documents.

129. For example, UN Security Council Resolutions 678 (1990) ("keep the Security Council regularly informed"); 929 (1994) ("report to the Council on a regular basis," the first report within fifteen days); 940 (1994) ("report to the Council at regular intervals," the first report within seven days); 1031 (1995) ("report . . . at least at monthly intervals," the first report within ten days); 1080 (1996) ("provide periodic reports at least twice monthly," the first report within twenty-one days); 1088 (1996) ("report . . . at least at monthly intervals"); 1101 (1997) ("provide periodic reports, at least every two weeks," the first report within fourteen days); 1244 (1999) ("report to the Council at regular intervals," the first report within thirty days); 1264 (1999) ("provide periodic reports," the first report within fourteen days); 1386 (2001) ("provide periodic reports").

130. UN Security Council Resolution 794 (1992).

131. During the Council debate on the transition in Haiti, the U.S. delegate stressed the planned continuity of the operation: "My government has worked hard with the Multinational Force and the Secretariat staff to ensure a seamless transfer of responsibility—a transition without marked change. More than half of the military personnel and about one-third of the civilians in UNMIH will be veterans of the Multinational Force. Overall, there will be no dramatic alteration in mission size, troop capabilities, or quality of command"; UN Doc. S/PV.3496 (1995), p. 11. Similarly, when UNAMSIL took over for ECOMOG in Sierra Leone in 2000, Nigerian ECOMOG troops were "re-hatted" and remained as part of UNAMSIL; see UN Doc. S/PV.4099 (2000), pp. 4–5.

132. For example, UN Security Council Resolutions 786 (1992); 836 and 844 (1993).

133. UN Security Council Resolution 1270 (1999).

CHAPTER 6: UN TECHNICAL COMMISSIONS

1. UN Security Council Resolution 674 (1990).

2. For example, Article 36 of the draft articles produced by the International Law Commission in 2001 on the responsibility of states for internationally wrongful acts provides that "the state responsible for an internationally wrongful act is under an obligation to compensate for the damage caused thereby, insofar as such damage is not made good by restitution. The compensation shall cover any financially assessable damage including loss of profits insofar as it is established." The official commentary to this article states that "financially assessable damage encompasses both damage suffered by the state itself (to its property or personnel or in respect of expenditures reasonably incurred to remedy or mitigate damage flowing from an internationally wrongful act) as well as damage suffered by nationals, whether persons or companies, on whose behalf a state is claiming within the framework of diplomatic protection"; United Nations, Report of the International Law Commission, Fifty-Third Session, UN Doc. A/56/10 (2001), pp. 243, 246, http://www.un.org/law/ilc/reports/2001/2001report.htm.

3. See, for example, David J. Bederman, "Historic Analogues of the UN Compensation Commission," in *The United Nations Compensation Commission,* ed. Richard B. Lillich (Irvington, N.Y.: Transnational Publishers, 1995), 258–68.

4. See generally Charles Nelson Brower, *The Iran–United States Claims Tribunal* (Boston: Kluwer Law International, 1998); George H. Aldrich, *The Jurisprudence of the Iran–United States Claims Tribunal* (New York: Oxford University Press, 1996).

5. More than $2.1 billion has been awarded to U.S. claimants and more than $1 billion to Iran and other Iranian claimants. See the tribunal's website, www.iusct.org.

6. There were 2,388 claims in this category. See the tribunal's website, www.iusct.org.

7. UN Doc. S/22559 (1991).

8. UN Doc. S/22661 (1991).

9. UN Doc. S/22643 (1991).

10. UN Security Council Resolutions 692 and 705 (1991). See generally, Alvarez, *International Organizations as Law-Makers,* 424–28.

11. UN Doc. S/AC.26/1991/1, paras. 10–13. The departure claims are known as "Category A" claims, and the claims for death or injury are known as "Category B" claims.

12. See "Status of Claims Processing" on the UNCC website, www.unog.ch/uncc/status. A claimant could receive more than one $2,500 payment if he or she qualified under more than one criterion, subject to limits of $10,000 per family for death and $5,000 for departure.

13. UN Doc. S/AC.26/1991/1, paras. 14–16. These are known as "Category C" claims.

14. See "Status of Claims Processing" on the UNCC website, www.unog.ch/uncc/status, and "Claims Processing," www.unorg.ch/uncc/clmsproc.

15. See ibid. This included the following categories: "D claims," or claims of individuals above $100,000; "E claims," or claims of corporations and public-sector enterprises; and "F claims," or claims of governments and international organizations.

16. UN Doc. S/AC.26/1991/7/Rev. 1, para. 18.

17. See "Claims Processing" on the UNCC website, www.unog.ch/uncc/clmsproc.

18. See ibid., para. 35.

19. See "Status of Claims Processing" on the UNCC website, www.unog.ch/uncc/status.

20. See ibid.

21. See UN Security Council Resolutions 706 and 712 (1991).

22. See UN Security Council Resolution 778 (1992).

23. See UN Security Council Resolution 986 (1995) and subsequent Council resolutions renewing the Oil-for-Food Program.

24. See ibid.; UN Security Council Resolution 1153 (1998).

25. UN Security Council Resolution 1483 (2003).

26. Ibid.

27. UN Doc. S/AC.26/Dec. 17 (1994), paras. 2–5.

28. UN Doc. S/AC.26/Dec. 73 (1999); "Payment Procedure" on the UNCC website, www.unog.ch/uncc/paymproc.

29. UN Doc. S/AC.26/Dec. 100/Rev. 1 (2002).

30. See "Status of Process and Payment of Claims" on the UNCC website, www.unog.ch/uncc/status.

31. See, for example, John R. Crook, "The UNCC and Its Critics," in Lillich, ed., *The United Nations Compensation Commission,* 89–92.

32. UN Doc. S/AC.26/1991/1, para. 18; UN Doc. S/AC.26/1991/7/Rev. 1.

33. See Bederman, "Historic Analogues of the UN Compensation Commission," 291–93.

34. UN Docs. S/AC.26/1991/7/Rev. 1, para. 24; S/AC.26/1992/15, para. 3.

35. UN Doc. S/AC.26/1992/15, para. 5.

36. UN Doc. S/AC.26/1992/11.

37. UN Security Council Resolution 687 (1991), paras. 16, 17, 19. In recommending a deduction of 30 percent for the Compensation Fund, the secretary-general estimated that 22 percent would be required for the servicing of Iraq's external debt; UN Doc. S/22661 (1991).

38. For example, the Clinton administration proposed that Congress authorize the vesting of frozen Iraqi assets in the United States for use to compensate U.S. persons having claims against Iraq that were not within the jurisdiction of the UNCC, with priority for U.S. military personnel or their families. Unfortunately, a few members of the U.S. Senate insisted that preference be given instead to certain claims based on commercial letters of credit, which the administration strongly opposed, and in the end the legislation was not adopted. See "Statement of Michael Matheson, Principal Deputy Legal Adviser of the U.S. State Department, before the House Committee on Foreign Affairs (October 13, 1993)," in *American Journal of International Law* 88, no. 2 (April 1994): 314–19.

39. Such claims have been submitted by the UN Development Program (UNDP), the UN High Commissioner for Refugees (UNHCR), and the UN Relief and Works Agency for Palestine Refugees in the Near East (UNRWA); see "The Claims" on the UNCC website, www.unorg.ch/uncc.

40. UN Doc. S/AC.26/1991/1, para. 17.

41. See Crook, "The UNCC and Its Critics," 96–98.

42. See, for example, Ronald J. Bettauer, "Establishment of the United Nations Compensation Commission," in Lillich, ed., *The United Nations Compensation Commission,* 29–30.

43. UN Security Council Resolutions 731 and 748 (1992).

44. UN Security Council Resolutions 748 (1992), 883 (1993), 1192 (1998).

45. UN Security Council Resolution 1506 (2003).

46. UN Doc. S/25704 (1993), Article 24(3). The statute may be found on the tribunal's website, www.un.org./icty.

47. Rule 106. The rules may also be found on the tribunal's website.

48. Rwanda: Statute, Article 23, UN Security Council Resolution 955 (1994); Sierra Leone: Statute, Article 19, UN Doc. S/2000/915. These statutes may be found on the websites of the two tribunals: www.un.org/ictr and www.sc-sl.org.

49. General Framework Agreement for Peace in Bosnia and Herzegovina, December 14, 1995, 35 *International Legal Materials* 75, Annex 7, Article I. The commission was composed of nine members—four appointed by the Bosnian Federation, two by the Republika Srpska, and the remaining three by the president of the European Court of Human Rights. Decisions were by majority vote.

50. General Framework Agreement for Peace in Bosnia and Herzegovina, Article XIV. For a description and commentary on this process, see Eric Rosand, "The Right to Compensation in Bosnia: An Unfulfilled Promise and a Challenge to International Law," *Cornell International Law Journal* 33, no. 1 (2000).

51. Agreement Between the Government of the Federal Democratic Republic of Ethiopia and the Government of the State of Eritrea (December 12, 2000), UN Doc. S/2001/608, Annex II.

52. See the website of the Permanent Court of Arbitration, www.pca-cpa.org.

53. See "List of Cases brought before the Court since 1946" on the court's website, www.icj-cij.org.

54. See United Nations, *The United Nations and the Iraq-Kuwait Conflict* (New York: United Nations, 1996), 8–13; United Nations, Final Report on the Demarcation of the International Boundary between the Republic of Iraq and the State of Kuwait by the United Nations Iraq-Kuwait Boundary Demarcation Commission, UN Doc. S/25811 (1993), paras. 27–40.

55. See United Nations, *The United Nations and the Iraq-Kuwait Conflict,* 14–17.

56. UN Security Council Resolution 662 (1990).

57. UN Security Council Resolution 686 (1991); UN Docs. S/22320 and S/22321 (1991).

58. UN Security Council Resolution 687 (1991), sixth preambular paragraph and paras. 2–4.

59. Ibid., paras. 4–5; UN Security Council Resolution 689 (1991).

60. UN Doc. S/22456 (1991).

61. UN Doc. S/22485 (1991).

62. UN Doc. S/22558 (1991).

63. Ibid., Annex I-II.

64. See United Nations, Final Report on the Demarcation of the International Boundary between the Republic of Iraq and the State of Kuwait, para. 21.

65. Statement by the President of the Security Council, UN Doc. S/24113 (1992); United Nations, Final Report on the Demarcation of the International Boundary between the Republic of Iraq and the State of Kuwait, para. 112.

66. See, Statement by the President of the Security Council, UN Doc. S/24113 (1992); United Nations, Final Report on the Demarcation of the International Boundary between the Republic of Iraq and the State of Kuwait, paras. 44–102; M. H. Mendelson and S. C. Hulton, "The Iraq-Kuwait Boundary," *British Yearbook of International Law, 1993* (New York: Oxford University Press, 1995).

67. UN Security Council Resolution 833 (1993).

68. UN Doc. S/25963 (1993).

69. UN Doc. S/25905 (1993).

70. UN Doc. S/1994/1288.

71. See Vienna Convention on the Law of Treaties (May 23, 1969), 1155 *United Nations Treaty Series* 331, Article 52.

72. See Mendelson and Hulton, "The Iraq-Kuwait Boundary," 144–50.

73. See UN Security Council Resolutions 740, 743, 749, 752–55, 787 (1992).

74. See United Nations, *The Blue Helmets,* 3d ed., 401–03; UN Security Council Resolutions 915 and 926 (1994).

75. UN Security Council Resolution 1177 (1998).

76. See UN Doc. S/2000/643.

77. UN Security Council Resolution 1320 (2000).

78. Agreement Between the Government of the Federal Democratic Republic of Ethiopia and the Government of the State of Eritrea, Algiers, December 12, 2000.

79. See UN Doc. S/2002/744, para. 3; website of the Permanent Court of Arbitration, www.pca-cpa.org.

80. See UN Doc. S/2002/744, paras. 12–18; UN Doc. S/2003/257, paras. 16–20.

81. See UN Doc. S/2003/1186; website of the Permanent Court of Arbitration, www.pca-cpa.org.

82. See U.S. Arms Control and Disarmament Agency, *Arms Control and Disarmament Agreements: Texts and Histories of the Negotiations* (Washington, D.C.: ACDA, 1996).

83. Convention on the Prohibition of the Development, Production and Stockpiling of Bacteriological (Biological) and Toxin Weapons and on Their Destruction, April 10, 1972, Articles VI–VII.

84. Treaty on the Non-Proliferation of Nuclear Weapons, July 1, 1968, 21 *United States Treaties* 483, 729 *United Nations Treaty Series* 161, Article X; Treaty on the Prohibition of the Emplacement of Nuclear Weapons and Other Weapons of Mass Destruction on the Seabed and the Ocean Floor and in the Subsoil Thereof, February 11, 1971, 23 *United States Treaties* 701, 955 *United Nations Treaty Series* 115, Article VIII; Convention on the Prohibition of the Development, Production, and Stockpiling of Bacteriological (Biological) and Toxin Weapons and on Their Destruction, April 10, 1972, 1015 *United Nations Treaty Series* 163, Article XIII.

85. UN Security Council Resolution 687 (1991), paras. 7, 11. The treaties in question—to which Iraq was already party—were the 1925 Geneva Protocol on the Use of Chemical and Biological Weapons, the 1972 Biological Weapons Convention, and the 1968 Nuclear Nonproliferation Treaty.

86. UN Security Council Resolution 687 (1991), paras. 8, 10, 12.

87. Ibid., paras. 9, 12.

88. Ibid., paras. 9, 13.

89. Ibid., paras. 22, 24.

90. See UN Docs. S/22508 and S/22614 (1991).

91. See, for example, United Nations, *The United Nations and the Iraq-Kuwait Conflict*, 74–98; Murphy, "Contemporary Practice of the United States Relating to International Law," 471–72.

92. For example, UN Security Council Resolution 707 (1991).

93. See Murphy, "Contemporary Practice of the United States Relating to International Law," 472–77.

94. UN Security Council Resolution 1284 (1999). This was evidently included to address allegations within the Council that the last UNSCOM chairman had acted precipitously on his own authority in his reporting of Iraqi noncompliance.

95. UN Security Council Resolution 1441 (2002).

96. See, for example, Hans Blix, *Disarming Iraq* (New York: Pantheon Books, 2004); Central Intelligence Agency, *Comprehensive Report of the Special Adviser to the DCI on Iraq's WMD*.

97. See, for example, UN Docs. S/PV.4950 (2004), pp. 14–15 (Pakistan), pp. 23–24 (India), p. 30 (Cuba), pp. 31–32 (Indonesia), pp. 32–33 (Iran), S/PV.4950 (2004: Resumption), pp. 4–5 (Mexico), pp. 13–14 (Nepal), pp. 14–15 (Nigeria), pp. 16–17 (Namibia).

98. See UN Docs. S/PV.4950 (2004), pp. 2–3 (Philippines), p. 6 (Spain), p. 25 (Singapore), p. 28 (Switzerland); S/PV.4950 (2004: Resumption), pp. 2–3 (Egypt), p. 8 (Korea), pp. 10–11 (Jordan); S/PV.4956 (2004), p. 7 (Algeria), p. 9 (Philippines).

99. UN Security Council Resolution 1540 (2004), para. 5; UN Doc. S/PV.4956 (2004), p. 3 (Pakistan).

100. See UN Docs. S/PV.4950 (2004), p. 3 (Philippines), p. 7 (Spain), p. 12 (United Kingdom); S/PV.4956 (2004), p. 9 (Philippines).

101. One variation of such possibilities is the "Peacebuilding Commission" described in chapter 4, although it seems to be intended more as a recommendatory political body than a technical commission with legal authority to produce specific results.

CHAPTER 7: PROSECUTION OF CRIMES

1. These were the 1945 International Military Tribunal (Nuremberg) and the 1946 International Military Tribunal for the Far East (Tokyo). The 1919 Treaty of Versailles provided for ad hoc tribunals for German war criminals, but none were in fact created. See, for example, M. Cherif Bassiouni, *The Statute of the International Criminal Court: A Documentary History* (Ardsley, N.Y.: Transnational Publishers, 1998), 5–7; Virginia Morris and Michael P. Scharf, *An Insider's Guide to the International Criminal Tribunal for the Former Yugoslavia* (Irvington-on-Hudson, N.Y.: Transnational Publishers, 1995), vol. 1, 2–10.

2. See Agreement for the Prosecution and Punishment of Major War Criminals of the European Axis, August 8, 1945, 82 *United Nations Treaty Series* 279; Establishment of an International Military Tribunal for the Far East, January 19, 1946, *Treaties and Other International Acts Series* 1589.

3. UN Security Council Resolutions 670 and 674 (1990).

4. An account of the circumstances leading to the establishment of the tribunal can be found in Morris and Scharf, *An Insider's Guide,* vol. 1, 17–35.

5. UN Security Council Resolutions 764, 771, and 787 (1992).

6. UN Security Council Resolution 780 (1992).

7. UN Doc. S/25274 (1993).

8. UN Security Council Resolution 808 (1991).

9. Rapporteurs (Corell-Turk-Thune) under the CSCE Moscow Human Dimension Mechanism to Bosnia-Herzegovina and Croatia, Proposal for an International War Crimes Tribunal for the Former Yugoslavia, February 9, 1993.

10. A compilation of various proposals can be found in Morris and Scharf, *An Insider's Guide,* vol. 2.

11. UN Doc. S/25704 (1993), paras. 18–30.

12. UN Doc. S/PV.3217 (1993), p. 33 (China), p. 37 (Brazil).

13. UN Doc. S/PV.3217 (1993), p. 33.

14. UN Security Council Resolution 827 (1993).

15. Compare the Draft Charter proposed by the United States on April 5, 1993, reprinted in *American Journal of International Law* 87, no. 3 (July 1993): 437, with the statute proposed to the Council on May 6, UN Doc. S/25704 (1993), and approved by the Council on May 25, UN Security Council Resolution 827 (1993). The tribunal did not have various features proposed by others, such as *in absentia* trials and a collective prosecutorial body. See the compilation of national proposals in Morris and Scharf, *An Insider's Guide,* vol. 2.

16. The category of war crimes included "grave breaches" of the 1949 Geneva Conventions (Article 2) and violations of "the laws and customs of war" (Article 3). The category of genocide included any of a series of specified violent acts "with intent to destroy, in whole or in part, a national, ethnical, racial or religious group, as such" (Article 4). The category of crimes against humanity included any of a series of specified crimes "when committed in armed conflict, whether international or internal in character, and directed against any civilian population" (Article 5).

17. The tribunal has jurisdiction even over nationals of permanent members of the Council, as was demonstrated when the prosecutor considered and rejected allegations that NATO forces had committed crimes during the bombing campaign against Serbia during the Kosovo crisis.

18. Article 7 of the International Criminal Tribunal [for the Former Yugoslavia] Statute provides that "the official position of any accused person, whether as head of state or government or as a responsible government official, shall not relieve such person of criminal responsibility nor mitigate punishment."

19. *Prosecutor v. Dusko Tadic,* Decision on the Defense Motion for Interlocutory Appeal on Jurisdiction, October 2, 1995, para. 27; see www.un.org/icty/tadic/appeal. The Trial Chamber of the tribunal declined to consider any challenge to the legality of the tribunal, holding that it was not within the competence of a subsidiary organ of the Council to pass on the validity of the Council's action in creating it, but the Appeals Chamber disagreed and held that this question was an inherent part of the competence of any judicial organ like the tribunal.

20. Ibid., paras. 28–30.

21. Ibid., paras. 31–36.

22. Ibid., paras. 37–38.

23. Ibid., paras. 55–60.

24. UN Security Council Resolution 935 (1994).

25. These ideas were put forward by U.S. officials in July to the UN Secretariat and to representatives of the permanent members of the Council, followed by detailed U.S. proposals in early August for Council action.

26. UN Security Council Resolution 955 (1994).

27. Statute of the International Criminal Tribunal for Rwanda, Articles 11–12, annexed to UN Security Council Resolution 955 (1994).

28. Statute of the International Criminal Tribunal for Rwanda, Article 15.

29. In recognition of the clearly internal character of the Rwandan conflict, the statute of the Rwandan tribunal made explicit reference to the main international agreements governing internal armed conflict (Article 3 common to the four 1949 Geneva Conventions, and Additional Protocol II to the conventions), whereas these are covered in the Yugoslav tribunal by a general reference to the "laws or customs of war"; Statute of the International Criminal Tribunal for Rwanda, Article 4, annexed to UN Security Council Resolution 955 (1994); Statute of the International Criminal Tribunal [for the Former Yugoslavia], Article 3, annexed to UN Doc. S/25704 (1993). The jurisdiction of the Rwanda tribunal was limited to crimes committed during 1994, while the jurisdiction of the Yugoslav tribunal began on January 1, 1993, but had no specified ending date. The jurisdiction of the Rwanda tribunal included violations by Rwandan citizens in neighboring countries, while the jurisdiction of the Yugoslav tribunal was limited to violations committed in the territory of the former Yugoslavia; Rwanda Statute, Article 7; Yugoslav Statute, Article 8. These differences related to the fact that the Rwandan conflict had spread into neighboring countries, and to the fact that the Yugoslav conflict was far from ended at the time of the tribunal's creation. For a more detailed account of this process, see Virginia

Morris and Michael P. Scharf, *The International Criminal Tribunal for Rwanda* (Irvington-on-Hudson, N.Y.: Transnational Publishers, 1998).

30. UN Doc. S/PV.3453 (1994), p. 9 (Brazil), p. 11 (China).

31. The Rwandan delegation cited seven objections: (1) that the tribunal should have had jurisdiction over earlier episodes of alleged genocide in addition to the events of 1994; (2) that the tribunal should have had more trial judges and its own appeals chamber and prosecutor; (3) that its jurisdiction should have been limited to genocide, leaving the prosecution of the other crimes to Rwandan courts; (4) that countries that allegedly participated in the Rwandan conflict should not be permitted to nominate judges and participate in their election; (5) that convicted persons should be imprisoned only in Rwanda; (6) that capital punishment should be available for those convicted; and (7) that the seat of the tribunal should be in Rwanda; UN Doc. S/PV.3453 (1994), pp. 14–16. On the whole, Rwanda wanted more control over the tribunal than the international community was prepared to accept, and this difference of attitude provided a continuing source of friction for years afterward.

32. See, for example, Sean D. Murphy, "Progress and Jurisprudence of the International Criminal Tribunal for the Former Yugoslavia," *American Journal of International Law* 93, no. 1 (January 1999); Payam Akhavan, "Beyond Impunity: Can International Criminal Justice Prevent Future Atrocities?" *American Journal of International Law* 95, no. 1 (January 2001); John Hagan, *Justice in the Balkans: Prosecuting War Crimes in the Hague Tribunal* (Chicago: University of Chicago Press, 2003); Jane Stromseth, ed., *Accountability for Atrocities: National and International Responses* (Ardsley, N.Y.: Transnational Publishers, 2003), chapters 2–3; United Nations, Report of the Secretary-General on the Rule of Law and Transitional Justice in Conflict and Postconflict Societies, UN Doc. S/2004/616.

33. See *American Journal of International Law* 87, no. 3 (July 1993): 436.

34. Accounts of these inefficiencies and irregularities can be found in UN Docs. A/51/789 (1987) and A/52/784 (1998).

35. UN Security Council Resolution 1503 (2003).

36. UN Security Council Resolution 1481 (2003).

37. UN Security Council Resolution 1503 (2003).

38. See Tenth Annual Report of the International Criminal Tribunal for the Former Yugoslavia, UN Doc. A/58/297–S/2003/829; Completion Strategy of the International Criminal Tribunal for Rwanda, UN Doc. S/2004/341. The reliance on plea bargaining has been a matter of some controversy, with critics objecting that the resulting sentences were excessively lenient. Compare the Tenth Annual Report of the International Criminal Tribunal for the Former Yugoslavia, pp. 50–51, with "Plea Deals Being Used to Clear Balkan War Tribunal's Docket," *New York Times*, November 18, 2003.

39. For example, the U.S. representative in the Council debate on the adoption of the Yugoslav tribunal (Ambassador Madeleine Albright) stated, "Those skeptics—including the war criminals—who deride this tribunal as being powerless because the suspects may avoid arrest should not be so confident. The tribunal will issue indictments whether or not suspects can be taken into custody. They will become international pariahs. While these individuals may be able to hide within the borders of Serbia or in parts of Bosnia or Croatia, they will be imprisoned for the rest of their lives within their own land"; UN Doc. S/PV.3217 (1993), p. 13.

40. See www.un.org/icty.

41. See www.ictr.org.

42. See UN Security Council Resolution 827 (1993); Statute of the International Tribunal [for the Former Yugoslavia], Article 29, annexed to UN Doc. S/25704 (1993); UN Security Council Resolution 955 (1994), para. 2; Statute of the International Criminal Tribunal for Rwanda, Article 28, annexed to UN Security Council Resolution 955 (1994).

43. UN Security Council Resolution 1207 (1998).

44. See *Prosecutor v. Dokmanovic,* Order of October 22, 1997, No. IT-95-13a-PT; "Address by Ms. Carla Del Ponte, Chief Prosecutor of the International Criminal Tribunal for the Former Yugoslavia, to the North Atlantic Council," November 3, 2004, http://www.un.org/icty/pressreal/2004/p907-e.htm.

45. See, for example, UN Security Council Resolutions 1088 (1996), 1247 (1999), 1305 (2000), and 1357 (2001).

46. See Bassiouni, *The Statute of the International Criminal Court,* 10–18.

47. The Rome Statute can be found at www.un.org/law/icc/statute.

48. See www.un.org/law/icc/index.

49. Rome Statute of the International Criminal Court, Article 5.

50. Ibid., Articles 39, 42.

51. See, for example, the symposium on "Developments in International Criminal Law," *American Journal of International Law* 93, no. 1 (January 1999); the symposium on "The International Criminal Court," *Cornell International Law Journal* 32, no. 3 (1999); and Monroe Leigh, "The United States and the Statute of Rome," *American Journal of International Law* 95, no. 1 (January 2001).

52. See David J. Scheffer, "The United States and the International Criminal Court," *American Journal of International Law* 93, no. 1 (January 1999): 12.

53. U.S. Government Printing Office, *Weekly Compilation of Presidential Documents* 37, no. 1 (January 8, 2001).

54. Letter to UN Secretary-General Annan from Under Secretary of State Bolton, in U.S. State Department Press Statement, May 6, 2002. The reference to a lack of legal obligations was a tacit reference to Article 18 of the Vienna Convention on the Law of Treaties, May 23, 1969, 1155 *United Nations Treaty Series* 331, which obliges a state that signs a treaty subject to ratification to refrain from "acts which would defeat the object and purpose of a treaty" unless and until "it shall have made its intention clear not to become a party to the treaty."

55. A nongovernmental organization compilation of more than eighty such agreements may be found on the website of the Coalition for the International Criminal Court, www.iccnow.org.

56. The European Union took the position that the agreements proposed by the United States exceed the scope of this provision and that ICC parties would violate their ICC obligations by adhering to them. See Council of the European Union, Note from the General Secretariat of the Council, 12488/1/02 (September 30, 2002).

57. UN Security Council Resolution 1422 (2002).

58. UN Security Council Resolution 1487 (2003). Among other things, it was argued that Article 16 of the ICC statute was intended to grant immunity only for a specific situation, as opposed to the blanket immunity granted in 2002, and that the Council could not properly act under Chapter VII without a credible threat to the peace; see, for example, UN Doc. S/PV.4772 (2003), pp. 2–3 (Secretary-General), pp. 3–5 (Canada), pp. 5–6 (New Zealand), pp. 6–7 (Jordan), p. 7 (Switzerland), p. 9 (Greece), pp. 14–15 (Trinidad and Tobago), p. 18 (Nigeria), and p. 20 (Netherlands). In contrast to this blanket approach, the Council, in authorizing a multinational force for Liberia in 2003, specifically provided that officials and personnel of a contributing state that is not party to the Rome Statute would be subject to the exclusive jurisdiction of the contributing state unless that state waived its jurisdiction; UN Security Council Resolution 1497 (2003).

59. See "U.S. Drops Plan to Exempt G.I.'s from U.N. Court," *New York Times,* June 23, 2004.

60. Public Law 107-206.

61. United Nations, Report of the International Law Commission on the Work of Its Forty-Sixth Session, May 2–July 22, 1994, UN Doc. A/49/10 (1994), Draft Statute for an International Criminal Court, Article 23.

62. See United Nations, Report of the Preparatory Committee on the Establishment of an International Criminal Court, UN Doc. A/51/22 (1996), paras. 130–33.

63. Rome Statute of the International Criminal Court, Article 12. The Court's jurisdiction also includes crimes committed on board a vessel or aircraft under the registry of a state that has accepted its jurisdiction; Rome Statute of the International Criminal Court, Article 12(2)(a).

64. Ibid., Article 16.

65. Ibid., Article 11. Further, a state may, when ratifying, decline to accept the Court's jurisdiction for a period of seven years with respect to war crimes; Rome Statute of the International Criminal Court, Article 124. France and Colombia have exercised this option.

66. In addition to the limits of the definitions of crimes in Article 5, there will also be a detailed and restrictive set of Elements of Crimes pursuant to Article 9. Under Article 121, additional crimes may be added, or the scope of crimes already in the statute expanded, but only after seven years have passed since the statute's entry into force; further, this can only be done by an amendment process which requires ratification by seven-eighths of the parties, and amendments are binding only on parties that accept them.

67. Alternatively, there would seem to be no reason in theory that the Council could not create an ad hoc tribunal composed of some or all of the judges and prosecutors of the ICC if it determined that this was a more expeditious and effective means of international prosecution in a particular situation than attempting to create a new body from the ground up. (In fact, this is what the Council did in establishing the Rwanda tribunal, where it created an Appeals Chamber composed of the members of the Appeals Chamber of the Yugoslav tribunal and provided that the Yugoslav prosecutor would also serve as the Rwanda prosecutor.) In doing so, the Council could give its ad hoc tribunal greater jurisdiction than the ICC would have (for example, over terrorist crimes or previous war crimes), even while otherwise following the substantive and procedural provisions of the ICC statute.

68. Rome Statute of the International Criminal Court, Article 17.

69. Statute of the International Criminal Tribunal [for the Former Yugoslavia], Article 9(2), annexed to UN Doc. S/25704 (1983); Statute of the International Criminal Tribunal for Rwanda, annexed to UN Security Council Resolution 955 (1994), Article 8.

70. See, for example, Neil J. Kritz, *Transitional Justice: How Emerging Democracies Reckon with Former Regimes,* 3 vols. (Washington, D.C.: United States Institute of Peace Press, 1995).

71. See, for example, Michael P. Scharf, "The Amnesty Exception to the Jurisdiction of the International Criminal Court," *Cornell International Law Journal* 32, no. 3 (1999).

72. Rome Statute of the International Criminal Court, Article 16.

73. Ibid., Article 13(b).

74. For example, the Council's resolutions on the immunity of UN peacekeepers expressly decided, under Chapter VII, that states shall take no action inconsistent with its grant of immunity; UN Security Council Resolutions 1422 (2002) and 1487 (2003).

75. In the adoption of Resolution 1577 on the situation in Burundi, the U.S. representative stated that the United States only supported the resolution "based on the understanding that it in no way directed, encouraged or authorized ONUB [the

UN force in Burundi] to cooperate with, or support, the International Criminal Court"; see United Nations, Department of Public Information, Press Release SC/8258 (December 1, 2004).

76. See, "U.N. Votes to Send Any Sudan War Crime Suspects to World Court," *New York Times,* April 1, 2005.

77. UN Security Council Resolution 1593 (2005).

78. See generally, Laura A. Dickinson, "The Promise of Hybrid Courts," *American Journal of International Law* 97, no. 2 (April 2003).

79. UN Security Council Resolution 1315 (2000).

80. See UN Doc. S/2000/915 The negotiations were led for the United Nations by the assistant secretary-general for legal affairs, Ralph Zacklin.

81. See UN Docs. S/2001/228 (2001), para. 54; S/2001/857 (2001), para. 46; S/2002/679.

82. See UN Docs. S/2003/321 (2003) and S/2003/1201 (2003), www.special court.org.

83. UN Doc. S/2000/915 (2000), para. 9.

84. Statute of the Special Court for Sierra Leone, UN Doc. S/2000/915, Article 12.

85. Ibid., Article 15.

86. Ibid., Articles 2–4, 10. At the time of signature of the Lome Agreement, the UN special representative appended to his signature a disclaimer to the effect that the amnesty provision would not apply to international crimes of genocide, crimes against humanity, war crimes, and other serious violations of international humanitarian law; see UN Doc. S/2000/915, paras. 22–24. The crime of genocide was ultimately not included in the jurisdiction of the Special Court because of a lack of evidence of intent to destroy any national, ethnic, racial, or religious group as such; Statute of the Special Court for Sierra Leone, para. 13.

87. Statute of the Special Court for Sierra Leone, Article 5.

88. Ibid., Article 8.

89. Ibid., Article 14.

90. Ibid., Article 19.

91. Ibid., Article 20.

92. UN Doc. S/2000/915, paras. 64–65.

93. It is interesting to note that the Appeals Chamber of the Special Court has held that it is an international court and not a part of the Sierra Leonean justice system for the purpose of deciding that it is not obliged to give immunity to Charles Taylor as a former head of state of Liberia. See Special Court for Sierra Leone, Press Release, May 31, 2004, www.sc-sl.org.

94. See UN Doc. A/57/769 (2003), paras. 6–7.

95. UN General Assembly Resolution 57/228A (2002).

96. See UN Doc. A/57/769 (2003), paras. 9–30.

97. UN General Assembly Resolution 57/228B (2003).

98. Draft Agreement Between the United Nations and the Royal Government of Cambodia Concerning the Prosecution Under Cambodian Law of Crimes Committed During the Period of Democratic Kampuchea, March 17, 2003, Articles 3–4 (included as Annex to UN General Assembly Resolution 57/228B [2003]).

99. Ibid., Articles 5–7.

100. Ibid., Articles 1–2, 9.

101. Ibid., Article 11.

102. UN Doc. A/57/769 (2003), paras. 29–30.

103. UN Doc. S/1999/779 (1999), para. 66.

104. United Nations Mission in Kosovo, "On the Establishment of an Ad Hoc Court of Final Appeal and an Ad Hoc Office of the Public Prosecutor," UNMIK/REG/1999/5 (September 4, 1999), http://www.unmikonline.org/regulations/1999/re99_05.pdf.

105. United Nations Mission in Kosovo, "On the Authority of the Interim Administration in Kosovo," UNMIK/REG/1999/1 (July 25, 1999), http://www.unmikonline.org/regulations/1999/re99_01.pdf; idem., "On Appointment and Removal from Office of Judges and Prosecutors," UNMIK/REG/1999/7 (September 7, 1999), http://www.unmikonline.org/regulations/1999/re99_07.pdf.

106. United Nations Mission in Kosovo, "On Assignment of International Prosecutors/Judges and/or Change of Venue," UNMIK/REG/2000/64 (December 15, 2000), http://www.unmikonline.org/regulations/2000/re2000_64.htm; UN Doc. S/2001/926, para. 49. A useful description of the international prosecutorial effort in Kosovo can be found in Gregory L. Naarden and Jeffrey B. Locke, "Peacekeeping and Prosecutorial Policy: Lessons from Kosovo," *American Journal of International Law* 98, no. 4 (October 2004).

107. Naarden and Locke, "Peacekeeping and Prosecutorial Policy."

108. See UN Docs. S/2003/996, paras. 19–22; S/2004/348, para. 42.

109. United Nations Mission in Kosovo, UNTAET/REG/1999/1; "On the Establishment of the Customs and Other Related Services in Kosovo," UNTAET/REG/1999/3 (August 31. 1999), http://www.unmikonline.org/regulations/1999/re99_03.pdf.

110. See UN Docs. S/2000/738, para. 42; S/2002/432, paras. 17–19.

111. See UN Doc. S/2000/53, para. 46.

112. See UN Docs. S/2001/719, para. 30; S/2002/432, paras. 36–37; S/2004/669, para. 20.

113. See UN Doc. S/2004/669, para. 16–19.

114. UN Security Council Resolution 1483 (2003).

115. Coalition Provisional Authority, "Delegation of Authority Regarding Establishment of an Iraqi Special Tribunal with Appendix A," Order Number 48 (December 10, 2003), http://www.iraqcoalition.org/regulations/20031210_CPAORD_48_IST_and_Appendix_A.pdf.

116. Ibid. The statute had of course been worked out with the coalition, and the coalition administrator reserved the right to alter or rescind the statute "if required in the interests of security."

117. See John F. Burns, "The Struggle for Iraq: Justice; Defiant Hussein, Lashing Out at U.S., Goes on Trial," *New York Times,* October 20, 2005; Council on Foreign Relations, "Iraq: Saddam's Trial," http://www.cfr.org/publication/8750/iraq.html.

118. Coalition Provisional Authority, Order Number 48, Appendix A (Statute of the Iraqi Special Tribunal), Articles 10–14.

119. Ibid., Articles 6–8.

120. Council on Foreign Relations, "Iraq: Saddam's Trial."

121. See, for example, Geneva Convention Relative to the Protection of Civilian Persons in Time of War, August 12, 1949, 75 *United Nations Treaty Series* 287, Article 146; International Convention Against Torture and Other Cruel, Inhuman, or Degrading Treatment or Punishment, December 10, 1984, 1465 *United Nations Treaty Series* 85, Articles 5–7; Montreal Convention for the Suppression of Unlawful Acts Against the Safety of Civil Aviation, September 23, 1971, 974 *United Nations Treaty Series* 177, Articles 5–7; International Convention for the Suppression of Terrorist Bombings, January 9, 1998, 37 *International Legal Materials* 249, Articles 5–8.

122. See UN Security Council Resolution 731 (1992).

123. See Case Concerning Questions of Interpretation and Application of the 1971 Montreal Convention, Order of April 14, 1992, para. 30.

124. UN Security Council Resolution 731 (1992).

125. UN Security Council Resolution 748 (1992).

126. For example, UN Docs. S/PV.3033 (1992), pp. 13–15 (Libya); S/PV.3063 (1992), p. 46 (Cape Verde), pp. 52–53 (Zimbabwe), and pp. 57–58 (India).

127. UN Doc. S/PV.3063 (1992), p. 65. The five abstainers were Cape Verde, China, India, Morocco, and Zimbabwe.

128. Case Concerning Questions of Interpretation and Application of the 1971 Montreal Convention Arising From the Aerial Incident at Lockerbie, paras. 1–11.

129. Ibid., paras. 25–29.

130. Ibid., paras. 41–46.

131. UN Security Council Resolution 1192 (1998).

132. Letter Dated April 5 from the Secretary-General Addressed to the President of the Security Council, UN Doc. S/1999/378.

133. *Her Majesty's Advocate v. Abdelbaset Ali Mohmed al Megrahi and Al Amin Khalifa Fhimah,* High Court of Justiciary at Camp Zeist, January 31, 2001, 40 *International Legal Materials* 582. The second defendant was acquitted in the absence of proof that he knew that the assistance he had provided was to be used for the purpose of the destruction of the aircraft. Al Megrahi appealed his conviction through the Scottish appellate system, and that appeal was denied; Opinion of the Court in *Appeal Against Conviction of Abdelbaset Ali Mohmed al Megrahi against Her Majesty's Advocate,* March 14, 2002, No. C104/01.

134. UN Security Council Resolution 1044 (1996).

135. UN Security Council Resolutions 1054 and 1070 (1996).

136. UN Security Council Resolution 1372 (2001).

137. UN Security Council Resolution 1267 (1999).

138. UN Security Council Resolutions 1333 (2000) and 1363 (2001).

139. UN Security Council Resolution 1390 (2002).

140. UN Security Council Resolution 1373 (2001).

141. See http://www.un.org/Docs/sc/committees/1373/.

Conclusion

1. See, for example, Fassbender, "Pressure for Security Council Reform," and idem., *UN Security Council Reform and the Right of Veto,* 220–75.

2. Europe has less than 10 percent of the world's population but a third of the membership of the Council and 40 percent of its permanent members. Asia, on the other hand, has 60 percent of the world's population but only 20 percent of the membership of the Council and of its permanent members. (Europe is likewise greatly overrepresented in the General Assembly, the International Court of Justice, and other bodies.) By comparison, Africa has less than 15 percent of the world's population but 20 percent of the Council and the court, and more than 25 percent of the Assembly. Latin America has less than 10 percent of the world's population, but more than 10 percent of the Council and the court, and more than 15 percent of the Assembly.

3. See, for example, Fassbender, *UN Security Council Reform,* 234–55.

4. United Nations, *A More Secure World,* paras. 249–60.

5. See Malone, ed., *The UN Security Council.*

Selected Bibliography

Primary Sources

1. Resolutions of the United Nations Security Council

Afghanistan: 1189, 1193 (1998); 1267 (1999); 1333 (2000); 1363, 1368, 1373, 1383, 1386 (2001); 1388, 1390, 1401, 1413, 1444, 1453 (2002); 1510 (2003); 1526 (2004).

Albania: 1101 (1997).

Angola: 864 (1993); 1127, 1135 (1997); 1173 (1998); 1237 (2000); 1412, 1432, 1439, 1448 (2002).

Burundi: 1545 (2004).

Central African Republic: 1125 (1997); 1159 (1998).

Congo: 143, 161, 169 (1960); 1080 (1996); 1291, 1484, 1493 (2003).

Cote d'Ivoire: 1479 (2003).

East Timor: 384 (1975); 1264, 1272 (1999); 1410 (2002).

Ethiopia/Eritrea: 1177 (1998); 1297, 1298, 1320 (2000).

Falkland/Malvinas Islands: 502 (1982).

Haiti: 841, 861, 875 (1993); 917, 940, 944 (1994); 1529, 1542 (2004).

Impact of armed conflict: 1314, 1325 (2000).

International Criminal Court: 1422 (2002); 1487, 1497 (2003).

International terrorism: 1189 (1998); 1368, 1373 (2001); 1390 (2002).

Iran-Iraq: 598 (1987).

Iraq: 660, 661, 662, 664, 665, 667, 669, 670, 674, 678 (1990); 686, 687, 688, 689, 692, 700, 705, 706, 707, 712 (1991); 778 (1992); 833 (1993); 986 (1995); 1137 (1997); 1153, 1175, 1210 (1998); 1284 (1999); 1302, 1330 (2000); 1382 (2001); 1441, 1454 (2002); 1483, 1500, 1511 (2003); 1538, 1546 (2004).

Lebanon: 426 (1978).

Liberia: 788 (1992); 813, 866 (1993); 985 (1995); 1343 (2001); 1497, 1509, 1521 (2003); 1532 (2004).

Libya: 731, 748 (1992); 883 (1993); 1192 (1998); 1506 (2003).

Korea: 83, 84 (1950).

Palestine: 54 (1948).

Peacekeeping operations: 1308, 1318, 1327 (2000); 1353 (2001).

Rwanda: 918, 925, 929, 935, 955, 965 (1994); 1503 (2003).

Sierra Leone: 1132 (1997); 1156, 1162, 1171, 1181 (1998); 1260, 1270 (1999); 1289, 1306, 1313, 1315 (2000); 1389 (2002).

Somalia: 733, 794 (1992); 814, 837 (1993); 897, 954 (1994); 1425 (2002); 1474 (2003).

South Africa: 134 (1960); 181 (1963); 190, 191 (1964); 282 (1970); 418 (1977); 569 (1985); 591 (1986).

Southern Rhodesia: 217 (1965); 221, 232 (1966); 253 (1968); 277 (1970); 314, 320 (1972); 326, 327, 333 (1973); 386, 388 (1976); 403, 406, 409 (1977); 423 (1978); 460 (1979).

Spain: 4 (1946).

Sudan: 1044, 1054, 1070 (1996); 1372 (2001).

Yugoslavia (including Federal Republic of Yugoslavia, Bosnia, Croatia, Kosovo, and Macedonia): 713, 724 (1991); 740, 743, 749, 752, 753, 754, 755, 757, 760, 761, 764, 770, 771, 776, 777, 780, 786, 787 (1992); 807, 808, 816, 819, 820, 824, 827, 836, 844 (1993); 908, 942, 943, 958 (1994); 970, 981, 1021, 1031 (1995); 1037, 1088 (1996); 1199, 1203, 1207 (1998); 1244, 1247 (1999); 1305, 1326 (2000); 1357, 1367 (2001); 1481, 1503 (2003).

Weapons of mass destruction: 1540 (2004).

2. Statements by the President of the Security Council (UN Docs.)

Aghanistan: S/PRST/2000/12.

Angola: S/PRST/1994/45.

Congo: S/PRST/2000/15.

Iraq: S/22485 (1991); S/24113 (1992); S/25091 (1993); S/PRST/1996/36; S/PRST/1998/1.

Libya: S/PRST/1995/36; S/PRST/1996/18, S/PRST/1996/10; S/PRST/1999/10.

Rwanda: S/PRST/2003/18.

Sierra Leone: S/PRST/1998/13.

Yugoslavia (including Federal Republic of Yugoslavia, Bosnia, Croatia, Kosovo, and Macedonia): S/PRST/1996/34; S/PRST/2002/16.

3. Proceedings of the Security Council (UN Docs., unless otherwise specified)

Albania: S/PV.3758, S/PV.3791 (1997).

Haiti: S/PV.3238 (1993); S/PV.3413 (1994), S/1994/828; S/PV.3496 (1995).

International Criminal Court: S/PV.4568 (2002); S/PV.4772 (2003).

Iraq: S/PV.2932, S/PV.2938, S/PV.2963 (1990); S/PV.3858, S/PV.3939 (1998); S/PV.4644 (2002); S/PV.4726 (2003), S/2003/51, S/2003/52, S/2003/350, S/2003/352.

Libya: S/PV.3033, S/PV.3063 (1992).

Palestine: *Official Records of the Security Council,* May 19, 1948.

Rwanda: S/PV.3453 (1994).

Sierra Leone: S/PV.3822 (1997); S/PV.4099 (2000).

Somalia: S/PV.3143, S/PV.3145 (1992).

South Africa: *Official Records of the Security Council,* August 7, 1963.

Weapons of mass destruction: S/PV.4950, S/PV.4956 (2004).

Yugoslavia (including Federal Republic of Yugoslavia, Bosnia, Croatia, Kosovo, and Macedonia): S/PV.3009 (1991); S/PV.3106 (1992); S/PV.3217, S/PV.3228 (1993); S/PV.3356 (1994); S/PV.3512, S/PV.3607 (1995); S/PV.3937 (1998); S/PV.4011 (1999).

4. Actions of Subordinate Bodies of the Security Council (UN Docs.)

International Criminal Tribunal for Rwanda: S/2004/341.

International Criminal Tribunal for the Former Yugoslavia: S/2003/829.

UN Compensation Commission: S/AC.26/1991/1, S/AC.26/1991/7/Rev. 1; S/AC.26/1992/9, S/AC.26/1992/11, S/AC.26/1992/15; S/AC.26/December 17 (1994); S/AC.26/December 23 (1999); S/AC.26/December 10, Rev. 1 (2002).

UN Iraq-Kuwait Boundary Commission: S/25811 (1993).

UNMIK (Kosovo): 1999/1, 1999/3, 1999/4, 1999/5, 1995/7, 1999/9, 1999/20, 1999/24, 1999/779, 1999/1250; 2000/64; 2001/926; 2003/1.

UNTAET (East Timor): 1999/1, 1999/3; 2000/1.

5. Resolutions of the General Assembly

Congo: 1474 (1960).

Korea: 337A (1950).

Peacekeeping: 60/1 (2005).

Sanctions: 53/107 (1998); 54/107 (2000); 58/80 (2004).

Sierra Leone: 57/228A (2002); 57/228B (2003).

Sinai: 997, 1000 (1956).

6. Reports and Statements of the Secretary-General (UN Docs., unless otherwise specified)

Afghanistan: S/2002/278; 2003/333, 2003/754, 2003/1212; S/2004/634; S/2005/616.

Cambodia: A/57/769 (2003).

East Timor: S/1999/513, A/54/654 (1999); S/2000/53, S/2000/738; S/2001/719; S/2002/432; S/2003/449; S/2004/669.

Ethiopia-Eritrea: S/2000/643; S/2001/45; S/2001/608; S/2002/744; S/2003/257, S/2003/1186.

Haiti: S/1994/828; S/2004/300.

Iraq: S/22320, S/22321, S/22456, S/22480, S/22485, S/22508, S/22558, S/22559, S/22614, S/22661, S/22643 (1991); S/25091, S/25811, S/25905, S/25963 (1993); S/1994/1288; S/2004/625.

Liberia: S/22133 (1991).

Libya: S/1999/378.

Peacekeeping: *An Agenda for Peace,* in 31 *International Legal Materials* 956 (1992); Supplement to *An Agenda for Peace,* S/1995/1.

Rwanda: 3402 (1994); A/51/789 (1997); A/52/784 (1998).

Sanctions: S/1995/300; A/54/383 (1999); SG/SM/7360 (2000).

Security Council reform: A/59/565 (2004).

Sierra Leone: S/2000/751, S/2000/915; S/2001/228, S/2001/857; S/2002/679; S/2003/321, S/2003/1201.

Transitional justice: S/2004/616.

Yugoslavia (including Federal Republic of Yugoslavia, Bosnia, Croatia, Kosovo, and Macedonia): S/23592 (1992); S/25274, S/25704 (1993); S/1997/767, S/1997/953; S/1999/779, S/1999/1250; S/2003/996, S/2003/421, S/2003/996; S/2004/348, S/2004/613; S/2005/335.

7. Other UN and UN-related documents

A More Secure World: Our Shared Responsibility. Report of the Secretary-General's High-Level Panel on Threats, Challenges, and Change, A/59/565 (2004).

Interim Report, Independent Inquiry Committee into the United Nations Oil-for-Food Program, New York, February 3, 2005, www.iic-offp.org.

Letter Dated April 13, 1995, to the President of the Security Council, S/1995/300.

The Management of the United Nations Oil-for-Food Program, Independent Inquiry
Committee into the United Nations Oil-for-Food Program, New York,
September 7, 2005, www.iic-offp.org.

Provisional Rules of Procedure of the UN Security Council, S/96/Rev.7 (1983).

Report of the International Law Commission, 46th Session, A/49/10 (1994);
53rd Session, A/56/10 (2001).

Report of the Panel on United Nations Peace Operations ("Brahimi Report"),
A/55/305–S/2000/809 (2000), http://www.un.org/peace/reports/peace_
operations/.

Report of the Preparatory Committee on the Establishment of an International
Criminal Court, A/51/22 (1996).

8. Decisions of the International Court of Justice

Case Concerning Questions of Interpretation and Application of the 1971 Montreal
Convention Arising from the Aerial Incident at Lockerbie *(Libyan Arab
Jamahariya v. United States of America),* Request for the Indication of
Provisional Measures, Order of April 14, 1992, 1992 *ICJ Reports* 114; Order of
September 10, 2003, 2003 *ICJ Reports* 152.

Certain Expenses of the United Nations, Advisory Opinion of July 20, 1962, 1962
ICJ Reports 151.

Legal Consequences of the Construction of a Wall in the Occupied Palestinian
Territory, Advisory Opinion of July 9, 2004, 2004 *ICJ Reports* 136.

Legal Consequences for States of the Continued Presence of South Africa in
Namibia (South West Africa) Notwithstanding Security Council Resolution
276 (1970), Advisory Opinion of June 21, 1971, 1971 *ICJ Reports* 16.

9. Decisions of other international tribunals

*Her Majesty's Advocate v. Abdelbaset Ali Mohmed al Megrahi and Al Amin Khalifa
Fhima,* High Court of Justiciary at Camp Zeist, January 31, 2001, 40
International Legal Materials 582; *Appeal Against Conviction of Abdelbaset Ali
Mohmed al Megrahi Against Her Majesty's Advocate,* March 14, 2002, No.
C104/01.

Judgment of the International Military Tribunal, September 30, 1946 (reprinted in
American Journal of International Law 41 [1946]: 186–218).

Prosecutor v. Dokmanovic, International Criminal Tribunal for the Former
Yugoslavia, Order of October 22, 1997, No. IT-95-13a-PT (reprinted in
Annotated Leading Cases of International Criminal Tribunals, vol. 3 [Antwerp:
Intersentia, 2001]).

Prosecutor v. Dusko Tadic, International Criminal Tribunal for the Former Yugoslavia, Decision on the Defence Motion for Interlocutory Appeal on Jurisdiction, October 2,1995, 35 *International Legal Materials* 32.

10. International agreements

Agreement Between the Government of the Federal Democratic Republic of Ethiopia and the Government of the State of Eritrea, December 12, 2000, UN Doc. S/2001/608, Annex II.

Agreement Concerning West New Guinea (West Irian), August 15, 1962, 437 *United Nations Treaty Series* 274.

Agreement for the Prosecution and Punishment of Major War Criminals of the European Axis, August 8, 1945, 82 *United Nations Treaty Series* 279.

Agreement on a Comprehensive Political Settlement of the Cambodia Conflict, October 23, 1991, 31 *International Legal Materials* 183.

Basic Agreement on the Region of Eastern Slavonia, Baranja, and Western Sirmium, UN Doc. S/1995/951 (1995).

Charter of the United Nations and Statute of the International Court of Justice, June 26, 1945, 1 *United Nations Treaty Series* 16.

Convention on the Prohibition of the Development, Production, and Stockpiling of Bacteriological (Biological) and Toxin Weapons and on Their Destruction, April 10, 1972, 1015 *United Nations Treaty Series* 163.

Draft Agreement Between the United Nations and the Royal Government of Cambodia Concerning the Prosecution Under Cambodian Law of Crimes Committed During the Period of Democratic Kampuchea, March 17, 2003, annexed to UN General Assembly Resolution 57/228B (2003).

Establishment of an International Military Tribunal for the Far East, January 19, 1946, *Treaties and Other International Acts Series* 1589.

General Framework Agreement for Peace in Bosnia and Herzegovina (Dayton Peace Agreement), Paris, December 14, 1995, http://www.ohr.int/gfa/ga-home.htm.

General Treaty for the Renunciation of War (the "Kellogg-Briand Pact"), August 27, 1928, 46 Statute 2342, 94 *League of Nations Treaty Series* 57.

Geneva Conventions on the Protection of War Victims, August 12, 1949, 75 *United Nations Treaty Series* 31-417.

Geneva Protocol for the Prohibition of the Use in War of Asphyxiating, Poisonous, or Other Gases, and of Bacteriological Methods of Warfare, June 17, 1925, 26 *United States Treaties* 571.

International Convention Against Torture and Other Cruel, Inhuman, or Degrading Treatment or Punishment, December 10, 1984, 1465 *United Nations Treaty Series* 85.

International Convention for the Suppression of Terrorist Bombings, January 9, 1998, 37 *International Legal Materials* 249.

Montreal Convention for the Suppression of Unlawful Acts Against the Safety of Civil Aviation, September 23,1971, 974 *United Nations Treaty Series* 177.

Rome Statute of the International Criminal Court, July 17, 1998, www.un.org/law/icc/statute.

Treaty on the Nonproliferation of Nuclear Weapons, July 1, 1968, 21 *United States Treaties* 483, 729 *United Nations Treaty Series* 161.

Treaty on the Prohibition of the Emplacement of Nuclear Weapons and Other Weapons of Mass Destruction on the Seabed and the Ocean Floor and in the Subsoil Thereof, February 11, 1971, 23 *United States Treaties* 701, 955 *United Nations Treaty Series* 115.

Vienna Convention on the Law of Treaties, May 23, 1969, 1155 *United Nations Treaty Series* 331.

11. U.S. documents

Comprehensive Report of the Special Adviser to the DCI on Iraq's WMD, Central Intelligence Agency, September 30, 2004, www.cia.gov/cia/reports/iraq_wmd_2004/index.html.

Executive Order 12722 (August 3, 1990), 55 *Federal Register* 31803.

International Emergency Economic Powers Act, 50 U.S.C. App., sec. 1701-06.

The National Security Strategy of the United States of America, The White House, Washington, D.C., September 2002.

Presidential Decision Directive on Peacekeeping, 33 *International Legal Materials* 1705.

Hearings on UN Sanctions Against Rhodesia, Senate Foreign Relations Committee, 92nd Cong., 1st Sess. (1971).

Letter of March 20, 2003, from the Permanent Representative of the United States to the United Nations, UN Doc. S/2003/351.

Letter from Under Secretary of State Bolton to Secretary-General Annan, U.S. State Department Press Statement, May 6, 2002, Washington, D.C.

Statement of Michael Matheson, Principal Deputy Legal Adviser of the U.S. State Department (October 13, 1993), in *American Journal of International Law* 88, no. 2 (April 1994).

Trading with the Enemy Act, 50 U.S.C. App., sec. 1-5.

United Nations Participation Act, 22 U.S. Code, sec. 287.

12. Other documents

Coalition Provisional Authority Order Number 48 (December 10, 2003), www.cpa.iraq.org.

Conclusions of the Peace Implementation Council [Bosnia], December 10, 1997, http://www.ohr.int/pic/default.asp?content_id=5182.

Decisions of the High Representative [Bosnia], August 28, 1998, March 5, 1999, www.ohr.int/decisions.

Letter from the Permanent Representative of Sweden to the (UN) Secretary-General, February 18, 1993, UN Doc. S/25307 (1993), containing CSCE Proposal for an International War Crimes Tribunal for the Former Yugoslavia by Rapporteurs under the CSCE Moscow Human Dimension Mechanism to Bosnia-Herzegovina and Croatia, February 9, 1993.

Letter from UK Foreign Minister Straw to Secretary-General Annan [Afghanistan], December 19, 2001, UN Doc. S/2001/1217.

Note from the General Secretariat to the Council of the European Union, 12488/1/02, September 30, 2002.

Press Release of Special Court for Sierra Leone, May 31, 2004, www.sc-sl.org.

Statute of the Iraq Special Tribunal, www.cpa-iraq.org.

Statute of the Special Court for Sierra Leone, UN Doc. S/2000/915, www.sc-sl.org.

SECONDARY SOURCES

1. Books, chapters, and articles

"Agora: Future Implications of the Iraq Conflict." *American Journal of International Law* 97, no. 3 (July 2003).

"Agora: The Gulf Crisis in International and Foreign Relations Law." *American Journal of International Law* 85, no. 3 (July 1991).

Akhavan, Payam. "Beyond Impunity: Can International Criminal Justice Prevent Future Atrocities?" *American Journal of International Law* 95, no. 1 (January 2001).

Aldrich, George H. *The Jurisprudence of the Iran–United States Claims Tribunal.* New York: Oxford University Press, 1996.

Alvarez, Jose E. *International Organizations as Law-Makers.* New York: Oxford University Press, 2005.

Bailey, Sydney D., and Sam Daws. *The Procedure of the UN Security Council.* 3d ed. New York: Oxford University Press, 1998.

Bassiouni, M. Cherif, ed. *Postconflict Justice.* International and Comparative Law Series. Ardsley, N.Y.: Transnational Publishers, 2002.

———, ed. *The Statute of the International Criminal Court: A Documentary History.* Ardsley, N.Y.: Transnational Publishers, 1998.

Bassiouni, M. Cherif, and Peter Manikas. *The Law of the International Criminal Tribunal for the Former Yugoslavia.* Ardsley, N.Y.: Transnational Publishers, 1996.

Blix, Hans. *Disarming Iraq.* New York: Pantheon Books, 2004.

Bowett, D. W. *The Law of International Institutions.* 4th ed. London: Stevens & Sons, 1982.

———. *United Nations Forces: A Legal Study.* New York, Praeger, 1964.

Brower, Charles Nelson. *The Iran–United States Claims Tribunal.* Boston: Kluwer Law International, 1998.

Brownlie, Ian. *International Law and the Use of Force by States.* New York: Oxford University Press, 1981.

Buergenthal, Thomas, and Sean D. Murphy, *Public International Law in a Nutshell.* St. Paul, Minn.: West Publishing Group, 2002.

Buergenthal, Thomas, Dinah Shelton, and David P. Stewart, *International Human Rights in a Nutshell.* St. Paul, Minn.: West Publishing Group, 2002.

Burg, Steven L., and Paul S. Shoup. *The War in Bosnia-Herzegovina: Ethnic Conflict and International Intervention.* Armonk, N.Y.: M. E. Sharpe, 1999.

Caron, David. "The Legitimacy of the Collective Authority of the Security Council." *American Journal of International Law* 87, no. 4 (October 1993).

Carter, Barry E., and Philip R. Trimble. *International Law.* 3d ed. Boston: Little, Brown, 1999.

Cassese, Antonio, ed., *United Nations Peacekeeping: Legal Essays.* Boston: Brill Academic Publishers, 1978.

Chesterman, Simon. *Just War or Just Peace: Humanitarian Intervention and International Law.* New York: Oxford University Press, 2001.

Claude, Inis L. *Swords into Plowshares: The Problems and Progress of International Organizations.* 4th ed. New York: Random House, 1971.

Conlon, Paul. "Lessons from Iraq: The Functions of the Iraq Sanctions Committee as a Source of Sanctions Implementation Authority and Practice." *Virginia Journal of International Law* 35, no. 3 (Spring 1995).

———. *United Nations Sanctions Management: A Case Study of the Iraq Sanctions Committee.* Ardsley, N.Y.: Transnational Publishers, 2000.

Cortright, David, and George A. Lopez. *The Sanctions Decade: Assessing UN Strategies in the 1990s.* Boulder, Colo.: Lynne Rienner, 2000.

Damsosch, Lori F., ed. *Enforcing Restraint: Collective Intervention in Internal Conflicts.* New York: Council on Foreign Relations Press, 1993.

———. "The Role of the Great Powers in United Nations Peacekeeping." *Yale Journal of International Law* 18, no. 1 (Winter 1993).

Damrosch, Lori Fisler, et al., eds. *International Law: Cases and Materials.* 4th ed. St. Paul, Minn.: West Publishing Group, 2001.

Damrosch, Lori Fisler, and David J. Scheffer, eds. *Law and Force in the New International Order*. Boulder, Colo.: Westview, 1991.

de Vet, Erika. *The Chapter VII Powers of the United Nations Security Council*. Portland, Ore.: Hart, 2004.

"Defensive Quarantine and the Law." *American Journal of International Law* 57, no. 3 (July 1963).

Dickinson, Laura A. "The Promise of Hybrid Courts." *American Journal of International Law* 97, no. 2 (April 2003).

Dinstein, Yoram. *War, Aggression, and Self-Defense*. 2d ed. New York: Cambridge University Press, 1994.

Durch, William J., ed. *UN Peacekeeping, American Politics, and the Uncivil Wars of the 1990s*. New York: St. Martin's, 1996.

"Editorial Comments: NATO's Kosovo Intervention." *American Journal of International Law* 93, no. 2 (April 1999).

Elliott, Kimberley Ann. "The Gulf War: The Law of International Sanctions." *Proceedings of the 85th Annual Meeting of the American Society of International Law*. Washington, D.C.: American Society of International Law, 1991.

Fassbender, Bardo. *UN Security Council Reform and the Right of Veto: A Constitutional Perspective*. Boston: Kluwer Law International, 1998.

Franck, Thomas M. "Lessons of Kosovo." *American Journal of International Law* 93, no. 4 (October 1999).

———. "The 'Powers of Appreciation': Who Is the Ultimate Guardian of UN Legality?" *American Journal of International Law* 86, no. 3 (July 1992).

———. *Recourse to Force: State Action against Threats and Armed Attacks*. New York, Cambridge University Press, 2002.

Goodrich, Leland M., Edvard Hambro, and Anne Patricia Simons. *Charter of the United Nations: Commentary and Documents*. New York: Columbia University Press, 1969.

Goodrich, Leland M., and Anne P. Simons. *The United Nations and the Maintenance of International Peace and Security*. Washington, D.C.: The Brookings Institution, 1955.

Gowlland-Debbas, Vera, ed. *United Nations Sanctions and International Law*. Boston: Kluwer Law International, 2001.

Graham-Brown, Sarah. *Sanctioning Saddam: The Politics of Intervention in Iraq*. New York: St. Martin's, 1999.

Gray, Christine. *International Law and the Use of Force*. New York: Oxford University Press, 2000.

Hagan, John. *Justice in the Balkans: Prosecuting War Crimes in the Hague Tribunal*. Chicago: University of Chicago Press, 2003.

Henkin, Louis. "Kosovo and the Law of Humanitarian Intervention." *American Journal of International Law* 93, no. 4 (October 1999).

Higgins, Rosalyn. *Problems and Process: International Law and How We Use It.* New York: Oxford University Press, 1994.

Hill, Stephen M., and Shahin P. Malik, *Peacekeeping and the United Nations.* Brookfield, Vt.: Dartmouth Publishing Group, 1996.

Hirsch, John. *Sierra Leone: Diamonds and the Struggle for Democracy.* Boulder, Colo.: Lynne Rienner, 2001.

Hoffman, William B. "Global Mandate, National Law." *Proceedings of the 89th Annual Meeting of the American Society of International Law.* Washington, D.C.: American Society of International Law, 1995.

Hufbauer, Gary C., and Barbara Oegg. "Targeted Sanctions: A Policy Alternative?" *Law and Policy in International Business* 32, no. 1 (Fall 2000).

International Committee of the Red Cross. *Commentary on the Geneva Conventions of 12 August 1949.* Vol. 4, *Geneva Convention Relative to the Protection of Civilian Persons in Time of War.* Geneva: ICRC, 1958.

"The International Criminal Court: Consensus and Debate on the International Adjudication of Genocide, Crimes against Humanity, War Crimes, and Aggression." Symposium issue of the *Cornell International Law Journal* 32, no. 3 (Summer 1999).

Joyner, Christopher C. "Sanctions, Compliance, and International Law." *Virginia Journal of International Law* 32, no. 1 (1991).

Kirgis, Frederic L., Jr. *International Organizations in Their Legal Setting.* 2d ed. St. Paul, Minn.: West Publishing Company, 1993.

————. "The Security Council's First Fifty Years," *American Journal of International Law* 89, no. 3 (July 1995).

Kozal, Peggy. "Is the Continued Use of Sanctions as Implemented against Iraq a Violation of International Human Rights?" *Denver Journal of International Law* 28, no 4 (Fall 2000).

Kritz, Neil J. *Transitional Justice: How Emerging Democracies Reckon with Former Regimes.* 3 vols. Washington, D.C.: U.S. Institute of Peace Press, 1995.

Lavoyer, Jean-Philippe, et al. "Jus in Bello: Occupation Law and the War in Iraq." *Proceedings of the 98th Annual Meeting of the American Society of International Law.* Washington, D.C.: American Society of International Law, 2004.

"Legal Authority for the Possible Use of Force Against Iraq." *Proceedings of the 92nd Annual Meeting of the American Society of International Law.* Washington, D.C.: American Society of International Law, 1998.

Leigh, Monroe. "The United States and the Statute of Rome." *American Journal of International Law* 95, no. 1 (January 2001).

Lillich, Richard B., ed. *Humanitarian Intervention and the United Nations.* Charlottesville: University Press of Virginia, 1973.

——, ed. *The United Nations Compensation Commission.* Irvington, N.Y.: Transnational Publishers, 1995.

Lobel, Jules, and Michael Ratner. "Bypassing the Security Council: Ambiguous Authorizations to Use Force, Cease-Fires, and the Iraqi Inspection Regime." *American Journal of International Law* 93, no. 1 (January 1999).

Lopez, George A., and David Cortright. "Containing Iraq: Sanctions Worked." *Foreign Affairs,* July/August 2004.

Malanczuk, Peter. *Akehurst's Modern Introduction to International Law.* 7th ed. New York: Routledge, 1997.

——. *Humanitarian Intervention and the Legitimacy of the Use of Force.* Hingham, Mass.: Nijhoff International, 1993.

Malone, John M., ed. *The UN Security Council: From the Cold War to the Twenty-First Century.* Boulder, Colo.: Lynne Rienner, 2004.

Matheson, Michael J. "United Nations Governance of Postconflict Societies." *American Journal of International Law* 95, no. 1 (January 2001).

McCoubrey, Hilaire, and Nigel D. White. *The Blue Helmets: Legal Regulation of United Nations Military Operations.* Brookfield, Vt.: Dartmouth Publishing Group, 1996.

——. *International Law and Armed Conflict.* Brookfield, Vt.: Dartmouth Publishing Group, 1992.

MacKay, M. Jennifer. "Economic Sanctions: Are They Actually Enforcing International Law in Serbia-Montenegro?" *Tulane Journal of International and Comparative Law* 3, no. 1/2 (December 1994).

Mendelson, M. H., and S. C. Hulton. "The Iraq-Kuwait Boundary." *British Yearbook of International Law, 1993.* New York: Oxford University Press, 1995.

Merrills, J. G. *International Dispute Settlement.* 3d ed. New York: Cambridge University Press, 1998.

Moore, John Norton, Frederick S. Tipson, and Robert F. Turner, eds. *National Security Law.* Durham, N.C.: Carolina Academic Press, 1990.

Morris, Virginia, and Michael P. Scharf. *An Insider's Guide to the International Criminal Tribunal for the Former Yugoslavia.* Irvington-on-Hudson, N.Y. Transnational Publishers, 1995.

——. *The International Criminal Tribunal for Rwanda.* Irvington-on-Hudson, N.Y.: Transnational Publishers, 1998.

Murphy, Sean D. "Assessing the Legality of Invading Iraq." *Georgetown Law Journal* 92, no. 2 (January 2004).

———. "Contemporary Practice of the United States Relating to International Law." *American Journal of International Law* 98, no. 3 (July 2004).

———. "De Jure War in the Gulf." *New York International Law Review* 5, no. 2 (Summer 1992).

———. *Humanitarian Intervention: The United Nations in an Evolving World Order.* Philadelphia: University of Pennsylvania Press, 1996.

———. "Progress and Jurisprudence of the International Criminal Tribunal for the Former Yugoslavia." *American Journal of International Law* 93, no. 1 (January 1999).

———. "The Security Council, Legitimacy, and the Concept of Collective Security after the Cold War." *Columbia Journal of Transnational Law* 32 (1994).

Naarden, Gregory L., and Jeffrey B. Locke. "Peacekeeping and Prosecutorial Policy: Lessons from Kosovo." *American Journal of International Law* 98, no. 4 (October 2004).

Osterdahl, Inger. *Threat to the Peace: The Interpretation by the Security Council of Article 39 of the UN Charter.* Uppsala, Sweden: Iustus Forlag, 1998.

Ratner, Steven R. "The Cambodia Settlement Agreements." *American Journal of International Law* 87, no. 1 (January 1993).

Reisman, W. Michael. "Assessing the Lawfulness of Nonmilitary Enforcement: The Case of Economic Sanctions." *Proceedings of the 89th Annual Meeting of the American Society of International Law.* Washington, D.C.: American Society of International Law, 1995.

———. "The Constitutional Crisis in the United Nations." *American Journal of International Law* 87, no. 1 (January 1993).

Rosand, Eric. "The Right to Compensation in Bosnia: An Unfulfilled Promise and a Challenge to International Law." *Cornell International Law Journal* 33, no. 1 (2000).

———. "The Security Council's Efforts to Monitor the Implementation of Al Queda/Taliban Sanctions." *American Journal of International Law* 98, no. 4 (October 2004).

Rowe, Peter, ed. *The Gulf War 1990–91 in International and English Law.* New York: Routledge, 1993.

Sarooshi, Dan. *The United Nations and the Development of Collective Security: The Delegation by the UN Security Council of Its Chapter VII Powers.* New York: Oxford University Press, 1999.

Schachter, Oscar. *International Law in Theory and Practice.* Norwell, Mass.: Kluwer Academic Publishers, 1995.

———. "United Nations Law in the Gulf Conflict." *American Journal of International Law* 85, no. 3 (July 1991).

Scharf, Michael P. "The Amnesty Exception to the Jurisdiction of the International Criminal Court." *Cornell International Law Journal* 32, no. 3 (1999).

Scharf, Michael P., and Joshua L. Dorosin. "Interpreting UN Sanctions: The Rulings and Role of the Yugoslav Sanctions Committee." *Brooklyn Journal of International Law* 19, no. 3 (1993).

Scheffer, David J. "The United States and the International Criminal Court." *American Journal of International Law* 93, no. 1 (January 1999).

Schweigman, David. *The Authority of the Security Council under Chapter VII of the UN Charter.* Boston: Kluwer Law International, 2001.

Shaw, Malcolm N. *International Law.* 4th ed. New York: Cambridge University Press, 1997.

Simma, Bruno, ed. *The Charter of the United Nations: A Commentary.* 2d ed. New York: Oxford University Press, 2002.

Stone, Julius. *Legal Controls of International Conflict: A Treatise on the Dynamics of Disputes- and War-Law.* London: Stevens, 1954.

Stromseth, Jane E., ed. *Accountability for Atrocities: National and International Responses.* Ardsley, N.Y.: Transnational Publishers, 2003.

Swindells, Felicia. "UN Sanctions in Haiti: A Contradiction Under Articles 41 and 55 of the UN Charter." *Fordham International Law Journal* 20, no. 1 (June 1997).

Szasz, Paul. "The Security Council Starts Legislating." *American Journal of International Law* 96, no. 4 (October 2002).

Taft, William Howard, IV. "Pre-Emptive Action in Self-Defense." *Proceedings of the 98th Annual Meeting of the American Society of International Law.* Washington, D.C.: American Society of International Law, 2004.

Talmon, Stefan. "The Security Council as World Legislature." *American Journal of International Law* 99, no. 1 (January 2005).

United Nations. *The Blue Helmets: A Review of United Nations Peacekeeping.* 2d ed. New York: United Nations, 1990.

———. *The Blue Helmets: A Review of United Nations Peacekeeping.* 3d ed. New York: United Nations, 1996.

———. *The United Nations and the Iraq-Kuwait Conflict.* New York: United Nations, 1996.

U.S. Arms Control and Disarmament Agency. *Arms Control and Disarmament Agreements: Texts and Histories of the Negotiations.* Washington, D.C.: ACDA, 1996.

U.S. State Department. *Digest of International Law.* Washington, D.C.: U.S. State Department, 1962.

———. *Digest of International Law.* Washington, D.C.: U.S. State Department, 1978.

Warner, Daniel, ed. *New Dimensions of Peacekeeping*. Boston: M. Nijhoff, 1995.

Watson, Geoffrey R. "Constitutionalism, Judicial Review, and the World Court." *Harvard International Law Journal* 34, no. 1 (Winter 1993).

Weiss, Thomas G. *Military-Civilian Interactions: Intervening in Humanitarian Crises*. Lanham, Md.: Rowman & Littlefield, 1999.

Weiss, Thomas G., et al., eds. *Political Gain and Civilian Pain: Humanitarian Impacts of Economic Sanctions*. Lanham, Md.: Rowman & Littlefield, 1997.

Weller, Mark. "The International Response to the Dissolution of the Socialist Federal Republic of Yugoslavia." *American Journal of International Law* 86, no. 3 (July 1992).

Wilde, Ralph. "From Danzig to East Timor and Beyond." *American Journal of International Law* 95, no. 3 (July 2001).

2. Special reports

International Commission on Intervention and State Sovereignty. *The Responsibility to Protect*. Report of the International Commission on Intervention and State Sovereignty. Ottawa: International Development Research Center, 2001, http://www.iciss.ca/pdf/Commission-Report.pdf.

Swiss Federal Office for Foreign Economic Affairs. Report from the "Expert Seminar on Targeting UN Financial Sanctions," Interlaken, Switzerland, March 17–19, 1998, http://www.seco.admin.ch/imperia/md/content/aussenwirtschaft/sanktionenundembargos/46.pdf.

INDEX

Michael J. Matheson was principal deputy legal adviser to the U.S. Department of State during 1990–2000, and acting legal adviser during substantial parts of that period. Currently he is a member of the international law faculty of the George Washington University School of Law in Washington, D.C., and a member of the UN International Law Commission. He is also on the board of editors of the *American Journal of International Law* and on the executive council of the American Society of International Law. He was a senior fellow at the United States Institute of Peace during 2001–2002.

Jennings Randolph Program for International Peace

This book is a fine example of the work produced by senior fellows in the Jennings Randolph fellowship program of the United States Institute of Peace. As part of the statute establishing the Institute, Congress envisioned a program that would appoint "scholars and leaders of peace from the United States and abroad to pursue scholarly inquiry and other appropriate forms of communication on international peace and conflict resolution." The program was named after Senator Jennings Randolph of West Virginia, whose efforts over four decades helped to establish the Institute.

Since 1987, the Jennings Randolph Program has played a key role in the Institute's effort to build a national center of research, dialogue, and education on critical problems of conflict and peace. Nearly 200 senior fellows from some thirty nations have carried out projects on the sources and nature of violent international conflict and the ways such conflict can be peacefully managed or resolved. Fellows come from a wide variety of academic and other professional backgrounds. They conduct research at the Institute and participate in the Institute's outreach activities to policymakers, the academic community, and the American public.

Each year approximately fifteen senior fellows are in residence at the Institute. Fellowship recipients are selected by the Institute's board of directors in a competitive process. For further information on the program, or to receive an application form, please contact the program staff at (202) 457-1700, or visit our website at www.usip.org.

John Crist
Acting Associate Vice President

COUNCIL UNBOUND:
THE GROWTH OF UN DECISION MAKING ON CONFLICT AND
POSTCONFLICT ISSUES AFTER THE COLD WAR

This book was set in the typeface Adobe Garamond; the display type is Adobe DIN Schriften. Cover design by Hasten Design Studio, Washington, D.C. Interior design, page makeup, copyediting, and proofreading by EEI Communications, Inc., Alexandria, Virginia. Production supervised by Marie Marr Jackson. Peter Pavilionis was the book's editor.